THE CARIBBEAN SHORT STORY: CRITICAL PERSPECTIVES

THE CARIBBEAN SHORT STORY:
CRITICAL PERSPECTIVES

EDITED BY

LUCY EVANS, MARK MCWATT
& EMMA SMITH

PEEPAL TREE

First published in Great Britain in 2011
Peepal Tree Press Ltd
17 King's Avenue
Leeds, LS6 1QS
UK

ISBN: 9781845231262

Supported by
ARTS COUNCIL
ENGLAND

CONTENTS

FOREWORD

EMMA E. SMITH

The Caribbean Short Story offers a collection of critical readings of short
fiction from the Caribbean and its diaspora, bringing together research by
scholars based across Britain, the US and the Caribbean. The project has
its genesis in a series of discussions between Lucy Evans and myself which
took place while we were both completing PhDs at the University of Leeds.
It began as a response to two observations: firstly, that there was an
extraordinarily rich heritage of short story writing from the Caribbean and
its diaspora; and secondly, that, while readers and teachers of fiction had
embraced the Caribbean short story, an extended critical book surveying its
forms and examining its significance was long overdue. We were approaching the subject from two directions. As academics, we were informed by
our research in Caribbean and postcolonial literature, as well as by my work
in narrative theory and Lucy's research in short story criticism; but we also
brought an understanding of the politics and pragmatics of Caribbean
publishing gained through our association with Peepal Tree Press, where
more than thirty short story collections have been published over the past
twenty-five years. Having both worked at Peepal Tree at different points
in our careers, we shared a clear sense of the material processes involved in
producing and distributing Caribbean short fiction, so were determined
that this collection would attend not only to the stories themselves but also
to some of the varied means by which they reach their audiences. In
inviting Mark McWatt to come on board as co-editor, we gained the
perspective of someone who is both a practitioner – a poet and award-
winning writer of short fiction – and an established academic based in the
region, where he is Professor Emeritus at the University of the West Indies
(Cave Hill).

This collection recognises and explores the short story's role as a mode
of creative expression deeply embedded in cultures and communities.
Drawing on oral and scribal traditions, and on multicultural roots which
tangle African, Indian, European, African-American, Amerindian and
other influences, the Caribbean and its diaspora has produced a flourishing
body of short story writing, manifesting a rich and diverse array of linguistic
and literary modes: from whispered bedtime tales to the call-and-response
performance of *crick-crack* stories; from social realist fictions voicing
narratives of the marginalised to complex experimentations with language
and form; and from self-published collections and individual stories in

newspapers and magazines with largely local readerships to stories appearing in print and, increasingly, electronic forms which reach out to global audiences.

The essays that follow explore the art of short story writing in the Caribbean, investigating its significance and some of the reasons for its abundance, as well as tracing how and where it has been produced and received. In a region without extensive investment in literary arts and with limited opportunities for publishing, the short story has long had a special value. Aesthetically, some writers find in the short story form closer links to folk narratives and oral modes of storytelling. For other writers, the flexibility of the form makes it a perfect canvas for innovation and exploration: Caribbean writers are constantly playing with shape and style and voice, finding possibilities for creolisation and cultural exchange within the rhythms of story and the patterns of story collections. Pragmatically speaking, the short story has been more readily and cheaply publishable, through newspapers and little magazines, and thus potentially accessible to a broad regional audience. It is also an effective route into literature, both for new writers and as a learning aid for young readers. And from the 1940s onwards, anthologies of short fiction have been gathering together, for both local and international readers, a diverse array of the region's writing. Peepal Tree Press itself has long been investing in the art of the short story, publishing collections that recognise the form's foundational position within Caribbean letters, and its vitality – in both senses of the word. It is therefore entirely appropriate that this first book of critical essays devoted to the subject should also find its home on Peepal Tree's list.

Bringing this book together has been a rewardingly collaborative process. First and foremost, we must thank our contributors for their fruitful responses to our call for papers, which asked: What makes the short story such a compelling literary mode for Caribbean writers? How have they employed it, and how has it been transformed in the process? We sought, and received, up-to-date critical perspectives on significant texts by established and emerging voices, so as to begin to map the ecology and the aesthetics of Caribbean short stories. The contributors have produced close readings of a century's worth of stories; they have drawn attention to little-known writers and brought new insight to well-established storytellers; they have made critical interventions into Caribbean cultural history, and addressed questions of community, nationhood, cultural exchange, language, form, aesthetics, and literary value. Within the book you will find conversation between different approaches and readings: points of contact and divergence are to be found, for instance, between the essays which take Trinidadian writing as their focus (see Evans, Peake, Procter and Ramcharitar). In drawing together a community – which is not to say *consensus* – of critical voices, this volume goes some way towards addressing the diverse communities of voice explored within Caribbean short stories, as well as the communities of writers and readers that give the stories life. But we also envision this book as joining a much larger conversation about Caribbean short story writing, building on valuable critical work that has come before (the bibliography at the back of this volume lists resources for further reading), and hopefully stimulating future dialogue. There remain so many more writers – from established voices, to fresh new ones, to those lying forgotten in the archives – who warrant new critical attention. And there is plenty more thinking to be done about, for example, reading and reception, environmental concerns, representations of sexuality, and the specificities of form and style, as well as a need to read short fiction across the linguistic divides of the region, engaging more fully with the writing of the French-, Dutch- and Spanish-speaking Caribbean than we have been able to do here.

In producing this collection, it is important to acknowledge not only the work of my fellow editors and our many contributors, but also the constructive input of several other people. In particular, this project was enriched by the editorial skill and subject knowledge of Peepal Tree's managing editor, Jeremy Poynting, who helped to define the contours of the collection and provided encouragement throughout the process. Additional thanks are due to Hannah Bannister at Peepal Tree for her ongoing support of the project and its editors, as well as to John McLeod at the University of Leeds for the inspiring introduction he gave both Lucy Evans and myself to the study of Caribbean literature.

Reading on, you will find that these essays offer many different pathways into Caribbean writing and the short story form. We hope that as well as informing intellectual study and birthing new questions for future research in both fields, this collection will also enrich the ways in which we all read and enjoy the extraordinary body of stories from the Caribbean, and beyond.

INTRODUCTION

LUCY EVANS

In *The Shape of That Hurt and Other Essays* (1992), Gordon Rohlehr suggests that in grappling with a 'New World situation of flux, historic and psychic chaos, cultural erosion',[1] Caribbean writers have developed 'a complex, multi-faceted, flexible sense of shape'.[2] Rohlehr's sense of a 'flexible' form generated by experiences specific to the Caribbean can be compared to Kenneth Ramchand's notion of an 'emerging Creole form' created through a fusion of the region's written and oral traditions. In 'The West Indian Short Story' (1997), Ramchand asserts that 'the history of West Indian prose fiction before 1950 is essentially the history of the short story', adding the self-consciously provocative statement: 'There are no West Indian novelists, only short story writers in disguise; no West Indian novels, only fabrications taking their shape and structure from the transfigured short stories they contain'.[3] Rohlehr's and Ramchand's comments touch on issues key to this collection of critical essays on Caribbean short stories. While Rohlehr's observations indicate how the form of Caribbean literary writing is inextricable from its subject matter and sociopolitical contexts, Ramchand's statements highlight the centrality of the short story form to the evolution of a Caribbean literary aesthetic, considering its impact on the development of not only short story writing but work in other genres.

Examining the significance of the short story to Caribbean cultural production across the twentieth and into the twenty-first century, *The Caribbean Short Story: Critical Perspectives* situates the formal characteristics of Caribbean short stories within the historical, cultural and socioeconomic background of the region and its diaspora. In doing so, the collection makes an important intervention into scholarly debate on the short story form. In order to clarify the nature and implications of this intervention, this introduction will first outline how short story theory and criticism has developed since it was established as a field of study in the mid-nineteenth century, briefly identifying changing methodologies and reflecting upon some of their values and shortcomings. It will comment on the inapplicability of many existing theories of the short story to the practice of Caribbean short story writing, with the aim of demonstrating the need for new approaches to the short story form. The latter part of the introduction will begin to explore the specifics of Caribbean short story writing, distinguishing its publishing history, aesthetics and cultural influences from the US and European short story writing traditions which have usually been the focus of theoretical and critical studies of the genre.

THE SHORT STORY: THEORY AND CRITICISM

Edgar Allan Poe's 1842 review of Nathanial Hawthorne's *Twice-Told Tales* has been repeatedly hailed by theorists and critics of the short story as the first example of commentary on the subject, and often presented as still pertinent to short story studies.[4] Poe's review and a later essay by Brander Matthews, 'The Philosophy of the Short-Story' (1901), also frequently quoted in studies of the genre, are concerned primarily to identify the short story's distinguishing characteristics, and in doing so to validate it as an art form in its own right, separate from the novel. For Poe, the short story's most important feature is 'unity of effect or impression' or a 'single effect'. Poe stipulates that the short story must be tightly structured, every detail necessary to this unifying effect.[5] Like Poe, Matthews seeks to illuminate aesthetic properties other than shortness which mark out the short story as a literary form: he argues that a 'true Short-story is something other and something more than a mere story which is short'.[6] He follows Poe in privileging unity, economy, containment and compression. Matthews explains that his choice of the term 'Short-story' over 'short story' is a means of differentiating between the 'genuine Short-story' and the 'brief tales to be seen in the British monthly magazines and in the Sunday editions of American newspapers' (Matthews, p. 75). For both Matthews and Poe, the compilation of aesthetic criteria for the 'true' or 'genuine' short story serves as a means of sifting the literary from the popular, removing a literary mode of short story writing from the commercial context of mass-produced magazines and newspapers in order to demonstrate its status as worthy of critical acclaim.

The process of defining and delimiting the short story – establishing its formal properties and distinguishing it from other genres – continued to underpin short story theory of the 1960s and 70s. These theorists often took a formalist approach, identifying general characteristics of the genre in the abstract and developing taxonomies of categories and sub-categories. While these theories are presented as universally applicable, the examples selected to illustrate them are almost exclusively limited to US and European male authors. The same names recur again and again: Nathaniel Hawthorne, Edgar Allan Poe, Herman Melville, James Joyce, Guy de Maupassant, Anton Chekhov, Joseph Conrad, Henry James, O. Henry, Sherwood Anderson, Ernest Hemingway, Rudyard Kipling.

Furthermore, the formalist aspect of these studies often sits uneasily alongside a simultaneous attempt to trace the literary history of the short story form back to Poe, as its progenitor, or sometimes beyond as far as Chaucer and Boccaccio. For example, Mary Rohrberger combines general claims on the structure of short stories with a conception of the short story as deriving 'from the romantic tradition'.[7] The same kind of tension between conflicting methodologies can be seen in Ian Reid's study, where universalising definitions of the short story form as an 'essential generic type' strain against a historicising approach to the genre.[8] While Reid is attentive to the short story's 'protean variety' as it has developed through the centuries, he nevertheless remains intent on 'delimiting the territory of the short story proper' (Reid, p. 3, p. 4).

A number of studies of the modernist short story published since the 1980s move away from the formalist approach of the critics discussed above, positioning short stories of the modernist period within the specific social and cultural context in which they were produced and consumed. The concern of these critics has generally been less to establish the generic boundaries of the short story form than to locate it within the wider literary culture of the modernist movement, whose spirit the form is often seen to encapsulate.

In an influential 1968 essay, Nadine Gordimer described the short story as 'a fragmented and restless form', proposing that 'it is perhaps for this reason that it suits modern consciousness' which is best expressed as a 'flash of fireflies, in and out, now here, now there, in darkness'.[9] Later critics have extended and developed this idea.[10] In singling out the short story as an ideal mode of writing for modernist literary experimentation and as especially apt for articulating the experience of modernity, critics of the modernist short story allude to various strategies and devices which they see as typical of modernist short fiction; for example, ellipsis, ambiguity, epiphany, symbolism, impressionism,[11] plotlessness, economy, and the foregrounding of style. These stylistic features are presented as a means of engaging with a sociocultural climate of 'fragmentation, dislocation and isolation' (Hunter, p. 47), 'social change and the break-up of community',[12] and 'the increasing loneliness and isolation of the individual in a competitive society' (Gordimer, p. 266).

Critics of the modernist short story do not, like Poe, Matthews and others, make general claims about the aesthetic value of the 'true' or 'genuine' short story, or the 'short story proper'. However, in their decision to limit their discussion to an elitist, high modernist tradition of short story writing, these critics continue to privilege a literary mode of short story writing over the popular forms of short fiction produced within a growing mass market at a time of rapid technological development. Furthermore, while they do not, like Reid and Rohrberger, attempt to create universally applicable taxonomies of the short story form, they nevertheless present a particular cultural tradition of short story writing as 'the' tradition rather than as one of many traditions developing in different parts of the world. Essays in this volume by Dave Gunning, James Procter, Jak Peake and Joanna Johnson explore experiences of modernity and forms of modernist short fiction distinct from those examined by critics of modernist short fiction such as Clare Hanson, Adrian Hunter, Paul March-Russell and Dominic Head.

Writing in 1987, W.H. New begins a study of the short story in Canada and New Zealand with a critique of existing theoretical and critical debate on the genre, observing that 'most commentary does not adequately apply to the practice of the short story outside America, England and continental Europe'.[13] New argues that 'an explanation of a formal cultural connection in one society does not transplant automatically to another', since 'in each society there has been a separate adaptation of literary form' (New, p. 16). Scholarly work on the short story form since the publication of New's book has begun to acknowledge the presence of multiple cultural traditions.[14] It is into this broader scholarly endeavour that we enter this critical collection, in recognition of the particular place that the short story holds within Caribbean literature.

The most recent monographs on the short story incorporate a last chapter on postcolonial short fiction: the final chapter of Paul March-Russell's *The Short Story: An Introduction* (2009) is entitled 'Voyages Out: The Postcolonial Short Story' and the closing section of Adrian Hunter's *The Cambridge Introduction to the Short Story in English* (2010) takes as its topic 'Postcolonial and Other Stories'. In both cases, the positioning of these chapters implies that they are afterthoughts rather than key components of the studies. Reading the short story form in relation to Gilles Deleuze and Félix Guattari's notion of 'minor' literature (Hunter, p. 139; March-Russell, p. 248), these concluding chapters build on arguments made by Mary Louise Pratt and Frank O'Connor. Focusing on the short story's 'status as minor and lesser genre with respect to the novel', Pratt reflects how in various parts of the world the short story has been 'used to introduce new regions or groups into an established national literature, or into an emerging national literature in the process of decolonization'.[15] This attention to the cultural politics of the short story form recalls O'Connor's earlier and often quoted association of the short story with 'submerged population groups' and 'outlawed figures wandering about the fringes of society'.[16] The limitation of this particular strand of short story theory is that in making a case for the short story form as a subversive mode of writing for marginalised groups everywhere, and – in the case of March-Russell and Hunter – collapsing a diversity of texts into the category 'postcolonial', it de-emphasises the specific histories and social contexts of different short story writing traditions.

Along with New's study of the short story in Canada and New Zealand, several monographs and essay collections deal with the specifics of short story writing in Canada, Australia, Africa and South East Asia.[17] Additionally, Jacqueline Bardolph's collection, *Telling Stories: Postcolonial Short Fiction in English* (2001) is divided geographically into sections on 'Canada',

'The West Indies', 'Southern Africa', 'India, Sri Lanka and the Diaspora', 'New Zealand', and 'Australia', and in 2004, a special issue of the *Journal of West Indian Literature* focused on the Caribbean short story. However, there is scope and indeed a necessity for further critical enquiry, if the significance of the short story form to a diversity of literatures in English is to be fully understood. In the introduction to the *JWIL* special issue, Hyacinth Simpson observes: 'It would seem that even a special issue devoted entirely to the West Indian short story would still not be enough to do justice to this single creative tradition', and hopes that the publication will stimulate '[f]urther exploration of the Caribbean short story'.[18] Taking its cue from Simpson's comment, the remainder of this introduction and the critical essays which follow will trace the development of the Caribbean short story through the twentieth and into the twenty-first century.

THE CARIBBEAN SHORT STORY

Writing in 2006, Alison Donnell comments on the 'extraordinary myth of a doubled spontaneous genesis' generated in discussions of Caribbean literature, the first of these being 'London in the 1950s with the "boom" of male writers (Lamming, Naipaul, Selvon)'. Donnell comments on the relatively few critical works which 'offer a sustained reading of writings from before 1950'.[19] According to Kenneth Ramchand, in the Caribbean region 'the short story held the field as it were until the 1950's', and the short story tradition 'went underground when our writers turned novelists on emigration to London in the 1950's'. From that point on, he suggests, 'the novel became the prestigious and preferred form' ('The West Indian Short Story', p. 22, p. 27). Ramchand's remarks illustrate that the 1950s 'boom' involved the emergence not only of male migrant writers but also of the Caribbean novel. Therefore, the privileging of writing produced in the second half of the century referred to by Donnell would seem to run parallel with a privileging of the novel over the short story as the subject matter of Caribbean literary criticism.

Charting the evolution of the Caribbean short story from the 1850s into the twenty-first century, this essay collection challenges the suggestion, made by George Lamming in 1960 and reinforced by later critics, that the notion of a pan-Caribbean aesthetic was first cultivated in England in the second half of the twentieth century.[20] While not contesting the significant contribution of West Indian migrants' experiences of London in the 1950s and 60s to the development of a Caribbean literary tradition, this collection begins from the premise that attention to the formation of a literary culture based in the Caribbean region in the early- to mid-twentieth century is crucial to a full appreciation not only of Caribbean short story writing, but of Caribbean literary and cultural production more generally.

In the first half of the twentieth century, the Caribbean region lacked the publishing houses, distribution channels and reading public necessary for the production of novels. However, a number of small magazines and newspapers in various parts of the region offered an outlet for the publication of short fiction and poetry.[21] These circumstances rendered the short story form central to the development of a regionally based Caribbean literary tradition. Contributions to this collection explore the role of local periodicals in the emergence of the genre within particular Caribbean national literary cultures; Raymond Ramcharitar's essay analyses short fiction appearing in Trinidadian newspapers and magazines from the mid-nineteenth century to the 1930s, and Suzanne Scafe's essay looks at the creative output of Jamaican newspapers and magazines from the late 1930s to the 1950s.

Reinhard W. Sander notes that many of the literary magazines which appeared in the first half of the twentieth century, such as *The Beacon* in Trinidad, *Bim* in Barbados, and *Kyk-Over-Al* in Guyana, were 'West Indian' in outlook, despite being based on particular islands.[22] According to Rhonda Cobham, their circulation between as well as within islands generated 'an exchange of creative work and cultural information across the region that facilitated cross-fertilization of ideas and interests'.[23] These critics' comments indicate how the region's literary magazines of the first half of the twentieth century performed a foundational role in forging connections between island cultures, generating a readership which extended across the archipelago, as well as in building up a tradition of short story writing within the anglophone Caribbean region. This process was aided by *Caribbean Voices*, a radio programme broadcast on the BBC which was contemporary with *Bim* and *Kyk-Over-Al*, and is discussed in depth in Alison Donnell's contribution to this volume. Organised by the British producer Henry Swanzy, and featuring short stories and poems by Caribbean writers, the programme broadcast this material from London back to the English-speaking Caribbean. *Caribbean Voices* not only facilitated the expansion of a Caribbean literary tradition and readership in practical terms, but also, with its insistence on 'local colour' conveyed though the setting and language of the stories,[24] actively intervened in the shaping of a regional Caribbean aesthetic.

Hyacinth Simpson describes how the literary magazines of the 1930s and 40s 'openly embraced nationalism and independence', building their 'cultural and political emphasis in tandem with their publication of short stories'.[25] She later comments that a 'direct connection between politics and literature was again strongly articulated in the 1970s, although with different effects on literary form in the short story' ('Patterns and Periods', p. 15). This collection examines short story writing produced at different historical moments: the period leading up to the independence of Caribbean nations, the period immediately following independence, and the late twentieth and early twenty-first century, where the question of independence has been replaced by other concerns such as globalisation, mass tourism and neocolonial pressures. Stories by a wide range of writers are situated within the specific histories and cultural traditions of various Caribbean regional and diasporic societies. The collection seeks to demonstrate how the close connection between the form and politics of Caribbean short stories has altered through time, manifesting differently in the fantastical experimentalism of contemporary writers such as Pauline Melville and Nalo Hopkinson than in the social realist barrack-yard stories of C.L.R. James and Alfred Mendes.

The tension between oral and literary influences has long been and remains a contentious and politically significant concern for Caribbean short story writers, related to issues such as anti-colonial resistance, nation-building, creolisation, and cultural authenticity. Short story theorists and critics of modernist short fiction have, in different ways, focused on distinctions between literary and popular modes of short story writing, often foregrounding the former as more worthy of critical attention. In the examples examined above, the aesthetic qualities of the 'short story proper' or the 'modernist short story' are defined against the supposedly formulaic character of mass-produced popular short fiction appearing in British and US newspapers and magazines of the late nineteenth and early twentieth century. However, as I have shown, critics regard the creative output of local newspapers and magazines as a basis for the formation of a Caribbean literary aesthetic rather than a threat to it. Furthermore, oral storytelling practices deriving from African, Indian and Amerindian culture have been seen as a vital component of the Caribbean literary tradition developing in the twentieth century. In a Caribbean context, then, popular modes of storytelling, oral and written, are less a foil against which the literary genre of the short story is showcased than a constitutive element of that genre. In the introduction to his 1982 anthology, *Best West Indian Stories*, Ramchand presents the West Indian short story as a 'bridge between the oral tradition and the highly literary appearance of the West Indian novel'.[26] Speaking of the francophone Caribbean, Édouard Glissant probes further into this question of how a Caribbean literary tradition has emerged from a 'tortured relationship between writing and orality'. The difficulty and friction of this relationship is, for him, a source of creativity, generating a 'synthesis of written syntax and spoken rhythms'.[27] Jamaican short story writer Olive Senior is similarly concerned with a productive interplay between the oral and the written, arguing that to 'claim the influence of the oral and assert its continued potency is not to devalue literary endeavour, but to enhance it'.[28]

In a study of the Indo-Caribbean short story, Frank Birbalsingh considers how oral storytelling practices have shaped the narrative structure of

Caribbean short fiction. He sees the short story form in the Caribbean as a 'direct descendent of a Caribbean oral tradition of folk tales' characterised by 'discursive, digressive, episodic and anecdotal literary patterns'.[29] While Birbalsingh's comment is based on an analysis of Sam Selvon's writing, the patterns he identifies can be found in the work of other Caribbean short story writers – for instance E.A. Markham and Robert Antoni, who deploy digression as a structuring principle within a maze of interlinked stories, anecdotes and asides.[30] While these two writers are not given substantial attention within this collection, their particular innovations merit my own brief digression here. Markham's and Antoni's writing challenges the frequently reiterated arguments of Poe and Matthews that short fiction is characterised by a 'single effect' and 'vigorous compression', and should be 'complete and self-contained' (Matthews, pp. 73–4). While the focus of much scholarly debate on the short story form has been on brevity and economy,[31] Markham's and Antoni's styles are deliberately and markedly uneconomical; never complete, their stories run into each other and expand to incorporate shorter embedded tales.[32]

As is implied in the comments of Ramchand, Glissant, Senior and Birbalsingh, the region's oral culture remains alive and buoyant in Caribbean literature, and continues to energise contemporary short story writing. The relationship between the oral and the written is therefore differently nuanced in Caribbean short fiction than in European or US short fiction. Paul March-Russell refers to the 'ghostly presence of oral and folk culture' in the work of Leskov, Kipling and Poe, relating this to the effects of modernity on cultural production. Clare Hanson makes a comparable point about Irish and Welsh short story writers Frank O'Connor, Sean O'Faolain and T.F. Powys who she suggests, 'can only look back self-consciously to a past offering a hypothetically organic "world of story" which has now vanished' (Hanson, p. 111). In Caribbean short story writing, orality is much more than a nostalgic echo of a disappearing art form. Oral storytelling practices not only continue to flourish as part of the region's popular cultural traditions, such as carnival and calypso, but are renewed and reinvented in its literature.

The issue of orality also has a very different bearing on the question of community in Caribbean short story writing. In the examples offered by March-Russell and Hanson, the writers' sense of dislocation from folk traditions is due to the breakdown of 'organic' communities bound by a shared culture as a result of urbanisation. Due to the social and economic changes effected by modernity, individuals are 'estranged from themselves and from each other' (March-Russell, p. 26). This chimes with O'Connor's notion that 'the short story remains by its very nature remote from the community – romantic, individualistic, and intransigent' (O'Connor, p. 21). In contrast, I suggest that community is at the heart of much

Caribbean short story writing, and that orality is often central to the articulation of community. In the first half of the twentieth century the region's literary magazines and the *Caribbean Voices* programme helped to generate communities of short story writers and communities of readers and listeners. In the early twenty-first century, the idea of community remains a dominant theme within Caribbean short fiction.[33] Olive Senior's reflections on her own writing process in 2005 show how an engagement with oral storytelling traditions enables her to explore collective histories and experiences. She explains that 'while writing is a private act, orality is a communal one; it implies a teller and a listener, as traditional song consists of call and response' (Senior, p. 49). Senior explains that in her writing she approximates this form of collective narration, deliberately choosing 'to write from the perspective of the many different people who make up the place I come from and not limit myself to any one point of view' in order to convey how within the Jamaican island community, '[e]very voice feeds into and takes from a larger collective voice' (Senior, p. 42).

As discussed above, critics of the modernist short story have related the formal features of short fiction to the individual experiences of loneliness, isolation, alienation and dislocation due to the break-up of community resulting from industrialisation and technological development. The aesthetics of Caribbean short fiction have emerged from a very different socioeconomic background, where communal experiences are emphasised despite the region's geographical and political fracture and the destabilising effects of mass migration. Cultural critics have conceptualised the Caribbean using models of association across difference: Caribbean cultural identity is presented by Glissant as a 'multiple series of relationships' (Glissant, p. 139), by Antonio Benítez-Rojo as 'a discontinuous series of recurrences'[34] and by Wilson Harris as a 'series of subtle and nebulous links'.[35] In a context where the concept of unity is strained and contested in a variety of ways, Poe's notion of the short story's 'unity of effect' becomes inappropriate as an analytical tool. At the same time, Nadine Gordimer's description of the short story as 'fragmented and restless', resembling momentary flashes of fireflies surrounded by darkness and in this sense expressing the 'loneliness and isolation of the individual in a competitive society' is not entirely applicable to Caribbean short story writing, where the question of community is often a central issue, examined alongside and in tension with themes of alienation and cultural dislocation. As this collection of critical essays aims to demonstrate, the study of Caribbean short stories requires new theoretical and critical paradigms sensitive to the specific histories and cultural traditions of the region and its diaspora.

BOOK STRUCTURE AND CONTENTS

The essays are divided into five parts which link them on the basis of shared concerns and subject matter, although these groupings are by no means discrete: there are of course multiple points of connection between sections. The first part of the collection focuses on publishing histories of Caribbean short stories, exploring the role played by newspapers, magazines, radio and cultural organisations in the genre's development in various parts of the region. Alison Donnell analyses women's short fiction broadcast on the BBC's *Caribbean Voices* programme in the 1950s, looking at stories by Edwina Melville, Marina Crichlow and Sylvia Wynter. She comments critically on the gender politics implicit in the programme's editorial processes, considering the marked difference in the literary profiling of male and female writers and the impact of this on the shaping of a Caribbean literary canon. Suzanne Scafe's essay examines Jamaican short fiction published in newspapers and small magazines or self-published from the late 1930s to the 1950s. By identifying the wide range of styles, strategies and political orientations of short story writing in this period, Scafe draws attention to the conflicts and tensions characterising the emergence of a national literary tradition. Raymond Ramcharitar discusses short stories published in the *Beacon* magazine in the 1930s. Arguing that these stories reproduce the discourse of the 'colonial Imaginary', his essay unsettles the critical consensus that the Beacon Group was foundational to the development of a Trinidadian and a West Indian literary tradition, making for an interesting dialogue with Jak Peake's essay in this collection. Shifting from anglophone to hispanic Caribbean writing, Patricia Catoira's essay explores the impact of revolutionary politics, and later, the economic crisis of the 1990s, on the production of Cuban short stories. Catoira proposes that whereas the Cuban novel has 'become hijacked' by global market forces, short story writers have acquired more creative autonomy in the twenty-first century.

    The second part of the collection consists of essays which highlight particular political and socioeconomic contexts underpinning the aesthetics of Caribbean regional and diasporic short fiction. Abigail Ward explores Ismith Khan's engagement with the legacies of Indian indenture, focusing on his portrayal of the Indian Caribbean subject as outsider, excluded by Trinidad's African Caribbean population and at odds with a British colonial education system. Elizabeth Walcott-Hackshaw examines how two contemporary Haitian writers – Yanick Lahens and Edwidge Danticat – manipulate the short story form in their creative response to the island's traumatic history of dictatorial régimes. Both Ward's and Walcott-Hackshaw's readings highlight tensions and overlaps between Caribbean experiences within and beyond the region. Claire Westall explores the representation of cricket and childhood in the short stories of six writers of varying social, cultural and ethnic backgrounds: Michael Anthony, Paul Keens-Douglas, Earl McKenzie, Ismith Khan, Raywat Deonandan and Elahi Baksh. Her analysis demonstrates the political significance of cricket in the Caribbean, touching on themes such as nationalism, community, social exclusion and racial divisions. Sandra Courtman's essay covers stories from Jamaica, Britain, Puerto Rico and Trinidad published between 1960 and 1991 (by John Figueroa, Stuart Hall, Rosario Ferré and Willi Chen). She emphasises the cross-cultural aspects of these stories, both in their simultaneous appeal to local and international reading audiences, and in the way that they creolise the short story form through linguistic and structural innovations.

The essays in part three focus on Caribbean short story writers' engagement with a modernist aesthetic and/or the notion of modernity. Dave Gunning offers a reading of Claude McKay's and Eric Walrond's short story collections of the 1920s and 30s. Emphasising the global dimensions of their work, Gunning considers these writers' conception of a 'black internationalism' which is crucial to, rather than at odds with, their depiction of Caribbean culture. The essay locates the modernist techniques of Walrond's stories within an experience of modernity specific to the Caribbean region. James Procter examines the form, content and publishing history of Seepersad Naipaul's short stories, challenging critical studies which place them in the shadow of V.S. Naipaul's novels. Focusing on the formal constraints of the short story and relating this to Seepersad Naipaul's depiction of an insular and isolated East Indian Trinidadian community, Procter explores the stories' articulation of tensions between Indian traditions and a creolised, urban modernity. Joanna Johnson explores Jean Rhys's economical, 'pared-down' mode of short story writing, evaluating the effects of rigorous cutting on the style, tone and subject matter of her stories and looking at her use of modernist techniques such as epiphany, ellipsis and impressionism. Offering a very different reading of the Beacon Group and its influence on later generations of Trinidadian writers than Raymond Ramcharitar's essay, Jak Peake considers how Lawrence Scott and Earl Lovelace remap Trinidad with their focus on relations between the local and the global, and between the Caribbean region and the Americas. The essay explores how their depiction of unbounded and relational Caribbean geographies is expressed through the form of interconnected stories.

Part four deals with vernacular influences, illustrating the ways in which folktales and oral traditions continue to shape the form and content of contemporary Caribbean short stories. Emily Zobel Marshall examines Andrew Salkey's reinvention of Anancy, the trickster spider figure, through his reworking of Caribbean folktales, themselves reinterpretations of stories told within Akan tribal communities. Comparing short story collections published in 1973 and 1992, the essay considers the changing social and political significance of Anancy stories. Gina Wisker looks at the combination of speculative fiction with European, African and Caribbean folktales in the short stories of Caribbean Canadian writer Nalo Hopkinson, exploring how this innovation enables Hopkinson to comment upon the constraints of racial and gendered identity, as well as to envisage alternative futures. Patricia Murray examines the distinctly Guyanese characteristics of Pauline Melville's stories, considering their formal and thematic engagement with myth, folktale and the carnivalesque. The essay identifies how Melville draws upon Alejo Carpentier's notion of the 'marvellous real' while adapting it to incorporate migrant experiences and diasporic locations. Melville's work is presented as politically charged, despite – or rather through – her exploration of 'spirit worlds on the move'.

The essays in the fifth and final part of the book focus on some of the ways in which writers push against the established generic boundaries of the short story form, blurring distinctions between short fiction and poetry, or the short story and the novel. Shirley Chew examines the various kinds of 'intertwinings' which have both shaped Olive Senior's life and featured within her writing: of ethnicities and cultural backgrounds, of folk traditions and colonial influences, of the oral and the written. In doing so, she offers insights into the generic 'intertwinings' of Senior's work, where short stories have the musicality of poetry and where poetry is structured as a story sequence. My own essay positions V.S. Naipaul's sequence of interconnected stories and prose fragments, *A Way in the World* (1994), alongside his first story sequence, *Miguel Street* (1959), considering how both the form of the sequence and the concept of a Caribbean community are renegotiated in the later text. Discussing recent collections of linked stories by Kwame Dawes and Mark McWatt, Andrew Armstrong examines the trope of the journey as it operates both thematically and formally, in these writers' crossing of the generic boundaries of the short story, novel and poem. Elaine Savory analyses Kamau Brathwaite's 'dreamstories', published in various forms at different points in his career. Drawing attention to the 'porous' borders not only between these continually revised stories but also between the genres of short fiction and poetry in Brathwaite's work, Savory considers his development of a 'postmodern' style which combines ancient storytelling practices with postmodernist experimentation.

As a whole, *The Caribbean Short Story: Critical Perspectives* presents the Caribbean short story not only as integral to the emergence of the region's literary culture, but also as a site of continuing invention and renewal. As the above outline indicates, the scope of the collection is culturally, geographically and historically extensive, and encompasses anglophone, francophone and hispanophone linguistic zones. Essays cover Caribbean writing from Jamaica, Guyana, Trinidad, Dominica, Barbados, Cuba, Puerto Rico and Haiti as well as Canada, the US and Britain, dealing with writers from a variety of ethnic backgrounds. Furthermore, ranging from discussions of James, McKay, Rhys and Walrond in the early twentieth century to Danticat, Dawes, Hopkinson and McWatt in the twenty-first century, the essays illuminate continuities and differences in the way the short story form has been employed by Caribbean writers through time, giving readers a broad sense of the genre's evolution. As such, the collection paves the way for more specialised studies of Caribbean short story writing in particular time periods or locales.

NOTES

1 Gordon Rohlehr, 'Author's Preface', in *The Shape of That Hurt and Other Essays* (Port of Spain, Trinidad: Longman, 1992), pp. vii–xiii (p. x).
2 Gordon Rohlehr, 'The Problem of the Problem of Form', in *The Shape of That Hurt*, pp. 1–65 (p. 2).
3 Kenneth Ramchand, 'The West Indian Short Story', *Journal of Caribbean Literatures*, 1:1 (1997), 21–30 (p. 27, p. 21).
4 See, for example, Charles E. May, *The Short Story: The Reality of Artifice* (New York and London: Routledge, 2002 [1995]), p. 1; Susan Lohafer, 'Introduction', in *The Tales We Tell: Perspectives on the Short Story*, ed. by Barbara Lounsberry, Susan Lohafer, Mary Rohrberger, Stephen Pett, and R.C. Fedderson (Westport, CT and London: Greenwood Press, 1998), pp. ix–xii (p. ix); 'Preface' to *Postmodern Approaches to the Short Story*, ed. by Farhat Iftekharrudin, Joseph Boyden, Joseph Longo, and Mary Rohrberger (Westport, CT and London: Praeger, 2003), pp. vii–xi (p. vii).
5 Edgar Allan Poe, 'Review of *Twice-Told Tales*', *Graham's Magazine*, May 1842. Reprinted in in *The New Short Story Theories*, ed. by Charles E. May (Athens, OH: Ohio University Press, 1994), pp. 59–72 (pp. 60–61).
6 Brander Matthews, 'The Philosophy of the Short-Story' [1901], in *The New Short Story Theories*, ed. by May, pp. 73–80 (p. 73).
7 Mary Rohrberger, 'The Short Story: A Proposed Definition' [1966], in *Short Story Theories*, ed. by Charles E. May (Athens, OH: Ohio University Press, 1976), pp. 80–82 (p. 81).
8 Ian Reid, *The Short Story* (London: Methuen, 1977), p. 4.
9 Nadine Gordimer, 'The Flash of Fireflies' [1968], in *The New Short Story Theories*, ed. by May, pp. 263–67 (p. 264).
10 See, for example, Dominic Head, *The Modernist Short Story: A Study in Theory and Practice* (Cambridge: Cambridge University Press, 1992), p. 6; Clare Hanson, *Short Stories and Short Fictions, 1880–1980* (London: Macmillan, 1995), p. 57; Adrian Hunter, *The Cambridge Introduction to the Short Story in English* (Cambridge: Cambridge University Press, 2007), p. 46.
11 See particularly Suzanne C. Ferguson's discussion of the impressionist movement's impact on early twenty-first century short story writing in 'Defining the Short

Story: Impressionism and Form', *Modern Fiction Studies*, 28:1 (1982), 13–24.

12 Paul March-Russell, *The Short Story: An Introduction* (Edinburgh: Edinburgh University Press, 2009), p. 26.

13 W.H. New, *Dreams of Speech and Violence: The Art of the Short Story in Canada and New Zealand* (Toronto, ON: University of Toronto Press, 1987), p. 4.

14 As well as the publications discussed below, see *The Tales We Tell: Perspectives on the Short Story*, ed. by Lounsberry, Lohafer, Rohrberger, Pett, and Fedderson, which includes an essay on the anglophone African short story; *Postmodern Approaches to the Short Story* (2003), ed. by Iftekharrudin, Boyden, Longo, and Rohrberger, which includes an essay on Iranian short fiction and an essay on the postcolonial short story; *The Postmodern Short Story: Forms and Issues*, ed. by Farhat Iftekharrudin, Joseph Boyden, Mary Rohrberger, and Jaie Claudet (Westport, CT and London: Praeger, 2003), which includes an essay on Canadian short fiction.

15 Mary Louise Pratt, 'The Short Story: The Long and the Short of It', *Poetics*, 10 (1981), 175–94 (p. 187).

16 Frank O'Connor, *The Lonely Voice: A Study of the Short Story* (London: Macmillan, 1963), pp. 19–20.

17 For example, F. Odun Balogun, *Tradition and Modernity in the African Short Story: An Introduction to a Literature in Search of Critics* (New York: Greenwood, 1991); Bruce Bennett, *Australian Short Fiction: A History* (Santa Lucia: University of Queensland Press, 2002); *The Short Story in South East Asia: Aspects of a Genre*, ed. by Jeremy H.C.S. Davidson and Helen Cordell (London: School of Oriental and African Studies, 1982); *The Canadian Short Story: Interpretations*, ed. by Reingard M. Nischik (Rochester, NY: Camden House, 2007).

18 Hyacinth M. Simpson, 'Introduction', *Journal of West Indian Literature*, 12:1–2 (2004), i–vii (p. i, p. vi).

19 Alison Donnell, *Twentieth-Century Caribbean Literature: Critical Moments in Anglophone Literary History* (London and New York: Routledge, 2006), p. 11.

20 George Lamming describes how the category 'West Indian' only 'assumed cultural significance' for migrants encountering one another 'in foreign territory', and proposes that '[i]n this sense, most West Indians of my generation were born in England' (*The Pleasures of Exile* (London: Pluto Press, 2005 [1960]), p. 214). Three decades later, Anne Walmsley presents the CAM, initially located in England, as 'the first genuinely Caribbean-wide cultural movement' (*The Caribbean Artists Movement 1966–1972: A Literary and Cultural History* (London and Port of Spain, Trinidad: New Beacon Books, 1992), p. 315).

21 See Louis James, 'Writing the Ballad: The Short Fiction of Samuel Selvon and Earl Lovelace', in *Telling Stories: Postcolonial Short Fiction in English*, ed. by Jacqueline Bardolph (Amsterdam & Atlanta, GA: Rodopi, 2001), pp. 103–08 (p. 104). James suggests that this situation is partly due to the geographic fragmentation of the region.

22 Reinhard W. Sander, 'The Thirties and Forties', in *West Indian Literature*, ed. by Bruce King, 2nd edn (London: Macmillan, 1995, pp. 38–49 (p. 40). The term 'West Indian', used by the editors of these magazines, concerns only the anglophone Caribbean, unlike the more inclusive terms 'Antillean' and 'Caribbean' used by later writers, critics and cultural theorists to refer to all linguistic zones.

23 Rhonda Cobham, 'The Background', in *West Indian Literature*, ed. by King, pp. 11–26 (p. 18).

24 Returning rejected manuscripts to the Jamaican-based editor Gladys Lindo in 1946, Swanzy regrets the 'complete absence of local colour'. Henry Swanzy, letter to Gladys Lindo, 13 August 1946, *Caribbean Voices* correspondence 1945–1953, folder 1, West Indiana Collection, UWI St. Augustine, Trinidad.

25 Hyacinth M. Simpson, 'Patterns and Periods: Oral Aesthetics and a Century of Jamaican Short Story Writing', *Journal of West Indian Literature*, 12:1–2 (2004), 1–30 (p. 12).

26 Kenneth Ramchand, 'The Short Story – An Introduction', in *Best West Indian Stories* (Kingston: Nelson Caribbean, 1982), pp. 1–5 (p. 2).

27 Édouard Glissant, *Caribbean Discourse: Selected Essays*, trans. by Michael J. Dash (Charlottesville, VA: University of Virginia Press, 1989 [1981]), p. 147.

28 Olive Senior, 'The Story as Su-Su, the Writer as Gossip', in *Writers on Writing: The Art of the Short Story*, ed. by Maurice A. Lee (Westport, Connecticut and London: Praeger, 2005), pp. 41–50 (p. 50).

29 Frank Birbalsingh, 'The Indo-Caribbean Short Story', *Journal of West Indian Literature*, 12:1–2 (2004), 118–34 (p. 125).

30 See, for example, E.A. Markham, *Taking the Drawing Room Through Customs* (Leeds: Peepal Tree, 2002) and Robert Antoni, *My Grandmother's Erotic Folktales* (London: Faber & Faber, 2000).

31 Here I include critics of modernist short fiction who often draw on James Joyce's self-conscious allusion to his own 'style of scrupulous meanness' in the writing of *Dubliners* (*The Letters of James Joyce*, Volume II, ed. by Richard Ellman (London: Faber, 1966), p. 134).

32 I discuss this in more detail in the following articles: 'Questioning Black Identity: Strategies of Digression in E.A. Markham's *Meet Me in Mozambique*', *Moving Worlds*, 9:2, (2009), 125–36; 'Local and Global Reading Communities in Robert Antoni's *My Grandmother's Erotic Folktales*', in *Postcolonial Audiences: Readers, Viewers and Reception*, ed. by Bethan Benwell, James Procter and Gemma Robinson (London and New York: Routledge, forthcoming 2011).

33 This issue is explored more fully in my book-length study, *Communities in Contemporary Caribbean Short Stories* (work in progress).

34 Antonio Benítez-Rojo, 'Three Words toward Creolization', trans. by James Maraniss, in *Caribbean Creolization: Reflections on the Cultural Dynamics of Language, Literature and Identity*, ed. by Kathleen M. Balutansky and Marie-Agnès Sourieau (Gainesville, FL: University Press of Florida, 1998), pp. 53–61 (p. 55).

35 Wilson Harris, 'Tradition and the West Indian Novel', in *Selected Essays of Wilson Harris: The Unfinished Genesis of the Imagination*, ed. by Andrew Bundy (London and New York: Routledge, 1999), pp. 140–51 (p. 140).

PART ONE

PUBLISHING HISTORIES

HEARD BUT NOT SEEN: WOMEN'S SHORT STORIES AND THE BBC'S *CARIBBEAN VOICES* PROGRAMME

ALISON DONNELL

It is now a much-repeated fact of anglophone Caribbean literary history that many of the internationally acclaimed writers whose names trip off the tongue – V.S. Naipaul, Derek Walcott, Sam Selvon and George Lamming – were given their first 'break' or 'airing' on the BBC radio programme, *Caribbean Voices*. The much-cited story of V.S. Naipaul tapping out the first pages of *Miguel Street* in the BBC offices forms the epicentre of its creative reputation. Indeed, most accounts of the success of this programme point to its role in the formation of the region's major male novelists. This chapter wishes to divert attention to the many short stories by women writers that were broadcast across the lifetime of this pioneering programme. These unresearched and unacknowledged early stirrings of Caribbean literary expression may not have led to the grand narratives of national self-definition that we still identify as the central, if male, canon, but perhaps this difference points to their distinctive value. These short stories by women – often focused on the domestic, the local, the intricately human – offer important glimpses of another Caribbean literary aesthetic and ethic that was quietly in the making in the 1950s. They also, in their careful rendering of the involved life of communities and their expression of a yearning for communication and literary intimacy, restore a fitting back-history to the works of accomplished Caribbean women short story writers today, such as Olive Senior, Lorna Goodison and Christine Craig.

The *Caribbean Voices* programme was first broadcast in March 1943 and came to an end in 1958. Initially a twenty-minute Sunday broadcast, the programme was fashioned by the Jamaican writer and journalist Una Marson. Indeed, if there is a woman's presence spoken of at all within the context of *Caribbean Voices*, then it is usually that of Marson. Marson, the first black woman employed by the BBC, was initially appointed programme assistant for *Calling the West Indies*, a radio programme which relayed 'morale-boosting' messages from servicemen based in the UK back home to the Caribbean. However, Marson's involvement in the BBC's prestigious poetry programme *Voices* and her impassioned commitment to Caribbean cultural nationalism shaped her vision and she started weaving readings of published works by Caribbean writers and reports of cultural events into her broadcasts. The success of this format garnered support for her idea of a 'Caribbean Voices' programme, unique among the Overseas provision, and the broadcasts soon gathered quite a following.

In the summer of 1946 when Marson's poor health necessitated her return to Jamaica, the BBC approached the now legendary Henry Swanzy, already a producer with the Overseas Service. The rest, as they say, is – Caribbean literary – history. Philip Nanton describes the programme's impressive statistics:

> Over the 15 years of its existence, some 400 stories and poems were broadcast, along with plays and literary criticism from around the region. There were 372 contributors in all, of whom 71 were women. Many writers, artists, and musicians who cut their literary teeth on the programme went on to achieve international fame, notably the Nobel Prize-winners Derek Walcott of St Lucia and Trinidad-born V.S. Naipaul; but also George Lamming and Kamau Brathwaite from Barbados; Sam Selvon, again from Trinidad; Edgar Mittelholzer, Wilson Harris, and Ian McDonald from Guyana; and Andrew Salkey, Gloria Escoffery, and John Figueroa from Jamaica.[1]

It is no coincidence that the programme's lifetime aligned with the 'boom' in West Indian literature and it deserves much credit as a formative literary platform. In many instances its modest annual budget provided the literal as well as literary sustenance to see fledgling talents safely out of the nest, as well as confirming the possibility of authorship as a profession. To be granted airtime on the BBC accorded these writings a proper value, aside from the inflated prestige associated with acknowledgement from the 'motherland'. What is more, the opportunity for writers to have their work broadcast to an interested audience allayed one of the main concerns about fostering positive conditions for writers within Caribbean societies. The programme quickly became a literary centre of gravity, attracting potential scripts from writers across the region through advertisements in local newspapers and by word of mouth. At the same time, its energy worked outwards, transmitting writings back across the region and thereby over-coming the problem of fragmentation and isolation that had constrained earlier island-based literary projects, such as the pioneering All Jamaica Library. Importantly then, *Caribbean Voices* did not only nurture the individual careers of several literary giants, but it also opened up a signifi-cant and influential cultural arena in which personal friendships and alliances between writers could be built. It offered a congregation point (both real and wireless, local and international) to which Caribbean writers and audiences could gather in excitement as weekly and varied expressions of a Caribbean literature were both voiced and heard.

Given that the *Caribbean Voices* programme is so emphatically and repeatedly linked to the success of Caribbean literary authorship, it is all the more regrettable that nearly all of the women writers whose work it broadcast remain unknown to readers and even researchers of Caribbean literature today. Talented writers such as Eula Redhead, Inez Sibley, Marjorie Brown and Edwina Melville remain unremarked upon. Louise

Bennett and Sylvia Wynter are the exceptions to this rule, although neither was particularly facilitated in their writing careers by the programme. Such a discrepancy between the visibility of male and female writers would seem to invite a gendered analysis, and the politics of gender influencing the profiling of literary authorship in this context was not a straightforward one.

Certainly, the recovery of Caribbean women's writing and other cultural activities during this period cannot be undertaken innocent of the homosocial character of many of the foundational organisations that facilitated cultural prominence for Caribbean writers. The League of Coloured Peoples, the BBC *Caribbean Voices* grouping, the Caribbean Artists Movement, the independent publishing scene of the 1960s and 70s, and the dub and reggae scene of the 1970s all operated as brotherhoods of sorts. This is not to say that they did not include women but rather that there is often a clear correlation between the secondary and supportive roles women occupied as assistants, secretaries, organisers and facilitators in these movements and projects, and their representation as marginal figures in, or complete absence from, historical accounts. Yet, even when women were on a seemingly equal footing, as with these writers whose works were selected for broadcast, their professional destiny remained dramatically different to that of men.

There is more than a hint of the boys' club atmosphere to be detected in the BBC groupings that formed the *Caribbean Voices'* pathways to literary visibility. Although the programme had come into being at the hands of Una Marson and was briefly overseen by Mary Treadgold, the gender profiling of the programme altered dramatically once Swanzy was appointed. The programme was managed by John Grenfell Williams and all subsequent gatekeepers were men, with V.S. Naipaul, Edgar Mittelholzer and Andrew Salkey all acting in editorial roles at various points. Gladys Lindo was appointed as the local representative in Jamaica, but her husband Cedric effectively took on the role, acting as 'a sort of coarse sieve merely to cut down on his [Swanzy's] work'.[2] Another unofficial but highly influential friend of Swanzy's was Frank Collymore, the editor of the pioneering literary little magazine *Bim*. Although edited and produced in Barbados, *Bim* attracted and supported writing from across the Caribbean and their correspondence led to a series of productive literary exchanges. Several of the women whose stories were broadcast on the programme had work published in *Bim*. In 1948, Swanzy introduced a more academic element to the programme and engaged two critics for special quarterly broadcasts based on a discussion of the literary value of selected works. Both were men. Arthur Calder Marshall, a progressive if not radical thinker in terms of colonial politics[3] and Roy Fuller, an English poet and a regarded literary reviewer of the period. Both clearly argued for Caribbean writers and writing at a time when this was not necessarily easy or popular.

My point is to suggest that this almost exclusively male cluster was inevitably shaped by a shared perspective on social, political and literary matters that was itself implicitly informed by masculine norms. In this regard, the women writers' focus on more domestic, intimate and interior worlds was not as immediately correspondent with the idea of Caribbean national cultural expression that sat at the centre of the BBC's West Indian programming mission. Indeed, while researching 'early' Caribbean women's writing in the 1990s I began a correspondence with Henry Swanzy and visited him to discuss women's contributions to the programme. In one letter, Swanzy pauses from his evaluations of various women writers to offer the following reflection:

> On reading this reply I am uneasily aware that I might be accused of male chauvinism. Possibly the same thing might be said of the various links in the chain of communication: Cedric Lindo, Frank Collymore, A. J. Seymour. I always think it [sad (crossed out)] odd that I never even heard of Jean Rhys.[4]

What Swanzy's reflection does suggest is the extent to which homosociality operated as an unwitting mechanism for inclusion, allowing West Indian men to build alliances with one another as well as with British (and in Swanzy's case, Irish) men, using already established modes of social exchange. In this context, Swanzy's sense of himself as a man among men was not a situation manufactured by his individual cultural habits.

One of the major factors that created the startling difference of literary fortunes for Caribbean male and female writers of this generation is that the women writers, or budding writers, did not migrate during the early Windrush years. Therefore their presence, while heard through these broadcasts, was not seen or felt in the same way as the active nucleus of male writers who occupied the metropolitan space and would frequently drop into the freelancers' room at London's Langham Hotel. Although the extent of the women writers' connections to one another remains unclear, it is doubtful that they had much contact as a group within island communities and there was no comparable sense of a band of emergent female writers. Of course, many West Indian women did migrate to the UK and other northern countries during this period to take work as domestics, nurses and teachers and their labour generated a significant portion of the remittance sent back to the Caribbean. However, it would seem that the women who had demonstrated their talents as writers did not transport their emergent literary identities or ambitions to London, the then epicentre of Caribbean literary activity. Yet, even if they had made this journey, who is to say that they would have benefited from the creative community any more than Marson, who appears to have serviced the career of other writers more than her own from this metropolitan base.

This gendered reality of Caribbean life certainly impacted on women's understanding of their identities as authors. Selvon and Lamming shared an 'Imperial' typewriter on the boat to England and travelled to London with a determined focus on their vocation of being a writer. Caribbean women writers have seldom shared that same exclusive focus on or privilege of a writing identity. It would be unhelpful to generalise about the social positions or lifestyles of the women who submitted work to the *Caribbean Voices* programme as, from the little biographical information that I have managed to glean to date, these appear to have been very varied. However, it seems reasonable to assume that none of them identified as a writer in the same way as Lamming or Selvon, or indeed as the self-confessed precociously assured and talented Derek Walcott. For some, such as H.V. Ormsby Marshall, who founded the Jamaica Centre of the international P.E.N. club in 1948 and served as its Hon. Secretary, writing was likely a leisure activity in a culturally busy middle-class life. For others, such as Gloria Escoffery, writing was one part of her involvement in expressive culture as she was a prominent reviewer and visual artist. The same is true for Marina Critchlow, later Marina Ama Omowale Maxwell, who came to Britain from Trinidad in the 1960s and was an active, radical member of the Caribbean Artists' Movement. Later, she founded the esteemed Yard Theatre Movement in Jamaica and wrote essays, poetry and plays. For Maxwell writing was a steady, committed but largely unac-knowledged pursuit. For Edwina Melville, writing was a gifted fraction of her remarkably full life. Melville took employment as a schoolteacher and shop-holder but she also served for many years as a Member of Parliament for the People's National Congress in Guyana where she represented the cause of the Amerindians.

But for most, such as Laurice Bird, Marjorie Brown, Connie McTurk, Eva Nicholas and Rose Auguste, who have left little trace, it was most probably because their economic, domestic and familial identities, as well as lived realities, meant that any such identity would have been unimagi-nable. Later generations of Caribbean women writers, especially those who remained in the Caribbean, such as Merle Hodge, Erna Brodber and Olive Senior, did not distinguish 'writer' as the identity to be pursued at all costs but rather wove the activity of writing into their intellectual and profes-sional lives. This is also true of migrant women. Although when Marson came to England in 1932 she had published two collections of poetry and seen her first play successfully staged in Kingston, she took up work as the secretary to the League of Coloured Peoples and was known at the BBC as an assistant. Arriving slightly later in the 1950s, Beryl Gilroy's first book *Black Teacher* (1971) was based on her experience as one of the first black head teachers in Britain at Beckford Infants' School, London. How exactly this apparent difference in conceptualising a writing identity impacted on women's literary careers is as difficult to measure as the reasons for the difference itself and yet it remains an enduring consideration to try to understand the starkly gendered disparity in literary fortune.

It would be wrong to underplay the support and assurance that being broadcast on the *Caribbean Voices* programme offered to its women authors and readers. Certainly, reliable employment at the BBC was safe haven to Marson, just as it was to Naipaul. The same is true of one of the programme's finest readers, Pauline Henriques. Although an accomplished actress, who in 1946 became the first black actress to appear on British television in Eugene O'Neill's *All God's Chillun' Got Wings*, stage work was difficult to find for Henriques and she even 'whited up' on occasion. Her employment at BBC radio as an actress and a broadcaster gave Henriques an enabling professional context. Yet neither Marson nor Henriques were employed as writers and it is in terms of expectations for a literary career that the gender gap becomes most marked.

It is known that Henry Swanzy and later Andrew Salkey acted as informal literary agents for promising writers, contacting London publishers and agents or making such contacts possible. The same gestures of creative nurture and door-opening were seemingly not offered to women. Another extract from Swanzy's letter offers a clue in this regard:

> Far away on the high savannas of the Rupununi in Guiana there was a particular favourite of mine, a girl called Edwina Melville, who was the only writer to send material direct to London. Her account of listening to the radio in her vast solitude was so well done that I was able to have it printed in the 20th anniversary number of the BBC external journal <u>London Calling</u>. I often wonder what happened to her. She was married to the Melville clan on the borders of Venezuela, against whom Forbes Burnham sent three planeloads of troops, to smoke them out.[5]

Swanzy's admiration and affection for Edwina Melville is not in question. All the same, his mention of this formidable woman as a 'girl' and as 'married to the Melville clan' begins to shrink the frame of possible representation for her as a serious writer. Swanzy's efforts to promote her literary reputation are not to be dismissed but recommending her captivating story, 'The Voice', to the BBC's Overseas Journal is hardly a gesture in the same league as recommending works to London publishing houses and is suggestive of a whole web of associations, assumptions and circumstances which came together to downplay the possibilities for women writers to find professional status, even those whose literary talents were not in dispute.

In considering literary profile and visibility, the short story form itself is certainly significant. The particular currency of the short story as a feminine form is often cited. Diminutive, domestic and often more provisional than a novel, the short story is often regarded as fitting a woman's sensibility but also the pragmatics of her writing life, if it comes in precious snatches of time.[6] Indeed, while this form suited the radio programme's format, the successful male writers who submitted prose all went on to be novelists. Sylvia Wynter was the only woman to have followed this transition from short story to novel writing, and the best known after Bennett. Since the economy of the short story form leads to an intensification of observation and to highly focalised scenes that coalesce person and place, the genre was well-suited to the programme's demands for demonstrably 'Caribbean' works. Yet, while these women writers arguably conformed to Lamming's now famous account of the West Indian writer as one who 'looked in and down at what had traditionally been ignored....',[7] it is worth recognising that the gendering of lives that emerges from within their stories' compressed frames is often depicted against the expectations formed by the reading of male canonical works, many from this same period. For Lamming, this task led to the restoration of 'the West Indian peasant to his true and original status of personality' (Lamming, p. 39). For these writers, acts of representation and restoration are more locally specific. Indeed, the Irish short story writer Frank O'Connor's observation that the form was particularly suited to expressing the conditions of 'submerged communities' seems most fitting to their work.[8] What is restored in these works are highly particularised communities, defined in part by the same historical concerns that shaped the works of the canonical male writers but often centred on Caribbean lives and situations still reaching for literary articulation today. Although there are very many stories that merit close critical reading, this piece will focus on stories by Edwina Melville, Marina Crichlow and Sylvia Wynter. To my mind, these works raise interesting questions around the voicing of gendered experience and demonstrate formal departures and innovations that give this voicing an aesthetic correlative.

Edwina Melville, whom Henry Swanzy told me was the only woman to send her scripts directly to London, is an interesting case study for a consideration of how the programme's short stories voiced both a woman's and a Caribbean world. Melville's three stories are strikingly different in terms of style and content but what unifies them is the lovingly detailed portrayal of grounded human and animal lives. Her first story, 'Fishing in the Rupununi Savannah, British Guiana' was broadcast on Sunday 9 August 1953. Although this piece relates a fishing trip, the narrative is arguably more fully engaged in sketching the relationship between the husband and wife and the story begins with the wife's sense of her inauspiciousness:

> She was beginning to think she was a 'Jonah'. You know, the bad luck person. A person that makes plans go all wrong the minute they put in an appearance. Last year they had planned a fishing trip and at the last moment down came the rain and they were prevented from even peeping out of doors for three days straight!

> Now the same thing happened this year, but added to the rain both [her] baby daughter and herself got fever the very same day we were supposed to have gone fishing.

The cancelled trip, which is taken instead by two Indians, leaves her husband 'furious', 'disappointed' and 'restless'. When he resolves to take the trip alone, his wife asks to accompany him. His initial response is negative: 'Not this time Babs. You're not well and it looks like rain again. I'm only going to Jacare. You know I always go there alone.' Yet, when he reappears and tells her to hurry as he is about to leave, 'She needed no second bidding and before you could say "Jack Robinson" she was on the back of that motor-bike and Coco [...] promised to look after the babies while she was gone.'

The story of their trip is rich in local detail. Yet the act of fishing with bow and arrow, and the naming of particular trees and fish, are all framed within the narrative of the wife struggling not to fall behind her husband, not to be a Jonah. There is a moment when Melville's sketching of the environment also seems to carry an allegorical function. The discovery of fish teeming and swarming with a hum equivalent to an engine is followed by Melville's explanation of the 'Ruar' fish. Her first comment seems significant: 'It is the male who makes the noise, the female just slithers silently along tired with the burden of eggs she carries'. Throughout, there is a strong sense of woman's yearning to participate in the world beyond the home, to engage equally with men in the pleasures of the land and the thrill of adventure (Melville was the first woman in Guyana to obtain a tractor driver's licence).

The original manuscript enacts odd shifts in perspective so that the female protagonist seems to be identified at some points as 'she', and at others as 'I' and once as 'Edwina'. The husband, Chas, also takes the first person narration at points. Unusually, the script for this story shows editorial changes throughout, seemingly by one hand. It would be difficult to speculate whether these changes were made by Swanzy who was the producer at this point (though they do not appear to be in his distinctive hand) or perhaps by the Guyanese writer Gordon Woolford who acted as reader for this piece, or by another BBC employee. Although frequent, these alterations serve mainly to standardise third person narration but there are a couple of more interesting interventions.

On page three of the manuscript, the editor has put a line through two paragraphs that comprise almost half the page and written the words 'Jump bit'. These paragraphs, presumably omitted from the broadcast, do not add to the detailed depiction of the Guyanese environment and could be seen as a digression from the fishing story. Rather, they offer an extended moment in the narrative for the wife's consideration of the emotional dynamic of her marriage.

> I began to wonder if he had brought me through these torturous brambles
> and gnarled tacubas on purpose. I was determined not to say I wanted
> to go home [...]. How gleeful my husband would be if I fell, although
> I really didn't have much more to soak.

Without these paragraphs, the story is more straightforwardly a tale of
action. It also becomes more clearly about the naming of the habitat and the
particular style of the encounter between human, animal and natural
worlds that occurs within the Rupununi savannah. This editorial stream-
lining would confirm what Griffith has called 'Swanzy's focus on the
Caribbean local and particular'.[9] What is lost is the story's interest in the
gendering of entitlements to such 'adventure' and the intimacy with place
that it affords.

The other editorial change of note comes on page three of the manuscript when the couple head off to another spot in search of fish. The
manuscript reads: 'Once again they clambered down steep sides and I
showed Edwina how the water was so high that it had covered what was an
old cart road at the side of the lake'. With the editorial changes, the story was
broadcast as 'Once again they clambered down steep sides and he showed
her how the water was so high...' The erasure of Edwina, of the announcement of the writer as a literary subject, clearly denies the auto/biographical
signature of this piece. While this gesture may seem both innocent and
possibly insignificant, Melville's more sustained and explicit identification
of herself within her second story suggests that it had significance to her
own understanding of her work.

'The Voice', broadcast on Sunday 20 June 1954, is a brief but compelling vignette centred, tellingly, on the broadcast 'event' of a woman's short
story in the Rupununi savannahs. The metatextuality of the piece, re-
hearsing with creative licence the moment when the first short story was
broadcast, is sharpened by Melville's description of the Indians listening
to the story,

> repeating now and then the names of people and places they knew. A
> few English words they could catch, and one of them so excited he wanted
> to tell others what he heard, translated one word – Coupau, he said
> clearly, 'fish'.

There is no mistaking the correspondence between these two 'fishing'
stories. Melville ensures that this second short story successfully delivers
the woman writer to the centre of her own text. Interestingly though,
having achieved this, the piece reaches out towards the literary inclusion of
another peripheral identity.

Opening with an appeal to the listener to make an imaginative journey,
Melville elegantly evokes the scale of the savannah landscape and the way
in which all life is dwarfed under the immensity of its sky. Aware of her
radio medium, Melville skillfully assembles acoustic imagery:

> Wispy rags of cloud stretch out across the moon's face; so much space up there, cloud, stars and a solitary moon – air, air that is full of voices. Limitless dome of heaven so full of sound. Some men build slender steel pyramids to clutch the sounds out of the sky and transmit them for all the world to hear. Others simply press their hands together and their fingers form a pyramid that points to the sky, not to clutch so much as to pray.

The piece draws a careful, respectful symmetry between new and old worlds, reversing the Eurocentric gaze so that the New World of the Caribbean becomes an already occupied land, shaped by the particularities of the Amerindian peoples. The story draws self-consciously on the way in which acts of communication, though precarious and difficult, act as a bridge between public and private worlds and between technology and the sacred.

It is Melville's concern to represent these 'others', those whose ceremonial hands the radio receiver's pyramid form mimics, that gives the piece its depth of form. Initially, the voices of the thatch and the heavens are forgotten as the mistress scrambles in excitement to hear the voice of the radio.

> 'Oh!' she prayed, 'let me find the station quickly.' The night was so hot, not a breeze, not a friendly sound. On the range-finder the needle, moving slowly, oh so slowly, trying to pick up London, the BBC.
>   Then a voice! The voice! The programme already started and the reader already half-way through the story. Her story! Her eyes shining in the glow from the radio's dial, Nancy suddenly leapt from her crouching position and shouted: 'Coco! Machek! [...] Call the vaqueros. Quick! Tell them to come!'

Although the anticipation and thrill of the mistress at hearing her own words voiced back through this magical device is unambiguous, the broadcast becomes an occasion for community and for the recognition of those 'others' rarely seen or heard in Caribbean literature, even today. As they gather around the radio, the vaqueros catch fragments of their world coming from the little box: 'Only the voice, clear and powerful, coming over, repeating now and then the names of people and places they knew'. While the mistress had sent word of their world to London, the BBC and this radio has sent back her world in her form and her excitement at her recognition from both near and far is made palpable by the narrative.

For the mistress, the broadcast voice of the radio makes thrilling and significant connections between her life and the distant world of the motherland, evoked in the story through a briefly lit portrait of the Queen. However, having ensured the writer her moment of recognition, the story tells how, for 'the boys', the connection remained immaterial, their bearings firmly set on the world they inhabited. As the batteries and the broadcast fade, the mistress's distress is set against the movements of the vaqueros who 'turned and went out first, laughing softly'. Not insignifi-cantly, the piece ends with the maid Nancy and a return to the thatch of the savannah house which now delivers its own, cherished voice: 'Yes, there was a breeze! She lifted her face and felt the sweet coolness of it and at the same moment she heard the thatch roof begin to whisper again.' The simplicity of this piece and its gathering up of emotional intensity only to deliver disappointment and the dispersal of interest delivers an affection-ately knowing portrait of the fragility of Caribbean connections to the motherland. More intriguingly, it also provides a subtle critique of the inclination towards voices centred elsewhere that may make Caribbean subjects deaf to the sounds of their own place.

Melville's third piece, though formally less interesting then the first two, certainly takes the task of listening to her own place very seriously. Described by Naipaul in his introduction to the programme as 'a somewhat leisurely piece of reportage', 'Tikerish-Din, The Fire Tiger' was broadcast on Sunday 18 September 1955. This story makes Melville's rendering of Amerindian subjects even more central. Although less sophisticated and engaging in its narrative style, the story weaves elements of folklore and translated observations from Wapishana language to craft an intimately observed natural history of the Rupununi. There is much to be admired in Melville's prose style and particularly in the way that she manipulates narrative perspective and authority. On these grounds alone it is regrettable that she did not develop her writing career further. It seems likely that Melville's writings were increasingly directed towards the urgent repre-sentation of those Amerindian subjects whom she represented politically as the MP for Guyana's Region 9. In 1956 she published *Rupununi: A Simple Storybook of the Savannah Lands of the Rupununi District, British Guiana* and there is no further record of her literary works.

Marina Crichlow's story 'Cane Harvest Barren', broadcast on 19 May 1957, is a beautifully written piece that focuses on the thoughts, feelings and actions of Angus, a sugar factory worker, the day after his wife dies when she collapses drunk on the factory's belt and 'the cutter… mutilated her warm, brown, inert body'. The story reverses the identity of the (archetypally) physically strong Caribbean male in order to articulate a remarkable emotional capacity. Given that the stereotyping of Caribbean masculinity according to physical prowess and machismo pride is still the subject of concern today and that the idea that women writers depicted men either as brutes or invalids still seems to be widely accepted, this early depiction by a woman writer of male grief, anguish and loss offers a clear and significant departure from dominant literary expectations. This re-versal is made clearer still by the fact that it is Angus's wife, Rona, who is the alcoholic and whose drinking leads to fatal consequences for the family.

Although the story is tightly focused within the domestic setting of their

home and especially alert to Angus's responses to his wife's death, it does
gesture at its beginning and end to the wider historical forces that inform
this personal tragedy. Angus is aware that his wife went to the factory
because she did not want him to find her drunk and yet the manner of her
death remains significant. Crushed like cane, Rona's body becomes a literal
victim of the sugar plantation. But the violence enacted on her body also
speaks more symbolically to the historic violence of the plantation that
created dependency and despair, and profited from the commodification of
its labouring bodies. The burden of plantation history is also suggested in
Angus's sympathetic representation of his wife's alcoholism:

> It wasn't her fault... he knew it... it couldn't be. It traced back to her
> home life... she was not to blame. He couldn't blame her. Her father
> drank, her mother drank, her sister and her two brothers too. How could
> she help it? She had grown up in it and it had grown with her... grown
> too big for her.

In another gendering that flows against expectation, Angus reflects on how
Rona 'had struggled for a long time against it... for six long months, so
bravely, not once... she had been his strong, little soldier'.

The nurturing, unconditional love that Angus expresses is certainly an
unconventional portrayal of Caribbean masculinity but the refraction of
grief into denial, anger, loss and despair is both effortlessly crafted and fully
recognisable. Most significantly, the story ends with Angus's empathetic
imagination of Rona's suffering, an experience that becomes unendurable:

> How had she felt to be chopped, cut up – Rona! His wife! He opened
> his clenched fist and stared dully at the deep gash across his palm. He
> ran out towards the high cane. The knife lay on the hard dusty, floor,
> gleaming, soiled.
>   He was never found, but the dripping blood marks were traced to
> the edge of the plantation river.

Through a one-line description, the blood-stained boundary of the plantation, like the sharp blades of the factory, speaks to, if not directly of, the
violence of lives prescribed by the colonial condition. 'Cane Harvest
Barren' is not a clichéd portrayal of an emasculated Caribbean man but a
persuasive and affecting depiction of a man with an inspiring capacity to
feel the suffering of another in spite of the dehumanising conditions of
plantation life that made the possibilities for mutually fulfilling, self-
defined relationships almost impossible to imagine.

Given Sylvia Wynter's imposing profile as a Caribbean intellectual and
her success as a novelist with the publication of her novel *The Hills of Hebron*
in 1962, it is perhaps not surprising that her short story, 'Paramour',
broadcast on 25 November 1956, already shows a marked confidence in
terms of her writerly style. Jamaican by birth, Wynter also wrote radio
plays, some with her second husband the Guyanese novelist Jan Carew,

and this short fiction shows both a skilled ear for and a delight in the 'voicing' of Caribbean experience. Written in the first person, 'Paramour' narrates the experiences of an adolescent girl, Victoria, who is both bookish and wild at its opening. Caught by a heavy storm walking back from school one day, she is beckoned by a woman's voice and takes refuge in 'a rambling T-shaped old house, made of timber and furnished […] like a palace'. Inside she meets Edna who appears to her as a heroine from one of her romance books: 'Her body was long and slender like the coconut palms and the sweet expression in her eyes belied their aloofness, her strangely slanting eyes set in a face that flared open like a poinsettia flower, and soft lips, and such a cascade of dark hair'. After drinking hot milk and promising to teach Miss Edna to read, Victoria returns home late. Her mother is waiting with the tamarind switch to punish her delay and the situation turns more grave still as Victoria relates the glamour and charm of the 'beautiful lady' who had given her shelter:

> Dat half chiney wretch, day common woman dat have a married man keeping her. You mean you go in the house of a kept woman after all the slave ah slave for you. You with your colour and education can get anywhere and now you want to be a slut….. a paramour like dat woman!

When the mother's anger turns to tears she begins to explain herself: 'Look Victoria, you know that all me heart set on you turning out a worthwhile woman who I could be proud of. Ah don't want you to associate with people like dat woman, dey kind to you but dey all set on making you like dem. People envious chile'.

Despite promising her mother that she would not visit again, Victoria rushes back the very next day and encounters Miss Edna and her young lover, Johnny. It is Johnny whom Edna hopes to marry in order to free herself from her life as the kept woman of an older, married man. Edna's wish for marriage reveals that she desires to be respectable and she tells Victoria, 'Life gwine to be different for me from now on Vicky. No more sweetheart life for me!' When Victoria visits again only the next day, Miss Edna's words have come true in tragic fashion and the girl is met with a terrible scene: 'On the divan Miss Edna lay stretched out; blood streamed from a hole in her chest. On an armchair beside her a man, a precise hole in his temple, sat quite still'. On one level this story seems to confirm the moral lesson delivered by a higgler woman, along with the family's vegetables – the 'wages of sin was death'. However, while the bare plot of the story may confirm the terrible penalties associated with sexual transgression, its voices clearly draw attention to female dependency. Moreover, the linguistic and literary energetics of the piece flow against any such ready or simple condemnation and invest instead in the power of language to transform lives and our understanding of lives. It is not insignificant that Miss Edna yearns to read and write in order to empower herself as a woman in a male world. Furthermore, Victoria's enchantment with the word paramour makes a new voicing of the term possible, as her acoustic relish delinks the word from its pejorative associations: 'The word paramour was new to me and beautiful. I couldn't understand why she should pronounce it with such contempt. "Paramour" sounded as she was, soft and sibilant and sweet, and from that moment in my mind she was Edna Paramour.'

In terms of formal innovation, the distinct Creole voices of Victoria, her mother and Edna create a textured piece, delicately but purposefully crafted to be heard. Wynter is aware of the way in which language register functions as an index of social standing and observes how Johnny's speech shows 'the careful enunciation affected by all elementary pupil teachers'. Perhaps most significantly, Wynter voices the nuanced movements along a Creole continuum through Victoria's mother's double response, rendering the subtle code-switching of a Jamaican woman as she seeks to modulate her emotions and gain authority in the act of parenting.

Notably, the delight in language here produces a self-reflexivity that is seen in the other stories too, and that seems to suggest an interesting leitmotif or point of connection. Given the demands of the *Caribbean Voices* programme for distinctly 'Caribbean' voices, it is interesting that these women short story writers appear less self-conscious about the Caribbeanness of their writings than they are about their writerliness. For these women writers it is the pull towards the idea of 'Voices' and the recognition of the power of language that marks a distinctive feature of their work. It is impossible to imagine how the writing of Melville and Crichlow may have developed, or even that of Wynter, if they had assumed professional authorship in the same way as Lamming or Selvon. All the same, their writings broadcast on the *Caribbean Voices* programme suggest that our understandings of Caribbean literature may have been somewhat different if this had come to pass. Of course, it is likely that these women writers, like the significant male writers of the period, would have looked towards the novel form as a means of consolidating their literary reputations. In this, they too may have turned towards more orthodox forms and versions of the 'knowable community' that Raymond Williams identifies with the realist novel,[10] but these communities would certainly have been configured and communicated in distinctive terms. While in all cases their comparatively short-lived literary careers are lamentable, these stories still present a valuable insight into the diversity of Caribbean lives and the ways in which acts of literary representation connected to the shared requirement to deliver understanding of lives and locales that remained unknown and almost unknowable to each other. Although brief, the glimpses that these short stories by women offer of a literary engagement with ideas of community, belonging, and the possibilities and restraints that condition human intimacy are notably different from the established norms of Caribbean literary representation within this period.

Just after he joined the *Caribbean Voices* programme, Henry Swanzy stated that the 'main value of a programme like *Caribbean Voices* is to provide an outlet for writers who would otherwise be mute'.[11] Although only twenty percent of the writers given voice through this forum were women, it is salutary to consider how small a fraction of those seventy are mute again today. While the tiny sample that I have discussed here represents a carefully selected cluster, my wider research of the scripts suggests that as a body of writing these works that were once heard but remain unseen present an archive from which Caribbean literary history still has much to learn.

SHORT STORIES CITED

Crichlow, Marina, 'Cane Harvest Barren', BBC *Caribbean Voices* manuscript broadcast 19 May 1957

Melville, Edwina, 'Fishing in the Rupununi Savannah, British Guiana', BBC *Caribbean Voices* manuscript broadcast Sunday 9 August 1953

____ 'The Voice', BBC *Caribbean Voices* manuscript broadcast Sunday 20 June 1954

____ 'Tikerish-Din, The Fire Tiger', BBC *Caribbean Voices* manuscript broadcast Sunday 18 September 1955

Wynter, Sylvia, 'Paramour', BBC *Caribbean Voices* manuscript broadcast 25 November 1956

NOTES

1 Philip Nanton, 'London Calling', *Caribbean Beat*, 63 (September–October 2003), 66–71 (p. 66).

2 Gladys Lindo, Private Correspondence with author, 15 August 1991.

3 Glyne Griffith, 'This is London Calling the West Indies', in *West Indian Intellectuals in Britain*, ed. by Bill Schwarz (Manchester: Manchester University Press, 2003), pp. 196–208 (p. 202).

4 Henry Swanzy, Private Correspondence with author, 23 March 1990.

5 Henry Swanzy, Private Correspondence with author, 23 March 1990.

6 For debates about the gendering of the short story form see Susan Lohafer and Jo Ellyn Clarey, eds, *Short Story Theory at a Crossroads* (Baton Rouge: Louisiana State University Press, 1989). See also Elizabeth Walcott-Hackshaw's essay in this volume.

7 George Lamming, *The Pleasures of Exile* (London: Allison and Busby, 1960), p. 39.

8 Frank O'Connor, *The Lonely Voice* (London: Macmillan, 1963), p. 18.

9 Glyne Griffith, 'Deconstructing Nationalisms: Henry Swanzy, *Caribbean Voices* and the Development of West Indian Literature, *Small Axe*, 10 (September 2001), 1–20 (p. 20).

10 Raymond Williams, *The English Novel from Dickens to Lawrence* (London: Chatto and Windus, 1970), pp. 14–16.

11 Henry Swanzy, 'Caribbean Voices – Prolegomena to a West Indian Culture', *Caribbean Quarterly*, 1.1 (1949), 21–28 (p. 28).

'THE LESSER NAMES BENEATH THE PEAKS': JAMAICAN SHORT FICTION AND ITS CONTEXTS, 1938–1950

SUZANNE SCAFE

The 1950s is frequently referred to as the 'boom' period in Caribbean literary production, the first 'genesis' of a literary tradition structured around the now canonical novels of a selected group of writers.[1] Obscured by the shadows of these canonical 'peaks' however, were many writers whose work has been neglected even in recent reconfigurations of a more inclusive, less linear narrative of Caribbean literary history.[2] Despite this critical neglect, their short fiction, published in newspapers, 'little magazines' or self-published in the period from the late 1930s to the 1950s, played a crucial role in the development of a national literature that was to define itself in opposition to a borrowed colonial aesthetic. The work of these writers, and the context of vigorous political and cultural debate in which it was produced, provide a powerful witness to the texture of a Caribbean quotidian, its class and colour struggles and the conflicts that reflect gender roles and difference. Their small, often realistically imagined canvasses provide a detailed record of ordinary lives, made exceptional through their representation in literature.

The title of this chapter, taken from Henry Swanzy's essay 'The Literary Situation in the Contemporary Caribbean' (1956), highlights the value of the work of these 'lesser names' and its importance to what he describes as a 'new creative phase of West Indian writing'.[3] He writes: 'As the mind ranges, it begins, indeed, to wonder whether the lesser names beneath the peaks may not have the real heart of the matter in them, so far as the development of a true canon of self-understanding is concerned' ('The Literary Situation', p. 251). Although, as Swanzy notes, their stars shone only 'for a season', these short fiction writers, who were so productive during this twenty-year period, illuminated a critical moment in the development of a national cultural consciousness.

In her discussion of the short story and its critical reception, Mary Louise Pratt draws attention to the problematic status of the short story written for a newspaper or magazine, arguing that the 'magazine context implies distracted reception in brief moments between activities'.[4] Furthermore, she adds:

> Magazine fiction is planned for obsolescence. Unlike books, the text actually becomes garbage after reading. There is no chance, not any procedure for the mortality or immortality of a work to be determined

on its merits. The whole point is to replace it with another, equivalent product in next week's or next month's issue. (Pratt, p. 110)

'Magazine fiction' is also associated with the commercialisation and mass production of literature and has come to be seen as 'the genre for which a technology had been elaborated to efficiently meet the demands of the market place, the one most tending toward standardization and a "lowest common denominator"' (Pratt, p. 110). For most writers writing in the Caribbean during this period, the absence of a publishing house meant that their only recourse was to publish in the daily or weekly newspapers and literary magazines. These provided an outlet for a wide variety of original, experimental work that, though ephemeral, reflected a desire for a new aesthetic that would accompany the formation of a new society.

The period of the 1930s in Jamaica is described, by those writing at the time or shortly after, as a period of cultural awakening. Una Marson, writing in 1937, makes an emphatic connection between the political and the cultural: 'There is no doubt that there is an awakening in Jamaica today. We see signs of it in the formation of the NRA, the organization of Hunger Marches, Citizens Associations [...] in this new era literature must take its place'.[5] Ten years later, Peter Blackman makes a similar point, arguing that a 'new and valid West Indian aesthetic will emerge from the struggle for nationhood, now beginning to take shape in the West Indies [...] based upon the hunger and frustrations of the common people',[6] and in her autobiography *The Long Run* (1961), Cicely Howland provides a heady description of the social and cultural transformations she witnessed on her return to Jamaica in 1938, the 'year of awakening':[7]

> A country school teacher who had been setting poems about blue eyes and daffodils for twenty years read a poem one day by a fellow Jamaican about the beauty of her black people and there and then she revolutionized her whole approach to her work. (*The Long Run*, p. 107)

Leading this call for a radically transformed aesthetic was *Public Opinion*, the newspaper established in 1937 to oppose the ideological grip of *The Daily Gleaner*, and to increase the support of the People's National Party and its demand for self-government, articulated most coherently and forcefully through the Jamaica Progressive League. Attention was repeatedly drawn to Jamaica's social and economic ills: the inadequacy of the education system; the intolerable condition of housing; the blight of tourism and the need for a legitimate labour movement. Interwoven with these pieces of social and political comment were equally uncompromising demands for more radical forms of cultural expression.

Writing in 1937, Frank A. Hill argues that the 'dominant feature' of what he terms the 'refined' arts – sculpture, painting, literature and music – should be 'national sentiment':

> In our literature and music, there should be primarily the raising to life of the familiar figures and scenes which have gone unregarded because of constant association with them. When we have lifted them out of their commonplace setting and made them into the vital, human creatures they are, we can say with well-founded pride that we have laid the foundations for an abiding culture [...]. If we are to turn back to our own soil, let us rid ourselves of the bondage of first principles.[8]

The declamatory tone of Hill's manifesto is characteristic of many of the paper's contributions. Like Marson's call to 'bend at our own shrines in our own country',[9] it urges the artist to turn inward and to create national symbols from the cultural practices of ordinary life. The image of an 'ebony peasant leading his donkey along a dusty road'; the 'sinuous, slithery motions of our peasant women'; 'our undulating hills' (Hill, p. 5) become the iconic, though not unproblematic, symbols of nationalism in the popular fiction of this period and in the visual art of Albert Huie, Gloria Escoffery, Carl Abrahams, Carl Parboosingh and others, whose work regularly appeared in *Public Opinion* and *Focus*. In place of the 'bondage' of colonial forms stands the body of the black peasant and an African-centred peasant culture, signifiers of an emerging nation that was and would, for several decades, be led by a white and brown elite.

   While *Public Opinion* was the most radical publication in circulation at this time and was the most unambiguous in its desire for a national culture, other publications, reflecting a wide spectrum of political opinion, provided a forum within which literary expressions of the cultural 'awakening' could be articulated. In her weekly publication, *Jamaica*, Esther Chapman wrote: 'It seems incompatible to ask for self-government and Jamaica for the Jamaicans, and in the same breath demand that existing and new industries be heavily subsidised. The man who plays the piper calls the tune'.[10] As editor of the influential 'little magazine' *The West Indian Review*, Chapman published literary pieces by writers whose work also appeared in *Public Opinion*, and by including contributions from francophone Caribbean writers, the magazine promoted an awareness of a regional rather than a merely national literature. Most journalists and writers of poetry, drama and fiction contributed to several of the publications established during this period and the appearance of their work in such politically different contexts suggests the existence of a network of connections between writers, publishers and editors that crossed political affiliations and interests.

   Education was one of the most consistent campaign topics of *The Daily Gleaner*. After its responsibility to its business interests, its ideal reader was the school teacher, the group who formed what its letter writers sometimes referred to as Jamaica's 'quiet middle classes'. The literary discussions conducted on its pages, the publication of short fiction and poetry, the annual short story and poetry competitions and, in 1949, the founding of the Pioneer Press, whose aim was to 'provide books in every home',[11] making books accessible to people living on low incomes, all fulfilled the newspaper's commitment to aiding the development of a literate, reading population – not least as a way of increasing its readership. As its editorial argues, with sales of 40,000 copies daily and an estimated readership of 240,000, the paper was not reaching the additional 360,000 literate members of the island. The writer concludes:

> Far too much time is wasted on strong and 'weak' verbs, on analysis, on History, on 'Literature', on Geography: [...] the all-important thing to aim at is that the school curriculum should be so arranged that it admits a great deal of silent reading by the children. Nothing else matters.[12]

Despite their limitations, the newspapers and periodicals of this period provided the means of extending the field of discursive possibilities available to writers: the transient status of these texts provided an opportunity for innovation and experimentation as fictional writing emerged in dialogue with rhetorical writing, reportage and literary criticism. Writers were able to exploit the range of short fiction available to them, from the pithy, plot driven structures used in the contributions by writers such as Maureen Shirley and Archie Lindo to the more abstract,[13] meditative short fiction of Roger Mais and Claude Thompson or the weekly sketches and vignettes written for the *Gleaner* by Thompson and Randolph Williams. Much of the fiction produced in these contexts did not merely mirror the demands of a narrowly defined political nationalism, nor did it uncritically celebrate a vernacular culture. In drawing attention to the conflicts and contradictions that were already a threat to the ideal of a new nation, these writers' work suggested the possibility of political and cultural liberation.

Some of the most effective interventions in the dominant expressions of Jamaican culture were those that privileged the use of Jamaican Creole, not as dialogue, a form to which readers had already become accustomed, but as either the narrative voice or as a means of articulating a complex interiority. Inez Knibb Sibley's very small column 'Quashie's Version', published under the pseudonym 'Pennib', which appeared in the magazine pages of the *Gleaner*'s Saturday paper, constituted a startling disruption of the values and assumptions reflected in the society gossip columns and beauty pages. The name 'Quashie' has a triple function: it serves to signal both the African identity of the speaker and the creolised transformation of that identity – from Kwesi to 'Quashie' – as evidenced in the speaker's use of Jamaican Creole. By exploiting its more popular, derogatory connotations, Sibley uses the term as a mask of ignorance and stupidity behind which the black social commentator, Hezekiah, subverts and opposes the ideologies that dominate the pages from which he speaks. In this column the Creole speaker is both subject and agent of his own narrative, positioned and ready to participate in a newly emerging narrative of nationhood. Sibley published her collection, *Quashie's Reflections (in native dialect)* in 1939 with illustrations by Carl Abrahams, and her sketches were republished in 1968 with a revised foreword by Philip Sherlock, who had also introduced the original version. In it he praises the indigenous, 'intuitive' character of the work, drawing attention to the value of its use of a specific cultural register:

> [...] the traveller, hurrying to write another book of impressions and highly coloured sketches will not have attempted this; the friend who finds another home here could not have achieved this; to both are denied the experience and the sense of belonging, which alone make possible the writing of sketches such as these.[14]

Though these comments are made twenty-eight years after its original publication, Sherlock still finds it appropriate to register the work's value as evidence of the creative potential of a cultural 'insider'.

In her artfully 'intuitive' use of Creole language structures, Sibley confers value on an often discredited language form, its speakers and the culture they represent. One of the sketches, 'The Wedding Ceremony', is a creolised revision of the ritualised exchange of vows: the narrator, Hezekiah, recounts:

> [...] an when de parson sey 'Jezebel Grasshoppy Stance will you hab this woman to be thy lawful wedded wife?' Im mek reply, 'Ah no dat me cum fa parson?' An me hab fe glad, cause lilly or nutten mek dem change dem mine dese days.[15]

The groom disrupts a culturally imposed exchange and its transmission of empty vows. He appropriates control of the wedding discourse for himself and other so-called 'Quashies' – Creole speakers without literary or cultural authority – thus reclaiming the ritual of marriage for the 'folk'. He cuts short the parson, releasing him from his insecure hold of the Standard forms of English he is required to master, and gains approval from the narrator for his well-timed intervention. His creolised declaration of intent is spoken from the heart and is thus, the narrator suggests, imbued with integrity: his words promise a more lasting union.

In his influential work *Modernism and the Harlem Renaissance* (1987), Houston A. Baker explores the importance of what he defines as 'sound' – dialect, song and other orally transmitted cultural forms – in early twentieth-century African American literature. He argues that these 'sounds' emanate from the 'slave world' where 'discourse was figured as hard won song and courageously expostulated black oratory (and written prose) designed to move the spirit of freedom'.[16] Sibley's Creole 'soundings' are creative transformations of an African past that look forward to political and cultural freedom. In 'A Case in Court', for example, her narrator begins: 'Sometimes back me hab a case in Court, one facey man cum tek me up sey me ah practise Obeah.' In the narrative that follows Sibley pits the wit, language and the 'insider' cultural knowledge of her Creole narrator, the Obeah practitioner, against the learning of the judge who, on conceding defeat, commends Quashie's 'logic' and 'argumentation'.[17] The tale thus marks a victory both for the discursive power of the narrator's Creole and for the survival of outlawed African practices: Quashie has the final word and uses it to confirm the judge's position as a colonial 'outsider': 'But larned as im is, im no noa eberyting, ef im tay yah lang nuff maybe im fine out' ('A Case in Court', p. 35).

As well as these sketches Sibley contributed several short stories to *Public Opinion* in the late 1940s and early 50s, some of which reappeared in *Focus* and were aired on the *Caribbean Voices* programme. One of her most popular was 'The Terror Bull and the Taunt Song' (1956) described by Swanzy in his six-month review of *Caribbean Voices* as a 'brilliant' expression of a daring imagination.[18] This story is an extended version of the ideas expressed in 'A Case in Court', celebrating the power of the word, both as demotic speech and as an expression of the wisdom and knowledge of the ancestors, continued in oral storytelling practices and song. The 'terror bull' (terrible) of the story is a seven-headed bull that wreaks havoc in the country villages, killing men, women, children and their animals, then throwing them into 'the awful sink-hole'.[19] Armed with a machete, Tobias, one of the story's protagonists, sets out to avenge the murder of his lover by single-handedly killing the bull. As he prepares for the task, the 'wraithlike' figure of his 'great, great, great grandfather' appears and warns that 'all the weapon you have caan do it', telling him instead to use an 'old time taunt song' and the bull's secret name to charm and madden him ('The Terror Bull', pp. 63–64). As the old man predicts, it is the 'sounding' of an ancient cultural memory that eventually kills the bull: each time Josiah repeats 'Shimmolimo oh! Me know you name Bear me up good tree bear up', one of the bull's heads dramatically rolls to the ground, freeing the community of their terror ('The Terror Bull', pp. 65–66), thereby ensuring the survival of the village and its oral traditions.

Other writers, such as W.G. Ogilvie, incorporate the 'sounds' of black oratory into their short fiction in equally self-conscious ways. Ogilvie's short stories appeared in the first two short story collections published by Pioneer Press and his two novels were published by Pioneer Press in 1953. Whereas his full-length novels rely on techniques of social realism to confer literary value on the cultural practices of ordinary, rural communities, the economies demanded by short fiction result in a more creative interconnection of language and culture. The back-room bar of the story 'The Great Kranjie' (1950) is a site of male bonding, a place where male authority is confirmed through the power of speech. The story opens with quiet irony as the 'village worthies' continue to drink amid the sounds of more productive activities; the narrator emphasises the harmony between the natural world, the villagers and the men in the bar:

> The night was warm with the sounds of crickets amid the bushes on the nearby hillside; while from the village square came the noises of people doing their final shopping. Within the backroom of Mass Joe's shop the village worthies sipped and drank in that spirit of tranquil comradeship such as can be understood only by those who have shared in similar gatherings.[20]

The final phrase positions the narrator 'inside' the culture that is being described, thus bridging the distance between the Standard English narrative voice and the characters. Shortly after the scene is set, Tata, 'their sage', is used to tell the story of Kranjie's triumph and final defeat. Like other stories in this collection, 'The Great Kranjie' has an allegorical function, revealing and, through its own storytelling, challenging relations of power between the strong and the weak. The eponymous Kranjie is a horse whose speed belies his appearance. Tata recounts: 'Him were not a big horse, Him did close-quarters, but well tallawah' ('The Great Kranjie', p. 32). His reputation for speed, however, spreads to neighbouring districts, and finally Tata's father is persuaded to race the horse in Kingston, where Kranjie is an object of ridicule: 'When all the backra folkses see the little close-quarters horse and them hear say that him was going to run 'gainst for them own, them laugh after we' ('The Great Kranjie', p. 33). But of course he is more than the sum of his appearance, and in Tata's account wins against the sleek, expensive thoroughbreds. This is not the end of the tale, however, for as Tata reveals, the win is disallowed: 'Them disqualify Kranjie on the claims that it were a races; and as 'cording to rules the horses must run. But Kranjie was flying' ('The Great Kranjie', p. 35). It is the perfect bar-room tale; lively and full of vivid exaggeration. It also contains a more serious message about the relationship between language and power, for although Tata is, in that moment of comradeship, master of the word, outside of Mass Joe's back-room discursive power lies with the 'backra folkses' who own the race course, the jockey on loan to Tata's father and the rules of the race: they determine who wins the 'plenty money' to which his father was entitled.

   In his discussion of these writers' contemporary, Edgar Mittelholzer, Kenneth Ramchand describes the use of Creole dialogue in the novel *Corentyne Thunder* (1941) as 'dialect' used in 'accordance with a strict realistic criterion of appropriateness': it reflects the way the character speaks in what Ramchand terms 'real' life. He adds that if the author/ narrator 'wishes to express anything complicated about the character, he has to work not directly through the character's consciousness or in the character's language, but by a mediating omniscience'.[21] Referring to the character Ramgolall, he writes: 'words and dialect are flat counters out of touch with the experience he has undergone' (*The West Indian Novel*, p. 81). The use of Jamaican Creole in the stories I have cited might at times seem heavy handed; reproduced literally, rather than creatively transformed. As Joan McLaughlin notes in her introduction to Sibley's work, however, the author's use of Creole is time- and place-specific, and should therefore conjure up for contemporary readers another time and place: she notes, for example, that Sibley's Creole contains 'some features which are now either obsolete or obsolescent'.[22] In addition, the languages used in these stories do not, unless intentionally, reflect what Ramchand describes as 'mutually exclusive social worlds' (*The West Indian Novel*, p. 97): these stories' Creole-speaking characters are knowing, articulate and socially engaged and the Standard English used in the narrative sections of this short fiction, can be imagined, as in Ogilvie's 'Kranjie', in a 'West Indian Standard voice' (*The West Indian Novel*, p. 74).

In addition to the use of a Jamaican vernacular and the exploitation of the language continuum available to Jamaican writers, the stories of this period are characterised by recurring tropes and sets of figurative and thematic oppositions: the country and the city; the figure of the car used in opposition to the bus and the tram; the bar, the barber shop and the digging-match. An embittered tone characterises the thoughts of the protagonist of Claude Thompson's 'The Children That Sit in Darkness' (1943): as the narrator walks the eight-mile journey to his new job as a scale clerk on 'Bananas Estate', a 'vast, feudal, industrial domain' that is over two hundred and fifty years old, he looks bitterly on at the cars 'whizzing' by, ignoring his attempt to flag them down: 'The occupants had sat aloof – looking neither to the right nor left – these "upper ten" people who were so desperately trying to be gentle folk; who looked like well bred people but were not'.[23] This scene, with its cynical reference to the ten percent of Jamaica's population that control the island's wealth and its social and cultural production, adds further irony to the story's earlier references to a slave and colonial past that refuses to die: 'It had been that ex-West India Regiment bugler blowing the last post as the sun was setting. People – his own dark people – had been laughing at the old black bugler […]. Verily the past was dead' (Thompson, pp. 41–42). The narrator angrily nurses the hurt inflicted by the assumed airs of those travelling in the comfort of their cars: they might have been the boys with whom he went to school and who had tolerated him then, 'You and Smith Major, the Doctor's son – you and Hones the parson's son', but now only speak to him when 'they could not help it' (Thompson, p. 40). For the black characters in this story, the dying days of colonialism do not herald a new dawn but merely the perpetuation of old injustices in new guises.

For most critics, these writers' work reflected 'a mature [West] Indian flavour and unmistakably Jamaican source and inspiration'.[24] Writers were intensely concerned with each other's work and were also influenced by the work of their European and American contemporaries: there were many articles that engaged in a critical discussion of the writing of Langston Hughes, Richard Wright and Zora Neale Hurston, whose folktales attracted considerable attention. Jamaican writers saw that the radical, expressive potential of the literary forms used by African American writers could be harnessed to their own desire for creative forms that would accompany a more inclusive, egalitarian and 'modern' nation. There were minor notes of discord, however: perhaps stung by his work's negative reviews in the *Gleaner* and *Public Opinion*, J.E.C. McFarlane describes the late 1930s as a period of 'extreme nationalism' that perpetuated an intolerance in literature and politics. He writes of a need to counter what he sees as a modern tendency in literary production that privileges 'jerky rhythms', and a 'vigorous, agitated and vehement' tone.[25]

Other writers such as John Figueroa viewed the trend towards what he saw as nationalist literature with some scepticism. While supporting the need for distinctly regional voices, John Figueroa is critical of what he sees as the partisan critical judgements and the narrow literary nationalism of 'cliques which did not welcome work which did not conform to their particular politics, policies or values'; he adds, '[t]he Caribbean *Life and Letters* had been captured by such a group and only their work appeared'.[26] A close examination of the Caribbean and 'Jamaica' issues of *Life and Letters* seems to suggest that what guided the selection of material for these issues of the journal was not so much the writers' networks or political affiliations but the works' use of 'local colour', a criteria on which Swanzy also insisted.[27] In 'What I look for in West Indian Literature', his introduction to the Jamaica issue of *Life and Letters*, the editor Robert Herring describes climbing Blue Mountain Peak on one of his visits to Jamaica:

> So Eustace, a trickified guide, who had already volunteered the information that the 'obeah situation fairly quiet', went across the hills to get some [rum]. At the top, we had one moment of sparkling clear view of Port Royal and long lines of coast.[28]

He continues, describing the appearance of a 'wandering youth' who came to play mento rhythms for Herring's party, 'four of his people and me, one buckra', and concludes with remarks about the appalling conditions for working people and the 'strong brave dignity of peasants met in the hills; a people too noble for poverty' (Herring, p. 3). It is implied in this introduction that, in addition to representations of social themes, the material selected should reflect the folksy, exotic character of the editor's own narrative. The result was the inclusion of material that was strong on local colour but not always representative of the wide range of themes and short fictional forms used by writers of the period.

The selection of R.L.C. Aarons's 'The Cow That Laughed' (1948) and

'The Road from St. Thomas' (1948) reflects this preference for exoticism.[29] Both stories treat their subject, obeah, with the amused disdain that characterises Herring's editorial. The protagonist of the 'The Cow That Laughed' is a 'trickified' obeah practitioner full of 'low cunning' who quite predictably succeeds in fooling his client: he comments on his own success, revealing to a reader 'outside' the culture of the narrative the extent to which obeah was integral to Jamaican culture: 'Fancy a man of that age believing in obeah. And he a church member too'.[30] In contrast to these stories, most of the short fiction in Aarons's self-published collection is much less sensational and, apart from occasional 'local' detail, could be set anywhere: the stories are quiet, controlled accounts of social ambition and class difference, focusing on Jamaica's lower middle classes: government clerks, teachers or hard-working tradesmen.

Despite this tendency, the material chosen for the journal was not, by any means, all sensational projections of exotic themes. Selections from the work of Claude Thompson, Vic Reid and Roger Mais provide Herring's journal with its political emphasis. Thompson's stories, like those of Reid and Mais, are characterised by a fragmentary narrative style associated with literary modernism: his prose also reflects the 'jerky', angular rhythms of jazz and blues, the more regular cadences of Caribbean mento and Shay Shay and the rhythms of oral storytelling. Like Mais and Reid, Thompson was less concerned with representations of 'real' dialogue than with approximating meaning through the silences and broken, half-formed sentences of his characters. The stories selected by Herring and Vic Reid, his assistant editor, for the 'Jamaica' issue of *Life and Letters* are from Thompson's collection *These My People* (1943). Both stories provide powerful social and political comment: one, 'A Man From Jamaica', is a historical narrative linking the struggle for freedom in the Caribbean in the early nineteenth century to the desire for political self-determination in the 1940s, and is centred around a tale of Simón Bolívar's visit to Jamaica and his delivery of the 'Jamaica letter'. The other, 'Monday Mawnin', is more firmly rooted in the context of 1930s Jamaica and ordinary people's experiences of joblessness and poverty. It is a melodramatic tale of a man who murders his girlfriend, having discovered that she is having an affair while he has been on the streets looking for a job. In the swirl of the story's impressionistic closing lines, fragmented and disconnected words are loosened from their conventional meaning: the mundane preoccupations of the policemen and their struggle to maintain rank are merged with the perpetrator's expressions of horror at his actions. Social and personal themes are interconnected as the protagonist's personal tragedy is heightened by the indifference displayed by those in authority.

Though Roger Mais and Victor Reid should not be considered the 'lesser names' beneath the peaks of Caribbean or Jamaican literary achievement, their work has suffered critical neglect in recent decades, and very little attention has been paid to their short fiction. Mais was the most prolific writer in Jamaica during the 1940s and early 50s, publishing short stories, novels, poetry and drama. He also produced angry, passionate political commentary and a series of satirical essays, written from prison, entitled 'They Lived in the Suburbs' (1945), in which he attacked fawning and uncritical journalists and a political system he was certain could not deliver true self-government. His short stories did not, however, reflect his political and social concerns: they were not, as Victor Ramraj has suggested 'exclusively protest pieces, complaining about the lot of the urban poor'.[31] In the most accomplished of his short stories he achieves a lyrical intensity that is not reflected in the work of his contemporaries. Many of his stories, like the better known 'Gravel in Your Shoe' (1986) and 'Listen, the Wind' (1986) and the less well-known 'Tig' (1941), do not use a conventional plot, focusing instead on relationships between individuals and the inadequacy of words to communicate their deepest feelings. Mais made several interventions into the long-running debate about the status and merit of literature in Jamaica that was conducted in *Public Opinion* between 1938 and 1945. In the article 'Why Local Colour' he defends the right of an author to be free to choose a literary style that reflects the broadest possible reading and a wide experience of culture. He writes: 'literature of any country is an imitation of the literature of all others; or better still, that is influenced by that of all the rest'.[32] In his discussion of the short story, he defends the absence of a 'thick plot' in his stories and his determination to be innovative, railing against the more 'popular mass-produce[d] art that is used to sell American magazines and journals, […] the kind of short story that the sort of people who teach things by correspondence course write about'.[33] It is ironic then that many reviewers praised his stories for their depiction of 'real' people and for their representations of 'the very colour and texture of Jamaica's earth'.[34]

The influence of Hemingway on both Thompson and Mais is evident in their fiction and in essays such as Mais's 'Words and So Forth' (1941) where he defends the muscularity of his prose,[35] its 'masculine vigour and directness symbolised by the straight line'.[36] The words, he argues, must speak for themselves. This terse, spare style certainly does characterise much of his short prose but it is most successful when it is combined with a lyricism that speaks of an emotional depth that belies the characters' silence or the unadorned word. An example of this lyricism is evident in the short story 'Tig' that lays bare the contradictory feelings threatening the characters' strong desire for each other: the unnamed young boy struggles with a complex set of emotions: anger, jealousy and awe, expressed through the repetition and interconnection of vividly drawn images. The moon is used to connect the feelings of the boy with the beautiful femininity of the girl but its shadows predict menace or disaster, sensed by the girl who, instead of meeting him as arranged, gives in to feelings of uneasiness and walks back to the village. She had been just within his reach:

> I've got that big ole moon inside my breast, Tig... an' when she blows up, a bit of it is goin' to stick against the roof of my head [...] She passes with playfully flapping skirts so close that he could have reached out a hand and touched her... she passes and is lost in the slow gloom just where the road dips. The moon, a brazen wonder, looks over the brink of a distant mountain... her long silken skirts of light reach down to the furthest fold of the valley.[37]

A similar effect is achieved in the moving and evocative 'You've Gotta Go Home' (1949), where the reader is positioned as an outsider, a sympathetic witness of the characters' anguish.[38] The story is constructed from the fragments of a conversation: the man repeating 'you go on home', an unexplained reference to a death – 'We've got to put him away decent you know' – and the woman's unsuccessful efforts to engage him. Their words constantly misfire, leaving both characters withdrawn and alone.

Ramchand describes a selection of Mais's stories featuring female protagonists as 'contributions to what is now called feminist literature',[39] arguing, for example, that in the short story 'Gravel in Your Shoe', the realisation the protagonist achieves is that in order to accept 'her man' as he is, she has to ignore the incessant 'gravel' of gossip in her shoe. She has to be alone and to believe in her own mantra: *'it's not the mountain you're climbing that wears you down but the gravel in your shoe'*.[40] With her man she is '[c]omplete, integrated, single, whole. Because they were held together by no such superficial bond as matrimony' ('Gravel in Your Shoe', p. 78), and though beset by her own doubts and the gossip of neighbours, she struggles to preserve the integrity of the relationship as the man conceives it. As they eat together at the end of the day, the female protagonist of 'Gravel in Your Shoe' offers 'her small conversation' and is happy if her man responds but forbearing if he is 'taciturn, dull, restless' ('Gravel in Your Shoe', p. 77). The personal freedom which he takes as an entitlement reflects and is a consequence of his need for intellectual freedom and is compromised by the personal commitment required by marriage. In contrast the woman is defined, even entrapped by her commitment. As he leaves in the evening, she thinks: 'He was not the one to make a fuss over her when he didn't mean it. Kissing when he didn't mean it [...]. She wouldn't want that, knowing him to be even then thinking about the other woman he was going to' ('Gravel in Your Shoe', p. 79).

Her desire to be alone is motivated by more complex factors than Ramchand suggests and her acceptance of her marriage is, the narrative implies, a daily struggle. The 'gravel in your shoe' represents not just the community's perception of the problem – the man's infidelity and lack of care – but the problem itself, which is both the mountain *and* the gravel it generates.

Whereas Mais's stories cannot be described as 'social protest' ('Introduction' to *Listen, the Wind*, p. xxii), many of Vic Reid's short stories are vehicles for social comment. Drawing attention to Reid's use of naturalism in some of his fiction, Henry Swanzy remarks that his is 'one of the few individual styles in the Caribbean, with its repetition and memories of Steinbeck and perhaps the Bible'.[41] Reid's more successful stories are his experimental vignettes such as 'Digging Match' (1948), 'Dead Drunk' (1948) and 'Waterfront Bar' (1948), all of which appeared in the early editions of *Focus*. 'Digging Match' is a swinging prose melody of voices and songs, '[a]ncient as Africa which was too ancient for them to know',[42] that offer lilting, repeated greetings to those who have come to work the ground, swinging their hoes: 'Into line, with room to swing; and as the furrows grow slowly along the hillside and reach from boundary to boundary then step back Joe and Amos and Davie and everybody' ('Digging Match', p. 50). The characters are connected to each other through work and song as they collectively offer to dig or 'match' the ground of one of their member and to continue the cycle of planting and reaping. A similar effect is achieved in 'Pattern' (1948), also structured around the song of a group of street boys who gather daily at the harbour to dive for the coins the tourists throw. Reid's prose gives beauty, energy and dignity to the sordid, cruel lives of these boys who are already men, particularly in the final lines when, after a brutal fight they follow the curve of the coin 'down through the sea in a swift seek for the shiny coin'.[43] Reid's stories use the rhythms of everyday songs to celebrate his characters' collective endeavour and loyalty even in the harshest conditions: they effect a 'resounding' of African orature, reformed in its passage from slavery to freedom.

It is not possible, within the space of a single chapter, to represent the full range of work published during this period, and several important writers have been omitted: Ethel Rovere's touching, allegorical portraits that confirm rural, village values; Cicely Howland's Rhys-like representations of rootless and alienated women; and the short fiction of writers such as H.D. Carberry, who became better known for their poetry. In addition, the chapter does not address the writing that reflects the patterns and experiences of migration, from Jamaica to Cuba or to Central and North America, and from the country to the city. The fiction that has been selected, however, represents a literature that is not confined to narrow nationalist themes and concerns. It is experimental, innovative and for the most part representative of not only a West Indian nationalist aesthetic but of a poetics of liberation: it is literary production that does not merely serve the nation but offers a critique of nationhood, even in its process of becoming.

NOTES

1 Alison Donnell, *Twentieth-Century Caribbean Literature: Critical Moments in Anglophone Literary History* (London: Routledge, 2006), p. 11.
2 Recent studies that focus on Caribbean literature in the period 1920–50 include Donnell's chapter, 'Difficult Subjects', in *Twentieth-Century Caribbean Literature*, Leah Rosenberg's *Nationalism and the Formation of Caribbean Literature* (New York: Palgrave Macmillan, 2007) and Mary Lou Emery's *Modernism, the Visual and Caribbean Literature* (Cambridge: Cambridge University Press, 2007).
3 Henry Swanzy, 'The Literary Situation in the Contemporary Caribbean', *Books Abroad*, 30 (1956), 266–74, repr. in *The Routledge Reader in Caribbean Literature*, ed. by Alison Donnell and Sarah Lawson Welsh (London: Routledge, 1996), pp. 249–52 (p. 252).
4 Mary Louise Pratt, 'The Short Story: The Long and Short of It', in *The New Short Story Theories*, ed. by Charles E. May (Athens: Ohio University Press, 1994), pp. 91–113 (p. 110).
5 Una Marson, 'Wanted: Writers and Publishers', *Public Opinion*, 22 May 1937, p. 6.
6 Peter Blackman, 'Is There a West Indian Literature', *Life and Letters*, 59 (1948), pp. 96–102 (p. 102).
7 Cicely Howland, *The Long Run* (London: Victor Gollancz, 1961), p. 162.
8 Frank A. Hill, 'Toss Away the Old', *Public Opinion*, 27 December 1937, p. 5.
9 Una Marson, 'Unsung Heroes', *Public Opinion*, 30 October 1937, p. 12.
10 Esther Chapman, 'Negro's "Public Enemy Number 1": Editor is a Woman', *Daily Gleaner*, 2 August 1939, p. 6.
11 'Notice', *Daily Gleaner*, 2 July 1949, p. 1.
12 'Better Education', *Daily Gleaner*, 2 January 1946, p. 8.
13 Maureen Shirley, 'Thou Fool', *Daily Gleaner*, 10 July 1951, p. 6 and 'The Thirteenth Step', *Daily Gleaner*, 5 September 1951, p. 8. Archie Lindo's stories were originally published in *Public Opinion* in 1937–8 and then later in the anthologies *My Heart Was Singing* (Jamaica: College Press, 1945) and *Bronze* (Jamaica: College Press, 1945).
14 Philip Sherlock, 'Foreword', in Inez K. Sibley, *Quashie's Reflections in Jamaican Creole* (Jamaica: Bolívar Press, 1968), pp. i–ii (p. ii).
15 Inez K. Sibley, 'A Wedding Ceremony', in *Quashie's Reflections in Jamaican Creole*, pp. 3–4 (p. 4).
16 Houston A. Baker Jr., *Modernism and the Harlem Renaissance* (Chicago: University of Chicago Press, 1987), p. 101.
17 Pennib, 'A Case in Court', *Daily Gleaner*, 25 February 1939, p. 35.
18 Henry Swanzy, 'Caribbean Voices – A Review of the Last Six Months', *Public Opinion*, 15 October 1949, p. 6.
19 Inez K. Sibley, 'The Terror Bull and Taunt Song', *Focus* (1956), pp. 60–7 (p. 60). This short story was originally published in *Public Opinion* in 1949.
20 W.G. Ogilvie, 'The Great Kranjie', in Vic Reid et al, *14 Jamaican Short Stories* (Kingston, Jamaica: Pioneer Press, 1950), pp. 31–35 (p. 31).
21 Kenneth Ramchand, *The West Indian Novel and Its Background* (Kingston, Jamaica: Ian Randle, 2004), p. 80.
22 Joan McLaughlin, 'Jamaican Creole', in *Quashie's Reflections in Jamaican Creole*, pp. iii–xi (p. xi).
23 Claude Thompson, 'The Children That Sit in Darkness', in Claude Thompson, *These My People* (Kingston, Jamaica: The Herald Printers, 1943), pp. 39–50 (p. 44).
24 Henry Fowler, 'Forward', *Focus* (1956).

25 J.E.C. McFarlane, *A Literature in the Making* (Kingston, Jamaica: Pioneer Press, 1956), p. 93.

26 John Figueroa, 'The Flaming Faith of those First Years', in *Tibisiri*, ed. by Maggie Butcher (Sydney: Dangaroo Press, 1989), pp. 59–80 (p. 72).

27 Glynne Griffith, 'Deconstructing Nationalisms: Henry Swanzy, Caribbean Voices and the Development of West Indian Literature', *small axe*, 10 (2001), 1–20 (p. 13).

28 Robert Herring, 'What I Look For in West Indian Literature', *Life and Letters*, 57 (1948), 1–3 (p. 2).

29 Both stories originally appeared in *Public Opinion* and in Aarons's self-published collection *The Cow That Laughed and Other Stories* (Kingston, Jamaica: Kingston Printers, 1944).

30 R.L.C. Aarons, 'The Cow That Laughed', *Life and Letters*, 57 (1948), pp. 50–57 (p. 53).

31 Victor Ramraj, 'Short Fiction', in *A History of Literature in the Caribbean*, ed. by James A. Arnold et al (Amsterdam, John Benjamin, 2001), pp. 199–223 (p. 206).

32 Roger Mais, 'Why Local Colour?', *Public Opinion*, 8 January 1944, p. 3.

33 Roger Mais, 'The Short Story', *Public Opinion*, 27 March 1943, p. 4.

34 Cicely Howland, 'Review: *Face and Other Stories*', *Public Opinion*, 9 May 1942, p. 6; and in the same edition K.J. Alexander, 'Review: *Face and Other Stories*', *Public Opinion*, 9 May 1942, p. 6.

35 Sandra Pouchet Paquet makes a similar observation in her essay 'The Fifties', in *West Indian Literature*, ed. by Bruce King (Basingstoke, Macmillan, 1995), pp. 51–62 (pp. 55–6).

36 Roger Mais, 'Words and So Forth', *Public Opinion*, 30 May 1942, p. 6.

37 Roger Mais, 'Tig', *Public Opinion*, 12 April 1941, pp. 8–10 (p. 8).

38 Roger Mais, 'You've Gotta Go Home', *Public Opinion*, 10 September 1949, p. 6.

39 Kenneth Ramchand 'Introduction', in Roger Mais, *Listen, the Wind and Other Stories* (Essex: Longman, 1986), pp.vi–xxx (p. xix).

40 Roger Mais, 'Gravel in Your Shoe', in *Listen, the Wind and Other Stories*. This story was originally published in Mais's collection *Face and Other Stories* (the collection was reviewed in *Public Opinion* in 1942).

41 Henry Swanzy, 'Caribbean Voices – A Review of the Last Six Months', *Public Opinion*, 10 October 1953, p. 5.

42 Vic Reid, 'Digging Match' *Focus* (1948), 48–61 (p. 48).

43 Vic Reid, 'Pattern,' *Focus* (1948), 52–56 (p. 56).

THE *BEACON* SHORT STORY AND THE COLONIAL IMAGINARY IN TRINIDAD

RAYMOND RAMCHARITAR

Introduction: Literature and the Colonial Imaginary

In examining literature in a former colony, particularly the literature's seminal moment during the colonial era, it seems evident that the characteristics of a crucial construct which affects the character of the literature – the 'national Imaginary' – and its relation to an overarching colonial Imaginary, are important.

Critical discussion of Trinidad's Beacon Group and its literary work, which are widely held to be the point of origin of contemporary Trinidadian (and West Indian) literature, has not broached the issue of the Imaginary, and the imaginative quality of the work, except in a tangential way. Gordon Rohlehr, for example, has described the emergence of West Indian literature as a phenomenon that was 'new and passionate and signaled the eruption into visibility of the colonial person' who had 'never quite articulated his deepest and most burning necessity in a fiction and language unmistakably his own'.[1] However to the primarily British publishers and readers, it signified something else. To them, 'our literature was being promoted as a quaint curiosity…whose meaning did not, and could not possibly matter' ('Trophy and Catastrophe', p. 294).

The imaginative dimension of the literature is alluded to here: the fact that the 'meaning did not [...] matter' was a consequence of the West Indian writer's discursive space, like his/her geographic space, being already colonised, and meanings and significations established in advance by interpretive and imaginative tropes. These meanings – the archetype of which was of a primitive frontier where civilisation had foundered – were established roughly with Shakespeare's *The Tempest*, and persisted via fictional, historical, and travel narratives like Daniel Defoe's *Robinson Crusoe* and Charles Kingsley's *At Last, A Christmas in the West Indies*,[2] and even the physical sciences which, up to the early twentieth century, 'scientifically' established the inferiority of the darker races.[3] The engine of these meanings was the imperial/colonial epistemology, and the fuel was authorised narratives describing and analysing colonial endeavour. These included the planter histories of Edward Long et al, Royal Commissions' and colonial government reports, and imperial travellers' and fictional accounts, such as Charles Kingsley's, Anthony Trollope's and James Anthony Froude's, in the nineteenth century, and later, the narratives of non-conventional media like fairs, exhibitions, travel documentaries and popular films.[4]

This link between the imaginative dimension of texts, and their role in producing self-knowledge and understanding via narrative as a vehicle for ideas or discourse, is apprehensible on the scale of a *nation*'s self-understanding. Raymond Williams, in his *Culture and Society, 1780–1950*, isolates the source texts that generated the foundational ideas of British democracy, and the phenomenon was discussed by Homi Bhabha and his contributors in the collection *Nation and Narration* (1990).[5] In Bhabha's collection Timothy Brennan argues that particularly post-colonial nations are 'invented' by interpellations of tradition, politics, and myth into the discourse of the socio-geographic entity that is evolving into a nation.[6] Once the discourse is produced, Simon During proposes a location: the 'civil Imaginary': a 'cultural space' which 'produces *representations of manners, taste, behaviour, utterances for imitation by individual lives*' [emphasis added].[7]

The effects of these narratives on creating the *character* of a nation's citizens are more literal than it would appear. Cultural psychologist Peggy Miller et al, examining narrative practices across cultures, propose that 'narrative reverberates through the lives of individuals, connecting them to other people... and *teaching them who they are or might become*' [emphasis added].[8] Furthermore, they conclude, 'when narratives are treated as situated practices rather than disembodied texts, it becomes apparent that storytelling is a dynamic process emerging from particular circumstances, shaped by the interests of narrative participants' (Miller et al, p. 603).

I will argue in this chapter, therefore, that a textual and discursive analysis of the social imagination that produced the *Beacon* stories, compared to the main elements of a colonial imaginary, will reveal that the Beacon Group was not, as suggested by other critics, the vanguard of an indigenous Trinidadian literature – labelled 'the Trinidad Awakening'.[9] I will show that they were (perhaps unwitting) agents perpetuating an ongoing colonial discursive program already identified, whose purpose was to create colonial subjects to the Empire's ontological specifications. (The dynamics of this programme have been described by Edward Said and Homi Bhabha et al.[10])

The colonial discursive programme comprised many synergistic components, of which written narrative was one, but diminished in importance with the advent of film from the early twentieth century. Once it was available, colonial discursive conditioning was dominated by the mass medium of film whose consumption had the desirable characteristic of not being dependent upon subscribers' literacy and communicating its ideas and values more subtly and to larger populations, which included the producers, consumers, and source subjects of the *Beacon*'s literature. Therefore, I do not propose to examine the effects of the *Beacon*'s literature on the Trinidad masses in this chapter. I will examine:

- The *Beacon*'s literature's characteristics *per se*, in relation to the themes and ideas in the pre-existent colonial imaginary;
- Its effects in creating perceptions among producers themselves, and their small group of subscribers, who all occupied positions of social power, which power was mobilised to shape a Trinidadian national culture post-1956; and
- I will conclude by briefly examining the consequences of this imaginative cathexis on the national literature of Trinidad.

THE COLONIAL IMAGINARY IN THE EARLY TWENTIETH CENTURY

Historian Carl Campbell notes that in nineteenth-century Trinidad, education was stratified according to class and economic status. The mass of the population was exposed to 'industrial' and 'agricultural' education, and secondary education was available to a few hundred candidates per year. It was only in the 1920s that secondary education became widespread, and even then, only to a small middle class.[11] The mass of people, therefore, was steeped in oral discourse: the Carnival, the Hosay, and the Hindu *Ramayana* tradition. Information and discourse were transmitted through calypso songs and masques during Carnival; public recitations and performances of Hindu texts, like the *Ramayana* at the Ram Leela; and the Muslim Hosay festival.[12] In such an environment of relatively low literacy, and the lack of unifying national narratives, the importance of film in transmitting a uniform set of ideas to the entire population was enormous.

Ella Shohat and Robert Stam observe that cinema 'partly inherited' the social function of the novel: 'films [...] idealized the colonial enterprise as a philanthropic "civilizing mission"', paradoxically, by showing Africans and Asians as 'human figures with kinship to specific animal species thus literalizing the colonialist zeugma, yoking "native" and "animal"'.[13] In Trinidad, they write, films served to condition the masses to accept authority vested in the white person and the symbols of empire, and this agenda was reinforced by law: 'the censorship code forbade "scenes intended to ridicule or criticize unfairly" British social life, "white men in a state of degradation amidst native surroundings, or using violence towards natives, especially Chinese, negroes [*sic*] and Indians" and "unequivocal situations between men of one race and girls of another race"' ('The Imperial Imaginary', pp. 125–126). British and American films were shown in Trinidad from 1911.[14] In 1912 the film company announced a free matinee for school children featuring 'special children's programmes' which would include 'travel and industrial pictures' after which the children would be encouraged to write essays.[15] By the end of the First World War, there were at least six cinemas across the island,[16] and that number steadily grew.

But these thematic staples of the colonial Imaginary – of the immutability of imperial authority, the innate inferiority of Africans and Asians, and the benevolence of empire – now disseminated and reinforced via film throughout the population, had been in circulation in Trinidad since the nineteenth century, and, I will demonstrate, were *reproduced* rather than *repudiated* in the *Beacon*'s fiction. Of importance here, to reiterate, is the imaginative character of the *Beacon* fiction, and its consequences on future literary production, and nationalist institutions.

A BRIEF HISTORY OF TRINIDADIAN SHORT FICTION TILL THE *BEACON*

The earliest known substantial local work of fiction published in the Trinidad press was a serialised novel, *Adolphus: A Tale*, a romance-revenge story whose protagonist was a mixed-race Trinidadian, in the *Trinidadian* newspaper in 1853. Its author was not identified.[17] (The first Trinidadian novel was E.L. Joseph's *Warner Arundell: Adventures of a Creole*, published in England in 1838, and set in various islands of the West Indies and Venezuela, and featuring non-white characters in substantial but secondary roles. Trinidadian novel-length narratives of the nineteenth century were rare: apart from M.M. Philip's *Emmanuel Appadoca* (1854), there appears no other than those identified.[18])

Short fiction appears intermittently in the nineteenth-century Trinidadian press, which was comprised of a large number of publications, many lasting only a few years, and usually operated by individuals. The fiction in the latter third of the nineteenth century had a few common characteristics, which can be found in a serial, 'Roses and Shamrocks', published from 14 September 1885, in the black-owned *New Era* newspaper. It was a detective story, set in England, with an all-white cast. By the turn of the century, short stories were more regular and the *Pioneer* serialised books and published local poetry and foreign fiction, which more or less conformed to these criteria: the protagonists were white, blacks were in secondary or minor roles, non-whites were inferior beings, and England was the centre, even if the story was located elsewhere.

A sampling of these narratives include 'Done!', a locally written story published in the *Port of Spain Gazette*, on 10 July 1898; 'A Rubber at Whist', also in the *Port of Spain Gazette*, 31 July 1898; 'A Curious Case' in the *Mirror*, 14 February 1899; and 'And Each Man in His Turn' in (installments in) the *Pioneer*, 8, 15, November 1899. 'Done' is a scandalous romance. Its heroine is the virtuous Ruby, who is pressured by her widowed mother to find a rich husband, even as her mother competes with her. 'Whist' is a supernatural thriller. 'Case' is a crime-courtroom thriller. They are set in India, England and the West Indies, but their protagonists are white, and all refer to England in some idealistic way.

Stories using the majority populations, even as backdrop, were rare. Graham Gorrie's 'The Masker of Carnival', published in the *Port of Spain Gazette* (24 February 1900), uses detailed descriptions of the Carnival celebrations to provide texture for the tragedy playing out in an aristocratic Spanish family. His descriptions of the non-white population conform to the dominant conceptions at the time:

> This band [...] are negroes. *The loud laugh, the vigorous, coarse gestures, the overflowing amount of animal spirits would betray them apart from their unmistakable gait.*
>
> And here, coming out of a side street [...] is a human counterfeit of a Royal tiger. [...] To these young East Indians there is no incongruity in this intrusion of the ancient mummery of the East to these new festivals of the new land of the West. [emphasis added]

These stories were consumed by a small number of literate people, who included the educated non-white 'radicals' who would instigate the political agitation at the turn of the century. At this time, black and coloured lawyers and professionals began to move aggressively to acquire political power. Their main media were the newspapers and the calypso, and their provocation would culminate in the Water Riots of 1903, a watershed event which altered the political trajectory of the island. Thereafter, the publication of literary works in the newspapers falls off, but the profusion of literary and debating societies throughout the society indicates that the interest in creative writing persisted among the literate, socially mobile segments of the population.[19]

By 1905, the only publication which maintained a significant literary output was the *Pioneer*, which serialised two books that year: Booker T. Washington's *Working with the Hands* and colonial official Hugh Clifford's *Sally (a Study) and Other Tales of the Outskirts*. In 1907, the first work of fiction to propose a black hero was published, though not in the newspapers: a novella, *Rupert Gray: A Tale in Black and White*, by Stephen Cobham. However, there was no further fiction in the daily press till the *Argos* in 1911 began to serialise foreign books and ran local poems.

Into this newly fomented environment World War I arrived, with Garveyism in its wake, and intensified race consciousness among the black population. The post-war era also saw the emergence of British Labour Socialism in Trinidad, and the growth in number and popularity of cinemas, their content filling a gap fiction might have occupied. Indeed, a hint of the force of the cinema in shaping local self-perceptions is available in the nomenclature of various Carnival bands, calypsonians, and later, steelbands: Alexander's Ragtime Band, Hellyard, Desperadoes, Casablanca, Renegades, Dixieland, Tripoli, West Side Symphony et al, were all derived from popular films of the time.

Fiction reappears in the newspapers in the mid-1920s. The Sunday edition of the *Port of Spain Gazette* in 1925 serialised lengthy foreign works, like *The Isle of Bigamaya*, by Ralph Vignale, and shorter individual pieces, located abroad, and featuring exclusively British characters.

The first Trinidadian Legislative Council elections were also held in 1925, and perhaps this combination of factors – long-desired, if limited, political autonomy, relative prosperity, a confident black and coloured middle class on the rise, and the lower classes in the thrall of the cinema – generated an urge for 'writing' the newly autonomous nation into existence. It also appears that these conditions were not only local, since similar literary movements appeared in all the islands by the 30s.[20] At any rate, through local or regional factors, the stage was set for the emergence the *Beacon* in 1931, and its direct antecedent, a short-lived precursor journal *Trinidad* in 1929 launched by C.L.R. James and Alfred Mendes.

TRINIDAD FACTION

From the data available in the press, early Trinidadian short fiction was preoccupied with British and colonial expatriate characters, but as far as representation of locals and the stories of their lives went, another stream of quasi-fictional discourse flowed consistently in the newspapers, and this is of premium importance in examining the *Beacon*'s fiction: this was the reportage on the quotidian lives of the majority population in the newspapers. A constant theme in the nineteenth-century press was the 'civilised' middle-class perspective on the lives of the majority Afro and Asiatic population, in sensational reports of crime, vice, obeah and violent Carnival activities. (This theme, civility versus savagery, was one of the characteristics of the British films of the early part of the twentieth century.)

Fair Play, owned by a French Creole, H.S. Billouin, commences its editorial on 1 March 1883, on 'Drum Dances', events which attracted the black urban underclasses, observing: 'It is an acknowledged fact that the animal organs of the African race are far more developed than their intellectual ones…'. Joseph Lewis, the black editor of the *New Era*, on 22 August 1881, complained about 'the spread and increase of the avowedly licentious classes about town' who 'created a moral nuisance on our midst'.

The reports of colonial expatriates were also critical, consistently painting them as decadent, corrupt, and incompetent. In 1878, *Fair Play* ran an extended campaign against one Dr. Crane, the colonial surgeon general, who, it claimed, had a fake medical degree. On 27 March 1884 the paper described the tenure of departing governor Sir Sanford Freeling as 'a striking lesson of the disaster of results which often ensue from infirmity of purpose and insincerity of profession'. The newspapers' praise was reserved for Creoles – white, coloured, and occasionally black men, who embodied the native 'Creole' ideal. On 9 June 1879 Lewis also wrote disparagingly of 'a proposed crusade' by the supporters of governor Sir Henry Irving to 'crush out by any means fair or foul the purely Creole element of the public service'.

The same newspapers had described the staples of urban underclass life – crime, miserable living conditions and obeah – since the 1860s.[21] For example, the *Gazette* editorial, of 10 September 1885, presented this description of the living quarters of the urban poor:

> The sheds or Barracks are divided into 6, 8, 10 or more rooms, the division being a wooden partition […] These rooms […] have one door, and an opening closed by a wooden shutter, as an apology for a window. […] The closet accommodation for all the inmates […] consists of one cesspit surrounded by a wooden hut […] Lavatories there are not; a 'wash' […] under a tap is the only thing approaching a bath.

As late as (12 April) 1912, an article in the *Mirror* provided this account of obeah:

> Our coloured servant, Susanna, was a firm believer in witchcraft […] On one of my periodical visits to her little cottage in Belmont […] I found Zanna […] in an unusual state of excitement. This she explained was due to someone having cast the evil eye on her favourite cow. 'You see mum,' she tole [*sic*] me dolefully, 'Bessie was a puffec beauty an' wen so many people keep puttin dey mouts pon she it made me [*sic*] nervous. Den pon a sudden she begin to fall off.'

All these themes and details would be repeated in the *Beacon*'s fiction. For example, C.L.R. James would write, in fiction ('Triumph', 1929), a story whose inciting event is obeah, practiced by poor black women:

> Every street in Port-of-Spain proper could show you numerous examples […] long, low buildings, consisting of anything from four to eighteen rooms, each about twelve feet square. […] In one corner of the yard is the hopelessly inadequate water closet unmistakable to the nose if not the eye; sometimes there is a structure with the title of bathroom […] he or she who would wash in it with decent privacy must cover the person as if bathing on the banks of the Thames....[22]

Thus, summing up the congruence between Trinidadian fiction, faction, and the colonial discourse on the indigenes of colonised nations, a few imaginative themes are common: a general lack of the graces of civilisation, evidenced by reports of crime, obeah, and violent entertainment; the superiority of imperial culture; and the general idealised representation of England. The *Beacon*'s thematic innovation was the corruption of colonial officials, but the virtue of the Creole middle class. Most significantly, this style, and indeed, *convention* of writing and interpreting the lives of the masses of the population had been established in the middle-class imagination, and the *Beacon* was comprised almost entirely of middle-class contributors.

THE *BEACON* IN TRINIDAD

The *Beacon* publication and movement are considered by influential critics to have been the vanguard of Trinidadian and West Indian fiction. Kenneth Ramchand identifies the moment with the consolidation of national artistic and literary talent and agendas. He writes: 'the literary pace setters [of the Beacon group] were Portuguese Creole, Alfred Mendes, and C.L.R. James'.[23] Later critics accepted this conclusion. Bruce King, introducing *West Indian Literature*, commented that the *Beacon* 'attempted to align creative writing with local radical politics'[24] which is closer to the truth, but his contributor, Reinhard Sander, while also acknowledging the wider *Beacon* agenda, is more definite: 'The *Beacon* and its precursor, *Trinidad* [...] mark the emergence of West Indian short fiction'. This meant that its 'editors insisted' that 'West Indian writing should utilise West Indian settings, speech, characters, situations and conflicts', in brief, they should be 'authentic' (Sander, p. 41).

But the critics have not commented upon its one crucial, unacknowledged pursuit: the *Beacon*'s undeclared war on colonial expatriates and reactionary locals, clergy, capitalists, and plantocracy – who belonged to the same social classes as some of the *Beacon*'s principals, like Alfred Mendes, Albert Gomes, and the de Boissierres. Ramchand quotes a personal communication from Mendes, describing the experience: 'We had 3 rip-roaring years of tearing into every sanctity and Pharisaism of the respectable folk. How hurt they were – but how much they enjoyed it' (Ramchand, p. 65). Mendes reiterated the importance the Beacon group's social location in a later interview: 'Most of us came from middle-class families. There was this dichotomy in terms. *Our background was too deeply embedded in us to overcome the growth of our intellect* from adolescence onwards, so that we still unconsciously hankered after what was behind us' [emphasis added].[25]

Seemingly oblivious of the significance of Mendes's admission and the copious textual evidence signifying it, many literary critics seem to agree that here was the 'authentic' point of origin of Trinidadian fiction. This is certainly in accord with what the *Beacon* felt its mission to be, as illustrated in a statement in its January–February 1932 issue, regarding submissions to its fiction competition:

> We fail utterly to understand [...] why anyone should want to see [a] Trinidad [...] where grave-diggers speak like English M.P.'s and vice versa. *The answer is obviously that the average Trinidadian regards his countrymen as his inferiors, an uninteresting people who are not worth his while. He genuinely feels this (and by this, of course, asserts his own inferiority) that with his people as characters, his stories are worth nothing.* [...]
>
> Sex is still the 'dirty little secret' but the local writer treats it with religious fervour..... (pp. 1–2 [emphasis added])

Here the group's social realism agenda is directly stated: to assert the agency of Trinidadians and the value of local experience and to devalue imitation of British models.

However, more recent critics have been less patronising in their evaluations. Harvey Neptune Jr. in examining the American occupation of Trinidad from 1941, examines the cultural-political environment of the precursor decade. He observes that the provocateurs in the Beacon Group took it upon themselves, via their organ, to 'banalise Britishness, to disturb its air of invulnerability' in response to 'Trinidad's pathological idealisation of Britishness'.[26] Neptune also notes that in the rush to idealise the indigenous, they 'proved guilty of romanticising blackness in a manner that flirted troublingly with metropolitan primitivism'. He continues that 'the degree to which the imaginations of the "common people" were captured by the nationalist intelligentsia cannot be known' (Neptune, pp. 20–21). Indeed, the *Beacon* agenda was distinct from the masses' agenda, which culminated in the riots of 1937, and even in contrast to the progressive agenda of the Labour movement. The Beacon group saw '[n]ationality rooted in outright resistance to contemporary Western ways' (Neptune, p. 50). This is demonstrated by the *Beacon*'s dismissal (in its May 1933 issue) of local literary and debating societies, which admired British literature and Arnoldian culture, as 'a popular malady, like typhoid fever or influenza' (p. 1).

This contempt materialised in the works of fiction published. Generally, the *Beacon* stories were realistic narratives – there were a few exceptions of 'lyric' short stories by Olga Yaatof ('Gasolene Station', April 1932 and 'The Stenographer', December 1932) and Kathleen Archibald ('Beyond the Horizon', June 1931) a few poor attempts at historical fiction (Michael Deeble's 'Yacua', June 1931), and some isolated attempts at humour and noir (like Percival Maynard's 'The Hunt that Failed' (September 1931) and Mendes's 'Damp' (August 1932)), but most stories were concerned with social realism: as direct reportage of the class and ethnic conflict in colonial Trinidad as could be reached in fiction.

Of forty-four stories published in the twenty-eight issues of the *Beacon* at least thirty could be described as belonging to the social realist genre. Of these, twenty-six are concerned with racial themes from the Creole middle-class vantage, the 'yard' theme, the 'decadent colonial' theme, and what can be described as 'exposé' stories, which revealed the sordid private lives of the colonial expatriates and reactionary locals.

At a distance of nearly eight decades, the exposé stories still evoke a thrill of scandal. They include Percival Maynard's 'Divorce and Mr Jerningham' (Jan–Feb 1932), Cecil Pantin's 'The Barrier' (September 1932), Alastair Scott's 'Brotherly Love' (August 1932), and Mendes's 'Snapshots' (December 1932) and 'Colour' (June–November 1933). The stories' subjects are anti-clericalism, divorce, incest, paedophilia and racial issues. Stories concerning particular issues (like divorce and censorship) appeared at times when debates were rife in the society. 'Divorce and Mr Jerningham', for example, was published at a time of a contentious debate over a divorce bill in the Legislative Council. It begins as the white, middle-aged Mrs Jerningham asks her husband his opinion on the bill, and he replies that 'I have not been lucky enough to have a personal experience of divorce'. Soon follows the arrival of a new 'well-proportioned though not particularly beautiful' typist, Doreen, in Mr Jerningham's office.[27] Mr Jerningham is snared, and when he admits to his adultery, Mrs Jerningham threatens divorce, which is now a possibility with the passage of the divorce bill. This real possibility brings the hero to his senses and saves his marriage.

The protagonists of 'The Barrier' begin an affair while vacationing in Barbados, whereupon the man (Travers) tells the woman (Angela) he cannot continue. They return home and Angela is invited by a friend to a party at another couple's home. She is told that her host has made her husband a cuckold which he must tolerate because divorce is not legal. Of course, the cuckolded husband turns out to be Travers.

In addition to the moral messages, given the small size of the white population at the time, it is likely that specific couples were being discussed, whose identities would be an open secret. The same strategy is evident in 'Brotherly Love', which relates the meandering of a young white man through the city in an inebriated state, recoiling at its denizens, all the while thinking of his sister at home in un-brotherly terms:

> Two black women passed him, *looking at him inquiringly*. They were horrible, he thought. His mind shifted to his sister [...]. He marveled that these ugly wandering creatures that had just passed him should be women just like she was a woman. He thought of her trim little figure, her delicate complexion, and wondered if she could have similar feelings to these others. [emphasis added][28]

By the time he reaches home, 'he began to forget she was his sister', and it is suggested that he acts on his amnesia. The story appears to be less concerned with art than exposing a specific situation.

Mendes actually achieves the artistic success absent from 'Brotherly Love', while maintaining the exposé agenda with the lengthy 'Boodhoo' (March–July 1932), the story of a young Eurasian plantation labourer fathered by a British overseer with a female labourer, who seduces his young British stepmother. Boodhoo's internal narrative as a Eurasian in the colony, his reflection on his antecedents and status, which would have been of real interest, are never broached. Boodhoo's (Indian) mother reveals her relationship to his stepmother, she says, simply to cause pain in return for the pain her husband caused her. Mendes portrays at great length Boodhoo's contempt for his Indian mother, and through extensive sitting room conversational scenes, his stepmother's, and the expatriates' revulsion at the non-whites in the society. While the broaching of the sexual congress between the male indigene and the female colonial is daring, its inner workings are never examined. Despite its artistic success (relative to its predecessors) 'Boodhoo' falls far short of its social realism agenda, achieving merely display, and not enlarging the national moral imagination with a treatment of the indigene as capable of complex moral motivation.

The exposé genre also found fertile ground in religion. The December 1932 issue of the *Beacon* opens with an editorial headlined 'The Muzzling of Thought' by Ralph Mentor, commenting on a cleric, Fr. O'Dea, who thought 'the literary movement in Trinidad should be held in check [and] instructed Catholics to burn such periodicals' – including the *Beacon* (p. 1). The majority of the fiction in that issue, Albert Gomes's 'Day-Dreams', Mendes's 'Snapshots', Percival Maynard's 'Peace', Ernest Carr's 'The Crime' and Cecil Pantin's 'Something for Nothing', is explicitly and unflatteringly directed at religion.

Gomes's 'Day-Dreams' places his distaste for religion in the mouth of a boy, Charlie, who is being forced to go to Sunday School: 'Everything about Sunday School frightened him [...] he didn't like the pictures of old men with gray beards and long dresses.'[29] Carr's 'The Crime' presents a mentally challenged protagonist, Wesley Calvin, who kills his employer who has molested and impregnated a young woman Calvin considered an angel. The 'moral' is clearly that colonial justice and morality are at odds. Pantin's 'Something for Nothing' introduces Bosco, a frail youth afflicted by an open sore, who is trying to get himself arrested to avail himself of the medical care and free meals in the public jail. He tries several means, including not paying bills and destroying public property, which end in his being saved by 'Christian charity'. He finally succeeds when he attempts to listen to a concert at an upper-class home standing outside the fence, and is arrested for loitering and trespassing. The irony is that Christian charity is practiced ritualistically, and fails those it is intended to comfort. When Bosco attempts to avail himself of beauty, in the form of music, this offends the purveyors of charity.

In 'Snapshots', the longest story, Mendes creates/reveals Mr Rose, who is mysterious, effeminate and Barbadian. He is hired by a Port of Spain businessman who has a wife and son ('little Dick'), to whom he becomes close, and establishes himself in the city's smart set. There is some curiosity in Rose's seeming immunity to the charms of eligible women. Then he is caught in a police raid at a transvestite party, which he manages to laugh off, and which is misinterpreted by the local elite in the following exchange:

> 'Surely [he knows] that sort of thing isn't done here?'
> 'What "sort of thing"?' Levitt asked...
> 'Why going out and drinking with coloured men,' he replied quickly.

The heavy-handed anti-clericalism is established by the narrator's descriptions of conversations between Levitt and his wife, who looks at her husband 'meekly' and with 'meek evangelicalism'.[30] The word 'meek' is used no fewer than four times in this context, throughout the story. 'Meek' echoes the Christian benediction, 'blessed are the meek', and its context here suggests the 'meekness' is weakness which enables evil. Indeed, no jibe is too small, as in 'anglicanism' being spelt with the lower case 'a' (rather than the customary capital A).

The story climaxes when, after the death of Rose, his trunk is opened by the police and reveals a hoard of sexual photographs of children, including little Dick. Obviously the moral is that the society is so enwrapped in its own hypocrisy, its denizens are unable to recognise real evil in its midst. The detail of the transvestite party also suggests that the incident was not entirely fictional.

In all the stories, the theme of race is pervasive, and Mendes makes a disastrous attempt to address it directly from June–November 1933 with 'Colour', of which the inciting event is the return of the coloured Frank, with his American wife Frieda, to colonial Grenada. The family's members ask questions like: 'isn't Frieda white […] And isn't it true that we are coloured?' The narrator assists with a description of Frank's complexion, that his 'skin had cleared up considerably and only the suspicious widening of his nostrils told the practiced eye he was not of European descent'.[31]

The other generic story-type was the moral study of the society's underbelly, of which James's 'Triumph' is the best-known example. It is an account of the lives of three women, Mamitz, Celestine, and Irene, in a barrack yard in Port of Spain in the 1920s. The story's inciting event is Mamitz's sudden reversal of fortune. Her relationship with the tram conductor who kept her ended with his beating her and leaving, and in the weeks before the story opens, no provider has emerged. Celestine is certain that 'obeah' was done to Mamitz and that the culprit is the jealous Irene. Celestine then contrives to have Mamitz treated for her condition, after which treatment Mamitz attracts the attentions of the louche Popo des Vignes and the stolid Nicholas the butcher.

The story begins with a detailed description of the barrack yard (already cited above), contrasting it with the standards of civility to which a British (and a Creole Trinidadian) reader would be accustomed. No member of the yard is allowed moments of interior reflection without the author's patronising commentary. For example, Mamitz's thoughts about the conflict regarding her competing swains: 'Mamitz accepted. She didn't like the butcher too much, but he liked her. And a pound of beef was a pound of beef.'

The story revels in the squalor of the yard-dwellers: the fact that the women are prostitutes, that they practice obeah, and even their men are without redeeming qualities. James describes Irene's provider as having 'a sore on his foot, which he had had for thirty years and would carry him to the grave [...] Syphilis *congenital and acquired* and his copious boozing would see to it there was no recovery' [emphasis added] ('Triumph', p. 39). A social 'insider' can sense the meta-text here of James's memoir, *Beyond a Boundary* (published much later) feeding a subtext that *he is not like that*, but is positioned to provide the seamy details for his subscribers, who, from the references, are white and British.

This posture to the lower orders would be repeated in the other yard stories in the *Beacon*. Percival Maynard's 'His Right of Possession' (April 1932) tells the story of Vera and Pedro, a poor, black couple. Pedro beats Vera and she leaves him. On her way to the police she meets her cousin who invites Vera to stay with her. They then decide to go to a calypso tent. Here Vera meets Donald, to whom she decides to succumb, then changes her mind, because she felt she 'belonged' to Pedro, and beating her was his right. More interesting than the ludicrous plot turns are the means by which the character expresses herself, and the author's representation of her interior narrative. The narrator reports that,

> Vera considered. She wondered if he wanted to make love to her. If he wanted her to go with him she would do so. That would prevent her from inconveniencing Olive. She didn't love him but what did it matter? What did anything matter – now?

But when she attempts to explain her action to her cousin, the character's sentiments are less eloquently expressed:

> Vera said: 'I suppose yo' dyin' to know why I here instead of wit' Donal'? Well I couldn' go an' live wid him – like dat. I said yes at fus because I did want to make Pedro see I coulda get somebody else [...] But I cahn go t'rough wid it.'[32]

Vera thinks sophisticatedly in the Standard English, but speaks in an inarticulate 'broken' Creole. The Creole is merely 'bad' English, and meant to signify the characters' wretchedness rather a viable idiolect or vernacular. We are also in the unusual position of knowing the editors thought that the author's 'treatment of Vera's psychology was excellent', and that he 'succeeded in pouring an amazing amount of local atmosphere into his story'.[33] This story won the *Beacon*'s short story competition, which announcement and encomium accompanied its publication in the April 1932 issue.

This examination of the lower orders' moral and material constitution continues in Mendes's 'Sweetman' (October 1931), 'Five Dollars Worth of Flesh' (September 1931), 'Ursula's Morals' (February 1933), and Maynard's 'His Last Fling' (May 1933). In no case is any of the lower orders allowed to rise above their interlocutors' preconceptions of their simple and simplistic morality, or lack thereof.

Norman Collingwood's two efforts focus on the sins of women: 'A Daughter of Jezebel' (March 1933), tells of Rosita, whose consort, Santos, who is 'a brute', mistreats her, and she retaliates by attempting to poison his tea and kills her cat instead. In 'The Dougla' (April 1933) Collingwood's barrack yard 'smell[s] of rum', and in this milieu he introduces Elaine, an 'Afro-Indian' who lived off many men because 'her seductive charm drove them mad'. She is, however, smitten by the worthless Tony, who rediscovers his love for her after he gets drunk and sees her with another man and seizes her to assert his ownership.

The stories are generally simplistic and artless, given to almost fetishistic descriptions of the squalor, and dialogue to establish the primitive 'otherness' of the characters through primary emotions: lust, greed, anger, jealousy, resentment. A small tributary diverges from the 'yard' stories: an examination of the rural peasantry, which is addressed in Mendes's 'Pablo's Fandango' (March 1931) and Percival Maynard's 'Francisco' (Feb 1933). But while the location has shifted in these stories, the perspective, of middle-class superiority, has not.

Outside the binary of decadent upper, and savage lower portions of society is the Beacon Group, illustrated in Mendes's 'Without Snow' (December 1931) as the antithesis of the 'yard' scenario. The characters are urbane Creoles, and the plot is what might be labelled today a 'suspense-thriller', about the narrator's brother-in-law, who is obsessed with his (the narrator's) wife. The story culminates at a soirée where the antagonist mesmerises the narrator's wife and attempts to murder her. The urbanity of the characters is established through leaden allusions to Bronte's Heathcliff, the music at the party which (we are told) is from Ravel, Stravinsky and Chopin, and the story climaxes to the Rachmaninoff Prelude. The antagonist's mysticism is not 'obeah' but mesmerism – à la the Golden Dawn Magical movement abroad in Europe at the time.[34]

THE *BEACON* IMAGINARY

A few things seem apparent from the foregoing. The *Beacon*'s discourse was a vehicle for a conversation between the colonial expatriates and the Trinidadian Creoles, which had persisted from the nineteenth century. Where the *Beacon* provocateurs diverged from their co-ethnic antecedents is, as Harvey Neptune points out, that they rejected the British Arnoldian ideal of culture and tried to establish wholly local standards, whose principal characteristic was that they 'resisted' Britishness. The *Beacon*'s description of literary clubs (May 1933) makes this evident:

> The 'literary club bug' does a great deal of harm. Nothing is so detrimental to the artistic development of the island [...] All [they do] is to inflate the already too inflated egos of our young men and women who as it is

are much too addicted to the belief that a Higher Certificate of a few appendages to ones name signifies a sine qua non of intellectual achievement.[35]

The positions that would be achieved later by the *Beacon*'s principals – Gomes and James – would embed this sophomoric rebelliousness into the nascent nationalistic cultural ethos and make 'resistance' a reflexive trope in Trinidadian (and West Indian) cultural discourse. Gomes would become the de facto Chief Minister in 1950, and James's protégé, Eric Williams, would succeed him in 1956 as premier, then Prime Minister for twenty years after independence. Gordon Rohlehr's fine essay, 'The Culture of Williams: Context, Performance, Legacy', makes this link explicit, and expatiates on the provenance and promotion of the agenda.[36]

To return to the beginning of this chapter, this programme, which was initiated by the *Beacon*, had severe consequences on the imaginative dimension of Trinidadian and West Indian discourse. Andrew J.M. Bundy, introducing the essays of Wilson Harris, introduces Harris's term the 'illiteracy of the imagination', which he perceptively ascribes to the agency of nationalist politicians, 'educated to the doctoral level in England'. This illiteracy, he writes, manifests as 'an attitude, a Philistinism taken up and worn like an inverse order of merit that has been one of the unanticipated legacies of independence'.[37] This shortcoming is crucial to the discussion of the Trinidadian national Imaginary, and the *Beacon*'s importance in furnishing it, since its material provided no alternatives to colonial morals, taste, opinions, behaviour, or artistic innovation. Indeed, the *Beacon*'s discursive centrality in Trinidadian fiction appears to have stunted the growth of a 'national' literature, since its topoi persist in the fiction that comes directly after it.

An exhaustive survey of contemporary Trinidadian fiction would require more space than this essay allows, but among the most successful Trinidadian writers of the twenty-first century, the *Beacon* themes persist. This is demonstrable through Earl Lovelace's oeuvre. His major novels, *The Dragon Can't Dance* (1979) and *Salt* (1996), institutionalise the 'yard' genre: they are peopled with mainly Afro characters, living in misery, poverty, and contempt for mainstream values under the omnibus label of 'resistance'.[38]

Finally, the paucity of imagination is not restricted to creative writers. The highly contestable ideas of critics cited here (King, Ramchand, Sander) have remained unchallenged for a generation. The consequences of epistemological stasis, or apathy, are displayed, to cite a single example, in the collection *Music, Memory, Resistance: Calypso and the Literary Imagination*, whose contributors attempt to fuse calypso, resistance, and ethnic primacy into a Trinidadian/West Indian national imagination. (The only reason this agenda is not yet in an advanced stage is the impotence of the academe in the Caribbean and the bankruptcy of the idea.) In the opening essay, the head of the Academy of Arts, Letters, Culture and Public Discourse of the University of Trinidad and Tobago (UTT) argues, without irony, that calypso ought to be given the status of social science, and makes explicit Eric Williams's agency in launching this academic-ontological trajectory.[39]

The major consequence of this simplification of a nation's experience and moral constitution is best captured by the American philosopher Martha Nussbaum who writes in her superb essay 'The Death of Pity': 'the intrinsic value of a human being is not innate. It is a developmental achievement and it can be blocked'.[40] This blockage is achieved when citizens are 'implicitly urged not to see complexities', since 'morality and liberal citizenship are achievements that have to be made and remade' ('Pity', p. 294). This continuous reconstruction of society is the work of artists and critics in conjunction with other, capable agents. The present social and cultural landscape of the West Indies shows clearly the folly that ensues after a generation of stifling the imaginative capacity of a region in the name of 'nationalism', or some other senseless slogan.

NOTES

1   Gordon Rohlehr, 'Trophy and Catastrophe', in *The Shape of That Hurt* (Port of Spain: Longman, 1992), pp. 293–94.

2   See Thomas W. Krise, 'Introduction', in *Caribbeana, An Anthology of British Literature of the West Indies, 1657-1777*, ed. by Thomas Krise (Chicago: The University of Chicago Press, 1999), pp. 1–15.

3   In Vol 1, No 7, of *The Beacon* (October 1931) Sydney Harland, a lecturer at the Imperial College of Tropical Agriculture, responded to an attack on him by C.L.R. James for his statement that 'the negro race is intellectually inferior to the white' (p. 18).

4   This is further developed and examined in Dennis Benn's *The Caribbean, an Intellectual History* (Kingston: Ian Randle Publishers, 2004).

5   Homi Bhabha 'Introduction', in *Nation and Narration*, ed. by Homi Bhabha (London: Routledge, 1994), pp. 1–7.

6   Timothy Brennan, 'The National Longing for Form', in *Nation and Narration*, ed. by Homi Bhabha (London: Routledge, 1994), pp. 44–71.

7   Simon During, 'Literature: Nationalism's other? The Case for Revision', in *Nation and Narration*, ed. by Homi Bhabha (London: Routledge, 1994), pp. 138–54.

8   Peggy Miller, Heidi Fung, Michelle Koven, 'Narrative Reverberations: How Participation in Narrative Practices co-Creates Persons and Cultures', in *Handbook of Cultural Psychology*, ed. by Shinobu Kitayama and Dov Cohen (London and New York: The Guildford Press, 2010), pp. 595–614.

9   The term is used in Lise Winer, 'Introduction', in E.L. Joseph, *Warner Arundell: Adventures of a Creole* (Kingston: University of the West Indies Press, 2001), ed. by Lise Winer et al, pp. xi–lii (p. xvi).

10 See Homi Bhabha, 'Of Mimicry and Man', in *The Location of Culture* (London: Routledge, 2004), pp. 121–31.

11 Carl Campbell, *Colony & Nation: A Short History of Education in Trinidad & Tobago* (Kingston: Ian Randle, 1992), p. 28.

12 See Gordon Rohlehr's *Calypso and Society in pre-Independence Trinidad* (Port of Spain: Gordon Rohlehr, 1990), pp. 43–86, Frank Korom's *Hosay Trinidad* (Philadelphia: University of Pennsylvania Press, 2003), and Sherry Ann Singh's 'The Ramayana Tradition and Socio-Religious Change in Trinidad, 1917–1990' (UWI, St Augustine: Unpublished PhD Thesis, 2005).

13 Ella Shohat and Robert Stam, 'The Imperial Imaginary', in *The Anthropology of Media: A Reader*, ed. by Kelly Askew and Richard R. Wilk (Oxford: Blackwell, 2002), pp. 114–48.

14 The *Trinidad Mirror* advertised, on 2 February 1911, the opening of the 'London Electric Theatre' in Port of Spain.

15 *Port of Spain Gazette*, 10 September 1912, 5; and 30 August 1912, 3.

16 This is according to an advertisement in the *Guardian*, 17 August 1919, 12.

17 This was republished in 2003 as *Adolphus: A Tale, & The Slave Son*, ed. by Lise Winer (Kingston: University of the West Indies Press, 2003).

18 See introduction to E.L. Joseph, *Warner Arundell—Adventures of a Creole* (Kingston: University of the West Indies Press, 2001 [1838]), by Lise Winer, Rhonda Cobham, Bridget Brereton, and Mary Rimmer, pp. xi–lii.

19 This is described in some detail by Lise Winer, Bridget Brereton, Rhonda Cobham, and Mary Rimmer in the introduction to Stephen Cobham, *Rupert Gray: A Tale in Black and White*, ed. by Lise Winer (Kingston: University of the West Indies Press, 2006), pp. ix–lv.

20 Reinhard Sander makes this point in 'The Thirties and Forties' in *West Indian Literature*, ed. by Bruce King, 2nd edn (London: Macmillan, 1995), pp. 38–51.

21 Example, the *Chronicle*, 4 February 1868, and sporadically for the remainder of the nineteenth century, as in the *Port of Spain Gazette*, 19 September 1885 and 16 July 1895.

22 C.L.R. James, 'Triumph', in *The Oxford Book of Caribbean Short Stories*, ed. by Stewart Brown and John Wickham (Oxford: Oxford University Press, 1999), pp. 35–49 (p. 35).

23 Kenneth Ramchand, *The West Indian Novel and Its Background*, 2nd edn (London: MacMillan, 1983) 2nd edn. 63

24 Bruce King, 'Introduction', in *West Indian Literature*, ed. by King, pp. 1–12 (p. 2).

25 Interview from *World Literature Written in English*, quoted in Rhonda Cobham, 'Introduction', in Alfred Mendes, *Black Fauns* (London: New Beacon, 1984), pp. i–xvi (p. xvi).

26 Harvey Neptune, *Caliban and the Yankees: Trinidad and the United States Occupation* (Chapel Hill: University of North Carolina Press, 2007), p. 27.

27 Percival Maynard, 'Divorce and Mr Jerningham', *The Beacon* (Jan–Feb 1932), 4–8 (p. 5).

28 Alastair Scott, 'Brotherly Love', *The Beacon* (August 1932), 10–12 (p. 10).

29 Albert Gomes, 'Day-Dreams', *The Beacon* (December 1932), 8–10 (p. 8).

30 Alfred Mendes, 'Snapshots', *The Beacon* (December 1932), pp. 11–17 (p. 17).

31 Alfred Mendes, 'Colour', *The Beacon* (June 1933), 14–18 (p. 17).

32 Percival Maynard, 'His Right of Possession', *The Beacon* (April 1932), 6–8 (p. 8).

33 *The Beacon* (April 1932), p. 2.

34 The Jan–Feb 1932 issue of the *Beacon* featured a profile of H.P. Blavatsky, one of the main figures in this movement, so it is certain the group was aware of European occultism.

35 'The Literary Club Nuisance', *The Beacon* (May 1933), pp. 1–2 (p. 2).

36 Gordon Rohlehr, 'The Culture of Williams: Context, Performance, Legacy', in *A Scuffling of Islands: Essays on Calypso* (Port of Spain: Lexicon, 2004), pp. 102–63.
37 Andrew J.M. Bundy, 'Introduction', in *The Selected Essays of Wilson Harris: The Unfinished Genesis of the Imagination*, ed. by Andrew Bundy (London: Routledge, 1999), pp. 1–33 (p. 30).
38 See, for an example of the critical adjunct to Lovelace's agenda, Gerard Aching's *Masking and Power* (Minneapolis: University of Minnesota Press, 2002), pp. 51–72.
39 See Hollis Liverpool, 'Eric Williams's Vision for the Development of Carnival' in *Music, Memory, Resistance: Calypso and the Caribbean Literary Imagination*, ed. by Sandra Pouchet Paquet et al (Kingston: Ian Randle, 2007), pp. 3–15.
40 Martha Nussbaum, 'The Death of Pity', in *On 1984: Orwell and our Future*, ed. by Nussbaum et al (Princeton: University of Princeton Press, 2005), pp. 279–99 (p. 294).

POLITICAL AND MARKET FORCES IN THE CUBAN SHORT STORY

PATRICIA CATOIRA

The breakup of the Soviet Union in 1991 plunged Cuba into a deep economic crisis. The island lost much-needed resources and subsidies it had obtained from the European bloc. Cubans entered the 'Special Period in Times of Peace' in which Fidel Castro asked his compatriots to prepare for sacrifices to confront the massive shortages of food, fuel, electricity, and consumer goods. The government began implementing a series of capitalist reforms to jumpstart the economy and obtain hard currency. Foreign investment was allowed for the first time in the form of mixed-capital ventures with the government. All of these initial efforts were directed towards the revitalisation of tourist infrastructure, which the revolutionary government had confined to the enjoyment of Cubans since 1959. Hotels and resorts, some dating from the 1920s, required massive renovations if they were to attract foreigners and compete with those of other Caribbean islands. The arrival of tourists and capitalist measures signalled the breakdown of Revolutionary Cuba's ideological pillars and its subjection to globalising forces.

The crisis transformed the dynamics of literary production as well. Paper – a Soviet import – became scarce and publishing houses almost ceased production during the first half of the 1990s. The short story proliferated during the Special Period for its minimal use of paper, its tighter engagement with the immediate reality, and its popularity in local *talleres* (literary workshops) and among young writers across the island. Shortages, prostitution, exile, and the increasing demoralisation of the population, while taboo in news media and public forums, became some of the common themes in the short fiction of the 1990s. As the state increasingly pushed for self-financing measures in the publishing sector, its control over the ideological content diminished and short story collections began to flourish outside the traditional literary circles of Havana. Cuba's incipient capitalisation of its resources also resulted in its openness to foreign markets. Collaborations with foreign editors and presses, and publishing abroad altogether, became the norm for the Cuban short story by the end of the 1990s and established a new set of publishing dynamics. After providing an overview of the emergence of the genre in Cuba and the influence of revolutionary politics on the creative process of short story writers, this essay will focus on the drastic changes the short story has undergone since the start of the Special Period.

The short story has a long tradition in Cuba as in the rest of Latin America. The genre benefited from its economy of space. Since the nineteenth century, national popular magazines and literary journals always reserved a section for a short piece of fiction.[1] In addition, the popularity of magazines among the reading public, mostly from the middle class, cultivated a liking for the short story. The first modest examples of the genre in Cuba appeared under the influence of the poetry-oriented Romanticism. José María Heredia (*Cuentos orientales*, 1829), Gertrudis Gómez de Avellaneda ('El aura blanca', 1860), and Ramón de Palma ('Matanzas y el Yumurí', 1837) targeted themes like freedom from tyranny, the noble savage, and impossible love which blended well with national discourses about independence and anxieties about miscegenation. Cuban writers adopted exotic settings inspired by their European and North American contemporaries (i.e. Lord Byron, James Fenimore Cooper, and François-René Chateaubriand). The short story continued as a marginal activity during fin-de-siècle modernism. The modernists showed a preference for aesthetics over content; even the politically active José Martí, considered Cuba's national patriot, left out social commentaries in his *La edad de oro* (1889).[2]

With the arrival of the twentieth century and the work of Jesús Castellanos (*De tierra adentro*, 1906) and Alfonso Hernández Catá (*Los frutos ácidos*, 1915; *Piedras preciosas*, 1924) the short story consolidated its place in the island's letters. In the newly established but unstable republic, both of these authors addressed issues regarding Cuban nationality, from life in the countryside to the role of the African and the Chinese in the new nation (Luis, p. 193). A key transitional figure between Castellanos and Hernández Catá and the following generation of the 1940s was Luis Felipe Rodríguez (*Relatos de Marcos Antilla*, 1932). His writings picked up the *criollista* themes of Castellanos by focusing on the life of the *guajiro* (Cuban peasant), but transmitted a political and social commentary that his predecessors lacked. Rodríguez's criticisms targeted, in particular, the dictatorship of Gerardo Machado (1925–1933), against which many intellectuals reacted. The sadistic and brutal behavior of the protagonist in 'Riguiñola' towards his dog is easily interpreted as an allegory of the Machadato.

The protests against the repression and the corruption of the Machadato rallied intellectuals around magazines such as *Revista de Avance* (1927–1930). One of its co-founders, Alejo Carpentier (*La guerra del tiempo*, 1956) became the first great writer of modern Cuba. With Carpentier, Lino Novás Calvo (*Cayo canas*, 1942), Lydia Cabrera (*Cuentos negros*, 1940), and Enrique Labrador Ruiz (*El gallo en el espejo*, 1953), the Cuban short story broke into the forefront of Cuban letters. These writers covered a wide range of themes from the African folklore of Cabrera's pieces to the political struggle and cosmopolitan modernity of Carpentier's work. In his attempt to portray Cuban life as realistically as possible, Carpentier, in particular, acknowledged the anachronism inherent in Latin American life; his writing explored how beliefs and customs labelled as magical and fantastic by Westerners because of their indigenous and African heritage are imbedded in Latin American life. 'Isn't the history of America but a chronicle of the marvellous real?', Carpentier wondered in the prologue of *The Kingdom of This World* (1949), giving a name to his theory.[3]

The last generation before the advent of the Revolution found its key figures in Virgilio Piñera (*Cuentos fríos*, 1956) and Jorge Cardoso (*El cuentero*, 1958). This group, also disillusioned with the political climate that culminated with Fulgencio Batista's coup in 1952, centred around the literary magazine *Orígenes* (1944–1954), which became the main publishing venue for their stories. Influenced by José Lezama Lima's preference for aesthetic experimentation over social message, Piñera, Cardoso, and his contemporaries turned their attention to the absurd and the fantastic. The post-1959 hard-line revolutionaries rejected this literature as escapist, while for the writers it was a way of capturing the irrational complexity of their realities. Despite their stylistic differences, Carpentier and Lezama Lima both recognise the 'fantastic' and 'marvellous' nature of Cuban reality.

The triumph of Fidel Castro and his *barbudos* revolutionised the literary world on the island. The state would now create and fund publishing houses such as *Letras Cubanas* and cultural institutions such as Casa de las Américas, and support writers' careers as long as they fulfilled their revolutionary commitments. The Castro government also promoted literature in general through a successful literacy campaign (1960–1961) and a series of reforms intended to provide free access to books and cultural venues. The Book Institute, founded in 1967 and in charge of publishing all types of books except textbooks, steadily increased the release of titles until 1989. In addition, Cuban publishers and literary contests became the outlet of much of the literary production from Latin American writers. Cultural production became tied to ideological expectations. Socialist realism provided the framework under which Cuban artists were to use their creations as vehicles to promote the ideals of the Revolution. Content prevailed over form in order for all Cubans to be able to grasp the message of the work. The heavy involvement of the state in literary production soon brought problems of censorship.

The short story from the beginning of the Revolution until the collapse of the Soviet Union enjoyed the same level of prominence as the novel. The instability in quality and quantity of collections since 1959 has generally coincided with different degrees of government control over cultural production, which can be divided in three periods: 1) revolutionary enthusiasm and commitment, 1959–1970; 2) the 'Five Grey Years' (*el quinquenio gris*), 1971–1975; and 3) regeneration, 1976–1990. The following overview of these three moments sets the context for the changes in the publishing sector and the creative process taking place in the Cuban short story with the beginning of the Special Period.

Two generations of short story writers coincided during the first decade of the Revolution. Those like Calvert Casey (*El regreso*, 1962), Humberto Arenal (*La vuelta en redondo*, 1962), and Antonio Benítez-Rojo (*Tute de reyes*, 1967) had been affiliated with the magazine *Ciclón* (1955–1959) – which reacted to the aestheticism of *Orígenes* – and often published their stories in the magazine *Lunes de Revolución* (1959–1962). The decadence of the bourgeoisie and its refusal to adapt to the revolutionary changes was a common theme of this generation, as seen in Arenal's 'El caballero Charles' and Benítez-Rojo's 'Estatuas sepultadas'. They registered the anti-Batista fight in urban settings, but in sharp contrast with their young contemporaries the atmosphere was sombre, as exemplified by the existential monologue of Casey's protagonist in 'El regreso'. After debating whether or not to return from exile to his homeland to join the revolutionaries, he does, and dies under torture. It was the group of young writers like Jesús Díaz (*Los años duros*, 1966), Norberto Fuentes (*Condenados de Condado*, 1968), and Eduardo Heras León (*La guerra tuvo seis nombres*, 1968; *Los pasos en la hierba*, 1971) whose writing propelled the Cuban short story into a golden era (*el quinquenio de oro*)[4] that for many was unsurpassed until the 1990s.[5] Díaz's *Los años duros*, winner of the Casa de las Américas Prize, inaugurated and represented the best of the so-called Narrative of Violence which focused on the fight against Batista and post-1959 counterrevolutionary forces. Despite the ubiquitous presence of violence, there was always an upbeat tone to their fiction that separated them from Casey's generation. When set before 1959, the focus turned to the fight against Fulgencio Batista. When the action took place after Castro's victory, the stories dealt with the Bay of Pigs invasion (1961), the fight against counterrevolutionary forces in Escambray (1960–1966), and the failure of the bourgeoisie to adapt to the Revolution. Although the narrative was often simple and linguistically plain as in the works of Lisandro Otero, many stories benefitted from the style and techniques of the Latin American boom such as multiperspectivism, *testimonio*, fragmentation, and magic realism. The stories in Díaz's *Los años duros*, for instance, favour the exposition of the action through the perspective of different characters, such as the three friends of 'Muy al principio'.

This stylistic complexity soon began to conflict with the didactic impositions of socialist realism, as exemplified in the marginalisation of writers such as Piñera and Lezama Lima. State officials feared that stylistic experimentation would eclipse the content. Works began to be censored not for speaking against the Revolution, as later writers explicitly would do, but for failing to praise it.[6] This period of revolutionary enthusiasm was nevertheless productive. Twelve volumes of short stories and three additional compilations of works of fiction in which the short story form predominated were released. In the same period of time, seventy single-author anthologies were published.[7] The ideological pressures surfacing in the last years of the decade were reflected in the absence of Benítez-Rojo in such anthologies due to his extensive use of magic realism (Mentón, p. 345).

The 1970s saw increasing censorship and persecution of antirevolutionary elements on the island as symbolised by the 'Padilla affair' of 1971.[8] This dark period, popularly referred to as *el periodo gris* or *quinquenio gris* (coined by Ambrosio Fornet in 1987), coincides with Cuba's complete adhesion to the doctrines of the Soviet Union. The rules for the 1970 short story contest 'XVI Aniversario 26 de julio', which was awarded to Manuel Cofiño's *Tiempo de cambio*, captured the spirit of the time: 'It must be noted as well that this contest has taken into account the political content as well as the artistic quality of each' (Alvarez, 'El cuento', p. 28, my translation). Further steps in state control over cultural production were taken the following year during the First National Congress of Education and Culture: 'It is necessary to establish a rigorous system for inviting foreign writers and intellectuals [to literary contests and awards] in order to avoid the presence of individuals whose work and ideology are in opposition to the interests of the Revolution'.[9] In this climate of censorship, some writers (Desnoes and Benítez-Rojo) went into exile, others (Heras León, Padilla, Díaz, N. Fuentes) were silenced and later left too, and a third group (Lezama Lima, Piñera) stayed marginalised for their cult of aesthetics and did not see their work published until the late 1980s or even the 1990s. No memorable short story collections came out of this dark period.

The creation of the Ministry of Culture in 1976 and the Colloquium of Cuban Literature celebrated in 1981 meant to clarify the relationship between state and literary production.[10] The government permitted a little more leeway to artistic expression, but a climate of censorship prevailed: 'It was still necessary to defend in some literary and official circles the short story's past/present disjunctions, independent characters, relevant message, resolution of conflict, incarnation of social ideas, and reflection of reality'.[11] Redonet stretches the grey years until 1982 and refers to the period as 'the bad time' [*la mala hora*] (Redonet, p. 11). Numerous artists left the island in the notorious Mariel boatlift in 1980 and throughout the decade that followed. Those who stayed began pushing the limits of their creative freedom within the régime, and their works began showing new themes and critiques of the government by focusing on the daily life of Cubans and unveiling their failed dreams and frustrations with the Revolution. The publication of these works in the 1980s coincided with the

Period of Rectification (1986–1990) which meant to critically assess the failures and successes of the Revolution. Of the literary climate in the 1980s, writer Senel Paz reflects:

> The current tension we live in is propitious for people who support hard measures, but I consider myself a defender and critic of the Revolution. One of the problems has been the idea that criticism and assessment are only patrimony of dissidents and counterrevolutionaries. Any controversial voice has been judged as trying to move away from the country. It is absurd and that is exactly what our new generation of Cuban writers is tired of. To reflect about the country is an eminently revolutionary act, the most necessary and revolutionary in today's Cuba.[12]

The short stories of the regenerative years generally focused on young characters who had grown up with the Revolution and were trying to find their place in the world; reason for critics to refer to this literature as one of discovery, adolescence, loss of innocence, bedazzlement, and ethical dilemma (García, p. 123). The leading exponents were Rafael Soler (*Noche de fósforos*, 1976), Miguel Mejides (*Tiempo de hombres*, 1977), the aforementioned Senel Paz (*El niño aquel*, 1980), Arturo Arango (*Salir al mundo*, 1982), Francisco López Sacha (*Descubrimiento del azul*, 1987), Mirta Yáñez (*Noche de sábado*, 1989), and Leonardo Padura (*Según pasan los años*, 1989). They injected new energy into the short story by addressing a reality beyond political ideologies, focusing, for instance, on death, fear, and morality (Alvarez, 'El cuento', p. 30). The style of this generation absorbs some of the techniques of the post-boom with its love of fragmentation, orality, popular culture, mix of genres, and depoliticisation.

Two representative stories of this decade deal with the traditionally taboo topic of homosexuality: Roberto Urías's '¿Por qué llora Leslie Caron?' (1988) and Senel Paz's 'El lobo, el bosque y el hombre nuevo' (1990).[13] In the first case, a young boy is publicly humiliated after 'coming out' to a friend. In Paz's story, a university student and member of the communist party sheds his homophobia through friendship with a controversial gay artist. Although the candid treatment of the controversial issue was welcomed as a breath of fresh air, the fact that these government-sanctioned criticisms found expression in gender issues suggests that the state did not feel threatened by such apparently marginal issues. Linda S. Howe points out, as other critics have, the double-edged sword of Paz's short story and its film version, Tomás Gutiérrez Alea's *Strawberry and Chocolate* (1993). They offer a critique of the government, but, by setting the action in the 1970s, they suggest that discrimination is a thing of the past.[14]

Writers were prolific in the 1980s. Alongside short story collections, many short stories appeared in literary journals such as *El caimán barbudo*, *Unión*, *Casa de las Américas*, *La Nueva Gaceta*, and *Revolución y Cultura*.

The coming of the Special Period unexpectedly provided the conditions for a cultural revolution within the Revolution. Beginning in 1990, book releases in Cuba decreased at a precipitous rate, reaching their lowest point in 1993. In that year, only 568 titles were published in total and print runs were also significantly reduced to barely two thousand copies. The Book Institute produced only 143 titles, a 75 percent decrease. Inflation and scarcity of crucial resources such as paper prompted a hike in the price of books. Even periodicals and journals were unable to keep up with their release schedule, and issues appeared in print as conditions allowed. As a result of this situation, government officials allowed for a series of reforms designed to revitalise book production in Cuba: they searched for sources of self-financing; they looked at the market in terms of national money and foreign currency; they sought to better respond to national talent and produce books appealing to foreigners; they looked at more efficient production processes; and they decided to reduce the number of titles from world literature.[15]

The regional *Centros Provinciales del Libro* also became more active in publishing books and spreading printing costs across the island. For a while, presses tried printing in *plaquettes*, a few pieces of cheap paper or semi-cardboard, often stapled together, but the process did not work very well due to the poor quality of printing and distribution. One successful measure consisted of forming joint editorial and printing ventures with foreign institutions, as in the case of the collaboration of Argentinian writers and editors in the 1994 publication of one hundred volumes of the Pinos Nuevos series. Unión Press also co-edited works with Spain, Puerto Rico, Colombia, Mexico and other countries, collaborations which made possible the release of nineteen books in 2002.[16] Similarly, a national cultural fund (Fondo para el Desarrollo de la Cultura) was created with foreign currency and was able to carry the costs of printing short text collections like La Rueda Dentada.[17] The prestigious institution Casa de las Américas, founded in 1959 to promote cultural exchanges and gatherings among Latin American artists, has published since 1994 the works from the series Premio Casa de las Américas, its famous literary contest, in partnership with the Ministry of Culture of Colombia.

In 1994, the Book Institute initiated its revitalisation by prioritising its goals. It gave preference to the release of national titles, especially under the auspices of Letras Cubanas, a press which absorbed 29.1 percent of the 1,047 titles published between 1994 and 1998. Most of the works published in this press were narrative fiction. Especially remarkable was the series Pinos Nuevos, a collaboration with Argentina, which in this period of 1994–1998 launched around 130 new writers, most of them young; an impressive fact hardly comparable to other first-world countries, where new authors struggle to get published (Más Zabala).

During this period of recovery and reform that started in 1994, print runs were sharply reduced to two thousand per title. To counterbalance a lower supply, many copies were sent to local libraries and cultural institutions to make books available to all. The Book Institute also made efforts to regularise the publication of magazines and journals. Some periodicals like *Temas*, *Marx Ahora*, and *La Revista del Libro Cubano* were able to go back to their normal rotation, but other magazines are still trying to stabilise their regular publishing. Significantly, from 1995 to 1999 twelve new magazines were created in an effort to maintain the interest of the reading public. Book prices have remained high and books are no longer a regular acquisition for Cubans. Other necessities have obviously taken priority.

Publishing under the shortages and difficulties since the 1990s has been challenging for writers. The state's decision to focus on the economy and its message to writers and publishing venues about finding self-financing strategies broke down the thirty-year-old relationship between the state and the work of its writers. In a way, the crisis created a tabula rasa that helped transform Cuba's literary scene. The ones hurt the most were well-established writers, most of whom were concentrated in Havana and preferred writing novels. To this group fits Howe's characterisation (and generalisation) of the effects of the crisis on Cuban writers and artists: 'disoriented' and 'in limbo' (Howe, p. 18). Because of their close ties to Havana's cultural institutions and government officials, ideological matters have always permeated their creative process. The authors who went into exile (e.g. Jesús Díaz and Zoé Valdés) throughout the decade were able to publish abroad their new as well as previously censored works. Among the novelists who stayed on the island, those who captured the crisis either directly (Pedro Juan Gutiérrez's 'dirty' novels) or indirectly (Padura's crime novels) benefited from the interest of foreign publishing houses, especially from Spain and Mexico. These publishing arrangements have provided much needed royalties and recognition for Cuban novelists while releasing them from the tight grip of government control.

The fate of the short story has been slightly different. The economic pressures imposed by the Special Period created a divide between the novel and the short story for the first time since the triumph of the Revolution. The genre proliferated especially among the *novísimos* (the newest), young Cuban writers who began writing in the 1980s but surfaced strongly in the 1990s – mainly through the Pinos Nuevos series – and solidified their presence as years passed. Since most of them had other professions they did not depend on writing for a living. Their peripherality together with the emphasis on self-financing probably contributed to their creative freedom, especially when compared with their contemporary novelists. Salvador Redonet's now classic anthology, *Los últimos serán los primeros* (1993), gathered the compositions of some of the first names of this generation, among them Andrés Jorge, Jorge Luis Arzola, and Raúl Aguiar. The variety of groups within this generation – whether established by the writers themselves or by the critics – attests to the wealth and richness of the Cuban literature that has been produced since the 1990s. They infused rage, irony, and other emotions into a laconic language that often resulted in the popular trend of micro short stories. They addressed issues of exile, violence, prostitution (*jineterismo*), marginality, and economic scarcity through a skeptical and existential lens. Their stories lost the discursive innocence – the subtle voice of a youngster coming of age – of the 1980s and became contestatory (García, p. 126). The *novísimos* also included an unprecedented large number of female voices which has continued into the twenty-first century. The *novísimas* and *postnovísimas* discuss similar issues to their male counterparts:

> As I see it, the most notable common denominator of women's writing in Cuba today is our special brand of realism: a realism that the women among the Cuban short story writers have fashioned, one which enlarges the frontiers of everyday life through the incorporation of the absurd and the supernatural. Behind us is the arena of politics, society and ideas.[18]

All the Cuban trends in the 1990s coincide with movements around Latin America such as *la nueva onda* in Chile, *la onda* in Mexico, the McOndo generation, and the Mexican crack generation.[19] With the arrival of the millennium, the short story continues to evolve. Jorge, who now lives in Mexico, and Arzola acknowledge the end of the *novísimo* wave and both no longer want to write about the same themes of *jineteras*, gays, and underground culture. Arzola, for instance, is now exploring *costumbrista* elements and the theme of the modern Cuban peasant in his works. The *postnovísimo* tendency strives to be even more creatively independent, polyphonic, and geographically bound by city or even neighbourhood, as in the case of los frikis, rockeros, and the group Diáspora, all based in Havana. As some of their names reflect, these groups of writers draw from and overlap with currents in the Cuban music venues of rap, rock, punk, and trova. The two worlds feed from each other in style and content.[20]

State officials have criticised the talk about scarcity, desperation, prostitution, and other social problems in Cuba since the 1990s as demoralising and counterproductive (Howe, p. 44). Many of the well-established novelists discussed above echoed the concerns of their government. Aída Bahr praises the promotion of new writers from the 1990s but believes that their movement is totalising and overly pessimistic, although she acknowledges that such is the world they confront in Cuba and elsewhere. She also sees the widespread presence of the *novísimos* in Cuban presses and national awards as problematic. She argues that some authors are copying the *novísimos'* style just to get published because it is the literary flavour of the week (García Hernández). Award-winning writer Miguel Barnet echoes the criticism: 'I do not see the value in the new Cuban narrative [...] they have not inaugurated anything new [...] lies are not information nor innovation'.[21] Padura also views the sudden popularity of the *novísimos* and *ultranovísimos* with caution. He disagrees with granting so much attention and laurels to writers who have only published a book or two:

> What this promotion will give, will give, but only as a result of time and work, and only if one stop thinking that they are the ones in charge of renovating Cuban literature, of making it transcendental and deep, of placing it in the field of postmodernity: because the problem, again, is to win over that simple little page on which we write, and that very often refuses to express what we want.[22]

Padura would prefer to wait and see if these promising writers fulfil in time public and critical expectations. The criticism from these established authors underlines the divide between the old guard of writers and the irreverent youth. The Cuban novelists seem to worry about the popularity of the younger generations generated by sales in foreign markets rather than through consensus among the literary elites of Havana.

The emphasis on self-financing since the 1990s has resulted in the decentralisation of resources and literary production away from Havana. The literary workshops created in the 1960s by the Revolution across the island were crucial in forming the *novísimos* and more recent generations of writers. Along with the Centros Provinciales del Libro, the vitality of the workshops helped release an unprecedented wealth of regional multi-authored collections: some examples include, from Sancti Spiritus, *Abrir ciertas ventanas: Antología del cuento espirituano* (Ediciones Luminaria, 2006); from Matanzas, *La hora: Antología del cuento en Matanzas* (Ediciones Aldabón, 2005); from Cienfuegos, *Como el aire en las orejas: Narradores en Cienfuegos* (Reina del Mar editores, 2004); from Santiago, *Para subir al cielo: Selección de narradores santiagueros* (Ediciones Santiago, 2006); and from Ciego de Ávila, *Nuevamente lunes: Panorama del cuento en Ciego de Ávila* (Ediciones Ávila, 2004). Local, regional and national literary contests have also helped young writers acquire much needed exposure and publication venues. Contests are usually linked to literary journals and cultural institutions such as Casa de las Américas or the UNEAC (National Association of Cuban Writers and Artists). Besides single-author collections, presses have been active in publishing volumes of participating, finalist, or winning short stories, as in the case of *Maneras de narrar: Cuentos del Premio La Gaceta de Cuba (1993–2005)* (Unión, 2005) and *Historia soñada y otros minicuentos: Premios, menciones, y finalistas, II Concurso Nacional de Minicuentos 'El Dinosaurio' 2003* (Ediciones Luminaria, 2005).

Traditional presses such as Havana-based Letras Cubanas and Unión have traditionally focused on the publishing of short story anthologies under a national prism encapsulated in the term Cuban. But during the

1990s their few releases left behind the well-established writers and mostly gathered the work of the *novísimos*. Besides Redonet's 1993 anthology mentioned above, other examples include *Fábula de ángeles* (Letras Cubanas, 1994) and *Poco antes del 2000: Jóvenes cuentistas cubanos en las puertas del nuevo siglo* (Letras Cubanas, 1997). Although women were included in these anthologies of *novísimos*, the 1990s saw the beginning of a series of volumes focused exclusively on the work of (*novísimo*) women. Mirta Yáñez's *Estatuas de sal* (Unión, 1996) sought to offer an overview of the work of Cuban women short story writers while Amir Valle's *El ojo de la noche: Nuevas cuentistas cubanas* (Letras Cubanas, 1999) focused exclusively on *novísimas*. All the dynamics taking place during the 1990s exploded in the new millennium. Thanks to the help of regional presses, short story collections from young authors (*Escritos con guitarra: Cuentos cubanos al rock*, 2005), women writers (*Cuentos infieles*, 2006), literary contests (*Trozos de la verdad: Antología de cuentos ganadores y finalistas del concurso anual de la revista de arte y literatura La Gaveta*, 2006), and Cuban authors in general (*Palabra de sombra difícil: Cuentos contemporáneos*, 2002) have multiplied across the island.

As the government grip over the means of literary production loosens, censorship practices have adopted more subtle and furtive means. Critic Armando Añel cites, for instance, that Valle's *Manuscritos del muerto* had been a finalist in the 1994 Casa de las Américas Prize in the short story category and was scheduled to be released in 1998 by Letras Cubanas. The volume was pulled out of print and Valle was not even notified. Soon after, one of the short stories from the same work, 'Mambrú no fue a la guerra', was excluded from the anthology *Cien Años del Cuento Cubano* despite the protests of its compiler, Alberto Garrandés, who eventually pressured Letras Cubanas to have the story published in his edited volume *Aire de Luz: Cuentos cubanos del siglo XX* (1999). The short story deals with the sexual and mental trauma of a veteran mutilated during one of Cuba's military involvements in Africa. Valle's story thus demystifies the revolutionary hero and reacts against the triumphalism of the Narrative of Violence. There are fewer cases of blatant censorship, as when well-known author Barnet declared that Valle's *Sade nuestro que estás en los cielos o la prostitución en Cuba*, first prize of Casa de las Américas testimonio category, would not be published as long as Barnet was a member of the national assembly.[23] Some have also suggested the scarcity of paper as a convenient excuse to not publish certain authors (García, p. 125).

Despite persistent problems with freedom of expression, notably during the crackdown on dissidents in 2003, there is nonetheless a sense of ideological renovation since the 1990s. Compilations dealing with previously questionable topics and genres such as sexuality and science fiction have surfaced (*El cuerpo inmortal revisitado: Cuentos eróticos cubanos*, 2004; and

Secretos del futuro: Cuentos de fantasía y ciencia ficción, 2005). These were previously considered as escapist. There have been tributes and awards presented to recent marginalised writers (i.e. Antón Arrufat) or those who were in the past (e.g. José Lezama Lima), as well as an effort to publish the works of writers in exile. In 1996 Yáñez included Lydia Cabrera in her famous anthology *Estatuas de sal* and defended the need to include writers in exile within the national corpus as the 2004 *Mi sagrada familia: Selección narrativa* collection from Oriente Press would do later with women writers. But the new efforts have also been ideologically tainted or perceived as such. Garrandés tried to include famous exile writers Guillermo Cabrera Infante and Norberto Fuentes in his anthology *Aire de Luz*, but in this case it was the writers who refused. In 2002 Letras Cubanas published a collection of short stories written by Cubans in exile, *Isla tan dulce y otras historias: Cuentos cubanos de la diaspora*. Carlos Espinosa, a Miami-based Cuban, made the selection and López Sacha, who is the president of the Writers Association of UNEAC, wrote the preface. Exile critic Matías Montes Huidobro praised the inclusiveness of the anthology but heavily criticised the ideological undertones of López Sacha's piece.[24] Despite these lingering resentments, what is important is that the inclusiveness of discourses from abroad along with an increasing freedom of expression has become a welcome trend since the 1990s.

If the work of exile writers is beginning to circulate more on the island as years pass, the same is true for Cuban writers in foreign markets. Since the crisis, Cuban authors have been increasingly proactive about submitting their work to international literary contests, which in return usually brings free promotion abroad and possible publication with a foreign press. The prestigious Juan Rulfo prize for short stories has been awarded, for instance, to more writers from Cuba than from any other country since 1990. Winning prizes abroad brings benefits to both the author and the government. On the one hand, the author gains an international audience and more potential remuneration. On the other hand, the government can boast about the high quality of the literature produced on the island despite the crisis. Authors can in this way enjoy access to foreign audiences and methods of self-financing without threatening the government.

The recent take-off of Cuban anthologies in international markets points to the growing popularity of the genre abroad as well. There is a genuine interest in the short stories produced on the island and by writers in the diaspora. Since the short story is not a hot commodity on the market, the genre has escaped the worst aspects of commercialisation associated with all things Cuban. As Ariana Hernandez-Reguant explains, 'during the 1990s, all sorts of entrepreneurs – music producers, literary editors, art dealers, journalists and academics – flocked to Cuba to be the first to publicise its cultural treasures' as symbolised by the film *Buena Vista Social*

Club (1999) and its discourse of authenticity.[25] The goal for these entrepreneurs was and still is to sell revolutionary Cuba before its dawn. Iván Rubio Cuevas and Esther Whitfield have argued that *novísimos* changed their themes of marginality from drugs and the underground world to the economic difficulties of the Special Period in order to cater to foreigners' desire to see a waning revolutionary Cuba.[26] I would argue instead that *novísimos* had to address scarcity and decay in order to explore the changing times in their country. That exploration coincided with the curiosity of foreign readers. But the Cuban short story since the 1990s goes beyond the portrayal of the hardships created by the economic crisis. There is science fiction, fantasy, eroticism, regionalism, and pop culture among other things. The heterogeneous nature of the Cuban short story since the last years of the twentieth century signals the creative independence of its writers. The novel is the genre that has become hijacked by the global forces of the market and where the Cuba of sex, tourists, hardships and revolutionary decay is being recreated.

Spanish and Latin American presses, for the most part, have been the main engine driving the Cuban publishing industry since the breakup of the Soviet Union. The increasing interest of US academic presses in Cuban literature and the short story, in particular, undoubtedly signals their incursion into the largest western capitalist market. All the publications abroad reflect the two main trends at work on the island: attention to young writers and women's writing. While a handful of volumes only include authors on the island, most anthologies published abroad include a mix of writers living on the island and in the diaspora. Equally, these publications from foreign presses have been edited by Cubans on the island, Cubans in the diaspora, by foreign scholars, or by a mix of the three.[27] All the editors see these collections in foreign presses as an opportunity to spread the vitality and high quality of the Cuban short story produced since the 1990s. For writers on the island, publishing abroad with foreign presses has brought the added benefit of receiving royalties in foreign currency, which means more economic security. Padura welcomes the openness of Cuban writers to foreign markets and a market-based industry. He contends that the market and its capitalist forces are a good way to fight Cuba's provincialism, lack of promotion, and lack of quality:

> Entering in that free system has shown that its laws are not as devouring as they made us think: in the system there is a diversity of spaces, for light literature and for a more artistic one, for the experimental and for the traditional, for the literature in favor and for the literature against, but above all, there is space for good literature. (Valle, *my translation*)

Padura's words and reference to his government's traditionally anti-market stand shows the level of renovation and increasing dialogue inside Cuba.

Publishing abroad also has its disadvantages. Texts in its original Spanish language tend to disappear or become harder to acquire when released
in translation. Anthologies published abroad are either out of circulation or
unaffordable on Cuban soil and lose what García calls their 'natural and
complicit reader: the one from here and now' (García, p. 127). In terms of
quality, the dangers of depending on the global forces of the international
market apply more to the novel. Being subjected to temporary trends and
consumers' taste endangers the quality and creativity of the writer. The
sexualisation and tropicalisation present in the Cuban narrative since the
1990s – as appealing to foreign readers as the current sexual tourism to
tourists in Cuba – is happening in the novels of writers like Pedro Juan
Gutiérrez, Zoé Valdés, and Daniel Chavarría. The short stories of the
novísimos and their successors have been able to remain independent,
contestatory, thematically eclectic, and stylistically innovating. So far,
globalisation has proven to have a more positive impact on the Cuban short
story despite the market's traditional preference for the novel. The decen-
tralising and self-financing publishing strategies on the island, the loosen-
ing of state control over cultural production, and the increasing interest of
foreign presses in spreading the prolific and refreshing work of Cuban
short story writers from the island and abroad, regardless of sales, indicate
the genre's growing vitality and popularity.

NOTES

1 Jorge Luis Arzola, 'La moda de la literatura cubana en el exterior es un gran mito',
   Interview with Aymara Aymerich, *La Jiribilla: Revista Digital de la Cultura Cubana*,
   10 (2001), p. 191 <www.lajiribilla.cu> [accessed 15 February 2005] (http://
   www.lajiribilla.cu/2001/n10_julio/264_10.html).
2 Leonardo Fernández Marcané, 'Panorama del cuento en las Antillas', *Baquiana*, 5
   (2003), 254–62 (pp. 254–55).
3 See Patricia Murray's essay in this volume for a discussion of Carpentier's 'marvellous
   real' in relation to the work of Guyanese short story writer Pauline Melville.
4 José B. Alvarez IV, 'El cuento cubano de 1959 a 1990: Un movimiento pendular',
   Southeastern Latin Americanist, 43:3 (2000), 21–36 (p. 25).
5 Luis Manuel García, 'Crónica de la inocencia perdida: La cuentística cubana
   contemporánea', *Encuentro*, 140–141 (1995), 121–27, p. 122.
6 Heras León received strong criticism for *Los pasos en la hierba* which demystifies
   the figure of the revolutionary. Heras was fired from the editorial board of *El
   caimán barbudo* and was sent to work for three years at a factory (Alvarez, 'El cuento',
   pp. 27–28).
7 Seymour Mentón, 'El cuento de la revolución cubana: Una visión antológica y
   algo más', in *El cuento hispanoamericano ante la crítica*, ed. by Enrique Pupo-Walker
   (Madrid: Castalia, 1973), pp. 338–55 (p. 338).
8 Heberto Padilla won the UNEAC award for his book of poetry *Fuera de Juego* in
   1968, although with a note of protest from some of the judges labeling him

counterrevolutionary and anti-Soviet. In 1971, Padilla and his wife, Belkis Cuza Malé, were arrested and incarcerated on the grounds of engaging in anti-revolutionary activities. The international controversy and outcry that grew around the incident peaked when Padilla was forced to make a public confession and express his repentance. The event was taped and transmitted all over the world with the intention of rebutting a denouncement of the arrest signed by well-known foreign writers such as Mario Vargas Llosa, Octavio Paz, Juan Rulfo, and Gabriel García Márquez. Padilla was later allowed to leave Cuba and went into exile to the United States in 1980.

9 'Declaración del Primer Congreso Nacional de Educación y Cultura', *Unión*, 1–2 (1971), 6–13 (p. 7).

10 Salvador Redonet, 'Para ser lo más breve posible', in *Los últimos serán los primeros* (Havana: Letras Cubanas, 1993), pp. 5–31 (p. 15).

11 Francisco López Sacha, 'Current Tendencies in the Cuban Short Story', *The South Atlantic Quarterly*, 96:1 (1997), 181–98 (p. 185).

12 Arturo García Hernández, 'Literatura en la Isla, hoy', *La Jornada* (my translation) <www.jornada.unam.mx> [accessed 24 September 2002] (http://www.jornada.unam.mx/ultimas/2002/09/24/literatura-en-la-isla-hoy/).

13 Urías's story won the 13 de Marzo Literary Competition sponsored by the University of Havana and Paz's was awarded the prestigious Juan Rulfo Prize.

14 Linda S. Howe, *Transgression and Conformity: Cuban Writers and Artists After the Revolution* (Madison, Wisconsin: University of Wisconsin, 2004), p. 15.

15 Carlos Más Zabala, 'Las nuevas del libro en Cuba', *La Revista del Libro Cubano*, 3:1 (2000), 49–52.

16 Waldo González López, 'En la Unión está la fuerza', *Bohemia*, May 2002 <www.bohemia.cubaweb.cu> [accessed 1 December 2008].

17 'Literatura cubana finisecular: un balance posible', *Inter Press Service*, 2004 <www.ips.org> [accessed 2 October 2007] (http://ips.org/cuba/enflitcu.htm).

18 Mirta Yáñez, 'Introduction', in *Making a Scene: Cuban Women's Stories* (London: Mango, 2004), pp. 5–13 (p. 12).

19 Patricia Valladares Ruiz, 'Lo especial del período: Políticas editoriales y movimiento generacional en la literatura cubana contemporánea', *Neophilologus*, 89 (2005), 383–402 (p. 390).

20 See López Sacha's 'Current Tendencies in the Cuban Short Story' for a thorough discussion of the different groups.

21 José B. Alvarez IV, '(Re)escritura de la violencia: El individuo frente a la historia en la cuentística novísima cubana', *Chasqui*, 26:2 (1997), 84–93 (p. 85, my translation).

22 Amir Valle, '"No soy un bestseller": Conversación franca y abierta con Leonardo Padura', *Librusa*, August 2000 (my translation) <www.librusa.com> [accessed 2 October 2004] (http://www.librusa.com/entrevista4.htm).

23 Armando Añel, 'Censura y autocensura en la literatura cubana de los noventa: una observación y algunos apuntes', *Revista Hispano Cubana*, 13 (2002), 71–78 (p. 77).

24 Matías Montes Huidobro, 'Transgresiones y transgresores', *Encuentro*, 28–29 (2003), 273–85 (p. 84).

25 Ariana Hernandez-Reguant, 'Writing the Special Period: An Introduction', in *Cuba in the Special Period: Culture and Ideology in the 1990s* (New York: Palgrave Macmillan, 2009), pp. 1–18 (p. 13).

26 Iván Rubio Cuevas, 'Lo marginal en los narradores novísimos narradores cubanos: estrategia subversión y moda', in *Todas las islas la isla*, ed. by Janette Reinstädler and Omar Ette (Madrid and Frankfurt: Iberoamericana & Vervuert, 2000), pp. 79–90 (p. 81); Esther Whitfield, *Cuban Currency: The Dollar and 'Special Period' Fiction* (Minneapolis: University of Minneapolis Press, 2008), p. 73.

27 Here are some examples by country or region. Spain: *La isla contada: El cuento contemporáneo en Cuba* (1996), ed. by Francisco López Sacha; *Para el siglo que viene: (post)novísmos narradores cubanos* (1997), ed. by Salvador Redonet; *Nuevos narradores cubanos* (2002), ed. by Michi Strausfeld; *La memoria hechizada: Escritoras cubanas* (2003), ed. by Madeline Cámara; *Voces cubanas: Jóvenes cuentistas de la isla* (2005), ed. by Eduardo del Llano; and *Voces y pálpitos: Nueva narrativa cubana* (2006), ed. by Eduardo Heras León. Latin America: *El ánfora del diablo: novísimos cuentistas cubanos* (Mexico, 1996), ed. by Salvador Redonet; *Cuentistas cubanas de hoy* (Mexico, 2002), ed. by Marilyn Bobes; *Cuento cubano del siglo XX* (Mexico, 2002), ed. by Jorge Fornet and Carlos Espinosa; *Caminos de Eva: Voces desde la isla: Cuentistas cubanas de hoy* (Puerto Rico, 2002), ed. by Amir Valle; *Cuentos cubanos contemporáneos: La línea que cruza el agua* (Venezuela, 2005), ed. by Rogelio M. Riverón; and *Nueva narrativa cubana* (Chile, 2003), ed. by Jacqueline Shor. USA: *Narrativa y libertad: Cuentos cubanos de la diáspora* (1996), ed. by Julio E. Hernández Miyares; *Cubana: Contemporary Fiction By Cuban Women* (1998), ed. by Ruth Behar and Mirta Yáñez; *Open Your Eyes and Soar: Cuban Women Writing Now* (2003), ed. by Mary Berg; *New Cuban Fiction* (2006), ed. by Mary G. Berg; *New Short Fiction From Cuba* (2007), ed. by Esther Whitfield and Jacqueline Loss; and *Havana Noir* (2007), ed. by Achy Obejas.

PART TWO

SOCIOPOLITICAL CONTEXTS

TRACING SIGNIFICANT FOOTSTEPS: ISMITH KHAN AND THE INDIAN-CARIBBEAN SHORT STORY

ABIGAIL WARD

This essay explores legacies of Indian indenture in short stories by the late Trinidadian writer Ismith Khan. Indentured labourers were brought from India to compensate for the substantial loss of African labour in the period following the emancipation of African slaves in the British Caribbean in 1834. As A.N. SookDeo explains,

> Even before 1833, Trinidad's planters had recruited labourers from neighbouring islands, and from China, Europe, Fayal and Madeira, in part to demonstrate their independence from the freedmen. Overtures to foreign labour showed that planters would not negotiate with their former slaves. They resented freedmen who bought land.[1]

The first Indian indentured workers were brought to the region in 1838 and, before the demise of the system of indenture in 1917, more than 400,000 labourers had been brought to the British Caribbean,[2] 140,000 of these to Trinidad alone.[3] Despite the vast numbers involved in this mass relocation, the past of the Indian indentured labourer is a curiously neglected one. If Britain's involvement in the transatlantic slave trade has still not been afforded the due amount of historical representation, the role played by Indian indentured labourers is especially overlooked. Slavery continues to be conceptualised as a history of black and white which, as Marina Carter and Khal Torabully argue, fails to 'fully take into account the ethnic complexity of post abolition societies that developed in the Caribbean and Indian Ocean'.[4] Indian indentured workers played a crucial role in the Caribbean's economic, cultural and social life during this period of indenture, and the legacy of this role is evident in the region's continuing rich ethnic and cultural diversity and outstanding Indian-Caribbean creative output.

There were, as David Northrup has argued, 'striking resemblances' between the systems of slavery and indenture: '[e]specially in the early years of the trade, many indentured labourers were recruited through kidnapping and coercion or were seriously misled by unscrupulous recruiters about their destinations, duties, and compensation'.[5] Indians were transported in overcrowded vessels, and mortality rates on board the ships were high. Once in the Caribbean, indentured labourers often lived in the same huts and did identical work to slaves, although, unlike slaves, this was largely a voluntary migration. Indentured labourers were not considered the property of plantation owners; indenture was (on paper, at least) for a fixed period, and their children were born free (though parents were often coerced to sign them into indenture too).

My focus in this essay is on Ismith Khan's collection of short stories *A Day in the Country* (1994), in which he seeks to uncover the Indian presence amongst Trinidad's 'secrets of massacres and mutilations, slavery and Spaniards, and old English bones'.[6] Some of the stories in *A Day in the Country* were written much earlier than the 1994 publication of this collection suggests. 'A Day in the Country' was first published in 1964, 'The Red Ball' in 1972 and 'Shadows Move in the Britannia Bar', though first published as a complete story in 1980, was incorporated into Khan's novel *The Obeah Man* (1964). Despite the temporal gap between the stories, they form an interesting, and coherent, collection which traces the development of the Indian-Caribbean protagonists from childhood, to adultood, and subsequent migration from Trinidad to the US, a point I shall return to in a moment.

Although Trinidad's history of colonisation is dismissed as an 'insignificant footstep' by a lonely, Indian-Caribbean child in Khan's story 'The Red Ball',[7] throughout this collection he examines the deeply significant role played by Indian indentured labourers and their descendents in this past, particularly focusing on the legacies of Indian indenture in the 1940s' and 1950s' Trinidad of his youth. *A Day in the Country* may be seen as partly autobiographical, which is typical of Khan's work. His novel *The Jumbie Bird* (1961), for example, is loosely based on the life of his grandfather, Kale Khan, who was a militant killed by the colonial authorities in the Hosay massacre of 1884, when authorities opened fire on participants in the annual Hosay parade. Similarly, there are interesting correspondences between Khan's personal trajectory and the collection *A Day in the Country*. Khan was born in 1925 and attended Queen's Royal College in Port of Spain, before working for the *Trinidad Guardian*. He migrated to the US in the 1950s and studied at Michigan State University and the New School of Social Research in New York, before completing a Masters degree in Creative Writing at Johns Hopkins University. He taught at a range of universities in the US until his death in 2002.

Khan's choice of the short story form as a mode of storytelling would seem appropriate given the form's popularity in the Caribbean. As Louis James explains, because of the disparate geography of the Caribbean, where there was not the 'publishing facilities [or] the reading public to support the publication of its lengthy novels', shorter pieces of writing were more easily printed and disseminated in local newspapers and magazines.[8] Trinidad, in particular, saw a vibrant short story culture focused around literary magazines like *The Beacon* and *The Minerva Review*. It was arguably the short story form which won Caribbean literature its earliest critical reception; C.L.R. James's popular story 'La Divina Pastora' (1927) gained international recognition,[9] and Trinidad's most celebrated author, V.S.

Naipaul, began his literary career with the short stories of *Miguel Street* (1959).[10] While the short story flourished in diverse ways in the Caribbean across the twentieth century, there has been a tendency amongst critics to focus on the more humorous Caribbean short stories. One of the earliest writers and critics to do so was Andrew Salkey when, fifty years ago, in the introduction to his collection *West Indian Stories* (1960), he asserted that 'West Indian short-story writers wear the comic mask with more assurance than the tragic'.[11] The collection of stories by Khan explored in this essay, while by no means lacking in humour are, overall, serious stories. Khan takes a different approach to the jocular writing of Sam Selvon or V.S. Naipaul and engages with a more sombre body of Indian-Trinidadian writing that includes, for example, Seepersad Naipaul's *The Adventures of Gurudeva* (1943) and Harold Sonny Ladoo's *No Pain Like This Body* (1972). Both Naipaul's short story collection and Ladoo's novel are set in early twentieth-century Trinidad, and all three writers explore the harshness of existence for Indian-Trinidadians at this time, with their various portrayals of drunken fathers, extreme poverty and domestic abuse. Like Naipaul and Ladoo, therefore, Khan explores a grimmer side to Trinidadian life, depicting a world of poverty, alcoholism and domestic abuse, often seen through the eyes of children who, external to, or outside, the adult world, find the racial and social divides of Trinidad puzzling.

The political dimension characteristic of much Caribbean short story writing manifests itself in Khan's stories in terms of his interrogation of social inequalities, and I argue in this essay that three of these continuing inequalities are evident in *A Day in the Country*. Firstly, Khan is particularly interested in the figure of the Indian-Caribbean as outsider, or newcomer, in relation to the African-Caribbean inhabitants of Trinidad. Importantly, though, in Khan's stories this figure is moved from the margins to the centre of his writing. We also see his concerns with the related alienation of Indian-Caribbean subjects from the British colonial education system and, finally, with ongoing racial tensions, particularly between Indian-Caribbean and African-Caribbean people.

The short story collection, unlike the novel form, enables Khan to explore these differing, though interconnected, areas in succinct snapshots of life in Trinidad in this period. The first five stories – 'The Red Ball', 'Pooran, Pooran', 'The Magic Ring', 'Perpetual Motion' and 'A Day in the Country' – have child protagonists; from childhood, we then reach adulthood with the stories 'Uncle Rajo's Shoes' and 'Shadows Move in the Britannia Bar'. The final two stories, 'Uncle Zoltan' and 'Shaving', feature protagonists that have recently returned from the US to Trinidad, enabling the narrators to adopt a critical distance from which to think about Trinidad. I would suggest that the short story form is also especially appropriate given Khan's interest in the Indian-Caribbean outsider. Ian Reid has argued that short stories 'frequently focus on one or two individuals who are seen as separated from their fellow-men in some way, at odds with social norms, beyond the pale'.[12] It would seem, when considering the Caribbean short story generally, that Indian-Caribbean characters are more likely to be viewed as outsider figures; for example, we might think of the character of Miss Coolie from Olive Senior's story 'Arrival of the Snake-Woman' (1989). As Frank Birbalsingh has argued, although Indians made up 40 percent of Trinidad's population by the 1950s, they 'were marginalized no matter what percentage of the population they represented'.[13]

This marginalisation can partly be explained by the relative lateness of Indian arrival to the Caribbean (coming after slavery and European indentured workers) and by their roles on the plantations, doing work previously undertaken by slaves. Indian-Trinidadians were therefore integrated into the island in a different way to African-Trinidadians; Shalini Puri writes in *The Caribbean Postcolonial* (2004) that, after emancipation, there was 'the *subordinate assimilation* of Afro-Trinidadians and the *subordinate segregation* of Indo-Trinidadians. Afro-Trinidadians thus became subordinate natives, while Indo-Trinidadians became subordinate foreigners'.[14] In Khan's stories, we can detect a legacy of this moment in the persisting image of the Indian as foreigner, or alien, within the Caribbean. This sense of 'foreignness' is instrumental to Torabully's concept of 'coolitude', which he defines as:

> an aesthetic blend, a kind of mix of a complex culture, bringing to the *imaginaire* a part of the other. It calls to attention 'Indianness' in relation with 'Otherness' as a premise which leads to a transcultural awareness. This is in keeping with the fundamental attitude of creolization.[15]

In his conception of coolitude, Torabully quite clearly draws upon negritude; both share 'the need to redress the state of oblivion and neglect attached to the condition of the Negro [and...] the Coolie' ('Theoretical Premises', p. 143). However, Torabully is quick to point out that coolitude is 'not essentialist', though he concedes that 'the vast majority of those described as coolies and who settled in ex-slave societies of the Caribbean, Pacific and Indian Ocean, from the mid-nineteenth century onwards, originated in India' ('Theoretical Premises', p. 144). Like Torabully, Khan seems particularly interested in the notion of otherness in combination with Indianness. As we shall see, rather than leading to 'transcultural awareness', however, in Khan's stories this perceived difference leads to the alienation of the Indian-Caribbean person, which he traces from childhood through to adulthood. In 'Uncle Zoltan' and 'Shaving', Khan presents characters newly returned to Trinidad from the US who find themselves distanced from their old lives on the island and, hence, as US-Trinidadians, are 'outsiders' in a new way – this time, within their own Indian-Trinidadian community.

For Khan, the alienation of Indian-Caribbean men and women has been supported by the colonial education system. In his book *Arising From Bondage* (2000), Ron Ramdin explores the role of education in perpetuating myths and stereotypes of Indian-Caribbean people:

> even though they have for generations embraced their Caribbean homelands, they are nevertheless still stereotyped and their history and culture are largely misunderstood by other Caribbean ethnic groups, in the main, because of an educational system that was Eurocentric and tended to perceive and treat the 'Indians' more as aliens, exotic groups (on the periphery of society), rather than as an integral part of 'Caribbean Studies', which should include in its curriculum aspects of African and Indian/South Asian history and culture.[16]

We see the inadequacies of this system in Khan's story 'Pooran Pooran', where a British education is an obvious aspect, and tool, of colonisation. In this story, the young protagonist travels each day from his rural home in Tunapuna to the city to attend college, where he is singled out as being different by the wealthier children. As Pooran begins to eat his lunch of roti, he is interrupted by two classmates with the pointedly non-Indian names of Harry Sharpe and John Glenford: '"it's cardboard and grass… that's what this *native* boy is eating, cardboard and grass. He, he, ha, ha, ha." […] Glenford took a pencil and poked in and out of the spinach leaves, piercing tiny holes into the roti with his pencil point'.[17] In this encounter, in which Puri's distinction between 'native' and 'foreign' is clearly collapsed in the child's use of the word 'native' to mean rural and Indian, we see the conflict between the traditional Indian roti and the tool of education, the pencil. Their opposition of these items underscores the notion that, for Khan, colonial education may have furthered the suppression and alienation of Indian children. Like the roti, Indian traditions and cultural beliefs are ultimately shown to be much more palatable to Pooran than a British education.

Education enacts transformation in differing forms in Khan's characters; in the stories 'Perpetual Motion' and 'Shaving', to which I turn in a moment, the education of the respective protagonists is shown to be one of the factors that distance both young men from their parents and, in the case of 'Shaving', the narrator's previous life in Trinidad. Pooran's uniform so alters his identity that his own father cannot recognise him upon his return from college: 'Ramdath saw a boy about Pooran's height and build get out of the third-class carriage whom he did not recognise at first […] Ramdath was overwhelmed with the transformation now that he saw his son in the college uniform' (p. 20). The transformative nature of Pooran's education is reflected not only in his physical transformation, but also in his changing views of the world around him. There is a clash of Hindu beliefs and Western education when cells are explained to him:

> He felt that all of his life was a lie – that Ramdath, Leela and the Sadhu,
> the holy man, had filled his head with stories which he would now have
> to cast off, and he meant to ask them when he got home what Mr. Hopkins
> meant; but looking about him in the hut, he knew that he couldn't,
> that they wouldn't understand, because he had not himself understood,
> but had only a feeling of loss and despair. (pp. 22–23)

Education confuses and alienates Pooran and, as in 'Shaving', it also divides
generations, where a chasm appears between traditional Indian-Caribbean
beliefs, dismissed here as 'stories', and the Western world of science;
between old and new. In 'Pooran Pooran', the clinical and unfeeling nature
of a British education (and particularly science) comes to be represented by
the death of a puppy; in contrast, Hindu beliefs are represented by life and
the possibility of rebirth. While, ironically, Pooran had hoped for a happy
outcome from his new education – that he and the teacher, Mr Hopkins,
'would breathe life into things' (p. 29), he is complicit in the puppy's death
in the name of science ('[w]e'll pickle it tomorrow…', p. 31). It is not by
working together with Mr Hopkins that Pooran achieves a sense of
happiness, but by asserting his independence from him (and the education
system he represents) in accepting Hindu versions of creation:

> As he looked at Ramdath and Leela again, he knew how it was in the
> beginning, that Mr. Hopkins was wrong. He knew that the little gods
> and the big gods had put the world together one morning… with the
> smell of smoked herrings, and the taste of hibiscus stem, and the odours
> of eggplant frying in coconut oil. And as he thought these things, he
> heard his own voice in the midst of this first morning of creation when
> he spoke: 'Baboojji, can I go with you to plant the sugarcane fields?… I
> don't want to go back to learn any more in the big college.' (p. 33)

This extract recalls a moment in Rooplall Monar's short story 'Dhookie'
from his collection *Backdam People* (1985): 'Headmaster John shake he
head and say: "Dull or brilliant, they all end in the sugar canefield"'.[18]
Monar's stories are set in Guyana in the 1930s-1950s, and therefore suggest
that he and Khan are part of a widespread pessimism concerning the
impossibility of Indian-Caribbean workers leaving the canefields, despite
the end of indenture. In the above quotation from 'Pooran Pooran' we see
that it is the protagonist's acceptance of, and reassurance provided by, his
hybrid Indian-Caribbean identity – the gods' creation of the world accompanied by the smells of a Trinidadian breakfast – that leads to his desire to
continue his father's canefield work. The ultimate rejection of science,
education and Western ideologies can be found in this plea to join his father
in the canefields: '[a]nother generation of his ancestry had tumbled
through an opening in the clouds, plunged through the maze and mire of
the fields of insane sun and withered skin that he and his fathers knew'
(p. 33). Sugarcane fields take on an especial significance in this story; as it
opens, Pooran's father is said to be prematurely aged from years in the

canefields and he hopes Pooran will not work the fields (pp. 18–19). A few pages later, Pooran is exempt from chores, which include unloading sugarcane tops from the donkey cart (p. 21). The canefields are a visible 'footstep' – a clear physical legacy of slavery and indenture. In this sense, we see Pooran's rejection of one aspect of colonisation (a British education) for another (canefield work).

When children continue their education and do not return to the fields, we can see much more clearly the divide between generations of Indian-Caribbean people. Whereas, in the early stories, we are presented with children struggling with the British education system, in the last two stories, 'Uncle Zoltan' and 'Shaving', we see the possible consequence of excelling at school: namely, migration to the US. As I have indicated already, in both stories, the protagonists visit Trinidad – in the case of 'Shaving', returning again to the US before the story ends. In this story, Khan tells what he calls a 'cutlass to computer'[19] story of a son who lives in the US recalling an earlier visit to his parents in Trinidad. His higher education at an American university has left him scathing of the way in which his mother speaks; he mentally corrects her English:

> I needed a long extension cord for my electric razor. 'Shave in the big-bureau-mirror,' said my mother. 'One does not shave *in* the big bureau mirror, mother, one shaves…'
> 'You could plug in the bedroom electricity,' she went on.
> 'You do not *plug in* the bedroom electricity mother…you plug your razor into…' (p. 133)

His university education leaves him critical not only of the way in which his parents communicate, but also of their traditional ways of living in the Caribbean. The US offers new possibilities and a sense of optimism, which contrasts with the pessimism, and closed thinking, of Trinidad. When his electric shaver will not work on the island, due to humidity, the narrator wonders, '[w]hy can't we do things like Americans? Is it because for more than a century we have been told, "You can't…"[?]' (p. 134).

This story explores the apparent contrast between a new, hybrid and diasporic (Indian, Trinidadian, American) identity, which is represented by the electric shaver, and an older, and old-fashioned, generation of Indian-Trinidadians, corresponding to the Gillette razor. The importance of shaving in establishing manhood is also examined here, as the narrator recalls his 'secret' first shave performed without his parents' consent. At this moment, the barber Sookoo calls him Clark Gable, an alter ego that comes to symbolise his new 'American' Indian-Trinidadian identity:

> I said 'No-no-no,' He said 'Yes-Yes-Yes!' and this time it was the cutting edge of the razor. I knew that I dared not move a muscle no matter how my emotions tumbled in my heart.
> 'A regular Clark Gable, boy! It look as if you ready for Hollywood!' (p. 136)

The narrator might not be ready for Hollywood just yet but, within a few years, he does go to live in the US. Upon returning home from the barber, his parents are initially horrified by their son's desire to be grown up, telling him his moustache makes him 'look like a crook!' (p. 137). They arguably reject not only the hastening adulthood of their child, but also the apparently corrupt and modern American identity his moustache seems to represent. Like Pooran's college uniform, the narrator's 'American' moustache makes him almost unrecognisable to his parents.

 The story – and the collection – ends with the narrator back in his apartment in the US where, ironically, the electricity is not working. As he shaves by candlelight using the Gillette razor his mother insisted he keep, we see the theatricality of his 'Gablesque' performance:

> I lather up before the mirror and now all those ancient faces from its nether side fall back in silence, seated like an audience in rows of a darkened theatre. On this side of the mirror, other faces emerge, and I hear other voices... the principals of this small drama. (p. 142)

These are voices of his 'home' in Trinidad, and also of his new life in America – the story ends with a conversation between contrapuntal, disparate, voices. Unlike Gable's oeuvre, this is no Hollywood film, but a 'small drama', making evident the local scale of the performance. The story ends not with the blaze of theatre lights, or even candlelight, but in the blackout at the close of a performance: '[b]eyond the sound of water running freely, there is only silence. I see my audience stand, I see their long lost faces and their clapping hands... as in a dream... there is no sound. And then they disappear in the darkness' (p. 143). Shaving in this traditional manner connects him to these voices – in this sense, it is ritualistic and performative – but, ultimately, the narrator is left with silence. Education and his subsequent relocation have left a permanent rift; in Stuart Hall's parlance, '[t]he past continues to speak to us. [... but] our relation to it, like the child's relation to the mother, is always-already "after the break". It is always constructed through memory, fantasy, narrative and myth.'[20] While the performative aspect of shaving enables the narrator to recall those voices of the past – both recent and much older – it is entirely dependent on imagination and memory; he remains forever cut off from his previous life in Trinidad. This is the final story in the collection, and the most dialogic; the plural voices heard at the end of 'Shaving' suggest a momentary instance of connection and collaboration before darkness falls. In this way, despite the collection's disparate voices, the reader is left with a feeling of connectivity; of the exchange, and dialogue, between old and new Trinidad, and between the island and its diasporic children elsewhere. Khan's use of the short story collection emphasises the form's potential to communicate, simultaneously, polyphonic viewpoints and an overall sense of connection between these disparate Indian-Caribbean accounts.

I have suggested so far that, for Khan, education fuels the separation between generations and may partly be responsible for the casting of Indian people as outsiders by African-Trinidadians, in particular. In stories from *A Day in the Country*, Khan selects as his protagonists characters that previously may have been excluded from historical or literary accounts of Trinidadian life. I would suggest that this is one of the reasons that five of his stories in this collection have child protagonists but, whereas in 'Pooran, Pooran', the child's Indianness is a factor in his alienation, in 'The Magic Ring', a young boy called Patrick is distinguished initially because he is cross-eyed. The sympathy generated from his difference ensures that he is not chased out of shops like the other children: 'he sensed that it was because there was something special about him. And he sensed it was the same thing about him which kept him on the side-lines of other boys' games, which he was rarely asked to join'.[21] In this way, Patrick's disability is both a gift and a curse, but his greatest persecutor is his father, who physically and verbally abuses him, with the taunt 'Ko-kee-eye' (p. 35). When Patrick espies a Chinese good luck ring in an adult friend's jewellery shop, he believes that '[t]o wear something beautiful, like the ring, would in some way counterbalance that thing in him which was ugly' (p. 40). Patrick's disability arguably enables a different vision to that of his parents, in his belief in the magic properties of the ring; namely, that it might simultaneously bring wealth and correct his sight, so that 'his eyes would become perfect and centred like everyone else's' (p. 40). We learn that Patrick's disability was caused by a blow to the head as an infant from his father; correspondingly, after his father's angry reaction to the purchase of the ring, another blow uncrosses his eyes: '[s]o you don't want to talk today-today... I goin' to make you talk!' (p. 51). Ironically, the blow accompanying his father's request for speech leaves Patrick with uncrossed eyes, but mute:

> 'Talk, son, talk to me,' [his mother] pleaded, and the boy tried again; his lips and mouth moved, they opened and closed, the boy sounded as though he tried to reach deep down into his chest to reach something that had been there, but it had gone silent. (p. 52)

Khan chooses this moment to end the story; like 'Shaving', which closes with absolute silence and darkness, this story also culminates in silence. Most of the stories in this collection conclude with silence, disappearance, incomprehension, unconsciousness or death, indicating an overwhelming sense of withdrawal from the comfortless materiality of Indian-Caribbean life.[22] What Patrick sees around him arguably leaves him speechless and unable to communicate the horrors of poverty and abuse which are, in these stories, part of the Indian-Caribbean existence. Torabully has argued that the trope of muteness has been particularly relevant to the position of Indian-Caribbean migrants:

> This muteness, this 'frailty' of speech, is another form of the symbolic
> castration of the coolie as a result of his/her situation in History, in the
> plantocratic society, and as reflected in many writings, including those
> of *créolité* writers. This fictional treatment in fact emphasizes what has
> been repressed and what has to emerge, in a kind of therapy. I am here
> referring to the 'murmur from the hold' where memory has been repressed,
> speech inhibited and the relation to a complex identity forced into an
> attitude of recoil. ('Theoretical Premises', p. 179)

Torabully's claims provide a helpful way of thinking about Khan's story;
Patrick is now able to see clearly, but his relation to his Indian-Trinidadian
identity is in 'an attitude of recoil', and far removed from any possibility of
coolitude. History's metaphorical silencing, or 'symbolic castration', of
Indian-Caribbean people can be seen in the absence of their pasts from older
accounts of Caribbean, Indian and British histories, as well as from the
majority of revisionary accounts of the slave trade which, in tracing the role
of the African slave, subsequently tend to eclipse the significant part played
by Indian indentured labourers on the British plantations in the Caribbean.
As David Dabydeen has argued, '[s]cholarly research has been focussed
overwhelmingly on the African dimension, and in the resulting Afro-centric
view of the Caribbean, the Indo-Caribbean is relegated to a footnote'.[23]

It is significant that much of the anger felt by Patrick's father is generated
by his discovery that Patrick has been working for a Chinese shopkeeper:
'[s]o this is why you never come home after school… you want the
Chineeman to put you in a bag and sell you… You don't know how them
Chinee people is… they does tie up children in a bag and sell them in
China…' (p. 49). While Patrick's father here rallies against Chinese-
Caribbean migrants, by far the greatest racial hostility explored in Khan's
stories is between African- and Indian-Caribbean people. V.S. Naipaul
earlier wrote of this conflict in *The Middle Passage* (1962), claiming:
'Trinidad […] teeters on the brink of racial war. Politics must be blamed;
but there must have been an original antipathy for the politicians to work
on. Matters are not helped by the fierce rivalry between Indians and
Negroes as to who despises the other more'. Naipaul found this antipathy
'at first sight, puzzling […] At all levels they share the same language, the
same ambitions […] and, increasingly, the same pleasures. Their interests
don't clash' (*The Middle Passage*, p. 86, p. 85).[24] However, for all Naipaul's
apparent puzzlement – which is shared by several of Khan's characters,
including Patrick – this is a hostility we can trace back to the early days of
indenture, when those African-Caribbean people remaining on plantations were often resentful of the new Indian labour force. As Puri explains:
'[b]oth colonial "divide and rule" policies and the lowering of sugar wages
that resulted from the increased supply of labour exacerbated relations
between these two poorest segments of Trinidadian society' (Puri, p 172).

In Khan's work, we see the legacies of this moment of indenture in the continuing racial tensions in mid-twentieth-century Trinidad; perhaps the most striking moment comes late in 'Perpetual Motion', when an Indian-Caribbean inventor is murdered at a Black Power rally in Woodford Square. Khan's unnamed inventor is consumed by the desire to use perpetual motion to free people of hard labour: 'he always had some spark going in his head. He knew that if he could harness some force – like gravity – put it to work, he could free men from the horsepowers that horses should do'.[25] It is perhaps appropriate that the descendent of Indian indentured labourers should be trying to invent a machine to enact another emancipation, or freedom, from hard labour.[26] However, as his son, the narrator, recognises, perpetual motion may be a dangerous force where, once started, machines (like racial tensions, perhaps) gain momentum and spiral out of control. Just before the death of the inventor, his son has a premonition:

> That night as I lay in bed listening to the keskedees going to sleep, and the jumbie bird, the death bird of the night coming to life, I wondered how Papa would stop his perpetual motion machine. Once it got going, it would build up acceleration, go faster and faster until it destroyed itself. (p. 56)

These thoughts are punctuated by a minor incident in Woodford Square, and the next day he is told: '[o]nce again a speaker was talking about "sending back" one race or the other of the island's mixed population' (p. 57). As each racial group seeks to remove the other, the narrator reminds us that Trinidad, like other formerly colonised countries with a past of slavery and indenture, comprises a diverse mixture of peoples and languages. Correspondingly, there is a problem with translation in this story, where words like 'freedom' and 'enemy' mean different things to different people. The inventor makes clear that he is all too aware of the ambiguity of 'freedom' in the following encounter:

> 'What people go do when your machine is finish, Papa?' I asked.
> 'Freedom, boy... they go have freedom.'
> 'What's that, Papa?'
> 'Ah! That's the question.' (p. 58)

The inventor's understanding of freedom ominously is at odds with that of the black rally leader, as his son records: '[t]his Saturday the speaker had some kind of loudspeaker, and I could hear what was being shouted out. "Power! Power to Black People! Let's ship those bastards back! Freedom now!"' (p. 63). In his influential essay 'Cultural Identity and Diaspora' (1990), Stuart Hall writes of the significant differences between Caribbean countries which exist 'alongside continuity', arguing that '[t]he common history – transportation, slavery, colonisation – has been profoundly formative. For all these societies, unifying us across our differences. But it does not constitute a common *origin*, since it was, metaphorically as well as literally, a translation' (Hall, p. 396). While Hall suggests here that the experiences of the 'common history' have varied between Caribbean islands, I would add that this notion of difference in translation might also be relevant when considering the varying backgrounds of those living together *within* a particular island, such as Trinidad. The experiences of 'transportation, slavery, colonisation' were significantly different for African-Trinidadians and Indian-Trinidadians; correspondingly, the meaning of 'freedom', too, is variable. For all this collection suggests – in its grouping of often disparate voices – connections (despite differences) within the Indian-Trindadian community, there is a distinct lack of *national* community in these stories.

Perhaps unsurprisingly, then, the word 'enemy' is also understood differently by the Indian-Caribbean inventor and African-Caribbean speaker. The speaker asks: '[w]ho is the enemy?', and answers his own question with the response: '[e]very son-of-a-bitch who is not a black man!' (p. 63), but the narrator's father is stabbed as he offers an alternative answer to the question: '[f]riction… you fool… friction is the enemy!' (p. 64). This response refers at once to perpetual motion and to racial harmony in Trinidad. The meaning of 'friction' is plural, and three of its definitions are pertinent to this story. Firstly, it can relate to the 'action of one object rubbing against another', or it can mean the resistance encountered by an object in moving over another object. Finally, it may relate to a disagreement – specifically, a 'mutual animosity arising from disagreement'.[27] We might think about these various meanings in relation to the friction within multicultural Trinidadian society at this moment in history, with different racial groups 'rubbing against' each other, and the resistance encountered by people of diverse ethnicities in day-to-day life in Trinidad which, in many cases, results in mutual animosity.[28] In *The Middle Passage*, Naipaul wrote of the lack of community in the Trinidad of the early twentieth century: '[w]e were of various races, religions, sets and cliques; and we had somehow found ourselves on the same small island. Nothing bound us together except this common residence' (*The Middle Passage*, p. 45). This lack of empathy may also be seen in 'Perpetual Motion':

> There were some people who wanted all the white people to leave, people who were born on the island. Now those of African descent wanted to send those of Indian descent back to India, and the people from India wanted to send the Africans back to Africa; the same was true of the Portuguese, the Chinese, the Syrians and the Lebanese. The truth was that we were all imports from one or other part of the world, and those who could truly call it their homeland, the Amerindians, were extinct – killed off by the Spaniards long before this polyglot collection of peoples arrived. (p. 57)

Alongside a reminder of Trinidad's racial diversity, this quotation also raises the complexity of terms like 'home' or 'homeland', portrayed in Khan's stories as particularly nebulous and shifting words. As Khan has explained in interview, 'as independence comes in Africa, I think the Africans feel – and rightly so – you know, "This is our country, what are you guys doing here?" But there is no way that anybody can say that to anybody else in the Caribbean because nobody in the Caribbean is indigenous to the area' (Dance, p. 125). The short story form arguably offers Khan a means of articulating this sense of mobility and change, allowing him to explore how notions of 'home' are different for each of the characters, as each negotiates their unique diasporan identity. Recalling Hall's comment that the past is 'always constructed through memory, fantasy, narrative and myth', Avtar Brah argues in *Cartographies of Diaspora* (1997) that home is always, for diasporan people, a place of the imagination: '"home" is a mythic place of desire in the diasporic imagination. In this sense it is a place of no return, even if it is possible to visit the geographical territory that is seen as the place of "origin"'.[29] Home may be desirable but, as an imaginary location, is forever inaccessible; as the son of Kale Khan in *The Jumbie Bird* asks, 'what goin' to happen to us? We ain't belong to Hindustan, we ain't belong to England, we ain't belong to Trinidad.'[30] In *A Day in the Country*, Khan's characters – caught between a mythic Indian homeland, of which there is little mention, and dreams of a future in the US – view Trinidad as a temporary location, or impermanent place of residence. Despite the collection's assertion of the significance of their 'footsteps' in the region, therefore, this notion of unsettlement, or unbelonging, precludes a comfortable, leisurely read; the abrupt and unsettling endings propel the reader into the next story without attaining closure or, necessarily, finding answers to the difficult questions posed concerning personal and national identity and belonging. This unsettlement shapes the pervading pessimism of *A Day in the Country*, as characters wrestle against poverty, racism, the colonial education system and their continued alienation in the turbulent society of Trinidad in the decades immediately preceding its independence.

NOTES

1 A. Neil SookDeo, 'Involuntary Globalization: How Britain Revived Indenture and Made it Largely Brown and East Indian (Trinidad 1806–1921)', *Man in India*, 88:1 (2008), 5–28 (p. 8).
2 William A. Green puts this figure at more than 500,000. See Green, 'Emancipation to Indenture: A Question of Imperial Morality', *The Journal of British Studies*, 22:2 (1983), 98–121 (p. 98).

3 In citing 140,000 as the number of indentured Indians brought to Trinidad, I
   follow Bonham C. Richardson, 'Livelihood in Rural Trinidad in 1900', *Annals of
   the Association of American Geographers*, 65:2 (1975), 240-51 (241). SookDeo gives
   this figure as 144,000 (11); V.S. Naipaul as 134,000 – see Naipaul, *The Middle
   Passage: Impressions of Five Societies – British, French and Dutch – in the West Indies
   and South America* (Harmondsworth: Penguin, 1985), p. 57.

4 Marina Carter and Khal Torabully, 'Introduction', in *Coolitude: An Anthology of
   the Indian Labour Diaspora* (London: Anthem, 2002), pp. 1–16 (p. 1).

5 David Northrup, *Indentured Labor in the Age of Imperialism, 1834–1922* (Cambridge,
   New York and Melbourne: Cambridge University Press, 1955), p. 5.

6 Ismith Khan, 'A Day in the Country', in *A Day in the Country: And Other Stories*
   (Leeds: Peepal Tree, 1994), pp. 66–84 (p. 77).

7 Khan, 'The Red Ball', *A Day in the Country*, pp. 7–17 (p. 9).

8 Louis James, 'Writing the Ballad: The Short Fiction of Samuel Selvon and Earl
   Lovelace' in *Telling Stories: Postcolonial Short Fiction in English*, ed. by Jacqueline
   Bardolph (Amsterdam and Atlanta, GA: Rodopi, 2001), pp. 103–08 (p. 104).

9 As Louis James notes, the story was often reprinted, and was 'selected by E.J. O'Brien
   as one of the *Best British Short Stories of 1928*' (p. 103).

10 *Miguel Street* was the first work Naipaul wrote, though the third to be published.
   See James, p. 104. Naipaul records the influence of his father's short stories, *Gurudeva
   and Other Indian Tales*, on his own work in the introduction to the 1976 edition of
   his father's stories. See V.S. Naipaul, 'Foreword' in Seepersad Naipaul, *The Adventures
   of Gurudeva* (London: Heinemann, 1995), pp. 1–20 (p. 15).

11 Andrew Salkey, 'Introduction', in *West Indian Stories,* ed. by Andrew Salkey (London:
   Faber and Faber, 1979), pp. 9–12 (p. 11).

12 Ian Reid, *The Short Story* (London: Methuen, 1977), p. 27.

13 Frank Birbalsingh, 'Introduction', in Frank Birbalsingh, ed., *Frontiers of Caribbean
   Literature* (London and Basingstoke: Macmillan, 1996), pp. ix–xxiii (p. xvi).

14 Shalini Puri, *The Caribbean Postcolonial: Social Equality, Post-Nationalism and Cultural
   Hybridity* (New York and Basingstoke: Palgrave Macmillan, 2004), p. 176.

15 Carter and Torabully, 'Some Theoretical Premises of Coolitude', *Coolitude*, pp. 143–
   213 (p. 168). See also V.S. Naipaul's *The Middle Passage* for the perceived alienness
   of Indian people (pp. 87–88).

16 Ron Ramdin, *Arising From Bondage: A History of the Indo-Caribbean People* (London:
   I.B. Taurus, 2000), p. 330.

17 Khan, 'Pooran, Pooran', *A Day in the Country*, pp. 18–33 (pp. 26–27).

18 Rooplall Monar, 'Dhookie', in *Backdam People* (Leeds: Peepal Tree, 1987), pp. 11–
   18 (p. 18).

19 Khan, 'Shaving', in *A Day in the Country*, pp. 131–43 (p. 138).

20 Stuart Hall, 'Cultural Identity and Diaspora', in *Colonial Discourse and Post-Colonial
   Theory: A Reader*, ed. by Patrick Williams and Laura Chrisman (Harlow: Prentice
   Hall, 1993), pp. 392–403 (p. 395).

21 Khan, 'The Magic Ring', in *A Day in the Country*, pp. 34–52 (p. 35).

22 Although, when questioned on his recurrent use of death in *The Jumbie Bird*, Khan
   has suggested a more positive meaning: 'it has to do with the East Indian community
   and all of the very firm and fixed traditions that they had. It had to die in a certain
   sense. It had to adapt if it was going to survive. I think that is true of any cultural
   group that migrates' (Daryl Cumber Dance, 'Conversation with Ismith Khan', in
   New World Adams: Conversations with Contemporary West Indian Writers (Leeds: Peepal
   Tree, 1992), pp. 122–32 (p. 124)).

23 David Dabydeen, 'Preface', in David Dabydeen and Brinsley Samaroo, eds, *India in the Caribbean* (London: Hansib: 1987), pp. 9–12 (p. 10). Notable exceptions published subsequent to Dabydeen's comments include Madhavi Kale's *Fragments of Empire: Capital, Slavery, and Indian Indentured Labor Migration in the British Caribbean* (Philadelphia: University of Pennsylvania Press, 1998) and James Walvin's *Making the Black Atlantic: Britain and the African Diaspora* (London and New York: Cassell, 2000).

24 Somewhat contradictory, then, is Naipaul's later claim: 'Everything which made the Indian alien in the society gave him strength. His alienness insulated him from the black-white struggle' (*The Middle Passage*, p. 88).

25 Khan, 'Perpetual Motion', in *A Day in the Country*, pp. 53–65 (p. 53).

26 Although Khan does not provide the inventor's age, it seems likely that, if born by 1917, he will have been too young to have been an indentured labourer.

27 *The Oxford English Reference Dictionary*, 2nd Edn, ed. by Judy Pearsall and Bill Trumble (Oxford and New York: Oxford University Press, 1996), p. 554.

28 I use the term 'multicultural' with care; in this instance, I am using it in its broadest sense, defined by the *OED* as being 'of or relating to or constituting several cultural or ethnic groups within a society' (Pearsall and Trumble, p. 950), without any suggestion of equality between those ethnic groups. For an overview of the debate concerning this word, see the introduction to *The Politics of Multiculturalism in the New Europe: Racism, Identity and Community*, ed. by Tariq Modood and Pnina Werbner (London and New York: Zed Books, 1997), pp. 1–25.

29 Avtar Brah, *Cartographies of Diaspora: Contesting Identities* (London and New York: Routledge, 2002), p. 192.

30 Ismith Khan, *The Jumbie Bird* (Harlow: Longman, 1985), p. 54.

THE TEMPORAL AESTHETIC IN THE SHORT FICTION OF YANICK LAHENS AND EDWIDGE DANTICAT

ELIZABETH WALCOTT-HACKSHAW

INTRODUCTION: FORM AND FRAMES

The short story as a genre demands of its practitioner an acute sense of time and space. Time can be defined in its most mechanical sense: the story line, the temporal frame of events, and the sequencing of transitions. There is also the more subtle use of time in the way the writer uses it to pace the story, to trace shifts and nuances in characters or to vary temporal frames through landscapes, both physical and psychological. These landscapes can co-exist in a short story, allowing a character to live in an imagined, 'psychological' time while inhabiting the 'real' time of the story. In many ways the short story demands a precision that approaches the poetic since there is no luxury of the extended temporal space afforded to the novel. Time and space render these two genres, novel and short story, distinct. Many of the best short stories have been chiselled with a precise, sure, efficient hand that understands both the limits and possibilities of the genre.

Within these temporal and spatial frames of the short story, a drama takes place. This dramatic quality can be achieved with the subtlety of Canadian writer, Alice Munro, where lives unfold ironically, laconically and with a quiet complexity. Munro has written eleven collections of short stories. Many of her stories explore the notion of uncertainty and unpredictability in relationships. A rural setting is often the stage where layers of lives are peeled away to reveal hidden secrets. Avoidance of what is painful or ugly is a typical feature in Munro's characters; they are unable to face truths. In 'Royal Beatings', Munro claims that she was inspired by the unofficial town history of incest between a father and daughter and the fact that the town in which this happened claimed that 'no untoward incidents ever took place within its boundaries'.[1] Her stories address the complexity of such familial relationships and the face presented to the world outside. But even within the walls of the home these family portraits show how little we know about those closest to us.

Time in Munro's short stories often unfolds on a psychological level, whether consciously or unconsciously; her characters exist in the dual temporal layers of 'psychological time' dominated by thoughts about their past and the 'real time' of the narrative. Her characters do not always reflect upon their actions, but this lack of reflection invites her readers to untangle the complex yet seemingly ordinary lives of the characters. Many stories and collections like *Runaway* (2004) have privileged a female perspective. Although Munro locates many of her stories in a rural Canadian landscape, her thematic concerns of love, betrayal, secrets, abandonment and solitude extend beyond North American borders.

Alice Munro is not Haitian, nor does she write about the Haitian experience. However, I have introduced this Canadian writer as a point of departure for this chapter on the works of two short story writers of Haitian origin, Edwidge Danticat and Yanick Lahens. Lahens and Danticat, as I will argue, approach time in a manner that resembles Munro's, even though their narratives recall the ever-present drama of Haiti's history and politics. Lahens and Danticat also develop their short stories around a psychological drama that is often the result of their Haitian experience. Both of these writers create a space where the psychological drama unfolds. The chapter will also attempt to locate qualities that are characteristic of Lahens and Danticat, presenting them as at once distinctively Haitian and at the same time part of a wider body of short story writers. Haiti has a singular legacy and an imposing, overarching history as the first Black Republic of the New World. This historical legacy can be both a blessing and a burden for any writer of Haitian origin. The past looms large and the brutalities that have accompanied this glorious legacy continue to dominate the present hardships of the poorest country in the Western Hemisphere. In this chapter I will examine the role Haiti's historical/political drama plays in the works of these two writers. I will also explore how location affects the writer's subject. My primary preoccupation, however, is the way in which both of these writers use time structurally and thematically to create their short dramas and to explore the impact of the collective narrative on the personal.

WOMEN, WRITING AND TIME

The Haitian short story has long been considered a minor genre compared to Haitian poetry and the Haitian novel. As Kathleen Gyssel notes, this is a paradox since 'the short story most resembles indigenous narrative traditions'.[2] In recent decades the Haitian short story has blossomed and is particularly popular amongst women writers. However, even though the form has been adopted by women writers the question of silencing and censorship still remains. According to Gyssel:

> Writing is considered a male activity and a woman should not make public her feelings: that's how Haitian society censors female voices. Lahens also underscores the modesty associated with short story, contrasting it with ambitious projects of writing a 'roman à thèse' or a 'roman à clé.' In these respects, one can understand why the majority of female authors are short story writers. ('Haitians in the City,' p. 3)

Short story writing for women is directly linked to time in both mundane and enlightening ways. In an introduction to her collection of short stories entitled *Selected Stories* (1997), Alice Munro responds to some of her readers' questions about becoming a short story writer. She says: 'I did not "choose" to write short stories. I hoped to write novels. When you are responsible for running a house and taking care of small children [...] it's hard to arrange large chunks of time' (*Selected Stories*, p. xiv). These practical links, to time and Munro's domestic challenges, also inform the ways in which she sees her fictional world; in many of her stories there is a necessity to understand the most routine, the ordinariness of life. Munro has a great sensitivity to the quotidian.

Haitian critic Anne Marty has posed comparable questions to Yanick Lahens about time, writing and women short story writers. Marty suggests that women chose to write short stories not because they are less ambitious than their male counterparts but perhaps because the demands and rhythms of real life offer them only limited morsels of time:

> Les femmes, au contraire, favoriseraient-elles la production de nouvelles, non qu'elles aient moins d'ambitions que leurs collègues masculins, mais peut-être parce qu'elles les adapteraient mieux aux réalités humaines? En effet, leur rythme de vie davantage fractionné les rendrait plus sensibles aux limites de la temporalité, au morcellement du temps.[3]

It can be realistically argued that due to the nature of women's lives, particularly those who have small children, they have limited time for creative endeavors and perhaps find the short story a more adaptable genre. These acts of balancing flights of the imagination and quotidian reality constitute territory usually reserved for women. But beyond the realistic time constraints perhaps there are other reasons why the genre is attractive to these women writers. This is a path of inquiry that Lahens has already explored:

> I would say that our women (Caribbean) plunge more directly into what makes up the day-to-day fabric of our relationships. They bring to light this historical and cultural dimension that is usually kept hidden [...]. As for our men, however talented they may be, they are still hiding behind great theoretical screens, lofty philosophical positions...[4]

The short story allows for these entries into the daily fabric that do not necessarily feature in the grand narrative of the nation. Myriam Chancy echoes these sentiments when speaking about Haitian women writers in general: 'it becomes necessary to define the novelistic literary tradition of Haitian women as one that transgresses nationalistic ideologies and refor-mulates nation and identity through the lens of personal and communal exile'.[5]

The question of time in the context of the nation's historical narrative is a feature in the works of many Haitian writers. A writer's biography necessarily affects his/her subject; this is often the case for those who have been subjected to violent, tyrannical régimes. Writers like Lahens and Danticat have not shied away from social engagement both within Haiti and in the Haitian diaspora. The murder of writer Jacques-Stéphen Alexis in 1961 remains a symbol of a terrorising régime;[6] the tragic event left an indelible mark on the psyche of many Haitian writers. Still, there is the continual question of the writer's political role versus the creative. This is not a new debate; Russian short story writer Anton Chekhov made his famous declaration on freedom and truth in an 1888 letter to A.N. Pleshcheyev:

> I should like to be a free artist and that's all […] I hate lies and violence of all kinds […] I regard signs and labels as mere prejudice. My holy of holies is the human body, health, intelligence, talent, inspiration, love and the most absolute freedom imaginable, freedom from violence and lies, no matter what form these may take.[7]

Chekhov also argued in another letter against political engagement: 'major writers and artists should engage in politics only enough to protect themselves from it'.[8] But this idea of disengagement from the political finds a counter-argument in the ideas of Jean Price-Mars who wrote in 1957 that Haitian literature from its inception has always been 'une littérature engagée'. He defined engagement as an expression of a people's desire to fight openly or secretively for their rights.[9] Many of Haiti's famous writers, like René Dépestre, Jacques Roumain and Jacques-Stéphen Alexis, all faced exile or death as a result of their engagement and their anti-establishment ideology. Marie Vieux Chauvet was forced into exile for her explicit, erotic work, *Amour, Colère, et Folie* (1968). In this trilogy she denounced the brutalities of the Duvalier dictatorship and courageously implicated the powerful bourgeois, to which she belonged, for their silence. Lahens admires Chauvet both for her courage and for her penetrating psychological exploration of her female protagonists; according to Lahens, Chauvet 'opened the way for the modern novel in Haiti' ('Haitian Literature After Duvalier', p. 85). Chauvet was amongst many other Haitian women writers including Virgile Valcin, Annie Desroy, Nadine Magloire, Jan J. Dominique and Ghislaine Rey Charlier who used their narrative to create heroines who retell the salient events of Haitian history (Chancy, p. 10).

A short biography of Yanick Lahens and Edwidge Danticat points to two distinct locations: Lahens still resides in Haiti, while Danticat left Haiti at the age of twelve for the United States. Danticat is one of the most famous contemporary Haitian writers, the first to write in English, while Lahens is less well known by those outside the French-speaking literary sphere. Before Danticat, born in 1968, left Haiti, many families had already left to escape the terror of the Duvalier régime. The young and gifted Danticat would go on to create her own North American success story with what could be described as an almost immediate recognition of her talents. Still, Danticat has always made Haiti the subject of her stories even though her protagonists often reside in the Haitian North American diaspora. Her last work, *Brother I'm Dying* (2007), is a memoir that tells the tragic story of her uncle's death having been held by US immigration at the Krome detention centre in Miami attempting to visit his own dying brother, Danticat's father.

Born in Haiti in 1953, Lahens received her secondary and tertiary education in France. On her return to Haiti, she taught at the State University (l'École Normale Supérieure) until 1995. To date Lahens has published three collections of short stories: *Tante Résia et les Dieux, nouvelles d'Haïti* (1994), *La petite corruption* (1999), and *La folie était venue avec la pluie* (2006). She has also published two novels: *Dans la maison du père* (2000) and *La couleur de l'aube* (2008). As a writer, literary critic and activist still residing in Haiti, Lahens has experienced Haiti's trauma on many levels. She understands the challenges faced by writers like herself and the many others who continue to make Haiti their home. Lahens explores the complex notion of the writer's exile in the long essay: *L'Exil: entre l'anchrage et la fuite, l'écrivain haïtien* (1990). The essay describes the physical and psychological exile faced by the Haitian writer who struggles with an interior drama of collective inclusion and creative exclusion; to be an effective observer the writer must create a self-imposed distance from the subject of the work and yet to understand the subject there is also the need for inclusion and proximity. *L'Exil* expresses the precarious, ambiguous status of the Haitian writer/intellectual in a volatile society. Little has changed since the time when the essay was written; Lahens blames this on the lack of a social infrastructure that might shelter Haitian citizens from economic hardship and political instability.[10]

Lahens'short stories have often portrayed the struggles of an alienated individual in a society where national politics affect personal lives. 'Le désastre banal' tells the story of Mirna, a young twenty-year-old Haitian woman whose main ambition is to get out of her poor economic circumstances. Mirna lives with four brothers and sisters, her mother and aunt. The seven of them share a three room apartment with a living room and two bedrooms in a poor Port-au-Prince neighborhood. Mirna's own home, like all those in her neighbourhood, is dilapidated and fetid. In the story there is continual reference to the area as the home of the 'vaincus' [conquered].[11] The 'vaincus' do not support each other; in fact their anger about their condition is turned inward even though their rage should be directed outward to those responsible for their condition. Mistrust replaces love:

> Mais c'était malgré tout un quartier de vaincus. Et comme tous les quartiers de vaincus, les hommes et les femmes passaient le plus clair de leur

temps à se méfier les uns des autres. Si derrière ces murs, la méfiance remplaçait très souvent l'amour, c'est parce que ceux dont les vaincus auraient dû se méfier étaient trop loin. (*La petite corruption*, p. 10)

Although Mirna knows that she has come from a world and a family of 'vaincus', she has no intention of staying in a home where the inside plumbing does not work, where they must bathe outside just metres from the latrine, and where a heavy rain causes the house to flood. Her brother, Lucien, sleeps with the young maid, Anita, from the country, who works for the family for very little having come from an even worse situation; if she wishes to stay she knows that she cannot say anything about Lucien's nightly visits. Mirna's younger sisters, Norma, Simone and Nicole, spend much of their time listening to reggae, ragga, or zouk on the radio.

Although Lahens relates the story from a third person perspective, the reader is very aware that we have entered this world through Mirna's eyes. The harsh criticisms of Mirna's family and the life in the neighborhood are decidedly Mirna's; the idea of spending one more day trapped in these four walls becomes untenable: 'Mirna était irritée à l'idée de rester un jour de plus enfermée entre ces quatre murs' (*La petite corruption*, p. 10). Unlike her sisters, Mirna has a job as a receptionist in the town centre and she has also enrolled in classes at the university. However, like many of the other young ladies in Port-au-Prince, she sees the arrival of the American soldiers as an opportunity to finally move out of her intolerable existence. She intends to use her seductive beauty and charms as weapons against the Americans. When Mirna reads two-year-old magazines that she has pinched from her Dominican hairdresser she muses over the photographs of Madonna and Claudia Schiffer, imagining the power of their beauty and the possibilities of 'triomphe' [victory] (*La petite corruption*, p. 12). Magazine images, articles, lines from a Julio Iglesias song, all serve to create Mirna's illusion of power and propel her to act upon her ultimate goal of leaving these 'perdants' [losers] (*La petite corruption*, p. 10). Mirna is too young to have felt the effects of the first American occupation of Haiti from 1915–1934 which led to a strong anti-American sentiment. Several decades later, Mirna's generation sees this American occupation is an opportunity; it is a gift, even her destiny. She intends to benefit from the American presence and has a clear strategy to use her beauty and sexuality to secure a job with the Americans. From the moment she walks in she is quite certain that the officer in charge, William Butler, does not stand a chance.

Lahens structures the story around Mirna's illusion of conquest. The story opens with Mirna waking up in a beautiful seaside hotel room at dawn, lyrically described as a moment 'entre lune et soleil', in between the night (moon) and the day (sun) (*La petite corruption*, p. 5); the peaceful silence is only interrupted by the sound of the waves lapping the shore. The last scene of the story also ends with the hotel, completing the symmetrical, cyclical quality of the tale. In between, the reader is taken through the different locations in Mirna's life, including the thoughts in her mind. The story is structured in a cinematographic manner. The technique is effective, moving the reader from one frame to another using the narrator's voice to describe Mirna's world. But this visual quality also adds an invasive, voyeuristic element; the reader enters the most private locations in Mirna's life. The reader is in the hotel room when Mirna and William have sex and even more invasive is the manner in which their thoughts are exposed. The third person perspective used by Lahens is more effective than a first person narrator; the intimacy of the 'I' is replaced by the reader as the observer/voyeur in the room looking on as the scene unfolds.

One of the most outstanding characteristics of Lahens' storytelling techniques is her ability to interweave narrative threads. On one level Mirna's story describes a cycle of economic depression and despair. Mirna's use of her beauty and sex for material gain could be seen as a form of prostitution. There is an exchange of services; both parties benefit, including Mirna's family who readily accept all of William's gifts. Even Lucien, who is the supposed anti-establishment militant, happily gains from his sister's relationship with the American soldier. In fact the only person in Mirna's family who objects is not Mirna's mother but her Aunt Violette whom Mirna describes as 'une bigote' (*La petite corruption*, p. 17). Such a description is notable particularly in a Haitian context; it reflects an important change in a younger Haitian generation who no longer share the hatred for the first American occupation of Haiti from 1915–1934. But it is precisely Mirna's response to her aunt that complicates the simple explanation of prostitution. Mirna's inspiration for this quiet revolution that she hopes will allow her to break from her economic circumstances come from magazines that glorify pop icons like Madonna and models like Claudia Schiffer; Western hedonism of the 1980s has not bypassed Port-au-Prince. As such, the terms 'vainqueur' [conqueror] and 'vaincu' [conquered] have different meanings for different generations; they are in Mirna's context less ideological but decidedly material. Mirna interprets power, success and moving across to the side of the victors in very practical terms. Her strategy is clear and she knows she will have to act quickly since these 'relationships' generally last no more than eight days: 'Les fêtes de ce genre ne durent jamais au-delà de huit jours. Il me faut agir vite. Très vite' (*La petite corruption*, p. 14).

With the subtlety of recalling the first American occupation in the context of vainqueur/vaincu, Lahens plays an interesting game with the temporal. The Haitian past is continually evoked in the Haitian present but with revisions and omissions; the Americans have returned to Haiti but this time, their occupation is seen by one young ambitious young girl as an opportunity, even a gift. The ideological political rhetoric of the past is notably absent in Mirna's world. She has already decided that her people have abandoned any notion of a collective revolution to effect a change in their situation; Mirna must act alone, refusing to accept the title of 'vaincu'. She will not exist in this 'banalité quotidienne du désastre' [disaster's everyday banality] (*La petite corruption*, p. 10).

Lahens establishes a clear distinction between Mirna's and William's view of Haiti. William, at fifty, has as much 'faim' [hunger] for this young Haitian woman as she hungers for his money. William's psychological landscape recalls many 'old' colonial themes of whites coming to civilise the barbarians and humanise the Negroes. But his desire for Mirna is also based on an adolescent desire to have what was forbidden to him having grown up white in a white America ['Blanc dans une Amérique blanche'] where he knew nothing of 'des négresses' (*La petite corruption*, p. 16). While Mirna sees the occupation as a gift, for William, Mirna is *his* gift.

Lahens does not spend much time in the story explicitly commenting on the racial prejudice that still exists even in this more modern Haiti. Race is a thematic layer of the story but it is not reduced to obvious polemics of white conqueror versus poor black Haitian girl. The encounter between Mirna and William is complex and cannot simply been seen as simply an act of prostitution on Mirna's part. Prejudice, prostitution and politics are all intertwined in the story recalling Haiti's past and placing it in the context of Mirna's present. The first American occupation of Haiti (1915–1934) destabilised the nation in a profound manner and affected every aspect of Haitian life, culturally, politically and ideologically, as Michael Dash states:

> The intention behind and the nature of the American Occupation form an indispensable background to Haiti's political and literary movements in the twentieth century. The presence of white foreigners on Haitian soil, the authoritarian nature of this presence and the pseudo-colonial contact that was established between the invaders and the native population, not only disrupted the traditional function of Haitian society but served as a grim reminder of the days of Saint-Domingue prior to 1804.[12]

Fast forward to Mirna's situation and the ironic twists are startling if not tragic. The US, although no longer in the obvious colonial role, had re-entered the population through its media and culture long before William Butler arrived. This 1980s/1990s Haiti has not emerged from political, social or economic failures. Lahens's story creates temporal layers that evoke Haiti's revolutionary past, the first American occupation and the untenable present through Mirna's present experience.

At the end of the story there is a shift in the exchange of power. William is the conqueror while Mirna holds back a tear as she senses her defeat and wants to drown herself in silence and forget William's presence: 'Dans ce silence, elle voulait se noyer, oublier la présence de William' (*La petite corruption*, p. 20). Although she can imagine herself in a new life with

William in the US she recognises that in this new role she would have to wear a mask, hide herself. She realises that her exchange with William, the American, was not a fair one, nor could it have been, for the conqueror always has less to lose that the conquered. In the final twist we see a defeated Mirna who manages in the old cliché to win the battle but lose the war.

The silence that pervades the end of the story is in fact a major trope in Lahens' novel, *Dans la maison du père*. In this novel a young adult woman, Alice, returns to her home in Haiti where she is to inherit her father's house now that he has passed away. The novel focuses on Alice's past as a young girl under the rule of a tyrannical father; it traces Alice's eventual revolt through silent resistance to conform to her father's bourgeois dictates. Alice's actions rather than her words free her from her father's control. At the end of 'le désastre banal' Lahens also employs the trope of silence to describe a similar desire by her female protagonist to revolt against a life situation in Haiti that is no longer tolerable. Both Mirna's and Alice's characters describe personal tragedies that end with 'banal' acts of revolt. As with many of Lahens' narratives the ending is ambiguous; these quiet acts of resistance reflect psychological battles that do not end within the temporal frame of the narrative. Much like the complex collective situation in Haiti, Lahens does not offer easy solutions at the end of her stories.

DANTICAT'S 'SEVEN'

Edwidge Danticat's short story, 'Seven', is one of nine interconnected stories in her book, *The Dew Breaker* (2004). The book's main story focuses on the life of a 'Dew Breaker' or torturer who served in the Duvalier dictatorship and relocated to the US in order to escape retribution after the fall of the régime. Danticat frames the collection with stories about the Dew Breaker's life. The first story focuses on his confession to his young adult daughter, Ka, about his true identity. Her mother and father had created a new identity for her father in the US, thus Ka was brought up to believe that her father was one of Duvalier's victims; a prey rather than a predator. The last story in the collection retraces the history of Ka's father, describing how he met her mother, Anne; she too mistakenly thought that he had been a prisoner as opposed to one of the guards. The other stories in the collection are all connected to the Dew Breaker's tale either directly or indirectly, but ultimately all the characters have been affected by the traumatic political events in Haiti. The stories examine the way in which betrayal, secrecy and forgiveness affect relationships. Time becomes a major factor in the development of these overarching concerns as Danticat reveals the invasiveness of Haiti's political history in the personal lives of her characters. Many have had to recast their lives in a new homeland and, as Danticat shows, the Haitian American population is a broad demographic; there are famous singers, nurses, lower-, middle- and upper-class Haitians, drug addicts, soon-to-be deportees and of course torturers. Some of these Haitian Americans have been successful while others have faced alienation, discrimination and deadly racial attacks. Still, what they all seem to share is a longing for contact with Haiti; whether they have left willingly or under threat their stories are forever connected to a Haitian homeland that manages to transcend the most brutal realities. In Danticat's stories there is a profound connection with her place of origin that transcends the violence of Haiti's political past and the destabilising conditions of her exile; but despite this connection to Haiti, Danticat's treatment is never nostalgic; it is often critical, ambiguous and decidedly enigmatic. Haiti remains a haunting presence in Danticat's work with an ability to inspire and create ghosts like the Dew Breaker. Haiti occupies the physical and psychological landscapes of her characters' dramas.

'Seven', like Lahens' story 'Le désastre banal', tells the story of a relationship that must negotiate silences and secrets. It has been seven years since a husband now based in Brooklyn has seen his wife; his home is in the basement apartment that he shares with two other Haitian men, Dany and Michel. The owner of the apartment, as we come to learn, is the Dew Breaker. None of the men know about their landlord's true identity nor is it ever made an important part of the story's plot. Danticat focuses on the married couple and the reunion after this long-distance relationship:

> Seven – a number he despised but had discovered was useful marker. There were seven days between paychecks, seven hours, not counting lunch, spent each day at his job, seven at his night job. Seven was the last number in his age – thirty-seven.[13]

The first line of the short story, 'Seven', indicates that it has been seven years since the husband and wife have seen each other. We learn quite early on that the husband has had flings and one night stands with several women while away from his wife, and later in the story we learn that the wife has also had an affair with her neighbour. Neither side will reveal these infidelities but these secrets come to define their relationship in a profound manner.

At the airport Danticat affords the reader specific details that clearly illustrate the prejudice endured by many Haitians when they enter the United States. The wife is not sure why the customs officers are searching her suitcase; unfortunately she has been misinformed by her fellow Haitians as to how she should have avoided just this invasive searching by the custom officers: they have told her 'to gift-wrap everything so it wouldn't be reopened at the airport in New York' (*The Dew Breaker*, p. 39). This is clearly the wrong thing to do, and this scene on her entry into the US sets the tone for much of what is to come. In 'Seven', Danticat refers to two cases where this prejudice towards Haitians is taken to a tragic conclusion; Patrick Dorismond, the American-born son of a famous Haitian singer, who was killed by a policeman in Manhattan and Abner Louima who was arrested, beaten and sodomised by policemen in a station. These cases create a violent image of the US for the newly arrived wife who spends most of her days in the basement afraid to go outside. The alienation that she feels on arrival is explored by Danticat on several levels: racial, cultural and linguistic, since she does not speak English.

In the first few weeks while her husband is at work she cooks delicious Haitian meals for the three men but refuses to leave the basement. Her link with the outside world is through the Haitian radio station where she listens to and is happy to hear people speaking Creole. She writes letters that she sends to her family and her neighbor, a lover she had while her husband was away. After their initial days spent together, making love at least seven times by his count, 'one for each year they'd been apart', the time spent away from each other begins to create a feeling of distance between the couple, particularly for the wife. Although the husband does not believe that they should allow their union to become 'a victim of distance and time', it has ('Seven', p. 44).

Danticat uses several narrative strategies to create this distance: firstly the reader knows the names of the secondary characters in the story like Dany and Michel, but we never learn the names of the husband and wife. The pronouns he/she are used throughout. In this way their personal story becomes less specific, less intimate; they seem to reflect a more generic situation. We never hear them say each other's names. Secondly, Danticat uses very little dialogue in the story. We move in and out of their thoughts but seldom hear them communicating their ideas and feelings to each other.

The most important sign of the distance that exists between this couple is when the husband thinks about the first time they met at the seaside carnival in Jacmel. The fact that Danticat places this recollection at the end of the story is significant. The husband remembers his future wife being one of the official weepers who volunteer to perform this ritual of weeping when all the revellers go to the beach to burn their carnival masks and costumes the day before the end of the festivities on Ash Wednesday. He remembers her telling him that she could never fake weeping, that whenever 'she cried for anything, she cried for everything else that had ever hurt her' (*The Dew Breaker*, p. 49). It is interesting to note that in this new American home his connection to his wife is through these memories of the Haiti and the Jacmel carnival theatre. The husband recalls another part of the Jacmel carnival performance:

A bride and groom, in their most lavish wedding clothing, would wander the streets. Scanning a crowd of revelers, they'd pick the most stony-faced person and ask, 'Would you marry us?' [...] The joke was that when the person took the bait and looked closely, he or she might discover that the bride was a man and the groom a woman. The couple's make-up was so skillfully applied [...] that only the most observant revelers could detect this. (*The Dew Breaker*, pp. 51–52)

The wife also remembers the carnival in Jacmel when they played the game of dressing as a bride and groom: 'she disguised herself as the bride and he as the groom, forgoing the traditional puzzle' (*The Dew Breaker*, p. 52). She feels that it could easily be performed in the streets of this foreign land; there would be no need to speak, their performance could take place in silence. Using the carnival images of the couples' past life in Haiti at the end of the short story, Danticat demonstrates that the physical proximity between husband and wife has not brought them closer together. The silences and the secrets that they share have created a drama, a play, where their roles have been cast as husband and wife. Their life together in this country is now a performance of past memories.

Danticat has long been fascinated with the carnival at Jacmel; in her first memoir, *After the Dance* (2002), she writes of her longing as a child to attend the festivities when her family did not permit her to attend. It is only as an adult that she experiences the Jacmel carnival but this return is not only personal, it is a way of revisiting the island's tragic history. The contrast of the carnival revelry and the brutal reality is explained in the metaphor of the drum: 'After the dance, the drum is heavy. But during the dance, you're not thinking about the weight of the drum.'[14]

The story 'Seven' captures in many ways Danticat's subtle, complex rendering of human relationships where silences and secrets prevent complete connections between people. As in many of the other stories in the *Dew Breaker* there are puzzles that will never be completed. In the story 'Night Talkers', Claude is sent back to Haiti after being deported for killing his father while Claude was high on drugs. Claude on reflection realises that his life was in pieces and missing pieces, and that his return to Haiti has helped complete the puzzle: 'It's like a puzzle [...] I'm the puzzle and these people are putting me back together...' (*The Dew Breaker*, p. 102).

In both of these short stories by Lahens and Danticat silence and secrets have created everlasting distances. The characters have been cast in roles like actors; Mirna masks herself in a role and in 'Seven' both husband and wife realise they are part of a performance, a new carnival where the Haitian stage has been replaced by the American one. But unlike Danticat's carnival experience in *After the Dance*, there is no end to the drama of their performance. Another feature distinctive to both writers is the interweaving of the Haitian historical narratives in their works. Their treatment of this theme is not necessarily explicit; for example Lahens does not directly refer to the first American Occupation but it is a haunting presence, a temporal marker, a constant reminder of this traumatic moment in Haitian history. In 'Seven' there is no direct mention of the Duvalier dictatorship but the reader is aware that every character has been affected by the atrocities of this régime. However, although Danticat and Lahens create this historical layer in their narratives they privilege their characters' personal dramas, using the psychological landscape to explore the collective drama of Haiti's past and present.

Danticat has said that every writer is in the end political: 'even if we're not making our characters spokespersons, the things that concern us will absolutely find their way somehow into the work we do'.[15] In the tradition of Marie Chauvet these writers demonstrate the invasive quality of the collective historical narrative; Haiti remains a haunting presence with its enigmatic legacy. Time has always been an important part of the puzzle in trying to understand the inheritance of such a history but even more important is the way in which this history continues to affect the lives of Haitians. The short story form allows both of these writers to explore the collective Haitian drama. Danticat's interconnected tales in *The Dew Breaker* reveal both personal and collective life situations of a people; the short story form enables Danticat to create a structure that reflects separate, diverse narratives of a dispersed Haitian population and at the same time allows these narratives to produce a Haitian tableau. Lahens takes advantage of the genre's possibilities for brevity and ambiguity; the reader is seldom given the complete picture even as the characters' psychological landscapes are explored. Through her temporal poetics Lahens effectively illustrates the ways in which the present tense of the characters' experience is inevitably linked to the past tense of a collective history. In this way both Danticat and Lahens, writing from different locations and in different languages, reveal a similar desire to explore through these works of short fiction a temporal aesthetic that is equally preoccupied with Haiti's past and present.

NOTES

1 Alice Munro, *Selected Stories* (New York: First Vintage Contemporaries, 1997), p. xix.
2 See Kathleen Gyssels 'Haitians in the City: Two Modern-Day Trickster Tales', <http://social.chass.ncsu.edu/jouvert/v7isl/gyss.htm> [accessed 11/10/2008> [accessed 11 October 2008], p. 1.
3 Anne Marty, *Haïti en littérature* (Paris: Maisonneuve & Larose, 2000), p. 204.
4 Clarisse Zimra, 'Haitian Literature after Duvalier: An Interview with Yanick Lahens,' *Callaloo*, 16:1 (1993), 77–93 (p. 86).
5 Myriam Chancy, *Framing Silence: Revolutionary Novels by Haitian Women* (New Brunswick, New Jersey: Rutgers University Press, 1997), p. 10.

6 Jacques-Stéphen Alexis (1922–1961), is one Haiti's most famous writers. Alexis was a member of the communist party in Haiti and deeply influenced by Jacques Roumain. His political opposition to the Duvalier régime led to his death.

7 Anton Chekhov, Letter to A.N. Plescheyev, Moscow, 4 October 1888, quoted in Gordon McVay, 'Introduction', in Anton Chekhov, *Short Stories*, ed. by Gordon McVay (London: Folio Society, 2001), pp. xiii–xxiv (p. xviii).

8 Anton Chekhov, Letter to A. S. Suvorin, 1898, quoted in Zinovy Zinik, 'Foreword', in Chekhov, *Short Stories*, ed. by McVay, pp. ix–xii (p. xii).

9 Jean Price-Mars, *De Saint-Domingue à Haïti* (Paris: Présence Africaine, 1959), p. 13.

10 Yanick Lahens, *L'Exil: entre l'anchrage et la fuite, l'écrivain haïtien* (Port-au-Prince: Editions Deschamps, 1990), p. 6.

11 Yanick Lahens, *La petite corruption* (Port-au-Prince: Editions Mémoire, 1999), p. 8.

12 J. Michael Dash, *Literature and Ideology in Haiti* (London: Macmillan, 1981), p. 44.

13 Edwidge Danticat, *The Dew Breaker* (New York: Knopf, 2004), p. 35.

14 Edwidge Danticat, *After the Dance* (New York: Crown, 2002), p. 118.

15 See Mariel Brown's interview with Danticat, 'Finding Her Own Way Home,' in *Caribbean Beat*, 64 (November–December 2003), p. 57.

THE SHORTER FORM(S) OF THE GAME: CRICKET, CHILDHOOD AND THE CARIBBEAN SHORT STORY

CLAIRE WESTALL

Introducing *The Oxford Book of Caribbean Short Stories* (1999), Stewart Brown explains that while the collection hopes to 'remind readers that the Caribbean is a multilingual, multicultural space', it concentrates on stories from 'the cricket playing West Indies'. He contends that although this may reflect an English language bias, it is also a way of granting readers access to the traditions of Caribbean short story writing in a single volume.[1] His use of cricket as shorthand for Caribbean collectivity is both common and purposeful because the sport became a social institution able to demonstrate the potentiality of a united region on the world stage and it continues to hold a singularly significant place in the history, culture and popular imagination of the anglophone Caribbean. Cricket's ties to colonial history and anti-/post-colonial expressions of individual, national and regional independence have made it important to the identity construction and self-determination of the people and (is)lands represented by the West Indies team. The game's position – at the crossroads of colonial, postcolonial and globalising pressures – provides a sporting crystallisation of many of the socio-economic challenges faced by the Caribbean basin; issues which are also explored in Caribbean literature, sometimes via depictions of the game itself. Indeed, a sizeable number of writers have mobilised cricket in their work, with many, particularly within the short story form, drawing on it as part of their re-imagining of the Caribbean and their own childhood, often from a point of exile.

In the wider context of cricketing short stories by Sam Selvon, V.S. Naipaul, Beryl Gilroy, Jean Binta Breeze and Cyril Dabydeen, this discussion reads six works which concentrate on the engagement between the game, childhood and authorial reflections upon adolescent development and communal inclusion. To be explicit, these stories are: Michael Anthony's 'Cricket in the Road' from his 1973 collection of the same name; Paul Keens-Douglas's 'Me an' Cricket' from *Role Call* (1997); Earl McKenzie's 'Cricket Season' taken from *A Boy Names Ossie – A Jamaican Childhood* (1991); Ismith Khan's 'The Red Ball' from *A Day in the Country* (1994); 'King Rice' by Raywat Deonandan from *Sweet Like Saltwater* (1999); and 'The Propagandist' by Elahi Baksh from *Jahaji: An Anthology of Indo-Caribbean Fiction* (2000).[2] This cluster stretches across lands, races, religions and literary generations. Clearly, there is a strong gender bias, as one may expect, with male authors presenting young male protagonists, directly or loosely autobiographical, engaged in cricketing initiations. Pertinently, Valerie Shaw has described how the 'theme of initiation is more prominent in [short] stories dealing with boys, one reason being that their transitions into adulthood can be readily matched by events and settings which recall the conventions of narrative "adventures"'.[3] The rendering of cricket's physical challenges, group dynamics and moments of individual success seem to fit this sense of adventurous initiation and the game's relation to English tales of boyhood adventures which spread across the British Empire after *Tom Brown's School Days* (1857) is also relevant. Readers may notice that half the stories chosen are by authors of Trinidadian origin (Anthony, Keens-Douglas and Khan). As one of the larger, more affluent and culturally diverse islands, home to C.L.R. James and Brian Lara, this may not necessarily be restrictive. Markham has written that the 'short story from Trinidad has long been rich enough to represent the region's literature'[4] and we may see additional evidence for this claim. Finally, African- and Indian-Caribbean authors have been grouped separately not because communal segregation or animosity is supported but rather because the issue of communal antagonism is tackled more directly in the Indian-Caribbean pieces and these stories also lead us to patterns of exile and return more explicitly.

In *Caribbean Prose: An Anthology for Secondary Schools* (1967) – which included 'Cricket', the early prose poetry version of 'Rites',[5] Kamau Brathwaite's famous poem of cricketing/political 'indiscipline and irre-sponsibility'[6] – Andrew Salkey identifies the 'common factor' that 'shapes all short stories' as 'the writer's ability to highlight characterisation, human behaviour, or a small event, often an ordinary, everyday one, in such a way as to bring it alive for the reader as an immediately recognisable, meaning-ful entity'.[7] His sense of the vibrancy of the 'ordinary', the 'everyday', and the communicability of shared practices echoes Elizabeth Bowen's view of the short story as a composition just beneath 'peaks of common experi-ence'.[8] Such notions of the 'ordinary' and 'everyday' may also remind us of the social realism of barrack-yard fiction as pioneered by authors like C.L.R. James and Alfred Mendes and published in *The Beacon* and *Trinidad* literary journals in the 1920s and 1930s. The barrack-yard genre, with its concentration of short stories, worked to convey and explore the common experiences of poverty stricken lives in the yard spaces of Port of Spain, Trinidad, and developed a working-class literary lens for Caribbean au-thors to adopt and adapt for their own purposes. This tradition stands behind the stories addressed here and the essay presents cricket, and its literary depiction as a boyhood pastime in short stories, as demonstrating when and how the 'ordinary' is 'meaningful' in its densely politicised and social commonality. In addition, the game's relation to ideas of centre and margins, participation and exclusion, colonial exploitation and successful creolisation suggests such depictions can also be read within the larger argument that the short story is 'by its very nature [at a] remove from the community', as posited by Frank O'Connor in *The Lonely Voice* (1963).[9] In *Re-Reading the Short Story* (1989), Clare Hanson similarly sees it as 'a form from the margins, a form which is in some senses ex-centric',[10] and no sport touches upon the 'ex-centric' more overtly than cricket, the leisurely pastime most associated with the ex-centricities of Englishness; the game originally of England, the former (or 'ex') centre of the British Empire; and the sport now controlled by those previously colonised (the 'exes' of Empire) whose strength has relocated cricket's 'centre'.

Cricket is repeatedly portrayed by Caribbean short story writers as a form of exciting, animated, vivacious play used by young children, typically boys, as a means of finding themselves and their social connections, as a way of trying to relate to their peers and/or generational elders, as a means of (re)negotiating the social, political and economic restrictions that structure their lives, and as a means by which authors may examine experiences of alienation and marginality – national, racial, religious, communal and personal. It is also seen to teach boys about self-control, perseverance, concentration, humility, personal success and the rewards of collective endeavour. Although these lessons historically derive from imperial discourses of English dominance they have become locally profitable as strategies for exposing and resisting colonialism. Usefully, Susan Engel has outlined three key characteristics that writers representing childhood typically draw upon: 'emphasis on vivid sensation', 'dramatizing children's sense of intimacy with [...] and at the same time their sense of the distant weirdness of adults', and 'a quality of dysyncrony of time and space'.[11] These are certainly aspects found in these stories. Without wishing to imply that the short story is an appendage to, or a derivative of, the novel form, we may view the connection between cricket and childhood as part of a wider trend in Caribbean literature to repossess a younger self and thereby express the difficulties of 'establishing one's own voice'.[12] As Mary Condé argues, the representation of childhood can act as a 'refuge', a space of imaginative escape and return which allows authors to explore their former and current sense of self.[13] Further, in her book *Caribbean Autobiography: Cultural Identity and Self-Representation* (2002), Sandra Pouchet Paquet reflects upon James's classic text *Beyond a Boundary* (1963) and explains how his 'youthful passion for cricket and literature [is made to] coincide with the adult's passion for cricket, literature and politics in what appears to be a natural progression, linking childhood experience with the adult's perception of the truth'.[14] A parallel case exists in the way that cricket has been deployed in the Caribbean short story by authors reflecting back to cricket's place in the society of their own childhoods so that they can make their youthful experiences sit with their adult views of the world, the Caribbean and their own development.

APPROACHING THE GAME IN AFRICAN-CARIBBEAN STORIES

Michael Anthony's 'Cricket in the Road', the earliest of the examples discussed here, is in many ways typical of his writing style and his interest in sporting youth which is more substantially explored in *The Games Were Coming* (1963). Markham has posited that Anthony 'writes with a sincerity and charm, but the stories in *Cricket in the Road* (1973) seem slight, the tone sometimes uncertain' (Markham, p. xxviii). This criticism is certainly fair but Anthony's contribution is useful for the way in which cricket becomes an activity lost, desired and then recuperated. Set in coastal Mayaro, Trinidad, the short story draws upon a nostalgic recollection of Anthony's childhood in the early 1940s as he writes about things and places he knows and therefore 'believes in'.[15] He has acknowledged that although he only lived in Mayaro until he was nine he has repeatedly returned to this 'home' in his writing, feeling it to be an anchoring location for his imaginative repossession of the land of his boyhood, before he left, first for San Fernando as captured in *The Year in San Fernando* (1965), and later, in the mid-1950s, for England and a writing career that begin with the BBC's *Caribbean Voices* programme (Anthony, 'Discovering Literature', p. 86). Told in the first person, the immediacy and intimacy of Selo's narrative voice is compelling because of his innocence and emotional vulnerability. Kenneth Ramchand has written of Anthony's work with admiration for what he calls Anthony's 'open consciousness' which is largely 'achieved by a scrupulous adherence to the boy's point of view, in a deceptively easy style that carries the necessary sensuous burden while sustaining the illusion of adolescent reportage'.[16] His assessment, based primarily upon *The Year in San Fernando*, is also applicable to 'Cricket in the Road', though this story offers more 'resolution' than Ramchand sees in Anthony's novels of childhood.

Ensuring that the reader understands the emotional importance of the cricketing encounter to be described, the game is established as an ordinary activity but one whose rarity value is significant during the 'rainy season' when the children got 'few chances to play'.[17] The weather, the constant threat posed by a climate 'always overcast' (p. 40), betrays an impending interruption or disruption which is tied to a sense of anger, violence and doom as the sea and sky appear to haunt, chase and terrify the children and their game of cricket – most particularly Selo and his attempts to bat. There is a strong sense of localised oppression, of a 'death-like' threat (p. 41), with the sky acting as a 'low-hanging' ceiling (p. 40), holding everything down until eventually Selo hides under the bed, against the ground, beneath his warm sanctuary of sleep. Even the comfort and protection of his mother seems insufficient. Anthony situates Selo, and his boyish outbursts and fears, among a small community, and an even smaller group of friends, identified as the 'we' of 'the road' (p. 40). The simple tale of the separation and reunification of friends is concerned with the juxtaposition of 'we' – the collectivity – versus the 'I' of the isolated narrator, whose alienation only increases in the stormy weather and when he throws away his friend's cricket equipment because he is not permitted to bat first. As part of a 'we' playing cricket in the road, he is happy, content, excited and involved in a mini mixed-sex community. As an 'I', afraid of the weather, upset at feeling excluded, and outside of the brother/sister pairing of his friends, he is alone, frightened and inactive. This 'I' position, this individual as actor, is attached to his role as batsman, to his singular cricketing performance. Selo's re-entry into street cricket only comes when Vern and Amy invite him back, in the New Year, and allow him 'first bat' (p. 43), as he had desired (and thought was fair). The sense of his friends looking 'new' suggests his own reawakening and the distance caused by his outburst. 'Embarrassed', he accepts their gesture of friendship and 'crie[s] as though it were raining and [he] was afraid' (p. 43). The rain and tears of Selo, Vern and Trinidad are combined in youthful repatriation, in communal cricket and friendship. This can be read as a small example of Anthony's manifestation of a young nation. Commenting on both Anthony and Lovelace in an interview, James described them as 'native and national [writers] in a sense that the previous generation is not'.[18] Revisiting this view via Fredric Jameson's notion of 'national allegory'[19] and acknowledging Anthony's lack of overt nationalist content, Harney argues that 'nationalism for Anthony takes the form in allegory, of a coming to terms with what already exists as a community and nation in Trinidad'.[20] For Anthony was writing, first and foremost in his mind, 'to the Trinidadian' (Anthony cited in Harney, p. 34), and the community of cricketing children appears to represent his idealised version of the Trinidad of his (re)imagined past.

Moving on to a Trinidadian schoolboy's experience of cricket, Keens-Douglas's 'Me an' Cricket' offers a genre-stretching example which draws on his abilities as a performance artist and raconteur. In fact, he has repeatedly performed this piece as a kind of folk story and demonstrated its proximity to Reid's definition of a 'yarn', one of the short story's 'tributary forms'.[21] However, it is published in Role Call as a short story and meets Salkey's definitional criteria, making it an interesting example of the meeting point between oral and scribal traditions. Cynthia James positions Keens-Douglas as a transitional force in the move from 'Orature to Literature' in children's folk traditions between the 1970s and 1990s, asserting that he played an important role in the reclamation of a local folk voice and the literaturisation of creole orality.[22] As with most of Keens-

Douglas's work, humour and dialect are crucial to 'Me an' Cricket' as he tells an apparently 'autobiographical' but clearly exaggerated, if not fiction-alised, tale of his failed initiation into sport 'at school' in the 1950s.[23] His story claims that as a small twelve-year-old he realised that boys were defined by their size and sporting prowess and so attempted all of the three sports available to him: running, football and cricket. When he discovered that he had no talent for the first and no stomach for the physicality of the second he withdrew into cricket, the 'gentleman's game' (p. 42), where he initially enjoyed fielding in the deep, resting under the trees, and taking one big swing with the bat before returning to the shade. This pattern is upset when he accidentally takes a spectacular catch and his team mates lionise him as their new hero. However, when they discover that he actually cannot bat, bowl or field he retires from the game and takes up the 'de safest position in Cricket... Commentator' (p. 45).

What may appear a simple and unchallenging tale of comedic reminis-cence actually contains noteworthy moments of engaged social commen-tary. Throughout, Keens-Douglas undercuts the superficial criteria used to pick sports representatives – 'if yu look good yu get pick' (p. 41). He pokes fun at the clichéd 'cool pose' signified by dark 'shades' (p. 43) being worn while batting. He suggests that the stereotypical claim that West Indies cricketers are 'natural players' has some weight but that it derives from a lack of infrastructure, equipment, coaching, money and practice time which means that only those who seem talented at a very young age 'get pick' (p. 41). In addition, when asking 'Yu know how hard it is to keep yu head down and yu chin up?' (p. 43) he gestures toward a wider question about how any one in the Caribbean can keep their head 'down' in terms of work and simultaneously 'up' with optimistic hope for the future. Finally, Keens-Douglas mocks the tradition of finding a new player and claiming him a heroic saviour after a moment of individual glory. He narrates how his younger self accidentally took an amazing catch, was declared the 'nex' Sobers' and then approached for his 'autograph' by local people (p. 45). But this over-investment in a singular heroic moment and person is exposed as hollow, misplaced and a distraction from other performances in the team. Keens-Douglas's depiction of childhood is one that ironises cricket's assumed role in masculine development but also identifies how adult spectators/commentators/citizens, physically distant from the game, are still concerned with its social and political role – at the level of anecdote and critique. It is very different to other stories where individual moments of success are seen as fundamentally important to a boy's confidence and communal initiation.

Of the selected group, McKenzie's 'Cricket Season' is probably the most straightforward, positive and moral story of cricketing initiation. Set in the 1950s of McKenzie's own youth in Mount Charles, St Andrew, Jamaica, it presents Ossie as a well behaved and obedient young Jamaican boy who, having been given 'a coin' by his Uncle Basil, a 'hero' and soldier home on leave, earns and saves in order to buy an instructional cricket book.[24] After the money his father had taught him to save in the table-leg at home is stolen, along with the Sunday dinner, Ossie's luck is almost immediately turned around when he bowls out a sixteen-year-old local cricketing 'hero' (p. 22) to win a bet and begin his savings again, only this time with the institutional security of the Post Office. In this rural setting, McKenzie presents a strong, stable and supportive family structure, with an affection-ate father, being supplemented by communal education and the rewards of hard work. While the theft, seemingly by someone known but 'faceless' (p. 21), presents an internal danger and sense of social darkness, this is quickly overridden by Ossie's mother's charitable defence of the thieves as probably 'hungrier' (p. 22) than them. Nevertheless, it is through cricket that Ossie is able to define himself away from this protective domestic space. In the opening exchanges Ossie reveals himself as a 'spin bowler' (p. 19) and his uncle provides encouraging words of ambition stating he could grow up to be 'another Alfred Valentine' (p. 19). The reference to the Jamaican off spinner, one of the 'spin twins' who, along with Sonny Ramadhin, helped the West Indies defeat England for the first time in England during the 1950 tour, situates Ossie in a tradition of cricketing achievement and identifies his possible contribution to a collective, inter-racial, national project, i.e. the 'national team' (p. 19), as his uncle calls it. The portrayal of cricketers as role models, as heroes to worship and emulate, is notable as it becomes important to Ossie's entry into a form of sporting maturity and allows the repeated references to his small size to be offset by his bowling achievements. When the 'cricket season' (p. 20) arrives it does so at the international, representational level of West Indies against England at Sabina Park. The cricket 'excitement spread even to the remotest village in the hills' (p. 20), reaching out to those, like Ossie and McKenzie himself, far outside of Kingston. Yet, cricket also arrives at the local village level and, as Beryl Gilroy has written, 'Village matches were usually played on a Sunday and *everybody* attended them'.[25] It is after the success of the local village team in their Sunday match that Ossie takes on Vincent to win 'a ten dollar bill' (p. 22). This moment of victory, of self-confidence and bowling competency, appears to mark his entry into a cricketing community, winning even though a 'boy' (p. 23). His father, jovial in his pride, jokes: 'you are earning money from cricket and you are not even a test player yet' (p. 23). In essence, Ossie learns that his patience, effort and talent, when combined, are the makings of his own success; success he privately nurtures and for which he is publicly appreciated.

Interestingly, Vincent, Ossie's opponent, is portrayed in remarkably similar terms to James's description of Matthew Bondman in *Beyond a*

Boundary. McKenzie writes, 'It was well known that Vincent did poorly at school. But put a bat in his hand and he transformed: he became expressive, confident, masterful. He said things with his bat that he could not put into words.' (p. 22) James recalls Matthew's 'pitiable existence' and batting in some detail, the essence of which is contained in the statement: 'Matthew had one saving grace – Matthew could bat. More than that, Matthew, so crude and vulgar in every aspect of his life, with a bat in his hand was all grace and style'.[26] Matthew is used by James to stand for cricket's aesthetic possibilities and their execution by players from all social classes and racial groups. In 'C.L.R. James on Cricket as Art', McKenzie places James's sense of 'significant form' (i.e. cricketing style) within the context of formalist and expressionist aesthetic theories and agrees that cricket is aesthetic. McKenzie 'find[s] the view that a cricketer can express his emotions through his playing convincing';[27] a statement supported by his cricketing story, though this was written before his encounter with James's writing. He goes on to examine James's claim that a knowing spectator (or spectators) can recognise and respond to the aesthetic dimension of cricketing action and concludes that there is a 'continuum' from art to sport, although he resists naming cricket an art form. McKenzie's stance – that cricket falls short of an art form but contains aesthetic dimensions – is played out in his short story as Ossie's aesthetic bowling is matched by dedication, self-control, patience and confidence which win out over the aesthetic performativity of Vincent and are understood as the key tools for masculine development.

NEGOTIATING WITH INCLUSION IN INDIAN-CARIBBEAN STORIES

Cricket's association with the legacy of slavery and anti-colonial nationalist movements has meant that it has been linked to the rise (and freedom) of the African-Caribbean population, despite Indian-Caribbeans constituting approximately an equal proportion of the population in Trinidad and Guyana and representing the regional cricket team. Frank Birbalsingh and Clem Seecharan have traced the contribution of 'Indo-Westindian' cricketers to the West Indies team (a contribution which has only increased in recent years) and Birbalsingh's survey article 'The Indo-Caribbean Short Story' (2004) lays the foundations for a consideration of cricket's appearance within such writing.[28]

Ismith Khan stands out as one of the few well-known Muslim authors from the Caribbean and his story, 'The Red Ball', is a third person narrative depicting a young Muslim boy's attempts to approach the centre of social life in Port of Spain after his family have moved there from rural Tunapuna and found economic survival harder than anticipated. Each day after school this boy lingers in Woodford Square and slowly, over an entire week, he creeps closer to the other boys playing cricket. That is, he 'stayed outside the centre' awaiting an opportunity for inclusion on his own terms.[29] Understandably, given Khan's familiarity with the location and scenario, the importance of Woodford Square is repeatedly underlined. The boy feels that is it the 'only place [...] where people were not chasing him down' (p. 9) as they were at school and at home. This is also the space left by the British and Spanish colonials for him, a boy from the 'sugarcane fields' (p. 9). In effect, he is the inheritor of all that has been and stands at the heart of the nation, in the public space that would become, for Eric Williams and his generation, the site for the University of the Masses, the People's Parliament. Passing his time on the periphery, he wades in the water of the fountain, a gift from the Scottish Governor George Turnball in 1866, admires the strength of Triton, son of Poseidon and god of the sea, and seeks comfort from the surrounding female figures. The boy repeatedly resists the diminutive calls of 'Thinney Boney' (p. 7) despite his desire to participate, to be included, until he is finally invited to play and asked his name. He identifies himself – first as Bolan and then as a new and devastating fast bowler. As for Ossie, the cricket ball is Bolan's weapon of self-articulation, a 'red hot' (p. 10) bolt of self-knowledge and confidence being used to gain admiration and acceptance as he bowls them 'all down before they could see the ball' (p. 10). Yet after such cricketing triumph he is forced to make 'indefinite gestures' (p. 11) to the sausage vendor because of his poverty, pushing him back to the edge of the group until he feels compelled to 'disappear' (p. 11), retreating homeward. When he returns the next day the boys are 'waiting for [him]' (p. 15), marking his inclusion, his acceptance based on merit. He is now their 'star bowler' (p. 15) and he reveals a 'shiny red cork ball, brand new' (p. 15). Bolan's journey toward the city of his nation and the community of his peers is charted in his sporting journey from the old tennis balls of the wealthy in Tunapuna to his own new red cricket ball. He reinforces his claim to social entry by buying the group the sausage he previously could not afford. However, the arrival of his father shatters this moment of camaraderie as it is revealed that Bolan has paid for the ball and food by taking his family's savings and must now be punished at home.

The move back toward home occurs twice, each time after his cricketing encounter, ensuring that it is a place/space away from his sense of hope and enjoyment; a point captured by the juxtaposition of laughter 'all around' (p. 11) and silence or arguments inside. Living, like Khan himself, at the end of Frederick Street, Bolan's home is just outside the centre. His father, a cutlassman, is struggling with the new life which appears to cause his clothes to smell of grass and his body of rum and cigarettes. He attacks Bolan's education and mocks the way that this education has altered Bolan's pronunciation of the word 'nowhere' so that to his father's ear it sounds like a dismissive response of 'nowhere' when he demands to know where Bolan has been after school (pp. 11–12). By always failing to use Bolan's name, his father refuses to grant him the individual recognition his mother demands and which he gained among his cricketing peers. Yet his father's verbal assaults are repeatedly unfinished, stuck in his throat as he pauses, 'swallows hard' (p. 13) or falls asleep. Knowing that he uses his mother as a 'defence' (p. 16), Bolan is shown to fear his proximity to the unhappiness of his parents and their poverty. When at home he is understood as 'waiting for something he couldn't describe' (p. 13), something he was 'released from' (p. 13) when playing cricket and which must be acceptance and recognition. After Bolan 'thief' (p. 16) the family savings, his father's physical punishment draws 'red welts' (p. 16) on his son's skin and only ends when fatigue allows the mother to intercede and reclaim her half of Bolan's flesh and blood. On seeing the cricket ball she knows what has occurred and asks her son if he 'remember[s] how to bowl' (p. 17) because she understands that this was the physical competency that had secured his social acceptance and made him happy. His mother uses the water pipe in the yard to help heal his wounds and offer him comfort, reminding the reader of the consolation/reassurance Bolan earlier sought and gained from the Triton's female followers. That night, as he lies in pain on the floor asleep, Bolan dreams that the man from the fountain, that figure of Triton is speaking to him, declaring his love and affection, but the smell of his father reveals that his imaginary Triton is really his father laying beside him and attempting to connect, in silence and anonymity, with his sleep-filled son. The father, by becoming combined with Triton, becomes the voice of the nation, a collective nation of the sea, of those brought across the water now struggling not to drown.

Also touching upon journeys across the vast water are 'King Rice' and 'The Propagandist', remarkably similar stories emerging from the diaspora in Canada and readdressing childhood experiences of cricket 'mad' characters who are fanatical supporters of their local village teams in Guyana, 'back home' as Deonandan writes. The texts share the tone, humour and style of Naipaul's *Miguel Street* (1959) and like Naipaul's 'Man-man' or 'B Wordsworth', the leading figures have communal identities based on their actions and the social acceptance of their behaviour as Bungy the 'funny man' becomes 'King Rice'[30] and Ramkissoon 'the godlike peasant' becomes 'The Propagandist'.[31] Both men are deemed to be, to some degree, insane and it is the extremes to which they go that increases the ironic humour and compelling humanity of these stories.

In 'King Rice' Deonandan describes how 'the entire village was made for cricket' (p. 17), with Bungy 'rallying' (p. 18) the support for the local team by attending every game – home and away – by ritualising his attendance by taking a 'lucky' (p. 19) bat and packed lunch, and by defending the reputation of his team and their chances of success to the point of 'physical

violence' (p. 17). He is claimed as 'our hero' (p. 19) and presents the voice
of political dissent by wearing a noose instead of a neck tie and introducing
himself to the new governor, Mr Carruthers, as 'a slave' (p. 19). In such
ways he is the communal showman and performer, their voice and reveller,
their leader and collaborator. The story's pivotal action is the grand finale
of the Demerara Cup 'between the rice farmers of Windsor Forest and the
sugar plantation workers of neighbouring Eyeflood [...] this match would
pit the imperialist sponsored sugar team against our intrepid heroes from
the autonomous mudlands' (p. 18). Deonandan goes on to contrast the
cricket grounds of the two teams: 'And the venue would be the enemy's
home fortress, the Eyeflood Cricket Ground, built and maintained splen-
didly with imperialist sugar money; a far cry from the dung-scattered
sandtrap against the seawall back in Windsor Forest' (p. 18). The fact that
the Windsor team has to play on the low lying land, where games are
interrupted by the 'rising water level' (p. 18), is presented as a hindrance:
'Not many people have played cricket well *under* the Caribbean' (p. 18).
This is the division, the political and cricketing opposition that structures
the story, determined, above all else, by land ownership and occupation.
When Bungy is late and without his bat, the travelling Windsor supporters
worry over the bad omen and this is exacerbated by the 'terrible start'
(p. 19) of their team. Yet: 'Bungy reached into his bag and pulled out a
handful of the finest Guyanese rice [...]. He scattered them over his
audience, bellowing: "King Rice!" Then, in a more guttural tone [...]
"Slave sugar"' (p. 20) at those who are wearing the 'brilliant white cotton
uniforms' (pp. 19–20) as if to reinforce their moneyed support, their white
connections and their exploitative relationship with slavery (cotton and
sugar). This fails to change the outcome of the game, Windsor Forest still
lose, but they find their way into the game, they play with pride and
'courage' (p. 20). This mad-man leader forces them to show the resilience
of their independent community on the field of imperialist-sponsored
play. As Seecharan has articulated, '[i]ngrained in the Indo-Guyanese
psyche is the idea of being a victim of King Sugar' and the ascension of 'King
Rice' subverts this authoritarian dominance.[32]

Seecharan also unpacks the way a 'strong sense of Indian identity [...]
emerged on the Guyanese estates' (Seecharan, p. 72) and this side to the
sugar estate legacy is revealed in 'The Propagandist' where the key protago-
nist/propagandist tells tall tales in order to aggrandise himself but on
winning a substantial cricket-based bet he fails to pay a fair proportion to
the anonymous boy narrator who had helped prove him right. Baksh
presents Ramkissoon as a self-declared 'born coolie' (p. 15) with a body
shaped and coloured by 'years of cutting and loading sugar cane' (p. 15)
with which he imitates or adopts independence by squatting on the land
and overseeing his wife and daughter's cultivation of a garden. Ramkisson

becomes the 'Propagandist' after continually using the word to dismiss the opinions of others in order to 'pontificate' (p. 17) and valorise his own thoughts, most of which he has gleaned from the recycled newspapers of the narrator. 'Propaganda', the narrator says, 'was a completely new word for us, and by its length and weight alone, it was somewhat mysterious. None of us knew what it meant' (p. 17). It is through such confident mystification that Ramkissoon becomes 'honoured as a reliable commentator on the current affairs of Guyana, the Caribbean and the world' (p. 18) and he uses this new power to reject the social initiatives of the new British Director of the Sugar Estate and to speak of India and Indian cricket, sprinkling his view with 'a few words of Hindi' (p. 18) to legitimise himself and evoke an emotional allegiance to those looking back across the water to where their ancestors had originated. The narrator knows of the Propagandist's lies and embellishments – including the claim that Lala Amarnath, the Indian captain, had punched an umpire – but he is also surprised to discover that the Propagandist's greatest claim – that Vijay Hazare, captain between 1951 and 1953, scored two centuries in a game, something at that time only achieved by one West Indian player, the great George Headley – was actually true. (Hazare did this against Australia in 1947/48.) The Propagandist wins a bet with this information but the narrator, who found the evidence, only receives 'a twelve-cent coin' (p. 23). He feels cheated and cannot, even as an adult, forgive him.

This bet, which pits West Indian pride against Indian achievement, brings into focus the key aspect of the story: the way that the Propagandist is allowed to bring out the racial divisions, pride and jealousies between the Indian and African Guyanese communities and the way these tensions were filtered through cricket when the Indian team toured the Caribbean in 1953. Those who had never seen a cricket match are described as journeying to Georgetown, the centre, 'simply to catch a glimpse of these cricketers, who, if they were not film stars, were at least true Indians' (p. 19), as ideas of originality and authenticity are brought to the surface by their presence. The narrator confesses that the community 'only pretended to be shocked by the Propagandist's partiality towards India while we joined in instinctively with the humour of his racist jokes putting down West Indian cricketers who were mostly Afro-West Indian' (p. 19). He remembers feeling that he 'longed to see those Afro-Guyanese swallow their racial pride' (p. 21) and is surprised that no violence breaks out between the two groups over the Propagandist's stance. This racial division is then seen in the political groups and election campaigns that follow as the Propagandist takes up a new role as the local heckler of political speakers, as he takes bribes from all sides while siding with none. Eventually the PFP candidate wins, as was expected. The close of the story brings about two moments of telling change, one with the election after which 'nothing in

Guyana would ever be the same' (p. 28) and another with the death of the Propagandist, which the adult narrator has recently heard of and which sparks this recollection. This ending, this movement away from the land and characters of Baksh's childhood, seems to remind the narrative/authorial voice of the forces which pushed the Propagandist out, away from his peers and community, especially the unresolved historical legacies of indentureship, continuing political exclusion, enduring communal divisions, and a perpetual sense of limited personal and collective horizons. Baksh says: 'the world that drove him to death has also driven me into exile' (p. 30) and our bond is a 'bond that links more than the two of us' (p. 30). Here he appreciates this 'bond' as uniting the diaspora, calling together creole speakers who may face a sense of enforced expulsion, of being pushed back, outside, toward a periphery that is a Western centre.

The authors considered here, living abroad or working with international horizons, re-cross time and water to revisit, perhaps even re-embody, the cricketing boyhood of their own personal or at least cultural past. By presenting the game, one saturated in local and regional politics very much understood by its participants and viewers, as play and promise, as potential inclusion and as evidence of social exclusion, they reawaken their own feelings of separation, alienation and marginalisation, most often from 'home' and male acceptance. At the same time, cricket is seen to provide boys, and the men writing of them, with a sense of freedom and confidence that indicates youthful, communal and national potential. This sense of possibility is still being worked through in the Caribbean and its short story tradition.

NOTES

1 Stewart Brown, 'Introduction', in *The Oxford Book of Caribbean Short Stories*, ed. by Stewart Brown and John Wickham (Oxford: Oxford University Press, 1999), pp. xiii–xxxiii (p. xiii).
2 Almost all of the short stories discussed here will appear in *The Bowling Was Superfine: West Indian Writing and West Indian Cricket*, edited by Stewart Brown and Ian McDonald. However, for reference purposes they have been taken from their original publications and the page references for each of these stories can be found in the bibliography. Although V.S. Naipaul's story 'Hat' from *Miguel Street* would seem to be within the bounds of this discussion, I have previously explored this work elsewhere.
3 Valerie Shaw, *The Short Story: A Critical Introduction* (London: Longman, 1983), p. 198.
4 E.A. Markham, 'Introduction', in *The Penguin Book of Caribbean Short Stories*, ed. by E.A. Markham (London: Penguin, 1996), pp. xi–xlv (p. xi).
5 Edward Kamau Brathwaite, 'Rites', in *The Arrivants: A New World Trilogy* (Oxford: Oxford University Press, 1973), pp. 197–203.
6 Hilary McD. Beckles, *The Development of West Indies Cricket: Volume 1. The Age of Nationalism* (London: Pluto, 1998), p. 107.
7 Andrew Salkey, 'Introduction', in *Caribbean Prose: An Anthology for Secondary Schools*,

ed. by Andrew Salkey (London: Evan Brothers, 1967), pp. 7–11 (p. 8).

8 Elizabeth Bowen 'Introduction', in *The Faber Book of Modern Stories*, ed. by Elizabeth Bowen (London: Faber, 1937), p. 19.

9 Frank O'Connor, *The Lonely Voice: A Study of the Short Story* (London: Macmillan, 1963), p. 21.

10 Clare Hanson, 'Introduction', in *Re-Reading the Short Story*, ed. by Clare Hanson (Basingstoke: Macmillan, 1989), pp. 1–9 (p. 2).

11 Susan Engel, 'Looking Backward: Representations of Childhood in Literary Work', *Journal of Aesthetic Education*, 33:1 (1999), 50–55 (pp. 51–53).

12 Judith Misrahi-Barak, 'The Detours of Narrative Voice: a Precondition of Self-Narration in Caribbean Literature', *Commonwealth Essays and Studies* 19:1 (1996), 71–79 (p. 71).

13 Mary Condé, 'Unlikely Stories: Children's Invented Worlds in Caribbean Women's Fiction', *Commonwealth Essays and Studies* 15:1 (1992), 69–75 (p. 70).

14 Sandra Pouchet Paquet, *Caribbean Autobiography: Cultural Identity and Self-Representation* (Madison: University of Wisconsin, 2002), p. 150.

15 C.L.R. James and Michael Anthony, 'Discovering Literature in Trinidad: Two Experiences', *Journal of Commonwealth Literature* 7 (1967), 73–87 (p. 82).

16 Kenneth Ramchand, *The West Indian Novel and Its Background* (London: Faber, 1970), p. 212.

17 Michael Anthony, 'Cricket in the Road', in *Cricket in the Road* (London: Heinemann, 1973), pp. 40–43 (p. 40).

18 C.L.R. James, 'Interview', in *Kas Kas: Interviews with Three Caribbean Writers in Texas*, ed. by Ian Munro and Reinhard Sander, pp. 23–41 (pp. 30–31).

19 Fredric Jameson, 'Third World Literature in the Era of Multinational Capitalism', *Social Text*, 15 (1986), 65–88.

20 Steve Harney, 'Nation Time: Earl Lovelace and Michael Anthony Nationfy Trinidad', *Commonwealth Essays and Studies*, 13:2 (1991), 31–41 (pp. 35–36).

21 Ian Reid, *The Short Story* (London: Methuen, 1977), p. 33.

22 Cynthia James, 'From Orature to Literature in Jamaican and Trinidadian Children's Folk Traditions', *Children's Literature Association Quarterly*, 30:2 (2005), 164–78 (p. 170).

23 Paul Keens-Douglas, 'Me an' Cricket', in *Role Call: Poetry and Short Stories by Paul Keens-Douglas* (Trinidad: Keensdee Productions, 1997), pp. 41–45 (p. 41).

24 Earl McKenzie, 'Cricket Season', in *A Boy Names Ossie – A Jamaican Childhood* (Oxford: Heinemann, 1991), pp. 19–24 (p. 19).

25 Beryl Gilroy, 'Village Cricket', in *Sunlight on Sweet Water* (Leeds: Peepal Tree, 1994), pp. 101–04 (p. 101) [emphasis added].

26 C.L.R. James, *Beyond a Boundary* (London: Serpent's Tail, 2000), p. 4.

27 Earl McKenzie, 'C.L.R. James on Cricket as Art', *Caribbean Quarterly*, 40:3&4 (1994), 92–98 (p. 95).

28 See Frank Birbalsingh, 'The Indo-Caribbean Short Story', *Journal of West Indian Literature* 12:1&2 (2004), 118–35; Frank Birbalsingh and Clem Seecharan, *Indo-West Indian Cricket* (London: Hansib, 1988).

29 Ismith Khan, 'The Red Ball', in *A Day in the Country and Other Stories* (Leeds: Peepal Tree, 1994), pp. 7–17 (p. 8).

30 Raywat Deonandan, 'King Rice', in *Sweet Like Saltwater* (Toronto: TSAR, 1999), pp. 16–20 (p. 16).

31 Elahi Baksh, 'The Propagandist', in *Jahaji: An Anthology of Indo-Caribbean Fiction*, ed. by Frank Birbalsingh (Toronto: TSAR, 2000), pp. 15–30 (p. 15).

32 Clem Seecharan, 'The Shaping of the Indo-Caribbean People: Guyana and Trinidad to the 1940s', *Journal of Caribbean Studies*, 14:1&2 (1999/2000), 61–92 (p. 71).

PART THREE

MODERNITY AND MODERNISMS

CLAUDE MCKAY, ERIC WALROND AND THE LOCATIONS OF BLACK INTERNATIONALISM

DAVE GUNNING

Claude McKay (born Jamaica, 1890) and Eric Walrond (born in British Guiana 1898, but raised also in Barbados and Panama) each came to particular prominence in the United States of the 1920s, as part of the movement still most commonly known as the Harlem Renaissance. Walrond produced only one major work, the collection of stories, *Tropic Death* (1926). McKay was already a well-regarded poet when he turned to fiction, and is now probably best remembered for his three completed novels. However, he also produced a collection of stories, *Gingertown* (1932). In this essay I wish to explore some of the ways in which McKay has been located as working within a particular network of global black consciousness, but also to question why this reading so often concentrates on his novels when *Gingertown* seems to offer such clear evidence of this strand of his thought. Walrond's stories of the Caribbean also offer a sense of the international, but articulate this vision very differently to McKay's. Recent work by Brent Hayes Edwards and, especially, Michelle Stephens, has challenged the notion of locating these writers solely within the context of the Harlem Renaissance as too limiting. The current essay wants to build on this work in the hope of finding appropriate ways to read these important collections of short stories which emphasise their internationality.

Suffering from ill health, as well as financial difficulties not unrelated to the worsening global impact of the Great Depression, Claude McKay left France in 1930, where he had lived for the previous six years, and settled in Tangiers, Morocco.[1] He would live there until the end of 1933 and complete both *Gingertown* and his last novel *Banana Bottom* (1933) from this North African base. His publishers, Harper, were awaiting the delivery of his third novel as he left, but he decided instead to submit to them his first collection of stories (a mini-collection of stories written while he was in Russia was published in Moscow in 1925 under the title *Sudom Lincha*, but was not translated back into English until long after his death).[2] While McKay hoped that his collection would restore his financial stability, *Gingertown* received, at best, mild praise from American critics, and at worst, outright censure. For the reviewer at the *Boston Evening Transcript*, the collection could be 'no help to the Negro race', as it depicted its black New Yorkers as 'lewd, wanton, gross, vulgar, vicious, incestuous and generally obsessed with a desire to break the bounds of racial barriers'.[3] The review is reminiscent of the storm that greeted his first novel, *Home to Harlem*,[4] which was condemned from across the African American political spectrum for its gritty portrayal of a seedy urban existence (while Marcus Garvey described the author of *Home to Harlem* as a 'literary prostitute', W.E.B. Du Bois famously wrote that 'after [reading] the dirtier parts of its filth I feel distinctly like taking a bath').[5] However, while *Home to Harlem* was a bestseller that seemed to cement McKay's reputation, *Gingertown* sold poorly and its failure contributed to McKay's eventual decline into poverty. Nonetheless, the collection of twelve stories, with six set in Harlem, four in Jamaica, one in Marseilles, and one in North Africa, seems to offer a useful fictional tracing of the multiple locations in which McKay himself found residence throughout his itinerant life and to capture some sense of the movement which defined him (Mary Conroy notes that he had wanted to give his 1937 autobiography, *A Long Way from Home*, the far less nostalgic title *Keep on Going*).[6] In particular, an examination of *Gingertown* can offer an interesting way into exploring McKay's specific relationship to those ideas of connection and affiliation that have become known as black internationalism.

Towards the end of *A Long Way from Home*, McKay tells the story of an encounter with a Moroccan *chaoush* (a 'native doorman and messenger'), sent from the British Consulate to enquire as to McKay's nationality:

> I said I was born in the West Indies and lived in the United States and that I was an American, even though I preferred to think of myself as an internationalist. The *chaoush* said he didn't understand what was an internationalist. I laughed and said that an internationalist was a bad nationalist.[7]

This sense of living within an international frame of reference, even when that can be best defined in opposition to the comforts offered by national belonging, is intrinsic to McKay's conception of himself throughout his autobiography and beyond. For Michelle Stephens, the local struggles for national status in which black people participated were constituted against global imperialist forms; the quest for self-determination 'would have to occur as a transnational one' and the political vision of such figures as McKay tended naturally therefore to '*international racial* formations, transnational race-based networks'.[8]

In their important 2000 position paper that seeks to open up the concept of diaspora to account for the international connections and continuities of influence among black communities, Tiffany Patterson and Robin Kelley locate black internationalism as articulating around a conception of shared difference that need not retreat to a sense of racial essentialism: 'black internationalism does not always come out of Africa, nor is it necessarily engaged with pan-Africanism or other kinds of black-isms'.[9] Diaspora is considered as process, based on an experiential sense of what may link diverse African-descended communities without the need for a point of origin which serves to unify these manifestations into a single determined narrative. Brent Hayes Edwards's *The Practice of Diaspora* (2003) serves as one of the most important studies which takes this sense of a global, though multifaceted, consciousness to examine a particular manifestation of black cultural production. Edwards's focus is the Harlem Renaissance, which he looks to free from its customary location within the national racial narratives of the United States. Instead, he wishes to explore the flourishing of creative talent that is understood to constitute this movement and which seems centred around post-1919 New York and to place it within a new, transnational framework, to recognise that 'the "New Negro" movement is at the same time a "new" black internationalism'.[10] His key site that informs this revisionary enterprise, offering an interlocutionary location against which the Harlem movement plays itself out, is the city of Paris, to which so many of the ideas and ideals that shape the Renaissance are transported, and from which they return, finding new forms and reinvested with new power. However, the danger remains that, in rejecting the single dynamic location of New York in favour of this transatlantic connection, Edwards instead offers a still-limited focus on just two locations, neglecting other crucial sites of cultural development.

For Stephens, this 'sense in which Paris becomes a new abstraction' is especially flawed for its neglect of another space which provides both source and crucible for many of the key changes Edwards wishes to address – the Caribbean:

> [T]he Caribbean [is] an alternative locality that eludes him, Caribbeanness, West Indianness, Antilleanness – the historical consciousness that radical West Indians bring with them to metropolitan sites – is a key context for their internationalist turn as they constructed Pan-African and Pan-Caribbean solidarities in both Europe and the United States throughout the early twentieth century.[11]

A recognition that the Caribbean origin of many of the crucial figures of the New Negro movement is central to understanding its particular internationalist inflection is, for Stephens, the missing element of Edwards's *The Practice of Diaspora*. She sees the 'shadow haunting Edwards's account' as precisely its failure to explore black internationalism in relation to the familiarity with the past and continuing imperialism under which Caribbean radicals were formed, 'the black subject's revelatory and radicalizing experience of his or her own alienated structural relationship, as a colonial subject, to the metropolitan state' ('Disarticulating Black Internationalism', p. 107). In her own full-length study of the manifestations of black internationalism, the Caribbean is seen as the location within which the impulse toward global racial unities might best be understood:

> [T]he Caribbean has the potential to enact multiple identifications among
> colonial populations of different races and to create societies that could
> model the types of multinational and multiracial democratic formations
> that were beyond the limits of Europe's and America's global political
> imaginations in the world created after 1919. (*Black Empire*, p. 30)

McKay's second novel, *Banjo* (1929), is central to both Edwards's and
Stephens's models of black internationalism (Stephens explicitly locates it
as 'a more truly transnational text in form and content than either *Home to
Harlem* or McKay's later novel, *Banana Bottom*' (*Black Empire*, p. 177)).[12]
However, it is in both of these critics' identification of the form of the novel
as central to its internationalist flavour that we can find one useful way into
examining *Gingertown*, the collection of stories that followed it.

Edwards notes that 'nearly all the contemporary reviews of *Banjo*
comment on the subtitle [*A Story without a Plot*], often in order to claim the
book is not a novel at all' (*The Practice of Diaspora*, p. 190). He goes on to
suggest that the loose picaresque structure of the novel provides an ideal
mirroring (indebted to musical forms) of the 'vagabond internationalism'
that McKay wants to portray (*The Practice of Diaspora*, p. 198). Stephens
takes this further. Having first suggested that McKay's turn from poetry to
the novel in the mid-1920s 'can be interpreted as his attempt to write the
New World Negro into the nation' (*Black Empire*, p. 142), she then reads
his open structure as itself a challenge to a nationalist imagination:

> If narratives of nationhood are also narratives of the self, fictions of identity,
> a story without a plot gives reader and writer a certain latitude in writing
> and imagining the self. It also frees writer and reader from imagining
> that self within the limited confines of the nation, as African American,
> African, and Caribbean characters move through a metropolitan, rather
> than a colonial landscape. (*Black Empire*, p. 195)

The freely colliding stories that make up *Banjo*, then, seem to embody the
contingent and ever renewable axes of connection that make up transnational
diasporas. But, given this notion that the fluid form might serve to capture
the complicated cultural location of the novel, we can perhaps begin to
understand how the stories that make up *Gingertown* extend this sense of
plurality and can be seen as an attempt to move away from the novel form
because of the restrictions its totality enforces upon the types of diasporic
identities that might be expressed.

'The Jungle and the Bottoms', the novel on which McKay was working
for Harper in 1930, was to have a similar picaresque structure to *Banjo*, and
was also set in Marseilles. However, McKay grew increasingly unsure as to
whether he felt able to complete the project, or whether he even wanted to.
He increasingly complained to friends that he had wearied of writing in the
picaresque mode. Convinced that his short stories would prove a welcome
and inventive change of form, he wrote to Max Eastman, 'they will show

that I am a writer of many moods and open the way for any book or any theme I may choose to write instead of my being taken solely as a writer of picaresque stories' (quoted in Cooper, *Claude McKay*, p. 269). Few critics have taken seriously McKay's view here that the stories might open up new conceptions of form for him, and that the collection might therefore profitably be examined as a whole. Even the critics who begin their discussion of *Gingertown* by noting that 'the collection illustrates the importance of the short story in the development of his fiction', find by the end of their discussion that the only praise they can offer is in relation to the longer works: 'Even though the Harlem stories cannot withstand the criticism of being a trifle artificial, his Jamaican stories dealing with less hackneyed subjects are quite authentic [...]. Indeed, they serve as a prelude to *Banana Bottom*.'[13]

Yet attention to the stories in their own right might perhaps allow us to conceive of another way of expressing black internationalism; the form allows McKay to conceptualise black internationalism differently to the novels, and in a way that moves from the Romantic individualism that can be so easily associated with his longer works. Both *Home to Harlem* and *Banjo* end inconclusively, as the protagonists move on to further adventures without taking the reader with them. The compressed space of the short story, however, tends much more easily to closure. If the sense of Jake, Ray and Banjo continuing to live within the fluctuations of global black cultures is vital to the denouements of the novels, the short stories have more definite endings, framing neatly their status as contained moments within these cultures, shaped by the unending processes of changes but available at any time for synchronic analysis. The multiple points of entry into and egress from international black experience afforded by the story collection also allow for productive disjunctions which cannot have the same power in the novels; while the Haitian Ray (who is a supporting figure in the first novel, and the main protagonist of the second) can experience a overwhelming sense of the diversity of black life as he moves from the Caribbean, to the United States, to Europe, and beyond, the cultural force of this multiplicity is nonetheless muted through its containment within the narrative of a single individual. The glimpses of plural black experiences that make up *Gingertown*, however, gain their unity only through an authorial or readerly consciousness willing to bring them together. The title directs us towards the local, to contained and knowable community. The intercontinental movement of the stories seems to push in the other direction, but is nonetheless unified by a sense of the imagined communities that might connect these distinct American, Caribbean, European and African locations.

'Brownskin Blues', the opening story of *Gingertown*, begins within the rain of a 'sloppy, disagreeable evening' on Lenox Avenue. The physicality of black Harlem is present, even as the weather forbids the usual activities of the 'young joy-lovers' and 'colored gangsters' who usually animate the place. As the action focuses upon a basement cabaret, we are introduced to the as-yet unnamed Bess and Jack in terms that wilfully combine the human, the social, and the external physical world: she wears 'a nigger-brown frock'; his 'complexion [is] the color and coarseness of brown wrapping paper'.[14] A mood is set that will dominate much of the six Harlem-based stories that begin the collection: the reality of skin colour is the dominant social signifier in McKay's vision of the city, whether in the divisions between black and white most clearly laid out in 'Near White' and 'Highball' or the wish for seemingly more desirable lighter brown skin that eventually leads Bess to disfigure herself with bleaching creams in 'Brownskin Blues'. Harlem is a place full of human vitality, but nonetheless remains a prison of sorts for its black residents, restricting them in ways that are simultaneously physical, social, and experienced at the level of the individual body. Angie, the heroine of 'Near White', who finds in her brief romance with the white John West a chance to experience the 'vast pleasure world' of the city, distinct from 'the narrow life of Harlem', is tempted by the seductive appeal of 'passing' as white (*Gingertown*, p. 81). Yet when she broaches the topic in order to sound the water with her lover, the realities of racial discrimination hit home hard:

> 'Supposing it was you, John, with a quadroon girl or octoroon, could you still love her?'
> 'Me! I'd sooner love a toad!'
> Her heart stopped dead. (*Gingertown*, p. 102)

The chance of mobility is abruptly curtailed and Angie is confined again not only to Harlem, but also to her abject body, now not just black, but that of a beast. Harlem here is a space of defined and inflexible boundaries; a location that enforces stunted identities among its black inhabitants.

The sense of Harlem as a racial ghetto which dehumanises those who are confined within it lends a bleak note to the stories. Even 'Mattie and her Sweetman', which Conroy characterises as the most 'humorously' offered of the stories ('The Vagabond Motif', p. 20), pulls the reader up with the chilling description of Mattie strangling at birth the child she had conceived with a white man (*Gingertown*, p. 60). Yet the collection does not wholly rule out the possibility of hope. The six and seventh stories, 'Truant' and 'The Agricultural Show', form a hinge at the centre of the collection that allows a fuller understanding both of how internationalism might revivify Harlem, and also of its role within Caribbean culture. Barclay Oram, the protagonist of 'Truant', is the only West Indian character given a major role in the Harlem section of *Gingertown* and his status as an educated man working as a Pullman waiter suggests a strong autobiographical link to McKay (see *A Long Way from Home*, pp. 3–9). On a run to

Washington, Barclay feels an irresistible urge to go 'truant', and fails to board the train back to New York. When he does return, he is suspended from work for ten days. Finding in the suspension a sense of freedom, he is dismayed when his wife fails to share his enthusiasm. Left alone to baby-sit, his thoughts turn to the vision of Harlem as a prison, a vision mobilised through his nostalgic memories of a Caribbean past: 'Why was he, a West Indian peasant boy, held prisoner within the huge granite-gray walls of New York?' (*Gingertown*, p. 152). This is not a simple acclamation of a simple rural life offered in opposition to urban discontentment, as the reference to the peasantry might suggest. In fact, Barclay is open about his love for the city and refuses the distinction between the pastoral and metropolitan life: 'The steel-framed poetry of cities did not crowd out but rather intensified in him the singing memories of his village life. He loved both, the one complementing the other' (*Gingertown*, p. 159). It is not the modernity of cities which alienates him, but the oppressive philosophies bound up within them: 'Oh, he could understand and love the poetry of them but not their law that held humanity gripped in fear' (*Gingertown*, p. 161).

As Barclay flees New York in favour of a life of 'eternal inquietude' (*Gingertown*, p. 162), the collection too leaves Harlem, and does not return. 'The Agricultural Show', which details the organising of the titular event in a small Jamaican village, might seem the complete opposite of the urban claustrophobia of the story which precedes it. Robert Bone certainly found in it the antithesis of Harlem chaos, offering a folkish sense of timelessness craved by McKay after his years of itinerancy:

> McKay's Jamaican pastoral with its images of racial harmony and social peace, is an objective correlative of the inner harmony that he so desperately seeks. Split and shredded by his contact with the Western world, he returns in his imagination to Jamaica in order to reconstitute his soul.[15]

Bone's reading is similar to those that find a simple retreat to a folk heritage in *Banana Bottom*; it is also equally misguided.[16] The 'folk' as seen in 'The Agricultural Show' are by no means straightforward and the story continually reminds us that the Caribbean forever looks outwards, even when articulating a sense of authenticity rooted in its own soil (Matthew Bright's refusal to rename the Agricultural Show a 'Parish Fair' can perhaps be seen as an instance of this rejection of parochialism (*Gingertown*, p. 171)). The key figures of the community who come together to stage the exceptionally successful show speak of an international set of connections that have little to do with an unproblematic folk consciousness: Matthew is a druggist whose career is made possible by studying under a doctor who in turn attended a European university; the second most active member of his committee is Madame Daniel, the wife of the local 'Aframerican' preacher; and the two families of greatest influence in the town are that of the

Panama-returned 'yellow native' Mr Andry and the creolised white Busha Glengley. At the show itself, the visiting Governor is presented with an 'old Negro exhibit': a ninety-six-year-old man, old enough to remember slavery and abolition. Yet, as David Nicholls points out, the presence of the nonagenarian is not a testament to the preservation of an old way of life but instead allows the changing history of the region to be mapped 'as an alternative figuration within the discourse on Jamaican modernity'; one in which the modern world is simultaneously imported into and forged within the island's rural spaces.[17] While 'Truant' demonstrates that a future-orientated vision is only possible in Harlem once its inhabitants find ways to connect productively across international spaces, 'The Agricultural Show' might be seen to make exactly the same point about rural Jamaica. Their contiguity within *Gingertown* not only reminds us of the similarity of these ideas, but also suggests that they may in fact be part of a single process of black internationalism. The form of the short story collection, in which diverse geographical locations can be placed in productive contiguity, provides an exploration of internationalism as a set of coterminous yet discrete acts, carried out among diasporic peoples who need not be aware of the ways in which their lives are continually conditioned by events beyond their immediate location, but will nonetheless experience the effects of this breadth in their daily lives.

While Stephens's insistence on the centrality of the Caribbean as a region to the formation of transnational impulses within the Harlem Renaissance – 'geohistory matters' ('Disarticulating Black Internationalism', p. 107) – can seem poorly evinced in the exclusion of McKay's Caribbean-based works from her analysis, she seems to remedy this in her essay on Eric Walrond's *Tropic Death*. For Stephens, these ten short stories set across the Caribbean region show their author 'attempting both to imagine and represent in literature a more hemispheric conception of the modern Americas'.[18] She regards Walrond's portrayal of the Caribbean as a strategy 'that identifies colonialism as the historical force behind both modernism and the [First] World War' ('Eric Walrond's *Tropic Death*', p. 170).

Tropic Death's stories are set in both rural Barbados and within the 'Canal Zone' of Colón, Panama. In both locations the conditions under which people live and labour are brutal and desperate. As its title may indicate, the thematic unity of *Tropic Death* is granted partly through nearly every story ending with the death of a major character (the exception is the title story which concludes the collection, though Lucian Bright's imminent departure for the leper colony at Palo Seco functions in much the same way here).[19] Yet even in life a similarity of experience draws together the suffering individuals in the stories, whether under the old yoke of British colonial structures and plantation labour on 'Little England' or under the American imperialism that organised Caribbean labour to hew out the

Panama Canal. Indeed, as Stephens observes, a significant theme of the collection is the continuities and disjunctions between these two forms of subjugated West Indian labour: 'The characters in Walrond's stories clearly represent a peasantry undergoing proletarianisation, often mirrored symbolically in the simultaneous transformation of Caribbean space within "the Zone" of the Panama canal' ('Eric Walrond's *Tropic Death*', p. 170). She quotes from 'Tropic Death' Walrond's recognition that the rural workers of the islands become something else in Colón: 'now theirs was a less elemental, more ephemeral set of chores. Hill and vale, valley and stream gave way to wharf and drydock, dredge and machine shop' (*Tropic Death*, p. 188). This transformation does not, however, take the form of a simple erasure of older modes of being. Walrond's West Indians retain a 'folk' memory of previous experience and custom, even within the modernity of the Panama project.

That this connection often takes the form of an attachment to the supernatural has been attacked by Michael Dash in his reading of Walrond's 'The Voodoo's Revenge', a story that precedes *Tropic Death* both chronologically and thematically.[20] In this story, it is suggested that obeah is used to kill the Governor who callously imprisons a former supporter who was trying to consolidate a position within Panamanian society. Dash is cutting:

> The construction of the Panama Canal was a dramatic illustration of the way in which industrial development and the migration of the poor would inexorably affect the folk beliefs of the peasantry. But Walrond is not protesting against the intrusions of modern technology but indulging in a celebration of the supernatural, perhaps provoked – like his contemporary McKay – by a deep nostalgia for the Caribbean he had left behind.[21]

While Dash may have some justification for reading 'The Voodoo's Revenge' in this way, his charge oversimplifies Walrond's story. The 'Voodoo' of the title is the newspaper editor Nestor Villaine, whose presence and role in Panama speak of a complex social order. Villaine 'was a native of Anguilla who had come to the isthmus as a "contract labourer" to dig the canal', but who quickly rejected that role in favour of becoming a pamphleteer and then editor of the *Aspinwall Voice*, a vociferously Liberal Party-supporting newspaper ('The Voodoo's Revenge', p. 97). His betrayal by 'the hope of the Liberal Party', Alcade Manual Salzedo, is a case of political treachery and ingratitude. Throughout the tale, Walrond introduces characters from across the early twentieth-century imperial world, configuring Panama as a place of international modernity. Within such multiplicity, the poisoning of Salzedo seems less an expression of atavistic justice than an inevitable consequence of rapid change and uncertainty. The violence is not carried forward from a folk past, but created within a distinctly modern present.

In *Tropic Death*, the persistence and evolution of folk cultures in an age of rapid modernisation is shown never to lack nuance or intricacy. In the story which uses a supernatural folktale most openly, 'The White Snake', the young servant girl, Seenie, drowsily believes she is suckling her infant son before realising that it is a snake taking her milk. Even here though, Walrond allows for a level of metonymy as the snake has already been included within the list of signs of collapse that Seenie's employer sees as threatening Barbadian society. The lynching of 'some wife-killing Hindu' and the discovery of a black camoodie in a chandelier can equally be seen to emphasise the fragility of colonial civilisation, yet these things are not wholly prior to, or separate from, modernity, but inhabit it and continue to invigorate it (*Tropic Death*, p. 137). In 'The Vampire Bat', the white landowner, Bellon Prout, recently returned from fighting in the Boer War, is warned not to ride through the gully at night. Discounting the advice, he finds there and takes in what appears to be an abandoned black child, but later turns out to be a vampire bat which kills him. However, it is less his rejection of the advice that provides the interest of the story, than his persistent inclination to follow it; his familiarity with the 'legend[s] rooted deep in the tropic earth' is significant and made central to the insight we receive into his state of mind (*Tropic Death*, p. 156). The images of fire-hags – 'St. Lucia sluts, *obeah*-ridden, shedding their skins and waltzing forth at night as sheep and goats, on errands of fiery vengeance' – are revealed as his own fears, even as he queries 'surely the niggers can't be right[?]' (*Tropic Death*, p. 155). Ultimately, his scepticism wins this internal battle, and he therefore heads to his death; for Kenneth Ramchand, it is precisely 'the White Creole's attempt to deny the existence of early modes of feeling shared with the blacks' that results in his downfall.[22] The existence of a folk understanding is not racially exclusive, but does require the rejection, or at least adaptation, of philosophies generated elsewhere. Refusing to recognise this need for syncretism, of evolving a new understanding for a new environment, destroys Prout.

Ramchand suggests that the stories are often concerned to draw out the traces of a 'community of feeling', linking West Indians together. Walrond's exclusive focus on the Caribbean in the collection suggests that this is important to him, but as the example of Prout shows, this feeling of community is not necessarily restricted to black West Indians. The internationalism of the islands is necessarily multiracial and plural. Indeed, this can be seen as a contrast to the racial segregation which structures lives in the United States, as seen in McKay's Harlem stories and such early Walrond works as 'On Being Black'.[23] Tony Martin sees Walrond's increasing distance by the mid-1920s from his former hero Marcus Garvey as entailed by the writer's increasing comfort within the ranks of the black bourgeoisie, so much so that his distinctive West Indianness was slipping away (*Literary Garveyism*, p. 131). However, it could also be read as a dissatisfaction with the limited racial politics of Garveyism, and the USA in general. In Walrond's earlier 'Vignettes of the Dusk', a successful West Indian chooses not to become an American citizen, despite living there for twenty years: "'America is all right,' he'd say, "but I ain't taking no chances!'"[24] While the United States offers opportunities within the modern world, the community left behind can only be fully renounced at the migrant's own cost. The need to understand the international black experience leads McKay's *Gingertown* out of Harlem, and first to the Caribbean, then more widely out into the world; *Tropic Death* rejects North America altogether, but instead creates a Caribbean fundamentally internationalised. The stories strive for community, but not in terms of simple proximity within a locality.

Victor Ramraj sees Walrond's 'experiments with multiple narrators, parallel structures, and fragmentary forms, and [use of] dreams, fragments of songs, and stream-of-consciousness' as part of his desire to capture authentic Caribbean experience,[25] but it is striking that these modernist techniques seem less to illuminate individual experience than to invoke an impressionist sense of place and time. Even during the horrific scene of Coggins Rum listening to the sounds of his daughter's autopsy at the end of 'Drought', in which he is unable to let his consciousness remain fixed on this point of horror, there is little sense of an individual, but rather Walrond seems to make the death of this one little girl a further metonymy of the brutal relations across the society:

> It came to Coggins in swirls. Autopsy. Noise comes in swirls. Pounding, pounding – dry Indian corn pounding. Ginger. Ginger being pounded in a mortar with a bright, new pestle. Pound, pound. And. Sawing. Butcher shop. Cow foot is sawed that way. Stew – or tough hard steak. Then the drilling – drilling – drilling to a stone cutter's ears! Ox grizzle. Drilling into ox grizzle.... (*Tropic Death*, p. 32)

While this close internal style might seem to allow for an intimacy between character and reader, Walrond's protagonists remain in many ways unknowable. The impressionistic style leaves little room for the development of character across time, and instead focuses vividly on the present as experienced in intense emotion.

Repeatedly throughout the collection, Walrond insists on objects, people and places becoming indistinguishable; as the extremes are highlighted, the individual becomes obscured, like in the quarry of 'Drought', where the sun makes the landscape 'become whiter and the color of dark things generally grew darker. Similarly, with the white ones – it gave them a whiter hue' (*Tropic Death*, p. 25). The complicated histories of people are concealed within the powerful shine of the present. This is employed in *Tropic Death* to create a sense of immediacy, in which the particulars of protagonists are defined more in their relation to social forces than through actual biography. Miss Buckner, the brothel keeper in 'The Palm Porch', is a key instance of a moment where an uncertainty of origins becomes instead a telling glance into Panamanian cosmopolitanism:

> Whether she was the result of a union of white and black, French and Spanish, English and Maroon – no-one knew. Of an equally mystical heritage were her daughters, creatures of a rich and shining beauty […] The prudent Miss Buckner, who had a burning contempt for statistics, was a trifle hazy about the whole thing. (*Tropic Death*, p. 91)

This haziness is a key aesthetic strategy: in wanting to capture the international dynamics that create life in the Caribbean, Walrond rejects the novelistic tool of developed character. Instead, the particular social currents are channelled through monadic consciousnesses, evincing the moments made inevitable by the collision of cultures brought about in Caribbean modernity.

McKay captures the spirit of black internationalism in his short story collection through offering tales that refuse geographical limitation and instead move fluently across diasporic spaces. Nonetheless, he retains the attraction to character that so enlivens his novels. The autobiographical elements of 'When I Pounded the Pavements' still resonate in Barclay Oram's existential crisis in 'Truant'; the urge toward character development equally seems to be at work in the nostalgic-seeming prolepses that end both 'Nigger Lover' and 'The Little Sheik'. Despite his attempt to exploit the possibilities of the shorter form, McKay's novelist background can seem at times to haunt *Gingertown*. In Walrond's style, though, there is no hint of an inclination to the novel form; the preferred mode is the vignette in which the torment of an individual is briefly brought into focus before the stories, and the societies in which they are set, immediately move on.

The contrasts in style often reveal contrasting attitudes to black internationalism. While McKay's 'The Agricultural Show' relies on its objective, if slightly sardonic, narrator to connect the diverse characters together, showing an internationalism in the local that overcomes difference, *Tropic Death* can seem more often to paint the international migrations that shape the turn-of-the-century Caribbean as raising unsurpassable boundaries between people. In 'Panama Gold', the self-sufficient Barbadian smallholder, Ella, rejects the advances of the Panama-returned shopkeeper, Mr Poyah, citing the source of his wealth as the reason, though seemingly more turned off by the darkness of his skin. She seems to retain a fondness for him, and the reader is left feeling after his sudden death that a likely coming together has been denied. For Rhonda Frederick, 'the strangeness that characterises Ella and Poyal's relationship suggests that a union between modern and traditional cultures might be inevitable but fraught with problems'.[26] In fact, Walrond's sharp cynicism about the possibility of productive relations between individuals seems to go hand-in-hand with a vision of the inevitability of new social forms coming into being despite the emotional reactions of his protagonists.

Notes

1 Tyrone Tillery, *Claude McKay: A Black Poet's Struggle for Identity* (Amherst: University of Massachusetts Press, 1992), pp. 127–28.

2 Wayne F. Cooper, *Claude McKay: Rebel Sojourner in the Harlem Renaissance: A Biography* (Baton Rouge: Louisiana State University Press, 1987), pp. 267–69, 403; Claude McKay, *Trial by Lynching: Stories about Negro Life in North America,* trans. by Robert Winter; ed. by A.L. McLeod (Mysore: Centre for Commonwealth Literature and Research, University of Mysore, 1977).

3 Quoted in John E. Bassett, *Harlem in Review: Critical Reactions to Black American Writers, 1917–1939* (Cranbury, NJ and London: Associated University Presses, 1992), p. 132.

4 Claude McKay, *Home to Harlem* [1928] (Lebanon, NH: Northeastern University Press, 1987).

5 Tony Martin, *Literary Garveyism: Garvey, Black Arts and the Harlem Renaissance* (Dover, MA: Majority, 1983), p. 137; Michelle Ann Stephens, *Black Empire: The Masculine Global Imaginary of Caribbean Intellectuals in the United States, 1914–1962* (Durham, NC: Duke University Press, 2005), p. 133.

6 Mary Conroy, 'The Vagabond Motif in the Writings of Claude McKay', *Negro American Literature Forum*, 5:1 (1971), 15–23 (p. 16).

7 Claude McKay, *A Long Way from Home: An Autobiography* [1937] (London and Sydney: Pluto, 1985), p. 300.

8 Michelle A. Stephens, 'Black Transnationalism and the Politics of National Identity: West Indian Intellectuals in Harlem in the Age of War and Revolution', *American Quarterly*, 50:3 (1998), 592–608 (p. 605).

9 Tiffany Ruby Patterson and Robin D.G. Kelley, 'Unfinished Migrations: Reflections on the African Diaspora and the Making of the Modern World', *African Studies Review*, 43:1 (2000), 11–45 (p. 27).

10 Brent Hayes Edwards, *The Practice of Diaspora: Literature, Translation, and the Rise of Black Internationalism* (Cambridge, MA and London: Harvard University Press, 2003), p. 2.

11 Michelle Stephens, 'Disarticulating Black Internationalisms: West Indian Radicals and *The Practice of Diaspora*', *Small Axe*, 17 (2005), 100–11 (p. 105).

12 Claude McKay, *Banana Bottom* [1933] (London: Serpent's Tail, 2005) and *Banjo: A Story without a Plot* [1929] (London: Serpent's Tail, 2008).

13 Kotti Sree Ramesh and Kandula Nirupa Rani, *Claude McKay: The Literary Identity from Jamaica to Harlem and Beyond* (Jefferson, NC: McFarland, 2006), pp. 143, 145.

14 Claude McKay, *Gingertown* [1932] (Freeport, NY: Books for Libraries, 1972), pp. 1–2.

15 Robert Bone, *Down Home: A History of Afro-American Short Fiction from its Beginning to the End of the Harlem Renaissance* (New York: Putnam, 1975), pp. 167–68.

16 Bita Plant's reading of Pascal's *Pensées* certainly does not seem to reveal her, or *Banana Bottom*, rejecting the achievement of the West in favour of an unproblematic return to the folk. In fact, as Tom Lutz perceptively points out, 'McKay's interest

in the question of the primitive is itself literary and cosmopolitan', drawing perhaps as much from his admiration of D.H. Lawrence as any childhood memories of authentic being. See Raphael Dalleo, 'Bita Plant as Literary Intellectual: The Anticolonial Public Sphere and *Banana Bottom*', *Journal of West Indian Literature*, 17:1 (2008), 54–67 and Tom Lutz, 'Claude McKay: Music, Sexuality and Literary Cosmopolitanism', in *Black Orpheus: Music in African American Fiction from the Harlem Renaissance to Toni Morrison* ed. by Saadi A. Simawe (New York: Garland, 2000), pp. 41–64 (p. 50). For further discussion of how *Banana Bottom*'s staged primitivism is a key moment in the development of a distinctive Caribbean modernism see Dave Gunning, 'Caribbean Modernism', in *The Oxford Handbook of Modernisms*, ed. by Peter Brooker and others (Oxford and New York: Oxford University Press, 2010), pp. 910–25 (pp. 915–16).

17 David G. Nicholls, 'The Folk as Alternative Modernity: Claude McKay's *Banana Bottom* and the Romance of Nature', *Journal of Modern Literature* 23 (1999), 79–94 (p. 83).

18 Michelle Stephens, 'Eric Walrond's *Tropic Death* and the Discontents of American Modernity', in *Prospero's Isles: The Presence of the Caribbean in the American Imaginary*, ed. by Diana Accaria-Zavala and Rodolfo Popelnik (Oxford: Macmillan Education, 2004), pp. 167–78 (p. 175).

19 Eric Walrond, *Tropic Death* [1926] (New York: Collier, 1972), p. 191.

20 Eric Walrond, 'The Voodoo's Revenge' [1925], in *'Winds Can Wake Up the Dead': An Eric Walrond Reader*, ed. by Louis J. Parascandola (Detroit: Wayne State University Press, 1998), pp. 94–103.

21 J. Michael Dash, *Haiti and the United States: National Stereotypes and the Literary Imagination*, 2nd edn (Basingstoke and New York: Palgrave Macmillan, 1997), p. 57.

22 Kenneth Ramchand, 'The Writer Who Ran Away: Eric Walrond and *Tropic Death*', *Savacou* 2 (1970), 67–75 (p. 68).

23 Eric Walrond, 'On Being Black' [1922], in *'Winds Can Wake Up the Dead': An Eric Walrond Reader*, ed. by Louis J. Parascandola (Detroit: Wayne State University Press, 1998), pp. 76–80.

24 Eric Walrond, 'Vignettes of the Dusk' [1924], in *'Winds Can Wake Up the Dead': An Eric Walrond Reader*, ed. by Louis J. Parascandola (Detroit: Wayne State University Press, 1998), pp. 90–93 (p. 92).

25 Victor J. Ramraj, 'Short Fiction', in *A History of Literature in the Caribbean Vol. II: English- and Dutch-Speaking Regions*, ed. by James A. Arnold (Amsterdam: John Benjamins, 2001), pp. 199–223 (p. 201).

26 Rhonda D. Frederick, *Colón Man a Come: Mythographies of Panamá Canal Migration* (Lanham, MD: Lexington, 2005), p. 156.

'TO SEE OURSELS AS OTHERS SEE US!': SEEPERSAD NAIPAUL, MODERNITY AND THE RISE OF THE TRINIDADIAN SHORT STORY

JAMES PROCTER

Seepersad Naipaul sits at a certain distance from the prevailing narratives of postwar Caribbean literature. His literary language was regarded by contemporaries like Edgar Mittelholzer and George Lamming as archaic, and he continues to appear remote from the markers of artistic innovation and modernity associated with other pioneer short story writers in Trinidad such as C.L.R. James and Samuel Selvon. Despite holding a US passport, and in contrast to so many aspiring writers of the 1940s and 1950s, Seepersad never left the Caribbean.[1] He was, in the view of Vidia Naipaul, 'a purely local writer'; detached from 'an outside audience, his 'barbs are all turned inwards'.[2] The stories, in turn, appear both backward and inward looking in terms of what Arnold et al note is their 'expert knowledge of the workings of the village tribunal, or panchayat, of the rituals of engagement and marriage ceremonies, and of the techniques of stickfighting and the arcane skills of obeah'.[3] Seepersad's tight, restricted focus on the island's insular and illiterate East Indian communities demonstrates little in the way of a national let alone transnational consciousness. In all of these ways, Seepersad Naipaul would appear what Alison Donnell might term a 'difficult subject': 'almost unknowable to the frameworks and pathways that [have] been established for reading Caribbean literature'.[4] In short, he seems divorced from the burning issues of independence and anti-colonialism, modernity and metropolitan culture, migration and diaspora, cosmopolitanism and creolisation, that have been central, *critical*, to evaluations of the boom years of twentieth-century anglophone Caribbean writing.

As a result, while Seepersad's short stories are ritually cited in existing assessments of anglophone Caribbean literature, they tend to feature as flags or reference points, part of a nod to predecessors on the way to the more elaborated, or extended discussions of the next generation of writers. This process of critical reflection and construction is itself interesting because it creates a misleading time lag, granting Seepersad a certain antecedence which implies he is prior to, before, and in a sense outside the key phase of literary emergence in the 1940s and 1950s. It is worth reiterating in this context of critical isolation that Seepersad's mature short fiction was written in the late 1940s and early 1950s, the same years Selvon and V.S. Naipaul were to establish themselves through the short story form. Seepersad vied with these and other writers for air space on the BBC's *Caribbean Voices* programme, and regarded Selvon as a rival for his Indian Caribbean raw materials.[5]

One of the main effects of this time lag on the critical reception of Seepersad's short fiction has been to distort *Gurudeva*'s significance and singularity as a work of literature, reducing it to the status of a raw material that can be mined for an analysis of the longer works of V.S. Naipaul, notably his epic novel, *A House for Mr Biswas* (1961). Building on earlier discussions about the influence of Seepersad's stories on *Biswas* (White (1975) and Boxill (1983)), John Thieme (1987) has offered a meticulous reading of *Biswas* through the lens of Seepersad's 'They Named Him Mohun'.[6] The same study contains an appendix offering a chronology of Seepersad Naipaul including parallels with Vidia Naipaul's classic novel. More recently Helen Hayward (2002) reads *Biswas* in terms of its troubled 'textual relations' with Seepersad's biography and short stories.[7] Meanwhile, in the 1976 edition of his father's stories, V.S. Naipaul himself encourages readers to think of their significance primarily in terms of their provision of raw materials for his own writing career, and his novels in particular. For example, a disgruntled contemporary Muslim reader of Seepersad's stories provides Vidia Naipaul 'the beginnings of the main character of my own first novel [*The Mystic Masseur*]' (*Gurudeva*, p. 7). The process of publishing *Gurudeva* (1943), he tells us, 'was my introduction to book-making' (*Gurudeva*, p. 7). Vidia describes himself as a 'participant', an occasional amanuensis (*Gurudeva*, p. 8), a witness to the early stories, watching them grow, offering advice (*Gurudeva*, p. 10). Quite literally at times, V.S. Naipaul's writing appears to emerge directly from the materials of his father's stories: '...Henry Swanzy, at my father's request, asked me to read "Ramdas and the Cow" for *Caribbean Voices*. The reading fee was four guineas. With the money I bought the Parker pen which I still have and with which I am writing this foreword' (*Gurudeva*, p. 11). And a little later, 'my father's early stories created my background for me' (*Gurudeva*, p. 15).

Without wishing to question Seepersad Naipaul's fiction as an illuminating resource for reading V.S. Naipaul, the absence of studies that can account for Seepersad's short stories on their own terms has resulted in the critical neglect of one of the region's pioneering short story writers. To reduce Seepersad to a literary resource is not only to underestimate his *own* literary resourcefulness, it contributes to a deceptive narrative of progress, told with the benefit of hindsight, that flattens important generic differences in the early years of the emergence of West Indian literature. Specifically, the critical reenactment of the *novelisation* of Seepersad's short stories by V.S. Naipaul and others, is part of a wider tendency in accounts of Caribbean literature to retrospectively reduce the short story form to a supplement of the novel in a way that mutes and mutates its generic distinctiveness. As Kenneth Ramchand has put it, the tendency remains 'to regard short stories as appendages or as steps leading to the novels'.[8]

V.S. Naipaul's sense of his father's stories 'as a private possession' (*Gurudeva*, p. 19) has tended to foreclose a wider historical assessment of *Gurudeva* and its public place within the context of the rise of the Caribbean short story. In what follows, Seepersad Naipaul's stories will be located within a broader framework of influences and intertextual relations in order to suggest that their importance exceeds the kind of anteriority and interiority implied by the closed binary circuit of father and son; that despite being overdetermined by their 'past-ness', Seepersad's stories are marked by and respond to the same contemporary conditions of modernity that gave rise to the short story form elsewhere. Short stories (like poems) are especially susceptible to decontextualisation as they are republished and recollected within different settings, sequences and contexts, and *Gurudeva* is no exception. In order to possess Seepersad's stories in a different way from his son, we must begin here by first considering the stories them-selves, as they have circulated historically in different forms since the early 1940s.

FROM *GURUDEVA* (1943) TO *GURUDEVA* (1976)

While virtually all contemporary readers of Seepersad Naipaul encounter his stories through *The Adventures of Gurudeva*, the 1976 collection that was published by Andre Deutsch and edited and introduced by V.S. Naipaul, many of the stories first appeared elsewhere, in magazines and newspapers (e.g. 'In the Village' in *Caribbean Quarterly*), a collection of Trinidadian writing (e.g. *Papa Bois*, circa 1947), on the BBC *Caribbean Voices* pro-gramme ('Sonya's Luck' 26.3.50; 'Gratuity' 21.5.50; 'Shouters "Visit China" in the spirit world' 23.7.50; 'The Engagement' 14.1.51; 'Obeah' 15.7.51; 'Ramdas and the Cow' 19.7.53), and in a volume of stories produced at the author's own expense in 1943, *Gurudeva and other Indian Tales*. Collectively, these various venues suggest a less traditional and insular, more modern and mobile picture of Seepersad Naipaul's short fiction than the one with which this chapter opened. If Seepersad did not migrate, his stories clearly did, and while their content seems stubbornly fixed on the village, the stories themselves were circulated via the modern technologies of print and radio for a metropolitan audience outside the village and often beyond Trinidad. While Vidia Naipaul has noted the primary audience (and the majority of copies were sold locally) for this first edition was the local East Indian community, the original framing of the text anticipates a wider readership. In the 'Introduction to the Author' by Chas Espinet, News Editor at the Trinidad Publishing Company (removed from the 1976 edition), Espinet associates the book, contrary to more recent accounts, at the cusp of 'a West Indian literary naissance'.[9] The use of 'West Indian' is deliberate here and anticipates an outside audience for the book: 'To those who would like to have a peep into the Indian's tapia hut and get an insight into what goes on behind the Indian's mind and about life in the village which one has passed sprawling along the motor-road, there can be no better guide' (Espinet, no page). The stories' narrators are also interpreters, translators of East Indian culture, part of a self-conscious attempt to communicate with an English-speaking audience beyond the one Seepersad Naipaul is writing about. Thus, we are repeatedly told characters are speaking Hindu despite and because of the fact the narrator translates their words into English (p. 33, p. 38). Vernacular terms (pukka badmash, p. 25; orhani, p. 34) suggest an intimate, specialist, knowledge of the community, while being glossed in the text (e.g. 'The panch or community...', p. 81), or placed in italics to signal their foreign-ness to the outside reader.

Gurudeva and other Indian Tales (1943) was published by Trinidad Publications and printed by the Guardian Commercial Printery (the printers of the *Trinidad Guardian*), and had a print run of 1000, of which only two or three copies are thought to survive.[10] The collection is seventy-two pages long, its eye-catching turquoise cover carrying a roughly illustrated rural village scene, a depopulated landscape housing a single grass-thatched hut.[11] Almost undercutting the front cover's connotations of a pre-modern, or peasant rural community, the inside cover addresses a modern, literate, presumably metropolitan audience by inviting submissions of indigenous Trinidadian literature, particularly (though not exclusively) short literature: 'Trinidad Publications invite Trinidadians to write on Trinidad: Contributions in the form of short stories, essays, poems, novels or novelettes and other writings are invited' (inside cover). Submissions had to be typed.

Gurudeva and other Indian Tales opens with a sequence or cycle of seven stories charting the adolescence and young adulthood of the protagonist. In accordance with the wishes of his father, Gurudeva leaves his Canadian mission school at the age of fourteen to be married to twelve-year-old Ratni. The stories record Gurudeva's increasingly violent and sadistic behaviour which begins with the casual, but increasingly systematic beating of his wife, and which is regarded by the wider family network as merely Ratni's fate and karma. This indifference to Gurudeva's actions as well as his own premature departure from school form part of a critique of traditional Indian spiritual and cultural values, and are informed by Seepersad's firm belief in Hindu reform.[12] As he grows, Gurudeva's violence takes on a public face when he strives to fashion for himself a powerful masculine identity by becoming a 'Bad John' and stick fighter. However, the repeated glimpses of Gurudeva's cowardice (he declines to take on real stick fighters but goes on to beat an old drunk) reveal this masculinity as all performance and bravado. The sequence ends with Gurudeva's arrest after beating the old man and then turning his stick on a policeman. The Gurudeva sequence is followed by six further short stories: 'Panchayat', 'Sonya's Luck', 'Obeah', 'Gopi', 'The Wedding Came, But –', and 'Dookhni and Mungal'.

The posthumous 1976 edition, which Vidia Naipaul bases on the manuscript sent to him in England following his father's death in 1953 is quite different from the 1943 edition, and reference will be made to both in this chapter to avoid granting too much stability and authority to one or the other. Two of the original stories ('Sonya's Luck', 'Gopi') have been removed from the 1976 edition, and several others not in the original added ('They Named Him Mohun', 'My Uncle Dalloo', 'In the Village', 'The Engagement', 'The Gratuity'). As Vidia Naipaul notes, the stories in the 1976 edition span the years between the author's birth in 1906 ('They Called Him Mohun') and the American occupation of the 1940s. Further, the Gurudeva stories of the 1943 edition (written 1941–1942) are supplemented by a sequence of ten additional episodes in the 1976 edition (written just before his death 1950–2) following the protagonist's release from jail. In these episodes, Gurudeva, along with the Indian society around him, seems increasingly compromised by the modern, creolised culture of contemporary Trinidad, and the protagonist's turn to punditry is satirised against this backdrop. At the end of the sequence, Gurudeva falls in love with one of his students, a modern, independent and Americanised young woman who ultimately rejects him when he says she must adopt traditional Indian dress and values for them to be married.

The changing contents (and content) of the 1943 and 1976 editions suggests Seepersad Naipaul's growing preoccupation with the impact of modernity on an East Indian community looking to Hindu traditions for sustenance. It also indicates the author's rapid development as a Caribbean writer during the course of a decade. The archaisms that slip into some of the early versions of the stories are replaced by a modified West Indian dialect (at least within speech marks) that is comparable with Selvon of the same period. As Victor Ramraj notes, the later stories demonstrate a felicity with the formal features of the short story and its 'economy, aesthetic distance, narrative pace, and structural control' (Ramraj, p. 205). However, to explain away the formal qualities of Seepersad's short fiction merely in terms of the development of the author and the evolution of his texts would be to circumscribe to an 'apprenticeship' theory of the Caribbean short story which this chapter hopes to move beyond. As was suggested at the start of this essay, a broader conception of Seepersad's short writing is required if its relationship to the rise of the short story in Trinidad is to be better understood.

TRINIDAD AWAKENING

In the opening pages of *The Trinidad Awakening*, Reinhard Sander speculates on the reasons for the deferred and sporadic emergence of a literary culture in Trinidad until the 1920s and 1930s. He points to 'the island's linguistic diversity and its rapidly changing patterns of settlement [e.g. French, Spanish, Portugese, British, indentured labourers from India and China]' which worked to impede the establishment of English and the consolidation of a middle class when compared with islands like Barbados and Jamaica.[13] The emergence of a stable and shared social and linguistic medium of expression (English), Sander suggests, was at least partly responsible for the rise of an indigenous Trinidadian literature, embodied in the work of the Beacon group.

We might speculate here as to whether these same conditions also placed a particular emphasis on the short story form in Trinidad during the early decades of the twentieth century. The modern short story has been classically associated with the lack of unifying structures such as 'tribe, nation, family and church' and the kind of shared assumptions that produced the nineteenth-century novel.[14] In his classic study of the genre, Frank O'Connor suggests in *The Lonely Voice* that the short story is the product of 'submerged population groups', which have no shared points of reference, 'no signposts' (O'Connor, p. 18). These atomised groups, and the isolated or lonely voice of the writer which according to O'Connor they produce, seem to come into particular focus within the early Trinidadian short story, not only in the enclosed worlds of the barrack-yard stories of the Beacon group, but also in the isolated East Indian village communities of Seepersad Naipaul. As David Dabydeen, Simon Gikandi and others have reminded us, the legacy of the indentured East Indian labourers has been one of outside-ness: marginalised in terms of African slave culture and estranged from the wider national and colonial culture.[15] The short story's formal emphasis on aperture (restricted framing), on narrative containment or curtailment would all seem appropriate here. On one level, the short story form, with its stress on the part rather than the whole, was ideally suited to the framing of the relatively discrete, culturally discontinuous worlds comprising Trinidad at the turn of the century. As such it provided an appropriate container and space for the self-consciously restricted vision of Seepersad Naipaul.

Seepersad's 'My Uncle Dalloo', a short story that only appears in the 1976 edition, is typical of the author's more general use of circumscribed rural settings and self-contained plots to articulate the isolated vision of the East Indian community in Trinidad. Vidia Naipaul notes in his 1976 foreword how his father described it apologetically as a sketch, and hesitated over different versions of it, but that he also had ambitions for it as a novel. Meanwhile Vidia appreciates its 'detail; in a small space it creates and peoples a landscape…' (*Gurudeva*, p. 11). The story is set in the tiny, unchanging village of Chandernagore, a conspicuously enveloped setting, and a lagoon for six months of the year. Within its insular, superstitious and illiterate community, the narrator's Uncle Dalloo reigns supreme: he is highly regarded because of his knowledge of English, books, and the world beyond the village, his Brahminical background and his foreign-looking dress, all of which mark him out as an outsider in the village. The twist of the story is that Uncle Dalloo's standing is premised on a performance (Dalloo knows little English, and is himself only semi-literate) which he stages to ensure his own power and status in the village. Interestingly, it is the narrator, Uncle Dalloo's nephew and otherwise complicit accomplice, who exposes this fact to the reader, observing dispassionately that the man's true qualities were being 'perspicacious, conniving, and versatile' (p. 134). In a different setting, the narrator suggests, these qualities might not be enough, but Chandernagore is 'microscopic' (p. 134), a 'cul-de-sac' (p. 135), a 'bowl' (p. 136).

The enclosed form of the short story provides an important vehicle for this circumscribed setting. A fiction on one level about the limits of vision, the restricted aperture of the short story serves to further ring fence the text. These formal limits are carefully observed within the story: despite the apparent outsideness of Uncle Dalloo and the narrator, the story never drifts from this location, except through the elevated and semi-detached consciousness of these two men, whose rare external glimpses only serve to emphasise the boundary conditions of the story and the form. At the end of the narrative, Uncle Dalloo and the narrator perform a bogus religious ritual in order to identify the whereabouts of an elderly villager's daughter. While Uncle Dalloo 'magically' reveals to the villager that the daughter has run away with a boy named Jagna, the reader discovers he in fact already knew of her location: she is hiding in the next village. Significantly, this location is withheld from the villager, who remains caught within the microcosm of Chandernagore, unable even to see as far as the neighbouring settlement. We only physically see the village from the outside at one point in the text, and even here from just 'a quarter of a mile away' (p. 137), at which distance the village huts 'made you think of some gargantuan, prehistoric monsters that had rambled in the slime and slush of the lagoon and then, no longer able to carry themselves, had died, greyed, become fossilised, and remained rooted and inert for ever' (p. 137). The insularity and inertia of the village explain the success of Uncle Dalloo's characteristic versatility. At the same time, this striking glimpse of a petrified or fossilised village setting exposes the evolving modern consciousness of the narrator. There is a tension here in the writer's vision which is on the one hand invested in 'preserving' these landscapes as a resource for his fiction (though we shouldn't deny the wider affection displayed in his stories), while witnessing them as extinct, or outmoded communities. As in many of Seepersad Naipaul's stories, the narrator is caught between offering a parasitic, 'insider' account of the folk practices of the East Indian Trinidadian village and the articulation of a certain distance and alienation from them. This is arguably what makes the self-imposed imaginative limits of the short story so formally effective here. They allow Seepersad to offer privileged access to a self-contained culture, translating it for the eyes of an external audience without losing the integrity of the village, or abandoning it for elsewhere.

JOURNALISM AND CONFINED COLUMNS

The epigraph to the original 1943 version of tales, removed in the 1976 edition, seems to directly foreground the significance of perspective and distance in the construction of community:

> Oh, wad some pow'r the giftie gie us,
> To see oursels as others see us! – Robert Burns.

In these lines from 'To a Louse' (1785) the speaker laments and humor-ously mocks our incapacity to see ourselves as others do, a fact which leads to false pride and vanity. On one level the words speak directly to the anti-hero of the Gurudeva sequence, a young man whose inflated sense of self-importance is the subject of Seepersad Naipaul's satire. However, the lines ultimately speak metafictionally to the project of literary and artistic construction which sees Seepersad, the local artist, striving to situate himself at a distance from his own community in order to better see its flaws and imperfections.

If the use of Robert Burns carries connotations of a romanticised vernacular folk culture, the literary device of the epigraph signals an artistic self-consciousness that marks what follows as more than the spontaneous outpouring of life and experience. Seepersad Naipaul is often credited for his faithful, and authentic depiction of rural rituals and traditions within Trinidad's East Indian communities – depictions which draw 'from life not from literature' (Ramraj, p. 205). Such claims of immediacy and veracity not only tend to underplay the expressions of alienation and distance considered so far, they also mute the extent to which his short stories are self-conscious literary constructions, informed as much by readings of other short stories as by ethnography or autobiography. As V.S. Naipaul reminds us in his own autobiographical narrative, *Finding the Centre*, Seepersad's 'idea of the writer – as a person triumphant and detached... [was]... a private composite of O'Henry, Warwick Deeping, Marie Corelli (of the *Sorrows of Satan*), Charles Dickens, Somerset Maugham, and

J.R. Ackerley (of *Hindoo Holiday*)'.[16] While it is true to say that Seepersad Naipaul was also a keen reader of Hindu reformist literature (which influences the satire of the *Gurudeva* sequence) and, later in life, R.K. Narayan, his semi-detached perspective is informed as much by an 'external' Anglo-American literature of empire as it is by an immersion in East Indian folk culture, or by his own brahmin background (another influence V.S. Naipaul famously speaks to).

Nevertheless, it was probably journalism rather than literature that suggested the Burns epigraph to Seepersad, and gave him the confidence to defamiliarise the everyday world of the East Indian community in fiction. In 1929, the year in which the first and, as it turned out, penultimate issue of C.L.R. James's *Trinidad* magazine appeared, Seepersad Naipaul began working on the *Trinidad Guardian*. Together, James and Naipaul became short story pioneers in the region, the former writing some of the earliest Caribbean short fiction in the 1920s and 1930s, the latter publishing one of the first sequences of short stories as a collection in the 1940s. Yet, perhaps because of their different political orientations, ethnic and diasporic backgrounds, the two are rarely, if ever, considered in connection with one another. This is a pity because, once more, it allows us to overlook the wider constitutive history of the Trinidadian short story as mere coincidence. One of the key constitutive forces in terms of the formation of the Caribbean short story was the rise of those carefully delimited print spaces, the magazine and the newspaper: locations that provided new opportunities for short story production, and whose confined columns also gave the stories shape, moulded them, made them short. While there is no evidence to suggest Seepersad Naipaul was ever in contact with C.L.R. James and the Beacon group during the 1930s, they, and their short stories, were ultimately connected by the new cultural conditions made available by journalism and print. It is perhaps no coincidence in this context that the wife of Mr Gault MacGowan was chosen as the external judge for the *Beacon* magazine's short story competition in the spring of 1932.

Mr Gault MacGowan was the flamboyant former editor of the *Times* in England who played a major role in reinvigorating the *Trinidad Guardian* between 1929 and 1934. MacGowan had a major influence on Seepersad (who worked on The *Guardian* between 1929 and 1943, returning briefly in 1953), teaching him the craft of journalism, but also, as an overseas visitor to the island, helping him (to adapt Burns) to see his own East Indian community in Trinidad as others do: 'He [MacGowan] was new to Trinidad, discovering Trinidad, and he took nothing for granted. He saw stories everywhere; he could make stories out of nothing; his paper was like a daily celebration of the varied life of the island' (*Gurudeva*, p. 14).

So, for all its basis in insular, illiterate communities, Seepersad's writing was also founded upon the methods of modern print journalism and the ability to turn out economical and enclosed, or serial, narratives with narrative pace and structural control for the confined spaces of the daily newspaper. This fact was dramatically foregrounded in the publication of the 1943 edition of the stories, some of which were accidentally set, by the Guardian Printery, into the narrow columns of the newspaper.

ENCLOSURE AND UNRESOLVED MODERNITY

This essay has considered the formal enclosure of Seepersad Naipaul's short stories as part of the demarcation of an unresolved modernity. Available critical assessments have tended to overlook this fact, emphasising instead, antecedence, a before-ness that is confirmed by the writer's manifest emphasis on insular village traditions. In contrast, I have tried to suggest that the confined boundaries of Seepersad's short fiction are in fact permeable sites of translation between inside and outside that articulate an ambivalent encounter with modernity. I say ambivalent or unresolved because on the one hand these boundaries allow the writer to preserve the sphere of the village, keep it intact; on the other, they allow him to illuminate that sphere's smallness and redundancy, as it is beset by the modern world beyond it. Further, these boundaries are to a large extent determined and *set* by the modern conditions of print journalism, conditions that paradoxically prescribe Seepersad's agency as a storyteller, in terms of his *inside-ness*, his authentic access to past, or passing, rituals.

In Seepersad's earliest short stories, this outside world is kept at bay, beyond the fictional limits of the narrative. Yet, even here, the fragility of these limits are made jarringly clear when, at one point, an old stickman is described as 'A Donald Duck of a man' (p. 49). The Hollywood reference (Donald Duck was about ten years old at the time Seepersad would have been writing, undoubtedly younger in Trinidad) jumps out at the reader submerged in the interiority of Gurudeva's world, with its hoseys and *gatka-wallas*. The disjunctive analogy cannot be plausibly said to reside in the consciousness of the narrator, who is locked into the same premodern world of his characters. It erupts from outside the text, betraying the veracity of his otherwise pristine setting, while revealing the modern conditions of its construction.

The later tales of Seepersad's *Gurudeva* sequence, written in the last years of his life (early 1950s), are increasingly emphatic on this intrusion. In 'Ramdas and the Cow', the dilemma of Ramdas, about what to do with his barren animal, is situated within the context of changes in the increasingly mixed, metropolitan urban communities on the island. These changes contrast with life in the small village of Cacande, a 'little India, almost wholly Hindu-populated' (p. 81) where Ramdas lives:

> Times had changed. If you lived in St James or San Fernando or Arima, or in any of the other hotchpotch and polyglot towns of the island, you could be a Hindu and yet sell your cow to a butcher without anybody asking you a word about it ... But Cascane was not like St James or Arima or San Fernando. Carcande was not polyglot. (p. 81)

On a pragmatic level, Ramdas needs to get rid of the cow, but as a religious man under the watchful eye of Cacande's little India, realises he cannot. The satire of the Gurudeva sequence is directed at a backward looking or unchanging East Indian community in need of reform, and, within this story, the palaver over a cow this causes.

As the hotchpotch, polyglot towns beyond the boundary of Cacande suggest, the later Gurudeva stories are much more explicitly articulations of a traditional East Indian community in tension with creolised, urban modernity. In these stories Gurudeva undergoes religious conversion, and becomes a pundit and teacher. It is here, as Vidia Naipaul notes, that Seepersad's concern with Hindu reform is most emphatic, and Gurudeva becomes the butt of the writer's bluntest satire. When he is challenged about idol worship, Gurudeva goes to see his old teacher Mr Sohun, who advises him 'when in Rome do like the Romans' (p. 92). Asked to explain, Mr Sohun responds:

> It means that in a country such as the West Indies, Western culture and habits are the passport to progress. You people want to build a little India of your own in Trinidad. You are trying to dance top in mud. It cannot be done. The difficulty lies in the fact that you are too much of a majority to assimilate, too much of a minority to dominate. On every hand you are pressed by Western influences. You cannot be entirely Oriental, nor entirely Occidental; you can no more be entirely Western that you can be entirely Eastern; neither a hundred per cent European nor a hundred per cent Indian. You will be distinctly West Indian ... (p. 92)

Here Seepersad Naipaul articulates strikingly similar processes of creolisation to those Simon Gikandi associates with the depiction of modernity in Samuel Selvon's fiction:

> Because he is concerned with the place of East Indians in an emergent Trinidadian national culture and their recognition as part of the mosaic of the nation, Selvon uses his narratives as agents of national consciousness. In particular, he posits social creolization as a temporal movement that will propel East Indian peasants from sites fixed by the colonial economy (the sugar cane plantation) and Hindu culture to a new totality defined by consciousness of a mutually shared Caribbean 'creole' nationhood. (Gikandi, p. 111)

As Gikandi notes, however, creolisation is a troublesome process in Selvon's writing as it is bound up with a notion of modernity that rejects tradition in favour of western metropolitan and cosmopolitan values. This compromised creolisation registers something of the ambivalence in Seepersad's articulation of modernity, an ambivalence Gikandi also detects in Selvon.[17]

Towards the end of the extended *Gurudeva* sequence in the 1976 edition, Gurudeva falls in love with Daisy, a thoroughly modern Indian girl who has become a Christian, a mixer, she hangs around the American base, wears make up and the latest clothes. She signals Gurudeva's seduction by the modern secular culture of postwar Trinidad. Significantly the relationship fails. Daisy refuses to give up her trappings and adopt traditional Hindu ways. Nevertheless, the relationship suggests a similar dilemma to that of Ramdas, in terms of the emergence of a creolised society in which the choice between one culture and the other is beyond resolution. Like so many of Seepersad's stories, it locates modernity and creolisation (para-doxically perhaps) in an interregnum where the old is dying but the new cannot be born. It presents modernity as not just a seductive but a sensible alternative while withholding the sort of transformative vision such an alternative might allow.

In the 'other stories' that follow the Gurudeva sequence, modernity returns again and again to haunt the traditional scenes and rituals which remain the focal points of the narrative. In the semi-autobiographical piece, 'They Named Him Mohun' the traditional *barahi* celebrations held to mark the twelfth day after the birth of a son, are circumscribed by modern developments and diversions from ritual:

> Of writing invitations she was altogether ignorant. The printed card that so many of the villagers were nowadays using she deemed but a recent innovation. It was pretty, to be sure, but was it more impressive? Was it as Indian as the traditional saffron-dyed rice? No, with the printed card she had no affinity. (p. 129)

At the party, '[t]he more old-fashioned brought presents in the shape of parcels of flour and Irish potatoes and some salt; but these were few. For, in spite of the stern conservatism of Soomin … modernism had spread its tentacles in the village.' (p. 131). For these guests dollar bills replace food gifts, and as the evening wears on 'mongrel' music (p. 131) replaces nativity songs.

In 'Panchayat', a village tribunal (panchayat) is held by Moonia against her errant rogue of a husband. The villagers are interested in the event, not because of its mainstream, everyday occurrence, but precisely because:

> … in these amazingly modern times a panchayat was a rare event. The machinery of the village tribunal, which had in the past removed so many domestic cleavages as well as settled or imposed punishments for religious or social anomalies, had become rusty and obsolete. … People preferred the law courts nowadays … who cared about … ostracism in these amazingly democratic times – especially in this polyglot island of many races and creeds. Trinidad is not India. (p. 157–8)

All of this would suggest Seepersad Naipaul's equivalence rather antecedence to writers such as Samuel Selvon (a writer recently recovered in
terms of modernity). Seepersad shares what Simon Gikandi identifies in
Selvon's novels as a concern with the 'transformation of East Indian
cultures in the colonial and postcolonial Caribbean, the attempt of East
Indians to redefine their value system against the pressures of modernity
and modernization, and the quest for individual identities against the
claims of old Indian traditions' (Gikandi, p. 111). For sure, Seepersad's
short stories are more hesitant on this subject; their very shortness means
those individual identities (epitomised in Selvon's Tiger) remain partially
formed. Moreover, as Victor Ramraj notes, '[u]nlike Seepersad Naipaul's
stories… Selvon's are not restricted to the East Indian experience. Many
more are about the experiences of Afro-West Indians and of West Indian
immigrants in London and Canada…' (Ramraj, pp. 212–213). Nevertheless, I would argue that Seepersad's modernity and modernisation are the
constitutive outside to his preoccupation with folk traditions and rituals
and are best understood in this sense, not as a retreat from modernity, but
as an uncertain attempt to comprehend tradition at the moment of its
disappearance. In this sense the special meaning of the backward glance of
Seepersad Naipaul's stories is not faithful reproduction of tradition, but
rather an emergent modernity that brings the past more acutely into focus.

NOTES

1   In order to avoid confusion with either Vidia Naipaul, or with Shiva Naipaul, I
    have taken the precaution of using 'Seepersad', rather than 'Naipaul', whenever I
    shorten the writer's full name.
2   V.S. Naipaul, 'Foreword', in Seepersad Naipaul, *The Adventures of Gurudeva* (London:
    Andre Deutsch, 1976), pp. 1–20 (p. 11, p. 15).
3   Victor Ramraj, 'Short Fiction', in *A History of Literature in the Caribbean – Volume
    2*, ed. by Albert Arnold, Julio Rodriguez-Luis, Vera Kutzinki, Ineke Phaf-Rheinberger
    and J. Michael Dash (Amsterdam, Philadelphia: John Benjamins Publishing Company,
    2001), pp. 199–223 (p. 205).
4   Alison Donnell, *Twentieth-Century Caribbean Literature* (London: Routledge 2006),
    p. 11.
5   It could be argued for example that the later stories of Seepersad learn from and
    'borrow' the output of Selvon that was appearing alongside his, and vice versa.
6   John Thieme, *The Web of Tradition: Uses of Allusion in V.S. Naipaul's Fiction* (London:
    Hansib Publishing, 1987).
7   Helen Hayward, *The Enigma of V.S. Naipaul: Sources and Contexts* (Basingstoke,
    HT: Palgrave Macmillan, 2002), p. 6.
8   Kenneth Ramchand, 'The West Indian Short Story', *Journal of Caribbean Literatures*,
    1:1 (1997), 21–33 (p. 27).
9   Chas Espinet, 'Introduction to the Author', in Seepersad Naipaul, *Gurudeva and
    other Indian Tales* (Port of Spain, Trinidad: Trinidad Publications, 1943), no page.

10 I am grateful to the staff at the Naipaul archive, University of Tulsa, for allowing me access to this edition, and to the British Academy for funding the research trip.

11 In the sky floats the face of an Indian woman, heavily outlined. She seems less an ethereal figure or deity than an anchor for the scene's Indian-ness. The artist seems to be the same Alf Cudallo who contributes the illustrations accompanying the text of the stories. These pen and ink drawings were possibly taken from issues of the *Trinidad Guardian*.

12 Hindu reform movements, which began in India in the late nineteenth century, came to have a sporadic impact on Trinidad's East Indian community in the 1940s.

13 Reinhard W. Sander, *The Trinidad Awakening: West Indian Literature of the Nineteen-Thirties* (New York: Greenwood Press, 1988), p. 7.

14 Frank O'Connor, *The Lonely Voice: A Study of the Short Story* (New York: Harper Colophon Books, 1985 [1963]), p. 9.

15 Simon Gikandi, *Writing in Limbo: Modernism and Caribbean Literature* (Ithaca and London: Cornell University Press, 1992), p. 111.

16 Vidia Naipaul, *Finding the Centre: Two Narratives* (London: Andre Deutsch, 1984), p. 46.

17 As Vidia Naipaul notes, 'Mr Sohun's son has the un-Indian name of Ellway. But the boy so defiantly named doesn't seem to have done much or to have much to do. When Gurudeva calls, Ellway is at home, noisily knocking up fowl-coops: the detail sticks out' (*Gurudeva*, p. 21).

'I CUT IT AND CUT IT': JEAN RHYS'S SHORT SHORT FICTION

JOANNA JOHNSON

'Please don't think me pernickety but every word must be exact' (Jean Rhys, letter to Selma Vas Diaz, 12 November 1956)

'…these sketches begin exactly where they should and end exactly when their job is done' (Ford Madox Ford, Preface to *The Left Bank*, 1927)

'Jean used to say, "Cut, cut, cut, cut"' (Diana Athill, *Guardian*, 5 January 2009)

In the preface to Jean Rhys's first published collection of stories, *The Left Bank* (1927), Ford Madox Ford reveals how, contrary to his advice and with 'cold deliberation',[1] Rhys's 'instinct for form' (Ford, p. 24) meant she 'eliminated even such two or three words of descriptive matter as had crept into her work' (Ford, p. 26). For Rhys, to 'treat [her subjects] truthfully […] and to tell how things really were',[2] to achieve what she felt was 'dearer' (Ford p. 26), meant that clarity and concision were of paramount importance. Close examination of a selection of Rhys's short stories throughout her career – over fifty stories were written over a fifty-year period – reveals how their economy of form allowed her to tell things better and to express the truth as she saw it, insisting that getting to it meant simplifying and cutting.[3] Part of that truth included Rhys's Dominican upbringing, which never left her imagination and her writing. So Rhys 'hands you the Antilles with its sea and sky – "the loveliest, deepest sea in the world – the Caribbean!"' says Ford, 'but lets Montparnasse, or London, or Vienna go', eventually conceding '[s]he is probably right. Something human should, indeed, be dearer to one than all the topographies of the world' (Ford, p. 26). Rhys's desire to cut out what she sees as superfluous build-up of 'atmosphere' (Ford, p. 25) or 'descriptive matter', then, appears not to extend to the topography of her Caribbean childhood, a place 'dearer' to her than the landscapes of Europe. 'The emotions and passions of a child being so penetrative' (Ford, p. 26) mean Rhys's early Caribbean influences persist in her work despite her insistence to eliminate description and cut her writing.

As a child in Dominica at the turn of the last century, Rhys would have been 'taught the language and customs of a country [England] she had never seen while living in and being shaped by the reality of the West Indies',[4] while later as an adult in England she felt she was treated as an 'ignorant "colonial"' (Athill, *CSS*, p. xii). Such tensions result in writing that is difficult to categorise. Noted Caribbean critic Elaine Savory usefully points to the complex nature of critical readings of Rhys's work and frames them in a Caribbean context:

> Jean Rhys and her texts have been interpreted by different critics and theorists in strikingly different ways. She and they are in those readings: Caribbean, English, European; feminist and anti-feminist; elite, working-class, marginal; white and white Creole; outside and insider; ageless and of her time. But one identity can hold all of these contradictory facets: Rhys is a Caribbean writer.[5]

Rhys's Caribbean identity that allows her to hold all of the contradictory facets Savory points to is especially important here. Not only does she stand 'chronologically as a kind of ancestor' (Savory, p. 152) for Caribbean writers, but the formal innovations through which these contradictions are expressed also render her work influential in the development of a modernist tradition of short story writing. While Rhys's Caribbean background was often the cause of her marginalisation and thus her anguish, it often translated into an intense and acute perception of life as told in her short stories.

Rhys was born in 1890 in Dominica to a Creole mother whose family had lived there from around the turn of the previous century and a father who was a Welsh doctor recently emigrated. She left her island home in 1907 to go to school in England, returning to Dominica only once thereafter on a short visit with her husband in 1936. Some of those years were spent in continental Europe – Holland, Vienna and Paris – but she lived all her life from 1928 until her death in 1979 in Britain. Rhys's first publication, her short story 'Vienne', in Ford Madox Ford's *Transatlantic Review* (1924), came three years before her first collection of short stories, *The Left Bank* (1927). Over the following twelve years four novels were published: *Quartet* (1928 – also known as *Postures* in the UK), *After Leaving Mr MacKenzie* (1930), *Voyage in the Dark* (1934), and *Good Morning, Midnight* (1939). After her supposed disappearance for several years (when she was in fact living in various places around Britain), she produced her best-known work telling the story of *Jane Eyre*'s first Mrs. Rochester, *Wide Sargasso Sea* (1966). On the strength of that novel's critical and popular success, she published another collection of short stories very quickly thereafter, *Tigers are Better Looking* (1968), which included a selection from the earlier *Left Bank* collection as well as eight new stories, while Rhys's earlier novels were also republished. A short collection of three pieces, *My Day*, was issued in the USA in 1975, followed by Rhys's final collection of short stories, *Sleep it Off Lady* (1976).[6]

Of Rhys's short stories, some of those she wrote in the middle period of her career are often considered her finest, including 'Let Them Call It Jazz'

(1968) (Rhys's only work written in a Creole narrative voice), 'Pioneers, Oh, Pioneers' (1976), 'The Day They Burned the Books' (1969), 'Till September Petronella' (1976), 'Fishy Waters' (1976), and 'Good-bye Marcus, Good-bye Rose' (1976).[7] These short stories are somewhat longer than most of the early and late stories; indeed, 'Till September Petronella' was once a great deal longer than its final form. In a letter to her editor, Francis Wyndham, in 1960, Rhys admits that 'Till September Petronella' was once 'a full length novel. Almost. I cut it and cut it'.[8] That 'Till September Petronella' was once almost a novel is of note, since it resembles in its plot and young women protagonists Rhys's four early novels; distinctions between Rhys's short novels and longer stories are often less clear than the distinctions between her longer and shorter short stories, some of which are often so brief and pared down they might be better described as vignettes, or sketches.

In her introduction to *The Collected Short Stories* (1987), Diana Athill suggests that at the end of her life Rhys was too 'weary' (p. ix) to take on anything longer, being primarily concerned with finishing her autobiography, *Smile Please* (1979), and while this is certainly true – and shorter vignettes would require less revision than longer stories – Rhys returned to her early form also by replicating the very short sketches she started out with. Much of the writing is sparse and according to Paul Kotrodimos, 'episodic',[9] or, to use the modernist term, fragmented. Emotional states seem to have an inverse relationship to the honed prose: the more complex the emotion, the less Rhys's writing says about it. Kotrodimos notes that '[a]t first glance, inexperienced readers may be inclined to dismiss these pieces as trite or perhaps even meaningless snippets in the lives of characters whose degenerate and marginal states can have no interest or worth' (p. 359). Yet these 'meaningless snippets' of 'degenerate' and 'marginal' states reveal great interest and worth: in producing these very short pieces, Rhys asks her readers to play an active role in deriving meaning for themselves. One early review of Rhys's first published collection of short stories in 1927 reads thus: 'For the most part Miss Rhys's stories and sketches are very brief. Her method is to reject the descriptive and the expository, to reject for the most part structural plot, and even to reject fullness of characterization as we understand it'.[10] In this description we see two things: first, that Rhys's stories are indeed brief (even though this is a relative term), and second, that they are written in a style that rejects the form of the story in its traditional sense, requiring the reader to actively read into an otherwise meaningless snippet – a style characteristic of the wider modernist movement of which she was part.[11]

Most of Rhys's short fiction remains overshadowed in critical attention by *Wide Sargasso Sea*, her other novels, and particular short stories such as 'Pioneers, Oh, Pioneers' (1976), 'Till September Petronella' (1976), 'Vienne' (first published 1924), and 'Let Them Call It Jazz' (1968). Carole Angier's important biography *Jean Rhys: Life and Work* (1992) does not deal with Rhys's short stories – though she adds a prefacing author's note that this is for reasons of space and economy rather than because she sees them as any 'less good or important' (p. ix). Similarly, Sue Thomas's *The Worlding of Jean Rhys* (1999) details only three of the short stories, '[r]egrettably', she says, 'because of considerations of space'.[12] Elaine Savory redresses some of this imbalance in her comprehensive and significant critical study, *Jean Rhys*, and looks at several narrative devices in the short stories. She suggests, for example, that Rhys 'constantly worked to eradicate any superfluous words in her texts: the economy of the short story form was something she could therefore fully embrace' (p. 153).

Other critical readings have sometimes conflated Rhys's fiction with her life,[13] and although much of Rhys's writing is a fictional recasting of many of her own experiences, Rhys was very careful to disassociate herself and her life from her writing, believing 'an artist's work should be considered in separation from the facts of his or her life'.[14] To see Rhys, like her heroines, as a 'passive victim [...] doomed to destruction',[15] as she has sometimes been described, is to underestimate the considerable strength that she shows in her tireless reworking of her writing. Other critics have drawn attention to a unified view, namely that of the outsider, or the marginalised perspective: In 'The World of Jean Rhys's Short Stories' (1990), A.C. Morrell argues that Rhys tells the same story over again throughout her three volumes of short stories.[16] Cheryl Alexander Malcolm and David Malcolm suggest that Rhys's short fiction has a greater range of narrative technique than the long fiction, but accept Morrell's view that all Rhys's stories have a commonality.[17] Although the stories share some common ground, this view is somewhat reductionist, and does not do justice to the extensive differences that do exist between the stories. While a lot of Rhys's work focuses on the outsider, this is not always the case (perhaps the fact that critics label her protagonists as 'outsiders' may itself accord them such a status).

While the specific stories I examine below span fifty years in their publication dates, they share a number of noteworthy narrative strategies. These particular stories, for the most part, have not received much critical attention, but are representative of the many characteristics of Rhys's short stories: highly concentrated emotion, a last line serving to pull the whole together and to refocus the whole effect of the story (the modernist 'epiphany'),[18] and the story's title as focal point. As such these stories showcase Rhys's significance as a practitioner of the art of the short story.

Edgar Allan Poe's seminal contribution to the understanding and theory of the modern short story form is well-known, but bears repetition here as it is key to understanding how Rhys's highly concentrated form works. In his review of Nathaniel Hawthorne's short stories, Poe suggests that the 'skilful literary artist' creates a 'unique or single *effect*' (Poe, p. 47) that can be read in totality at one sitting.[19] Importantly, Poe also stresses that the act of the reader would be a 'kindred art'; by this, he means that 'a sense of the fullest satisfaction' (Poe, p. 48) comes from the reader playing an equal role in contemplating and constructing what modernist short story critic Dominic Head calls the 'aesthetic wholeness' of the story.[20] The story will often begin *in medias res*, will not have a linear plot, and instead achieves its meaning from the building up of fragmented images, thoughts, and inner musings to create an overall impression. Paul March-Russell draws attention to the influence of Poe's theory of the short story on modernist short fiction, commenting how 'it was relatively straightforward to graft Poe's single effect onto the early modernist notion of the epiphany'.[21] Poe's emphasis on selection and fragmentation, techniques also prevalent in modernist short story writing, suited Rhys's preference for cutting and paring down as a means of making the whole impression more realistic. Her stories require the reader to participate in constructing meaning. Athill notes that Rhys has an extraordinary 'ability to condense: everything about her that matters is in it, though sometimes touched in so lightly that it can escape the notice of a reader who is less than fully attentive' (Athill, *Stet*, p. 180). These light touches that could be easily missed by the inattentive reader are the same (modernist) touches that require readers' input to glean more meaning from otherwise seemingly inconsequential snippets of the quotidian and ordinary.

The modernist writer Ford Madox Ford played a profound role in Rhys's life, both personally and professionally. When her first husband was in jail, Rhys was taken in by Ford and his partner Stella Bowen to live with them their Paris home. Ford showed her much of the art of (modernist) writing, and was the first person to champion and publish her work in his magazine *Transatlantic Review* (1924). Veronica Marie Gregg illustrates one of Ford's specific influences on Rhys, namely the extent of the influence of the last line:

> You must state your argument, you must illustrate it, and then you must stick in something that appears to have nothing whatever to do with either subject or illustration, so that the reader will exclaim 'what the devil is the fellow driving at?' And then you must go on in the same way – arguing, illustrating and startling and arguing, startling and arguing until at the very end your conventions will appear like a raveled skein. And then, in the last few lines you will draw towards you the master-string of that seeming confusion, and the whole pattern of the carpet, the whole design of the net-work will be apparent.[22]

The last line, crucially, is the one where 'the whole design of the net-work will be apparent'. In her short stories, Rhys carefully crafts this line, often working and reworking the ending several times to effectively shape it.[23] The pulling together of the master string, as Ford puts it, might be seen as another way of describing the epiphanic moment that contributes to the overall impression of the modernist short story.

A particularly notable example of this is in the short story 'The Day they Burned the Books'.[24] Set on an unnamed Caribbean island, the young female narrator tells of her friendship with a 'fair' boy (CSS, p. 153), Eddie, whose English father has come to live on the island and married a local coloured woman (p. 151) to whom he is abusive. The story tells of the children's friendship and how it is Eddie who first 'infects' the girl with 'doubts about "home", meaning England' (pp. 152–53). Some weeks after Eddie's father dies, his mother, who has 'hated' (p. 152) her late husband's books and the room in which they are kept, decides to take them down from the shelves and sell or burn them. The two children each salvage a book from the boy's mother: the boy has a torn copy of *Kim*, while the girl waits to see hers, rushing home in the dark excitedly to see what she has got, knowing 'this book was the most important thing that had ever happened' to her (p. 157) and that she would read it 'from the beginning to the triumphant words "The End"' (p. 155). However, back home in her bedroom when she finally sees the book she 'was very disappointed, because it was in French and seemed very dull. *Fort Comme La Mort*, it was called...' (p. 157). The last line here re-focuses the emphasis of the story. First, the book now seems 'very dull' rather than exciting, thus subverting any expectation that the day the books were burned would yield anything more. But its dullness is also significant and ironic, given that earlier in the story the girl narrator counters the criticism that she's just a 'horrid colonial' (rather than 'real' English) (p. 153) by saying she thinks it would be much more fun to be French than English in any case (p. 153).

Throughout the story, the girl narrator has described herself and considered her own behaviour in relation to her colonial identity: she finds her relations with the few 'real' English boys and girls she has met to be 'awkward' (p. 153). She is admiring of Eddie professing not to like strawberries or daffodils, when the other English children talk of such English 'delights' (p. 153), yet she also walks 'sedately' trying to contain her excitement about the book she's salvaged because she fears the 'black children's ridicule' (p. 155). Eddie's mother has chosen to sell the 'big fat glossy ones – the good looking' encyclopaedic-type books, but burns the 'unimportant' ones on 'the poetry shelf' (pp. 154–55), which include the 'infinitely worse' (in the mother's eyes) books by women. Rhys's narrator is marginalised by the colonial and gender hierarchy, yet also 'alive' (p. 155) and excited and by the prospect of the book she has grabbed. The book symbolises the girl's own small but important resistance to the mother's rampages, to the English children's haughtiness, to the black

children's ridicule. The book represents the possibility of excitement and
of being 'alive' (p. 155) for the girl, but in the end yields little.

The last line shifts the reader's perspective perhaps more radically in
another story, 'I Used to Live Here Once' (1976). One of Rhys's very latest
stories, it was wholly written in her older age (unlike some of the other late
period stories, which were often begun several decades earlier). Rhys
frequently stays away from using overtly sentimental images, instead
preferring to imbue moments of seeming insignificance with weight and
poignancy; her protagonists rarely show outward emotion, the strength of
feeling coming instead from inference. The more complex the emotion,
the less that is said, leaving the reader to discern for herself the moment's
full significance. This story shows such avoidance of the sentimental, yet
remains exceedingly moving. Told in the third person, it begins with an
unnamed woman making her way across what is obviously a once very
familiar path of stones over a river towards the house where she once lived
in an unnamed Caribbean setting. Felled trees indicate that some time has
passed since she was last there, but she still knows the terrain well. Two fair
children are playing, but they don't acknowledge her when she greets
them, something she does three times; instead, they run inside the house
commenting that it seems to have turned cold. The woman's outstretched
arms fall to her side as she realises the children haven't seen her at all, and
the story concludes with the line, 'That was the first time she knew' (CSS,
p. 388), whereupon she and the reader recognise her presence is as a ghost
figure. The abruptness of the last line, after the slow building of tension,
where it is unclear in which direction the story is heading, is a classic
moment of epiphany. Her once outstretched arms falling to her side are an
unsentimental way of showing an intensely affecting moment, where her
tiny gesture of disappointment evinces great poignancy. In Rhys's stories,
small, apparently trivial details are often freighted with meaning, and
within the small movement of the woman's once outstretched arms is a
much greater emotion.[25]

The shorter the story, the more significant each word becomes, so that
in the end Rhys's stories resemble poetry in their stylistic concerns and
attention to form. She chooses the placement of every single word carefully, often showing the same degree of care one might find in poetry. One
of Rhys's early critics, Gladys Graham, describes her writing thus:

> It has something of the balance and beauty of verse. The shifting of a
> phrase would be a threat against the whole. Words are used like little
> weights, placed with an almost fractional delicacy. Phrases and words
> that are lovely and beguiling in their form but ruthless and explicit in
> their content march the pages deterred [sic]. (Graham quoted in Gregg,
> p. 38)

Rhys's writing resembles poetry not only in the careful choosing of individual words, but also in its form and appearance on the page, where very short lines can be fragmented and set out as in poetry. One such example is an early story, 'A Night' (1927), in which an unnamed female narrator frets and worries, trying to sleep during a restless night, but her mind races, contemplating suicide, or as she puts it, 'le saut dans l'inconnu' (the leap into the unknown):

> If I had something to hold on to. Or somebody.
> One friend....One!
> You know I can't be alone. I can't.
> God, send me a friend....
> How ridiculous I am. How primitive....
> Sneering at myself I start on childishnesses.
> I imagine the man I could love. His hands, eyes and voice.
> Hullo, he'll say, what's all the fuss about?
> - Because I'm hurt and spoilt, and you too late....
> - What rot....What rot!
> He will buy me roses and carnations and chocolates and a
> pair of silk pyjamas and heaps of books.
> He will laugh and say – but nicely:
> Finished! What rot!
> Just like that. (*CSS*, p. 48)

These are the stream-of-consciousness utterances or internal thoughts of a troubled, restless woman, presented in a form which could easily be that of a poem. Here there are no barriers between the genres of poetry and prose; Rhys erases the difference between the two, breaking down conventional boundaries.

Rhys often used ellipses to indicate the trailing-off of a thought; this fragmentation adds to the poetic quality of her writing. In the above extract, the night-time thoughts are troubling and strange, veering wildly between the mundane and the surreal. The woman considers different ways to die – shooting oneself, drowning – thinking how each one might feel, but the story ends with her declaring much more matter-of-factly, 'Ridiculous all this. Lord I am tired....A devil of a business....' (*CSS* p. 49), suggesting that the morning will give way to more clarity and rationality. The title 'A Night' ensures that the focus remains on the ways in which fears are disproportionately troubling at night, rather than on the nature of the thoughts themselves – a more expected title might otherwise be 'Le saut dans l'inconnu' (she repeats this phrase several times in the story) which would have the effect of the story being 'about' suicide, instead of being about the way night-time skews our perceptions of reality. Rhys uses the titles of her stories as a narrative device, another means of saying much with little, providing a – sometimes unusual or surprising – focus or emphasis on the story which inflects it throughout.

In another early short story from *The Left Bank*, 'In the Luxemburg

Gardens' (1927), the extreme brevity (it is barely one page long) means that, as in a poem, each word assumes greater significance to the whole, and its deceptive simplicity belies its great poignancy. The story begins: 'He sat on a bench, a very depressed young man, meditating on the faithlessness of women, on the difficulty of securing money, on the futility of existence' (*CSS*, p. 27). The positioning of this phrase as a one-sentence paragraph, the first line indented, invests it with significance. In just a few brief words, we are shown the inner workings of this man's mind, an insight into his philosophy on life, summed up and compressed into a short line. We are not told how this man looks, nor what he is wearing; rather, our understanding of his character comes from his inner musings. Children (Rhys refers to them as Raouls, Pierrots, Jacquelines – the plural form of the individual names reveals the man's point of view that these children are interchangeable with one another) run around, playing. The man is morose, finding the children around him quite distasteful. But then, 'instantly interest came into his eyes' when he sees a girl whose legs are 'not bad!'; his 'hunting instinct' awakened, he follows her purposefully, 'twirling his little moustache determinedly' (p. 27), catching her up under a tree:

> 'Mademoiselle...'
> 'Monsieur...'
> Such a waste of time, say the Luxemburg Gardens, to be morose.
> Are there not always Women and Pretty Legs and Green Hats. (p. 28)

These final lines shift the focus of the story, that final pulling of the 'master-string' to tie it all together, and they provide a contrast with the first line, where the man's despondency with the futility of existence is quickly replaced with his moment of flirtation. The perspective shifts; Rhys allows the Gardens to voice the man's thoughts.[26] The capitalisation of 'Women' parallels 'Pretty Legs' and 'Green Hats', revealing that in this man's world, women have value only to the extent of the way they look. This very short story has a number of Rhysian hallmarks: shifts in perspective, a sketch of life rather than a driven plot, the significant first line, and the narrative thread pulling the story together at the end. This story is a remarkable example of how Rhys is able, in such a short time, to capture the moment between utter despondency and complete awakening to the possibilities in life. Here, the last line shows a shift in the man's perception of what it means to be alive, in contrast perhaps to the girl in 'The Day They Burned the Books' where the final line highlights that a book which once felt 'warm and alive' (*CSS*, p. 155) should turn out to be disappointing.

In stories published much later in her life, Rhys often returned to the very brief form of her earlier work, and retained many of the same techniques. Rhys had originally given her story 'On Not Shooting Sitting Birds' (1976) a different title: 'Pink Milanese Silk Underclothes'.[27] Again, her change of title illustrates a shift she wished to draw in the story's dominant perspective (*CSS*, pp. 328–330): no longer is the reader alerted foremost to the woman's European-style underwear; instead, the rather unusual title sounds more like a personal essay, or reflection, rather than a piece of fiction, and refocuses the story to reflect a memory of the woman's Caribbean background.[28] The story begins quite simply, and very concisely: 'There is no control over memory' (*CSS*, p. 328). These few words are freighted with meaning. Rhys's narrator goes on to reflect how some important events are forgotten, while trivial memories may 'stay with you for life' (p. 328). This idea of engrained memory applies to the occasion when the first-person female narrator buys herself pink Milanese underclothes for a dinner date about which she is 'excited' (p. 328). But the date goes badly wrong, and a gulf 'yawned' (p. 329) between the pair. Trying to 'distract or interest' the man, she describes at length a fictitious shooting party from her Dominican childhood, fabricating and embellishing the story, especially since in the 'genuine' (p. 329) shooting party, the girl runs away and hides because she 'hated and feared the noise of the gun' (p. 330), and thus has no idea what really happened at all. But her dinner companion is incredulous and 'shocked' (p. 330) that her brother apparently shoots sitting birds, even though at this point she has no idea whether her brother really did so because she is so entangled in her fabrication. She cannot tell him what really happened for fear that he would think her a liar and a coward, and she is not sure she 'liked him at all' (p. 330) by now so stays silent. He takes her home soon thereafter, and she feels regret when taking off her silk underclothes, saying nonchalantly: 'some other night, perhaps, another sort of man' (p. 330). In this story we are offered a snapshot of someone who is negotiating her identity as both a woman and a 'colonial' in England, someone who 'imagined [she] knew all about the thoughts and tastes of various English people' (p. 329), yet finds very quickly she has badly misjudged this.

The last story I examine here, 'Kikimora' (1976), is another from the late collection *Sleep It Off Lady*, and features the act of cutting in a different way since it involves the woman narrator cutting away her 'feminine charm', this time by literally cutting up her own clothing (*CSS*, p. 334). The story's humour – an aspect in Rhys's writing that often goes unnoticed – challenges the assumption that Rhys was somehow a victim, or self-destructive.[29] Carole Angier, Rhys's biographer, reads this story as one that was apparently written about a dreadful and violent argument Rhys had had with her second husband Leslie Tilden Smith, and is a 'perfect example of the self-destructiveness of the heroine's revenges: the way that, however much she means to hurt someone else, the only person she *can* hurt is herself'.[30] But the humour in the story allows a reading that does not so easily conceive the narrator as a victim.

The title of the story, 'Kikimora', is the name of a male pet cat belonging to a woman, Elsa, who, along with her husband, is entertaining Baron Mumtael for the evening. Again, the story begins simply: 'The bell rang' (*CSS*, p. 331), but in this short simple sentence lies much weight, because waiting to come in is the 'intimidating' and 'mocking' (p. 331) Baron. The Baron spends the evening scorning Elsa and making her nervous and tense with his bigoted remarks about her appearance and her apartment, finding it to be a 'typical interior' (p. 331) of a woman and commenting on how 'the spoilt female is invariably a menace' (p. 332). Some time later, Elsa's husband finally arrives, and although the 'tension lessened' (p. 332), the Baron and Elsa still have awkward exchanges, one concerning a painting the Baron does not like but comments patronisingly that he finds it 'colourful' and 'painted by a woman, I feel sure' (p. 332), although he is wrong, as Elsa points out. Later in the evening, Kikimora, Elsa's cat, scratches the Baron quite badly and he is very upset, repeating: 'One can't be too careful with a she-cat' (p. 333), to which Elsa 'would always answer. He's not a she-cat, he's a he-cat' (p. 333). When the Baron eventually leaves, finger bandaged, Elsa and her husband have a disagreement: she thinks the Baron is 'horrible'; he thinks he was 'rather a nice chap' (p. 334). Elsa returns to stroke her cat, clearly pleased he scratched the man: 'my darling black velvet cat with the sharp claws' (p. 334), she says. When, at the story's end, her husband asks her what she is doing by cutting up the suit the Baron has mocked her for wearing, Elsa responds that she is destroying her feminine charm, referring to the Baron's earlier comment, and says 'I thought I'd make a nice quick clean job of it' (p. 334).

While there is no doubt that Elsa feels trapped by the constraints of traditional gender roles here, and feels distress from the Baron's sneering and mocking remarks concerning the typical behaviour of women, the Baron getting his comeuppance from the cat nevertheless adds a humorous touch to the story. I see Elsa's destruction of her clothes as less an act of self-destructiveness than an expression of defiance and determination to rid herself of that which is representative of her constraints. And once again, the title of the story ensures a distinct perspective: in this case, it foregrounds the cat's retribution for his owner's discomfort rather than stressing Elsa and her suggested entrapment. It is interesting that Elsa decides to cut up her clothes as an act of resistance; perhaps Rhys's own insistence on cutting her prose signifies a similar impetus to rid herself of all that is considered superfluous or unwanted, her own act of resistance against those, like Ford for example, who called for more description in her stories.

In the case of this last story, Rhys's protagonist does in fact resemble her creator in her determinedness, and in her willingness to rid herself of the kind of clutter that she feels constrains her attempts at getting to the truth. As Athill comments, when Rhys was working on her writing, 'out of her eyes, then, looked a whole and fearless being, without self-pity, knowing exactly what she wanted to do, and how to do it' (Athill, *Stet* p. 184). The need to achieve such precision was what prompted Rhys to painstakingly craft her writing, helped along by her perfectionism and her self-doubt that anything 'was much good'.[31] Rarely content with a story that even the most meticulous of writers would usually regard as finished, and often revisiting her stories several times, clarity, simplicity, and truth were always key for Rhys:[32] 'I know it seems stupid to fuss over a few lines or words, but I've never got over my longing for clarity and a smooth firm foundation underneath the sound and the fury. I've learnt one generally gets this by cutting' (Rhys quoted in Gregg, p. 39). So even though some of her stories are so condensed that they barely stretch to two pages on the printed page, as I have shown, they lose nothing of their poignancy and depth, with that short moment of life, *in medias res*, revealing immense profundity.[33] And throughout these stories, Rhys's Caribbean background shapes both her own 'truth' (Athill, *CSS*, p. viii) and her influence on short story writing of the twentieth century. Her stories enriched an early twentieth-century modernist literary movement dominated by European and US writers, extending its cultural and geographic parameters, and they remain a vital part of the ancestry of short story writing in the Caribbean.

NOTES

1 Ford Madox Ford, Preface to Jean Rhys, *The Left Bank and Other Stories* (New York: Books for Libraries Press, 1927 [1970]), pp. 7–27 (p. 26).
2 Diana Athill, 'Introduction', in Jean Rhys, *The Collected Short Stories* (London and New York: W.W. Norton, 1992), pp. vii–x (p. viii).
3 Diana Athill, *Stet: An Editor's Life* (London: Granta, 2000), p. 184.
4 Veronica Marie Gregg, 'Jean Rhys and Modernism: A Different Voice', *The Jean Rhys Review*, 1:2 (1987), 30–46 (p. 34).
5 Elaine Savory, *Jean Rhys* (Cambridge: Cambridge University Press, 1998), p. x.
6 Posthumous publications include her (unfinished) autobiography *Smile Please* (1981), *Letters* (1984) and *The Collected Short Stories* (1987).
7 Diana Athill sees three distinct groups in Rhys's short story writing: 'early work, written before Rhys's first novel'; 'stories written, or completed, in the sixties'; and finally 'stories written, or completed when she was an old woman' (*CSS*, p. vii).
8 Jean Rhys, *Letters*, selected and edited by Francis Wyndham and Diana Melly (London: Penguin, 1984), p. 185.
9 Paul Kotrodimos, 'Jean Rhys', in *A Reader's Companion to the Short Story in English*, ed. by Erin C. Fallon, Rick. A. Feddersen, James Kurtzleben and Maurice A. Lee (Westport, CT: Greenwood, 2000), pp. 357–63 (p. 358).
10 Anonymous reviewer, *The New York Times Book Review*, 11 December 1927. Quoted in Kotrodimos, p. 358.
11 In a discussion of modernist short fiction, Clare Hanson sees 'the rejection of

"story" in the accepted sense' as 'one of its leading characteristics'. She notes that modernist short fiction writers 'argued that the pleasing shape and coherence of the traditional short story represented a falsification of the discrete and heterogeneous nature of experience'. Clare Hanson, *Short Stories and Short Fictions, 1880–1980* (London: Macmillan, 1985), p. 55.

12 Sue Thomas, *The Worlding of Jean Rhys* (Westport, CT: Greenwood Press, 1999), p. 6.

13 Carole Angier, Rhys's biographer, in *Jean Rhys: Life and Work* (1992) frequently mines her fiction as a source.

14 Francis Wyndham, 'Introduction', in *Jean Rhys Letters, 1931–1966*, selected and edited by Francis Wyndham and Diana Melly (London, Andre Deutsch, 1984), pp. 9–12 (p. 9).

15 Elgin Mellown, 'Characters and Themes in the Novels of Jean Rhys', in *Critical Perspectives on Jean Rhys*, ed. by Pierrette Frickey (Boulder, CO: Three Continents, 1990), pp. 102–17 (p. 106), details this description of Rhys's heroines from Walter Allen's *New York Times* review of *Wide Sargasso Sea*, 18 June 1967. Mellown also notes that Stella Bowen, the Australian artist who lived with Ford and Rhys, 'saw this quality [of being a victim] in Rhys herself' (p. 106).

16 A. C. Morrell, 'The World of Jean Rhys's Short Stories', in *Critical Perspectives on Jean Rhys*, ed. by Frickey, pp. 95–102 (p. 95).

17 Cheryl Alexander Malcolm and David Malcolm, *Jean Rhys: A Study of the Short Fiction* (New York: Twayne, 1996), pp. xii–xiii.

18 A moment of epiphany is a distinctive trait of many modernist art forms, where a perspective, often otherwise banal, trivial or quotidian, serves to refocus the total aesthetic experience for the reader or viewer. James Joyce, in *Stephen Hero* (an early version of *A Portrait of the Artist as A Young Man* (1916)) first defined epiphany thus: 'a sudden spiritual manifestation, whether in the vulgarity of speech or of gesture or in a memorable phase of the mind itself' (New York: New Directions, 1963), p. 211.

19 Edgar Allan Poe, 'Review of *Twice-Told Tales*', in *Graham's Magazine*, May 1842. Reprinted in *Short Story Theories*, ed. by Charles E. May (Athens, OH: Ohio University Press, 1976) pp. 45–51

20 Dominic Head, *The Modernist Short Story* (Cambridge: Cambridge University Press, 1992), p. 9.

21 Paul March-Russell, *The Short Story: An Introduction* (Edinburgh: Edinburgh University Press, 2009), p. 165.

22 Ford Madox Ford, quoted in Gregg, 'Jean Rhys and Modernism: A Different Voice', pp. 39–40.

23 Gregg outlines one such ending's evolution in the short story 'Before the Deluge' (1976) in 'Jean Rhys and Modernism: A Different Voice', pp. 38–40.

24 Even though it is a 'middle period' story and a little longer than the others I examine, the force of the last line makes it an exemplar of the technique and worthy of inclusion here.

25 As Malcolm and Malcolm point out, 'the smallest things matter. Seemingly inconsequential details carry considerable weight for her protagonists' (p. 91).

26 This shifting point of view, or focalisation, is reminiscent of Virginia Woolf's short story, 'Kew Gardens', which was published a few years earlier (1919/1921), and with which Rhys would have been very familiar. Helen Carr outlines other connections between Woolf and Rhys, most notably between Woolf's *Three Guineas* (1938) and Rhys's own political analyses (Carr, *Jean Rhys* (Plymouth: Northcote House, 1996), pp. 51–53).

27 The unpublished drafts of this story housed at the McFarlin library at the University of Tulsa show this change in title.

28 The title echoes another of Virginia Woolf's writings, 'On Not Knowing Greek', from *The Common Reader* (1925).

29 Athill mentions humour as 'one of the devices by which [the powerless] manage to survive' (*CSS*, p. ix).

30 Carole Angier, *Jean Rhys: Life and Work*. (London: Penguin, 1992), p. 367.

31 The miniscule changes Rhys insisted on meant she felt her manuscript was never quite finished. In the foreword to *Smile Please*, Rhys's unfinished autobiography, Athill describes this perfectionism: 'Some five years after the publication of *Wide Sargasso Sea* she said to me out of the blue: "There is one thing I've always wanted to ask you. Why did you let me publish that book?" [...] I asked her what on earth she meant. "It was not finished," she said coldly. She then pointed out the existence in the book of two unnecessary words. One was "then," the other "quite"' (Diana Athill, 'Foreword', in Jean Rhys, *Smile Please* (London: Andre Deutsch, 1979), pp. 5–15 (p. 8).

32 Critics such as Veronica Marie Gregg ('Jean Rhys and Modernism') and Elaine Savory (*Jean Rhys*) have extensively charted the long evolution of a Rhys draft from the first manuscript to the finished product.

33 The cover of *The Collected Short Stories* quotes a review which suggests that 'the force of her stories lies in the fusion of elegant prose with an uncanny penetration into the darker reaches of the soul' (*Washington Post Book World*, cover *CSS*).

REMAPPING THE TRINIDADIAN SHORT STORY: LOCAL, AMERICAN AND GLOBAL RELATIONS IN THE SHORT FICTION OF EARL LOVELACE AND LAWRENCE SCOTT

JAK PEAKE

The more he thought about the island, its history, geography, topography and geology [...] spurred on by the insistence of fate to an exact knowledge of the place, he was encouraged to return to save himself and to write a story.

Lawrence Scott[1]

[I]f we take the Caribbean and America, the Americas to be the New World. I think the New World is not simply a matter of the discovery by Columbus, but it suggests a new life, a new civilization and a new humanity.

Earl Lovelace[2]

The contemporary Trinidadian short stories of Earl Lovelace and Lawrence Scott owe much to the circle of writers who formed the Beacon group in the 1930s. The group, which included such figures as C.L.R. James, Alfred Mendes, Albert Gomes and Ralph Mentor, galvanised the modern topography of the Trinidadian short story in a number of distinct ways: firstly its local focus, secondly its examination of social conditions via sites such as the barrack yard and thirdly its anti-establishment and anti-colonial vision.

Though the Beacon group's short stories are far from uniform, ranging in location beyond both the barrack yard and Trinidadian shores to neighbouring rural environs or isles such as Martinique, Reinhard Sander and subsequent scholars have generally conceived of the barrack-yard stories as 'the most original' of the group's output.[3] Often set in an urban Trinidad, particularly Port of Spain or San Fernando, these stories present the barrack yard as a centripetal site of communal rented rooms, where kitchens are non-existent, squalor and poverty rife, and privacy scarce. These barrack-yard stories revolve around urban settings in which under-privileged, unmarried women and men seek loose companionships of convenience and 'keepers' for economic betterment. Intrigues, sex, violence and obeah are all common features of these brief narratives. Collectively, through the prism of the barrack yard, they present narratives of enclosure, containment and curtailment appropriate to the brevity of the short story form.[4] As Mendes suggests, the Beacon group 'established the norms – dialect, way of life, [and] racial types' for a future generation of Caribbean writers including V.S. Naipaul, George Lamming, Samuel Selvon, and Wilson Harris.[5]

In furthering the trend of focus on local *topoi*, Lovelace and Scott may be added to this list. Yet these writers approach the place of the yard from two different positions; Lovelace arguably writes from *within* the inherited yard tradition, a generation or two removed from its existence; Scott, however, writes from *without*, and yet in proximity to, the yard. In both writers' cases, the autobiographical aspect of their stories, though not always present, is often interwoven with the positioning of their narrators. Lovelace's Afro-Trinidadian heritage, his Methodist and Spiritual Baptist upbringing and his formative years in Toco, Tobago and Valencia are all reflected in his short story collection, *A Brief Conversion* (1988). Likewise Scott's *Ballad for the New World* (1994) betrays his French creole ancestry, Catholic upbringing and his childhood on a plantation as the son of an estate manager.

A historic distinction between the Beacon group, on the one hand, and Lovelace and Scott, on the other, is their positioning within the nation. In a 1972 interview, C.L.R. James stated that Lovelace is 'native and national in a sense that the previous generation [Harris, Lamming, Naipaul and James] is not'.[6] This inference, equally applicable to Scott, somewhat belies the complexity of both writers having lived through a period of national independence. Born in 1935 and 1943 respectively, Lovelace and Scott grew up in colonial Trinidad and Tobago, Lovelace spending a significant portion of his youth in Tobago. Just prior to Eric Williams assuming the post of Chief Minister of Trinidad and Tobago as PNM (People's National Movement) leader in 1956, George Lamming observed in the political magazine *PNM Weekly*: 'what strange *conversion* [my emphasis], what magic, took place in Trinidad between 1950 and 1954'.[7] Whether these words resonated with the twenty-one-year-old prospective writer of *A Brief Conversion*, one can only speculate – however, the possible impact of this period of national galvanisation, political rallying, with the hint of a West Indian Federation ever present, cannot be overlooked.

By the time of Trinidad and Tobago's independence in 1962, Lovelace's debut novel *While Gods Are Falling* (1965) was soon to be published.[8] Meanwhile, Scott was just a year away from embarking on his training as a Benedictine monk in Gloucestershire, England. As both writers grew up under the mantle of colonialism, becoming 'nationals' as adults after the fated collapse of the West Indian Federation, neither writer can be easily described as wholly 'native' nor 'national'. Lovelace's and Scott's short stories are roughly contiguous with their own biographical timelines: with most childhood stories generally set in the forties and fifties, around the period of Trinidad's US base occupation, and more of the adult narratives – more markedly in Lovelace's case – set in independent Trinidad.

While Lovelace's short stories bear many similarities to the Beacon group's yard stories, they also differ considerably. In the eponymous, opening story of *Conversion*, the narrator Travey's aunt Irene appears as a figure not so dissimilar to the archetypal yard women of the Beacon group. Gap-toothed (a sign of lustiness in folklore as with Chaucer's wife of Bath), with a 'hoarse seductive voice' and coquettish charms, she 'attracts the men who enter [...the] yard'.[9] Yet where the seductress was often central to the barrack-yard stories, here she is balanced by her sister, Travey's mother Pearl, a sober, aspiring parent.

The affluence of the black and brown classes in Lovelace's stories is another example of how his characters differ from those of the 1930s yard story: where yards in these earlier stories are sparse, squalid loci and their inhabitants often on the poverty line or the brink of eviction, figures such as Irene and Pearl do not suffer the same level of economic deprivation. Pearl's yard possesses a 'verandah', while Irene owns the most fashionable Trinidadian dresses and pampers her son Ronnie with ice creams and cinema tickets (*Conversion*, pp. 4–5). Middle-class figures such as Miss Ross proliferate and the ostensibly more working-class figures of Mr Fitzroy, a caretaker, or Joebell, an ex-convict, have access to much more than their 1930s yard antecedents. The school yard, the office, the Community Centre, the Sports Complex and the Recreation club are additional places for the aspirant cast of Lovelace's stories. Blues, a tragicomic figure, who reappears in the trio of short stories, 'The Fire Eater's Journey', 'The Coward' and 'The Fire Eater's Return', bears certain hallmarks of a 'sweet man' – a prominent figure of the Beacon group's stories, generally promiscuous, unemployed and financially dependent upon women. And yet despite his passing similarity to a sweet man, Blues possesses many anomalous traits which play against this type. Though he talks salaciously of 'women like peas', he only ever appears with one girlfriend, Ayesha, in 'The Fire Eater's Return' (*Conversion*, p. 43). Also where the sweet man of the Beacon group's short stories is often emotionally stunted in his attitude towards his various girlfriends, Blues seeks emotional solace from Ayesha. It is his poverty, joblessness and desperation in this last story of the triptych that arguably draws him into the greatest alignment with the destitution of yard characters from 1930s Trinidadian short fiction.

In Scott's *Ballad for the New World*, the narrators or central protagonists through which the narrative is filtered are, in all but one case, white, middle-class creoles of generally French or Spanish descent. In these stories, the narrator or central protagonist's childhood or ancestral home is often an estate house standing in opposition to, yet closely quartered with, the barrack yard. 'The Fitful Muse' is typical of the collection, as the narrator drives his mother to her old home, 'La Mariana'. 'At the back of the old house', the narrator informs us, 'were the outbuildings where the labourers and servants lived, the barrack-rooms' (*Ballad*, p. 20). His mother describes these dwellers as 'like the family, our old nannies. They tucked us up in bed' (*Ballad*, p. 20).

In contrast to Lovelace's generally Afro-Trinidadian narrators or central protagonists, who enjoy greater freedoms than their slave ancestors, Scott's white counterparts are often anxious or overburdened by the colonial baggage of their ancestry. In 'The Fitful Muse' the narrator's mother has a nightmare in which she dreams of being whipped by a black man from the barrack rooms. Her anxiety, the corollary of 'one hundred years of accumulated guilt and fear', resembles the crisis Philippe (Philip) Monagas faces in reading Trinidad's past in 'The Question of the Keskidee' (*Ballad*, p. 23). Overwhelmed by Trinidad's and, indeed, the wider region's baleful and barbarous past, Philip dies unable to complete his history of the island (*Ballad*, p. 65).

The large majority of Scott's central narrators and protagonists inhabit worlds of fading glamour in which sugar or cocoa estates are soon to be obsolete or replaced by modern industry. 'Malgrétoute' is archetypal of the collection, opening and closing around the theme of decay. The line, 'Boy, when cocoa was king' recurs as an old saying, a remembrance of past glory which Mr Wainwright recalls prior to the spread of witchbroom, a tropical fungal disease which has laid waste to Trinidad's cocoa and his livelihood at La Mariana (*Ballad*, p. 1). Now a junior overseer on a sugar estate, he has been 'dumped', as he sees it, in Malgrétoute (*Ballad*, p. 1). Derided by his in-laws for not joining the burgeoning oil or motor-car industries, Mr Wainwright chooses instead to remain in a declining industry, fighting for promotion, as he caustically remarks, 'into dead men's boots' (*Ballad*, p. 5, p. 8).

REMAPPING THE LOCAL AND THE SINGULAR

The local focus of Lovelace's and Scott's short story collections bears an interesting relationship with the genesis of the short story form and short story theory in the nineteenth century. As the putative 'father of the short story', Edgar Allan Poe is often credited as being the first theorist of its form. As an innovator, he was 'mapping out the territory, fixing boundaries, naming routes, setting up a terminology for the exploration of short fiction'.[10] It is significant that Poe's blueprint for subsequent generations of writers has been global in outlook, just as his story settings are international, encompassing South Carolina, Java, the Norwegian coast, Batavia, Paris and even mysterious, unnamed, anonymous places.[11] Such is his technique that geographic locales are occasionally left unspecified, as is the case in 'The Fall of the House of Usher'.[12] The effect created by such a story is one in which geography is of secondary importance to the imaginary, in which events are projected onto a generic, identifiably North Atlantic world of the mercantile and industrial nineteenth century. Poe's use of global settings and geographic indeterminacy brings into sharp relief the local focus of the Trinidadian short story from the 1930s through to Lovelace's and Scott's collections.

In an 1842 review, Poe famously asserted that the short story form requires a '*single* effect' and 'unity of effect'.[13] If this unity of effect can be perceived as an integral component which has been crucial to the genesis and formalisation of the short story, then its claim on the Caribbean short story, especially in respect to Lovelace's and Scott's stories, is less secure. James Procter has drawn attention to Poe's influence on Lovelace, signalling the words 'singular effect', 'limited situation' and 'one aspect of character' scrawled on Lovelace's manuscript of *Conversion*.[14] Yet alongside this influence, Lovelace follows a distinctly Caribbean tradition of interlinked short story-telling, presenting the same characters in multiple stories within the collection.[15] In *Conversion*, a cycle or sequence of stories emerges ('The Fire Eater's Journey', 'The Coward' and 'The Fire Eater's Return') in which Santo and Blues reappear as narrator and protagonist respectively. Similarly in *Ballad*, Scott's protagonists are generally descendants of either the French creole Wainwright or the Spanish creole Monagas de los Macajuelos (Monagas) families. Tantalisingly Scott hints at a possible relation between the Monagas and Wainwright families in 'The House of Funerals', where the marriage of Cecile and Carlos unites the 'old French family to [...] the old Spanish family' (*Ballad*, p. 104). The overall result of each collection is not one in which the 'singularity of effect' dominates, leading consequentially to singular, self-contained short stories. As fragments, these stories appear related – almost literally in the case of Scott – within cycles or sequences of time, place, communities, peoples and families.

Just as Édouard Glissant proposes that Caribbean epistemology is rhizomatic, challenging Eurocentric, totalising pedagogy, so too does the Caribbean short story threaten to disturb the neat, monolithic dictums of short story theory. The Caribbean short story is arguably rhizomatic, having some rootedness in notions of 'singular effects' or singular narratives common to the short story more generally, yet not exclusively so. This hypothesis suggests two things: that the short story form is employed differently by Caribbean writers than by writers in the North Atlantic and, more generally, that the short story may not be an entirely singular or closed form. In this way, my discussion here goes against the grain of many leading short story theorists who pit the continuous themes of the novel against the singularity of the short story.

In 'The Philosophy of the Short-Story', Brander Matthews writes: 'The Short-story is the single effect, complete and self-contained, while the Novel is of necessity broken into a series of episodes. Thus the Short-story has, what the Novel cannot have, the effect of "totality", as Poe called it, the unity of impression'.[16] He continues, 'the Novel cannot get on easily without love, the Short-story can. Since love seems to be almost the only thing which will give interest to a long story [...] yet] the Short-story, being brief, does not need a love-interest to hold its parts together' (Matthews, p. 74). Similarly, in an introduction to the Spanish American short story, Edelweis Serra writes: 'The short story, then, is a limited continuity, in contrast with the "unlimited discontinuity" of the novel [...]. The short story is a relatively closed order of internal associations and correlations, and the novel a wide open order'.[17] As Mary Louise Pratt observes, the singularity of the short story is often defined both in relation to and distinct from the novel as a long, open-ended form. (Pratt, pp. 94–96). Pratt argues that the short story and novel are interdependent, defining the relationship as 'asymmetrical' with the former dependent upon the latter (Pratt, p. 96). As much as theorists and admirers of the short story have tried to keep the two forms apart, she surmises, the short story has nevertheless relied upon the prestige of the novel for its growth. This is evidenced by the many novelists' careers which begin with the publishing of short stories and by the form's image as an experimental genre in which writers cut their teeth – where investment for readers and writers alike is relatively lower than with the novel. Following Pratt's line of argument, this essay forwards three points: firstly, the short story and novel are related forms; secondly, the short story need not be entirely centred upon singular or closed events; thirdly, an open-ended continuum of effects may be more apt in describing the Caribbean and, particularly, the Trinidadian short story.

    In the case of both Lovelace and Scott, the fact that their short stories have been published as collections plays a role in the stories' interconnec-tion, shared thematic content and relational aspects. The considerable length of stories like Lovelace's 'A Brief Conversion' and Scott's 'The House of Funerals', both of which are divided into two and three sub-sections respectively, challenge notions of the short story's containment, closure and brevity. With Scott, the shared themes and content between his short story collection and his novel, *Witchbroom* (1992), suggest the former is imbricated with the latter's continuous or episodic form. The blight of witchbroom described in the opening story of *Ballad*, 'Malgrétout', serves as the crucial backdrop to *Witchbroom*, while the Monagas family who feature in almost half of the stories in *Ballad* are the central protagonists of *Witchbroom*.[18]

    Place or places serve as an important connector in Lovelace's and Scott's stories. Indeed, locales bind families, characters, memories and communi-ties; they belie the wholesale fragmentation of individual stories; and they reinforce a far more open-ended and interconnected form of narrative structure. Such loci need not necessarily be perceived as fitting within a national model. Stefano Harney, for example, considers Lovelace as working outside the frame of national allegory: 'Nationalism is too fragile, too inflexible, to assimilate and use Lovelace's text because, beneath the narrative [...] there is a deep rejection of group identity' (Harney, p. 44). An alternative reading, however, could be that Lovelace does not entirely discard group identity, but operates at a sub- or supra-national level, perceiving both the individual and community as operating below or around the radar of 'grand narratives of national identity'.[19] On a similar note, Patricia Murray delineates Lawrence Scott's novel *Witchbroom* as locating Trinidad within a 'South American' heritage, a position which in her opinion connects it to Lovelace's *The Dragon Can't Dance* (1979), as 'a reminder of the liminality of the nation-space'.[20] If Scott's and Lovelace's novels hint at ulterior, interior or overlapping apertures within, around or outside the nation, this tension is arguably more acute in their short stories.

In *Conversion*, the community centres around Cunaripo as the home place or village and Port of Spain as a place of work. Characters are generally born in Cunaripo and either travel, commute or move to Port of Spain. Thus the collection links stories in which the interaction between the urban capital and rural Cunaripo is a continual theme. Since Port of Spain generally features as an anonymous hub in which reputations are built or destroyed, it may be tempting to see Lovelace's oeuvre as slotting into a paradigm of corrupt city versus idyllic country. However, as Evelyn O'Callaghan contends, Lovelace avoids such simplistic binaries.[21] While avoiding such polarisation, Lovelace nevertheless accentuates the importance of remaining true to the local, whether through contact with the home village, suburb or people in which characters have roots. Nicknames – Scully, Belly, Police, Santo and Blues – are indicators of local knowledge, as they signal a person's identity or standing in the particular community. In effect, this means most characters have two identities: one that is local, familiar and informal, and the other which is impersonal, formal and state-acknowledged. Those referred to by their legal appellations – Mr Cabral, Mr Wilkins, Mr Rivers and Mr Norman – tend to represent characters who are either formal strangers to Cunaripo or members of a 'respectable' middle class.

In a speech delivered in St Thomas in 2000, Lovelace castigated 'the bacchanal elite', a group he considers as following its own shallow pursuits of entertainment and tourism, while remaining detached from 'ordinary people' (*Growing*, p. 105). In many respects, the cast of 'Call Me "Miss Ross" For Now' are analogous to this bacchanal elite. In this story, the eponymous heroine participates for years in Village Council meetings which are stultified and poorly attended. Attracted to the caretaker of the village hall, Mr Fitzroy, she cannot bring herself, as the story's title suggests, to disclose her first name to him.[22] As a respectable member of the council and community, she has too much to lose. Mr Rivers, the council president, complains of the lack of young attendees at meetings, while Mr Grannum boasts of the excellent membership during his premiership. Yet neither councillor suggests any action to improve the current low turnout. The ballot for the next president is negligently conducted by Mr Rivers. He asks those who wish to relieve him of his post simply to raise their hands, dismissing a secret ballot on account of its lengthiness. In name and action, the councillors are detached from the community. Their meeting is exclusive, their activities closed and their members self-congratulatory. Significantly, on the brink of her own conversion, Miss Ross ruminates over the name which would perhaps connect her to the local nicknames and heritage of the community, 'her other name [...] not spoken for years' (*Conversion*, p. 79). Finally, longing to rid herself of the shackles of the stuffy council, she runs out of the meeting after her friend Fedosia. Her act, heretical to the councillors, highlights her decisive effort to associate with her fellow villagers. 'Call Me "Miss Ross" For Now' highlights that the city need not necessarily be the root of modern corruption and that mismanagement of public interests is equally liable at the rural and local level.

Lovelace's communal stories again appear to contradict the conventions of the short story form as set out by theorists of the genre. Frank O'Connor writes that 'the short story remains by its very nature remote from the community – romantic, individualistic and intransigent'.[23] Lovelace's stories make individuals' narratives central devices and yet equally portray how these individuals comprise communities. Thus the Cunaripo Community Centre which features in both 'The Fire-Eater's Journey' and 'Call Me "Miss Ross" For Now' gives a sense of continuum between these distinct stories, demonstrating how the protagonists from different narratives share communal space.

With Scott's *Ballad*, ancestry serves as a key issue which binds his stories together as a collection. Indebtedness to Gabriel García Márquez is detectable in the tone, style and content of Scott's stories, as they chart lineage, family homes and ancestral memories.[24] In Márquez's *One Hundred Years of Solitude* (1996) the Buendía family members and home in Macondo serve as central figures around which plot and chapters are arranged.[25] Likewise, Scott's stories are connected by family relationships. 'Malgrétout', 'The Fitful Muse' and 'Rabbits' feature Wainwrights, or relatives who are all linked to some degree to the old family home of La Mariana. Alternatively, with their ancestral roots in the ancient town of San Jose de Orunya (modern-day St Joseph),[26] the Monagases appear directly or indirectly in 'King Sailor One J'Ouvert Morning', 'The Question of the Keskidee', 'I

Want to Follow My Friend', 'Sylvia's Room' and 'The House of Funerals'. 'The House of Funerals', perhaps most redolent of Márquez's fiction for its account of the death of one of the last members of a generation, focuses specifically on Cecile Monagas, her home and her relatives. Its sections roughly intersect the lives of different family members, jump-cutting through time and locale. The first and last sections track the movements of Gaston, Cecile's grandson, in the 'tumble-down town', while the second section lingers in Cecile's home 'on top of the hill' with its views of the gulf and the 'continental cordillera of mountains in the north' (*Ballad*, pp. 97–98). In this middle section, the third-person narrative backtracks to recount episodes from Cecile's life, particularly her widowhood. The final section cuts between Gaston's movements through the town, remembered episodes of Cecile's life and Cecile's funeral. As with *One Hundred Years of Solitude*, where the family line serves as the start and end point of the novel, Gaston's standing as 'the last descendant of the Monagas de la Macajuelos' is significant. His presence in the last story of the volume signals an appropriate close to a collection structured around ancestry. Via different means to Lovelace, Scott's collection challenges O'Connor's theorisation of the short story as a genre evoking isolation and individualism, as families, however incongruous or dysfunctional, bind the individuals and individual stories in his collection.

REMAPPING AMERICA

Lovelace's and Scott's stories' engagement with the yard, rather than reproducing the Beacon group's output, effects a remapping of narrative terrain. Their collections reflect both a more contemporary Trinidad and a more open and relational link to the wider continent of America and the forces of modern globalisation. In many respects their narratives can be read productively in terms of Glissant's notion of 'poetics of relation', which in Michael Dash's interpretation operate at a 'new global level'.[27] Their stories also show, in Glissant's words, that Caribbean communities can no longer seek 'unique origins', but are rather shaped by an 'unceasing process of transformation' from 'multiple cultural sources'.[28] Both writers demonstrate a vision of a shared regional perspective between Latin America and the Caribbean. In *Ballad*, Scott's references to the Orinoco, El Dorado and Venezuela recast Trinidad in terms of its relation to South American culture and geography. In the case of 'Chameleon', the protagonist Monty recalls his earlier life and childhood in the Venezuelan town of Villahermosa. Despite distinct historical and cultural differences – the afternoon siestas and militaristic heritage – the mainland shares many parallels with the isle of 'La Trinidad'. Indeed much of Monty's story is sparked by associations between his present life in Trinidad and his formative years in Villahermosa. The fountain in the 'botanical gardens' initiates a memory of a fountain in his home town; the old town houses remind him of Villahermosa and Cartegena (*Ballad*, p. 33, p. 37). Monty's learning of the cuatro and the song-forms '*joropo*' and '*aguinaldo*' also ties him to music which forms the backbone of Venezuela's and Trinidad's shared cultural heritage.[29]

In Lovelace's collection Trinidad's links with Latin America are less conspicuous but nevertheless present. In 'Joebell and America', the protagonist Joebell is encouraged by his brother to remain in Venezuela to work, but rejects the opportunity at his folly, as he is eventually deported upon attempting entry to the US. The implication is that Latin America is less prejudiced towards the Caribbean migrant and that opportunities for employment are available to the Caribbean émigré.

While both Lovelace and Scott perceive close bonds between the Caribbean and Latin America, both writers are attuned to the asymmetric and neocolonialist relations that exist between tropical America and the countries of the North. Where both writers deal with Trinidad's colonial legacies, they also perceive the fragility of the island in relation to the US. Their stories convey the uneven networks of flow – economic and otherwise – that mark the US as a dominant contingent in Trinidad and tropical America. Trinidad's precarious status is particularly evident in two stories of Scott's collection, 'Malgrétout' and 'Ballad for the New World'. Both stories are set around the 1940s, a period often dubbed as Trinidad's 'American [US] Occupation' in light of a number of US military installations that were constructed in Trinidad's northwest.[30] From the most north-westerly, peninsular tip of Chaguaramas, to huge swathes of the 'east-west corridor' and the docks around Wrightson Road, the US army gained a stake in Trinidad's most urban and densest residential areas.[31] Though the US bases brought newfound jobs and economic security to the island, prostitution flourished and sexual rivalry for Trinidadian women increased. A hint of the new sexual threat posed by affluent US servicemen, memorialised in Lord Invader's calypso, 'Rum and Coca-Cola' – a cocktail of Caribbean spirit and North American sweetness – is given in anaphoric refrain in 'Ballad for the New World': 'We were in the shadow of America a long time, a long time. "…Rum and Coca-Cola… working for the Yankee Dollar"' (*Ballad*, p. 51).[32]

In 'Ballad for the New World', the narrator's brother epitomises Trinidad's intermediary status via his attraction to and enthralment with the US. He is an 'all-American' Trinidadian, a figure who lauds Hollywood icons in his youth, living in the guise of a North American hero (*Ballad*, pp. 52–53). He lifts weights, has a dog called 'Mutt', after the comic *Mutt and Jeff*, rides a motorbike at the 'Wallerfield' US base and, after a few years as a car mechanic and a car salesman, works on a Trinidadian oil rig.[33] The trajectory of his life moves from his youth and his James Deanesque devil-may-care-attitude – swiftly brought to a close by a near-fatal car accident – to his more sober life as a capitalist company owner. His declaration that he is 'a self-made man' aligns him with a panoply of North American self-inventors, epitomised not only by the venerable Frederick Douglass or Benjamin Franklin, but also by J.D. Rockefeller, Joseph Smith or Al Capone.[34] By the close of the story, he is a millionaire but has lost his 'James Dean rebel smile'; phlegmatic and passionless, he is spent by his ambition (*Ballad*, p. 57).

The narrator's description of his brother's ambition presents a mapping of Trinidadian and US relations that suggest a historical link to Trinidad's colonial past. His oil rig enterprise is likened to the conquistadorial dream of El Dorado (*Ballad*, p. 57). Where the sixteenth-century dream of enrichment was predicated upon gold, now it rests on oil, the new 'black gold'. Consequently, the British Oil Company has been replaced by US-owned Texaco.[35] The two associated transitions imply that what is happening in Trinidad's more recent history bears parallels with its colonial past: the colonial factory has simply been replaced by the international conglomerate. The oil company's switch from British to North American, from colonial to neocolonial ownership, appears little more than a shift of hegemonic relations. The narrator claims his story 'begins to fade' as his brother is lost in 'his hallucination, *folies de grandeur*, the old madness of the ancestors of the savannahs of Monagas, the pampas of Bolivar'.[36] Scott sees the continuum of Euro-American, male hegemony that stems back through the Monagas family line and dovetails with the ambitions of Simón Bolívar, the celebrated general and liberator of Latin America. The brother's association with Bolívar suggests another association to wider terrain and ideology of American independence. The narrator flits between independence and colonial metaphors and events in his recollection of his brother, narrowing, and even submerging, the boundaries between pre- and post-independent Trinidad. Power and rapid consumption, the narrator implies, have been prevalent in both states. His inferences can be further delineated as such: that in the Americas power has generally been retained by Euro-American elites, who end in replicating their own circular, self-generating hegemonic myths ad infinitum.

Lovelace presents a similar character study to that of Scott's 'All-American' Trinidadian in 'Joebell and America'. The title is both opaque and ambiguous, implying two meanings: firstly Joebell's relationship with the US, for which America stands as a synecdoche, and secondly his association with the wider American continent. At the opening of the story, the narrative asserts Joebell's wish to emigrate to the US. Having grown up on a diet of Hollywood icons, he projects a fantasist vision of the US, imagining a paradisiacal, consumerist cornucopia: 'America, where everybody have a motor car and you could ski on snow and where it have seventy-five channels of colour television that never sign off (*Conversion*, p. 111).

Joebell's vision is of a dynamic, vital US in which the consumer is *king*. His consumerist aspirations could be deemed symbolic of a 'commodity fetishism' prevalent in the colonial era and greatly accentuated by the late 1970s oil boom in Trinidad. Anthropologists such as Kevin Yelvington, Steven Vertovec and Daniel Miller have discussed the growth of consumerism in Trinidad in the wake of the oil boom, precipitated by the rise in the price of oil initiated by the Organization of Petroleum Exporting Countries (OPEC) in 1973.[37] At its peak in 1976–83, Trinidad and Tobago was one of the richest countries in South America (*Producing Power*, p. 64).[38] As Vertovec observes, 'the island society quickly became absorbed in an "easy money", free-spending, consumption-dominated ethos which one popular calypso [...] described as "Capitalism Gone Mad"'.[39]

Joebell symbolises the paradox of interrelations between the US and Trinidad. In some respects he is modern and progressive; in another his actions are short-term, high-risk and ultimately wasteful. As Shalini Puri argues, Joebell's wastefulness correlates with his '*carnivalesque* values of risk, recklessness, and impetuosity'.[40] Perceiving 'waste' as an endemic attribute of Trinidadian society and colonialism as a whole, Lovelace writes: 'it is for these reasons [Trinidad's heritage of waste] that Independence [...] does not mean anything new' (*Growing*, p. 24). In Lovelace's analysis, Trinidad's culture of waste is retrogressive and neocolonial in that it mirrors the symptoms and inequalities of colonialism. In 1988, the same year in which *Conversion* was first published, the government-owned Iron and Steel Company of Trinidad and Tobago (ISCOTT) anticipated a loss of TT $160.6 million.[41] Alongside concerns over the PNM's corruption, ISCOTT, Eric Williams's brainchild, embodied the huge wastefulness of state resources.[42] Joebell's addiction to gambling acts as a local, national and regional allegory of wastefulness.[43] An alternative thesis suggests that wastefulness is an in-built factor of wealthy, 'developed' societies. As Henri Lefebvre states: 'Nobody today is unaware of the fact that the obsolescence of such products is planned, that waste has an economic function, or that fashion plays an enormous role, as does "culture", in a functionalized consumption that is structured accordingly'.[44] In this respect, Joebell's and, allegorically, Trinidadian aspirations can be read as conditioned by the paradigms set by more affluent societies.

Spending a thousand dollars on a fake passport with the winnings from a game of wappie only to lose eight hundred at poker, Joebell gambles with his prospects.[45] Joebell's behaviour is symptomatic of modern consumerism in extremis. Working legally in South America, according to Joebell, encompasses too much hard graft and language learning (*Conversion*, p. 119). His outlook is representative of a Caribbean vision of the North

Atlantic world, specifically North America, as the ultimate haven or refuge from poverty, frustration and unhappiness. In a strange quirk of life mirroring and even outdoing art, in August 1988 – the year *Conversion* was published – 208 Trinidadians entered Canada claiming refugee status due to a 'loophole' in Canadian legislation ('Trinidad', B469). A distinction of Joebell's story from the Trinidadians who exploited Canadian border-control laws is that where the latter did not claim to be anything other than Trinidadian, Joebell assumes a US identity. This act of mimicry links him to the carnivalesque tradition of masquerade, where participants inhabit different roles or characters.

While Joebell's performance in the Puerto Rican airport, as a belligerent Vietnam veteran from the US South, may seem like the negative display of a null mimic man, another arguably more complex and subversive plot emerges. Joebell's belief that his knowledge of the US is infallible, as 'he grow up in America right there in Trinidad', complicates the notion of his merely play-acting (*Conversion*, p. 121). Such is the impact of US airwaves on Trinidad, Joebell feels he has culturally traversed into US terrain. Though initially he might appear fake, not unlike Blues, his simulation, unlike Blues's, is temporary and adopted solely for the purpose of con-founding the customs officials. When caught out by his West Indian pronunciation of Z as 'Zed', his Trinidadian-ness is accentuated and he leaves the airport singing a calypso of his own authorship. It is perhaps no surprise that his calypso expresses aspirations to travel to a US city renowned for its carnivalesque spirit, New Orleans: 'We gonna travel far / To New Orleans / Me and ma baby / Be digging the scene' (*Conversion*, p. 124). The conjunction of North American parlance, 'digging the scene', in a Trinidadian calypso form is suggestive of Trinidad's tessellation with and adoption of North American culture. Joebell's deportation and arrest highlight the darker side of Trinidadian–US relations. While the northern superpower exports its way of life as one of freedom and democracy through television, radio and print, its doors remain closed, enacting an effective ban on all immigrants, who – for reasons of deprivation, poverty, lack of resources and want of opportunities – are deemed undesirable.

In engaging with similar Trinidadian terrain to the Beacon group, Lovelace and Scott remap and open out Trinidad in terms of wider, more modern and interrelated networks of geography. In doing so, they demon-strate prevailing continuities and discontinuities between the following: colonialism, postcolonialism and neocolonialism; the local and the global; family, community and the individual; tropical America (the Caribbean and Latin America) and the North Atlantic (Europe and North America). Ultimately their specifically place-bound stories, and the connections between them, force a rethinking of boundaries between the short story and the novel. That the former offers closed singularity and the latter an open continuum, or even a series of discontinuities, is untenable in the case of both Lovelace and Scott. Their short story collections suggest rather a syncretism of the longer and shorter narrative forms, in which individual stories are linked, interrelated and open-ended and far less singular than many modern theorists assert.

NOTES

1 Lawrence Scott, *Ballad for the New World And Other Stories* (Oxford and Portsmouth, NH: Heinemann, 1994), p. 66.
2 Earl Lovelace and George Lamming, 'Interview with George Lamming', *Caribbean Writer's Summer Institute Archival Video Collection* (University of Miami, 1992).
3 Reinhard W. Sander, *The Trinidad Awakening: West Indian Literature of the Nineteen-Thirties* (New York: Greenwood Press, 1988), p. 55.
4 I have borrowed these linked ideas of 'containment' and 'curtailment' from James Procter. See James Procter's essay in this volume.
5 Alfred Hubert Mendes and Reinhard Sander, eds, 'The Turbulent Thirties in Trinidad: an Interview with Alfred H. Mendes', *World Literature Written in English*, 12:1 (1973), 66–79 (p. 75). See Reinhard Sander and Peter K. Ayers, 'Introduction', in *From Trinidad: An Anthology of Early West Indian Writing*, ed. by Sander and Ayers (New York: Africana Pub. Co., 1978), pp. 1–20 (p. 9).
6 Ian Munro and Reinhard Sander, eds, *Kas-kas: Interviews with Three Caribbean Writers in Texas* (Austin: African and Afro-American Research Institute, University of Texas at Austin, 1972), p. 30. Quoted in Stefano Harney, *Nationalism and Identity: Culture and the Imagination in a Caribbean Diaspora* (London and New Jersey: University of the West Indies, 1996), p. 33.
7 Kirk Peter Meighoo, *Politics in a 'Half Made Society': Trinidad and Tobago, 1925–2002* (Kingston, Oxford and Princeton: Ian Randle Publishers; J. Currey Publishers; M. Wiener Publishers, 2003), p. 36.
8 See Earl Lovelace, *While Gods are Falling* (London: Collins, 1965).
9 Earl Lovelace, *A Brief Conversion and Other Stories* (Oxford: Heinemann, 1988), p. 4.
10 John S. Whitley, 'Introduction', in *Tales of Mystery and Imagination*, ed. by John S. Whitley (Ware: Wordsworth Classics, 2000), pp. vii–xxv (p. xi).
11 Edgar Allan Poe, *Tales of Mystery and Imagination*, ed. by Whitley, p. 3, p. 39, p. 48. See also Edgar Allan Poe, 'The Murders in the Rue Morgue', in *Tales of Mystery and Imagination*, pp. 62–90.
12 The 'tarn' that eventually engulfs the house suggests the setting is northern Europe, as the word has roots in Old English and Scandinavian. However, no indication is given of the specific country. See Edgar Allan Poe, 'The Fall of the House of Usher', in *Tales of Mystery and Imagination*, pp. 148–63 (p. 148, p. 63). See also John A. Simpson and Edmund Weiner, *The Oxford English Dictionary*, CD-ROM (Oxford: Oxford University Press, 1992).
13 Edgar Allan Poe, 'Nathaniel Hawthorne', in *The Works of Edgar Allan Poe*, vol. 3 (New York: Widdleton, 1849) pp. 196–97.
14 James Procter, 'A"Limited Situation": Brevity and Lovelace's *A Brief Conversion*', in *Caribbean Literature After Independence: The Case of Earl Lovelace*, ed. by Bill Schwarz (London: Institute for the Study of the Americas, 2008) pp. 130–31.
15 V.S. Naipaul employs the technique in *Miguel Street*, where characters such as

Hat and Bogart, dwelling on the eponymous street, reappear in different stories. In many of the Beacon group's short stories, though characters are not exactly reproduced in different narratives, names and types of characters are repeated; Mamitz is the key figure in both James's 'Triumph' and Mendes's 'Sweetman', the kept woman in the former, the keeper in the latter. Similarly, in Paul Keens-Douglas's collection of short stories and dialect poetry, *Is Town Say So!*, characters such as Bobots and Blackie feature in multiple stories. This tradition of short stories, involving reappearing characters, can no doubt be traced back to Caribbean folktales in which figures like Anancy feature in a variety of narratives. Tellingly, in an Oxford anthology of Caribbean short stories, Anancy features as the protagonist in Andrew Salkey's short story 'A Proper Anno Domini Feeling'. For the Beacon group's short stories, see Sander and Ayers, eds, *From Trinidad: An Anthology of Early West Indian Writing*. See also Stewart Brown and John Wickham, eds, *The Oxford Book of Caribbean Short Stories* (Oxford and New York: Oxford University Press, 1999). Paul Keens-Douglas, *Is Town Say So!* (Port of Spain: Keensdee Productions, 1981). V.S. Naipaul, *The Mystic Masseur & Miguel Street* (London: Picador, 2002).

16 Brander Matthews, 'The Philosophy of the Short-Story', in *The New Short Story Theories*, ed. by Charles E. May (Athens, Ohio: Ohio University Press, 1994), pp. 73–80 (p. 73).

17 Edelweis Serra, quoted in Mary Louise Pratt, 'The Short Story: The Long and the Short of It', in *The New Short Story Theories*, ed. by May, pp. 91–113 (pp. 94–95).

18 However, it must be noted that while the Monagas family feature in both *Ballad* and *Witchbroom*, the specific family members from one do not reappear in the other. Names such as Gaston Monagas reappear, although as distinct characters in *Ballad* and *Witchbroom*. The concluding episode from 'The Fitful Muse', in which the narrator's mother is awoken by the nightmare of being whipped by a black man, also features in *Witchbroom*. See Lawrence Scott, *Witchbroom* (Oxford: Heinemann, 1993 [1992]) p. 144.

19 Nicole King, 'Performance and Tradition in Earl Lovelace', in *Caribbean Literature After Independence*, ed. by Schwarz, pp. 111–29 (p. 113). Lovelace's appraisal of calypso suggests an acceptance of community that circumvents nationality, and is rather both local and regional. See Earl Lovelace, *Growing in the Dark*, ed. by Funso Aiyejina (San Juan, Trinidad and Tobago: Lexicon, 2003) p. 136.

20 Patricia Murray, 'Writing Trinidad: Nation and Hybridity in *The Dragon Can't Dance* and *Witchbroom*', in *Caribbean Literature After Independence*, ed. by Schwarz, pp. 94–110 (p. 95).

21 See Evelyn O'Callaghan, 'The Modernization of the Trinidadian Landscape in the Novels of Earl Lovelace', *Ariel*, 20:1 (1989), pp. 41–54.

22 Significantly, just as Fitzroy is kept in the dark regarding her name, so are the readers.

23 Frank O'Connor, *The Lonely Voice, a Study of the Short Story* (Cleveland: World Pub. Co., 1963) p. 21.

24 Scott's indebtedness to Márquez is especially apparent in *Witchbroom*, where the narrative makes intertextual references to *One Hundred Years of Solitude*, referring specifically to Márquez's fictional town of Macondo and his figure of 'Remedios the beautiful' (see *Witchbroom*, p. 26).

25 Gabriel García Márquez, *One Hundred Years of Solitude* (London: Penguin, 1996).

26 This refers to Scott's spelling of the ancient town of St Joseph, which is commonly spelt San José de Oruña. See *Ballad*, p. 59.

27 J. Michael Dash, *Édouard Glissant* (Ca–mbridge: Cambridge University Press, 1995) p. 179.

28 Édouard Glissant, *Caribbean Discourse: Selected Essays*, trans. by J. Michael Dash (Charlottesville: University Press of Virginia, 1981), pp. 140–42.

29 A parang band performs these song-forms at the close of Lovelace's short story 'Shoemaker Arnold', (see *Conversion*, p. 132).

30 Lloyd Braithwaite is one of the earliest scholars to discuss Trinidad's 'American Occupation'. See Lloyd Braithwaite, *Social Stratification in Trinidad* (Mona, Kingston, Jamaica: Institute of Social and Economic Research, University of the West Indies, 1975) p. 78. See also footnote 1 in Harvey R. Neptune, *Caliban and the Yankees: Trinidad and the United States Occupation* (Chapel Hill: University of North Carolina Press, 2007) p. 199.

31 As part of a 1940 agreement between Franklin Roosevelt and Winston Churchill, the installations granted the US military territory on lease for air and naval bases.

32 This refrain repeats with subtle variations throughout the short story, (see *Ballad*, p. 53, pp. 55–56, p. 58).

33 Tellingly, *Mutt and Jeff* was first published by All-American Publications.

34 Joseph Smith was the founder of the Church of Jesus Christ of Latter-Day Saints, or as it is commonly known, Mormonism. See Hugh Brogan, *The Penguin History of the United States of America* (London: Penguin, 1990) pp. 238–51.

35 In 1956, roughly six years prior to independence, Texaco bought out the British-owned Trinidad Oil Company (TOC).

36 The anaphoric phrase *'folies de grandeur'* reappears in singular form in 'Sylvia's room', even resurfacing in Scott's novel *Witchbroom* (see *Ballad*, p. 57, p. 91; *Witchbroom*, p. 63, p. 125).

37 Kevin A. Yelvington, *Producing Power: Ethnicity, Gender, and Class in a Caribbean Workplace* (Philadelphia: Temple University Press, 1995) p. 99.

38 See also Daniel Miller, *Modernity: An Ethnographic Approach: Dualism and Mass Consumption in Trinidad* (Oxford and New York: Berg, 1994) p. 204.

39 Steven Vertovec, 'East Indians and Anthropologists: A Critical Review', *Social and Economic Studies*, 40:1 (1991), 133–69 (p. 138).

40 Shalini Puri, 'Beyond Resistance: Notes Toward a New Caribbean Cultural Studies', *Small Axe*, 7:2 (2003), 23–38 (p. 29).

41 Kevin A. Yelvington, 'Trinidad and Tobago, 1988–89', *Latin American and Caribbean Contemporary Record*, 8 (1991), B459–77 (B468).

42 It was this legacy which perhaps led to the PNM's first ousting from office in 1986 by the National Alliance for Reconstruction (NAR).

43 Joebell is continually referred to as a gambler or via gambling metaphors. Entering Puerto Rico, he is described as 'betting on himself' (see *Conversion*, pp. 120–21).

44 Henri Lefebvre, *The Production of Space* (Oxford, UK and Cambridge, MA: Blackwell, 1991), pp. 328–29.

45 Poker owes its modern genesis to the New World and is generally considered, though internationally renowned, as most popular in the US. Tellingly Joebell loses at poker, while winning at the Trinidadian game of wappie. See Glenn McDonald, *Deal Me In: Online Cardrooms, Big Time Tournaments, and the New Poker* (San Francisco: Sybex, 2005) p. 38, p. 42. See also inc Encyclopaedia Britannica, in *The New Encyclopaedia Britannica*, ed. by Robert McHenry, 15th edn (Michigan: Encyclopaedia Britannica, 1993), vol. 9, p. 551.

PART FOUR

FOLKTALES AND ORAL TRADITIONS

'AND ALWAYS, ANANCY CHANGES':
AN EXPLORATION OF ANDREW SALKEY'S ANANCY STORIES

EMILY ZOBEL MARSHALL

Andrew Salkey is well-known as a prolific writer who helped develop the talents of many young authors and broadcasters of Caribbean origin in Britain, yet little critical attention has been paid to his re-telling of the traditional Caribbean Anancy folktales. This is unfortunate, as in his two collections of tales for adults, *Anancy's Score* (1973) and *Anancy, Traveller* (1992), Salkey creates a unique and innovative vision of Anancy and encourages the radical social and political development of the Caribbean people.[1] As we follow Salkey's Anancy on his journey through time and space, the trickster spider reveals the complexities of Caribbean history and invents new ways to tackle the problems of the present.

This essay intends to examine how the Anancy figure has been reinvented and reinterpreted by Salkey. It is contextualised through an overview of how the folk figure was once used to consolidate the social practices of the Asante community and went on to challenge the oppressive colonial order in the Caribbean. It illustrates how Anancy is used by Salkey to provide an astute social and political commentary in a post-independence context and engages with the pressures and problems facing the contemporary Caribbean and its diaspora.

Anancy, the trickster spider, originated amongst the Akan peoples, predominantly found in present-day Ghana. Although many Akan tribal groups told Anancy tales, he seems to have played a particularly important role in the culture of the Asante-Akan group.[2] Amongst the Asante, Anancy tales were told in a communal setting and could be used to air frustrations and resentments and the village Headman, or even the King of the Asante, could be criticised through the medium of an Anancy tale (Rattray, p. xi).

The Asante Anancy tales depict Anancy as capable of anything. Like Salkey's Anancy, who challenges the boundaries of the short story form, he never respects the rules and has free reign to mock and steal from the Asante Supreme Being, Nyame. It is also he who brings essential elements of human civilisation down from the realm of the gods to humankind, most importantly wisdom and stories. However, when he does bring these vital elements, he always does so inadvertently – normally the result of a failed plan or trick – and as well as bringing wonderful things to mankind, he also introduces debt, jealousy, diseases, contradiction, serpents and monsters into the Asante world (Rattray).

While Anancy is misbehaving, the tales show the people and animals around him adhering to the rules of society. Indeed, the Asante had a tightly structured social hierarchy and any deviation could result in severe punishment. Contemporary scholars of the Asante Anancy folktales, Christopher Vecsey and Robert Pelton, have interpreted Anancy's role amongst the Asante as both tester and upholder of the Asante social system; through depicting a character that breaks boundaries and by providing a medium for the Asante to air their frustrations and resentments, the Anancy tales helped the Asante defuse any rebellious drives – through the tales they could 'let off steam'. By breaking all the rules of the Asante world though his anarchic behaviour, the figure of Anancy paradoxically reinforced the Asante social structure.[3]

The tales were brought to the Caribbean by slaves transported across the Atlantic from the west coast of Africa. Whilst he can be found in the folklore of numerous Caribbean islands, it is in Jamaica that Anancy made the biggest impact and was eventually crowned the national Jamaican folk-hero. In Jamaica, Anancy came down to earth; in his physical form he adopted human characteristics as he became more man and less spider and pitted his wits against Tiger rather than the Asante god Nyame. In the plantation context of captivity and conflict, Anancy took on a renewed role. Instead of functioning as a tester of the chains, Anancy helped to break them. He shifted from being assimilated into the sacred world of the Asante to become representative of the Jamaican slaves' human condition. The Anancy we find in Jamaica is even more aggressive, violent and ruthless than his Asante counterpart. In the Asante Anancy tales where there was a testing of limits there were always signs of the enforcement of community rules, but this was not always the case in Jamaica for in his plantation setting Anancy could invert the social order without paradoxically upholding it. On the Jamaican plantations Anancy had the potential to function as the destroyer of an enforced and abhorrent social system rather than the tester of the boundaries of a West African society with compliant members. His actions were violent and remorseless and many elements of plantation life entered into the tales, such as Massa, the whip and the cane fields.[4]

In Jamaica Anancy's predominant character traits are those of cunning, greed, lewdness, promiscuity, slothfulness and deceit, yet he also has many charming qualities. He is a master wordsmith, an accomplished musician, a comedian and a creature of exceptional intelligence. Most importantly, he functions as a figure of resistance and survival against an imposed and oppressive colonial order. The Jamaican Anancy tales tell of how Anancy, the small spider, gets the better of strong animals such as Tiger and Alligator or powerful white humans like Massa, the King, Buckra[5] and Preacher. We find Anancy escaping the whip, tricking Buckra, stealing Massa's sheep or daughters, ambushing armies, killing the preacher, playing drums and working on his provision ground. Like the slave trapped in the plantation systems, he uses one of the only means available to him to gain an advantage in his daily struggle for survival; his brains, not his brawn. It is this quality in particular that Salkey, who was told Anancy tales as a child by his grandmother, celebrates in his reinterpretation of the trickster hero.[6] Salkey's Anancy describes himself as the epitome of 'tricks, cunning head, yes when you mean no, no when you mean yes, dodging, out and out lying and ringing rings round master class'. He also a deep thinker; he sits for hours in his 'considering chair' in the Caribbean and then travels across continents trying solve the problems facing both his homeland and the modern world (*Anancy's Score*, p. 27, p. 144).

Salkey was one of the leading figures in the first wave of post-war Caribbean writers who settled and worked in London. Born in Colon, Panama in 1928 to Jamaican parents, he moved to Jamaica in 1930 and then left for England in 1952. Salkey was chastised by his some of his contemporaries for leaving the Caribbean; at an address at the former University College of the West Indies in Kingston 1961, he faced a fierce volley of accusations from the audience; 'you have deserted us,' they said, 'you serve up what English publishers require'.[7] Perhaps in response to these allegations, Salkey writes in his poem *Away*:

Yes, I am one of those
Who left the island;
But I am also one of those few
Who remained behind;
I never left.[8]

While Salkey physically left the Caribbean, it became the focus of his writing and broadcasting, his muse and his obsession. After graduating from the University of London he worked as a freelance broadcaster in the Caribbean section of the BBC World Service at Bush House, where he was much commended for his reading of Anancy tales on air (Morris, p. 42). He was a regular contributor to the highly influential *Caribbean Voices* programme, a weekly half-hour slot which focused on literary outputs from the Caribbean – described by Kamau Brathwaite as the 'single most important literary catalyst for Caribbean creative writing in English'.[9] Salkey persuaded Caribbean writers based in Britain, among them Samuel Selvon and George Lamming, to contribute to the programme, which in turn became a launching pad for their careers. Salkey soon became a central figure in the British-based group of Caribbean writers and intellectuals and published his first novel, *A Quality of Violence*, in 1955, followed by *Escape to an Autumn Pavement* (1960), *Georgetown Journal* (1972), *Jamaica* (1973), *Anancy's Score* (1973), *Joey Tyson* (1974), *Come Home, Malcolm Hartland* (1976), *Danny Jones* (1980) and *Anancy, Traveller* (1992), alongside several collections of short stories and poetry. He also edited several anthologies of Caribbean writing and become a key figure in the formation of the Caribbean Artists Movement (CAM) and the publishing house for black writing in Britain, Bogle L'Ouverture.

In his both his novels and journals, Salkey's dominant themes are drawn from Caribbean history and twentieth-century political issues facing the region. In the 1960s and 70s he was strongly influenced by the political awakening gripping the Caribbean inspired, in part, by Caribbean intellectuals, Rastafarian thought and the Black Power movement in the USA. Salkey's radical political development can be traced through his literary outputs; he uses Dr. Walter Rodney's deportation from Jamaica in 1968, which sparked huge student demonstrations and ended in violent conflict with the police, as a point of departure in his novel *Joey Tyson* (1974). Salkey's Anancy tale, *The One: The Story of How the People of Guyana Avenge the Murder of their Pasero with Help from Brother Anancy and Sister Buxton*, first published in 1985 and then added to the *Anancy, Traveller* collection under the title 'The One', is also a direct response to Rodney's deportation and subsequent ban from the island. Here Salkey posits Anancy as a freedom fighter battling against 'One-manism', which he describes as an 'offensive and backward aspect of Caribbean politics'.[10] In the 60s, Salkey and other members of CAM, John La Rose, Kamau Braithwaite and George Lamming, pushed for a renewed relationship between Cuba and the rest of the Caribbean. Accompanied by La Rose and C.L.R. James, Salkey attended the Congress de Habana in 1968, a global gathering of artists and intellectuals and recorded his thoughts on the Cuban situation and the events that followed the Congress in his *Havana Journal* (1971). In 1976 Salkey became a professor of writing in Hampshire college, Massachusetts, where he lived until he died in 1995 (Morris, p. 39).

Cultural theorist Stuart Hall describes Salkey in an obituary in *The Independent* as a 'born story-teller' which Hall believes was a quality most evident in his unique vision of Anancy:

> His own gifts for vernacular narrative are, in my view, seen to best advantage in the wonderful versions of Anancy stories… Anancy's inventive double-dealings, folk-craftiness and mastery of language and the forked tongue of the vernacular were a perfect mirror for Andrew Salkey's explosive sense of humour, gifts of narrative and generosity of spirit.[11]

As Anancy stories are traditionally told orally in Creole, in *Anancy's Score* (1973) and *Anancy, Traveller* (1992) Salkey goes to great lengths to capture the nuances of an oral performance and uses a prose based on a hybrid of Creole and Standard English, much like Samuel Selvon in his seminal text *The Lonely Londoners* (1956). In his broadcasts and written work Salkey experimented with fusing Standard English and Creole which was characteristic of the first generation of Caribbean writers in Britain (Hall, n.p.). Salkey was not only acutely aware of the importance of the preservation of

Creole and its use in contemporary cultural forms, but viewed its continued use as a method of cultural resistance in the face of colonial oppression. Indeed, *Anancy's Score* begins with the following epigraph by Kamau Brathwaite, taken from his historical study *Folk Culture of the Slaves in Jamaica* (1970): 'It was in language that the slave was perhaps most successfully imprisoned by his master; and it was in his (mis) use of it that he perhaps most effectively rebelled.'[12] In these collections Salkey implements Anancy as a medium through which to reflect on the limitations of language, the writing process and his chosen narrative structure, in which he combines both prose and poetry. In both collections Salkey frequently introduces us to Anancy as an artist and writer engaged in, and challenged by, the creative process. Anancy the artist-creator has 'sparkling big brains and 'nough born promise', as he is capable of 'producing some real masterful language' (*Anancy's Score*, p. 129). Anancy is used to meditate on the challenges Salkey himself faces as a writer, spinning stories and struggling to express himself through the production of words on the page.

While Salkey has been criticised for his overly 'self-conscious' use of language by the likes of Helen Tiffin and Jean Purchas-Tulloch, who describes his Anancy tales as written in a 'stilted bourgeois patois', Salkey seems acutely aware of the type of criticisms that will be levelled at him for his narrative style and uses Anancy to defend his actions.[13] He slams the critic in the tale 'How Anancy Became an Individual Spider Person' in which Brother Dog, a critic, is described as 'a warmonger in disguise'. Salkey explains:

> This is something that most critic-persons in The Beginning usual grow to be. They start off a torrent, like promising poet-persons, and somewhere along the ol' life line, they just dry up like sapling gum in the sun on a dead branch of a mango tree. (*Anancy's Score*, p. 20)

In 'Spider Hell-Hole' Salkey and Anancy become one. Anancy, the writer, shuts himself away in his spider hell-hole to write. Isolated and surrounded by articles and editorials, he eventually finds his voice, combining, like Salkey, both prose and poetry: 'two special ways to put down things and such like f'Anancy: one way got to call itself prose business, like direct word using; the other way got to do with poem. Mix up the two ways and you getting something nearish a prose poem linking' (*Anancy's Score*, p. 129). Although this makes him feel as powerful as three spiders, he nevertheless worries about the critics' response to his work – in particular his 'change-ups', his revisions of his earlier work; 'he smile a wicked smile and think that all the critic people and what they going say. Then he get depress same time' (*Anancy's Score*, p. 130). These are references to both Salkey's own 'change-ups' of the traditional Anancy story and his 'change-ups' of what many people think of as the 'normal' patterns and structures of language (Morris, p. 42). The tale ends with the Salkey-Anancy figure reviewing his work, but with the pleasure of having succeeded in his enterprise, comes the pain of the writer's responsibility:

> When he done him prose poem exercise at week end, he sit back and reading them loud. And he get one surprise. He see one time *baps* that he the most signifying writer he know anywhere. And believe me: this worry him lot'. (*Anancy's Score*, p. 131)

Salkey's 'change-ups' of the traditional Anancy story are evident in both his narrative style and in the themes he addresses. His tales address themes of much greater complexity, and while traditional tales are comprised of short sentences and primarily made up of dialogue between Anancy and his adversaries, Salkey often uses third-person narration and focuses on the descriptive; in *Anancy, Traveller* the narrator sets the scene and explains Anancy's predicament to the reader. Furthermore, they do not centre on a single trick, as the traditional tales do, or contain the songs and musical scores found in early collections.[14]

However, Salkey's tales are similar to traditional stories in their length and use of Creole. Anancy tales were customarily short stories told orally in a communal setting after a day of work. As there was little leisure time among the Asante or on the Caribbean plantations, a long story would not have been suitable. They were also short, with short songs often repeated throughout the tale, so they could be committed to memory. The repetition of songs, sentences and themes created a rhythm throughout the tale which Brathwaite compares to a verbal melody or a jazz 'riff'. He sees the Anancy story as 'an almost perfect example of improvisation, in the jazz sense, where tone, rhythm and image come together to create a certain kind of effect'.[15] To some extent, Salkey creates verbal melodies through repetition in his collections; for example the colour green is used as a recurring theme and symbol of hope. In 'Political Spider' Anancy's friends call Anancy 'Hope', 'which, as you know, is a green thing' (*Anancy's Score*, p. 31) and his speeches start with 'Me name is Anancy is spider is Hope is a green t'ing' (*Anancy's Score*, p. 37).

Salkey not only uses the short story form to experiment with narrative style and structure, but also to illuminate key aspects of Caribbean life and history, like a 'flash of fireflies' in the dark, to quote South African author Nadine Gordimer. Gordimer reflects that short story writers are able to juggle with chronology and 'throw narrative overboard' as they produce an impression of the world for the reader which is 'like the flash of fire-flies, in and out, now here, now there, in darkness'.[16] In *Anancy's Score* the short story form allows Salkey to focus on key themes without having to provide a great deal of context. Like many short story writers, Salkey expects his readers to meet him half way – to work at creating meaning. Salkey uses similar devices to short story writers of the modernist period, such as James Joyce and Katherine Mansfield, whose tales begin *in media res* – in the middle of things, without a formal introduction or explanation of scene or setting. Joyce and Mansfield celebrated fragmented form, discontinuous narratives and a self-conscious style of writing which drew attention to itself as an art form and challenged readers' literary preconceptions. Similarly, Salkey creates a narrative which is full of stylistic and thematic experiments and coupled with his use of a hybrid of Creole and Standard English, the tales in *Anancy's Score* are difficult to decipher and deliberately ambiguous; they ask the reader to allow themselves to enter into the bizarre and fantastical world of Anancy and not be frustrated by the lack of clear interpretations and meanings.

Another difference between Salkey's collections and the classic Anancy tale, in which Anancy is depicted as a devious character who does not operate within a moral framework, is his focus on principles. Classic tales blur and challenge distinctions between 'good' and 'evil' as dictated by Christianity and celebrate ambiguity. As Jamaican sociologist Barry Chevannes states, one must suspend moral and ethical judgements where Anancy is concerned. He points out that, 'many Jamaicans don't think of Anancy as a sinful [...] in the same we don't think of the man that pulls off the clever trick as sinful. You may take advantage of somebody else but you may say the person deserves to be taken advantage of'.[17] Salkey, on the other hand, cannot resist adding a moral dimension to his stories, which is also found in the majority of contemporary adaptations of Anancy tales published for children. Whilst on the Jamaican plantations the Anancy stories reflected the brutal and unpredictable lives of the slaves and the lengths they had to go to in order to survive, Salkey's uses Anancy to outline his vision of a better, more ethical, world.

In *Anancy's Score* (1973) Anancy is depicted as a politicised freedom fighter and symbol of resistance and hope who guides his people through a troubled history, but remains confusing, contradictory and tricky. Global political issues of war and nuclear power are addressed in 'Vietnam Anancy and the Black Tulip' and 'Anancy, the Atomic Horse'. In 'Anancy, the Atomic Horse' Anancy is a greedy, dangerous nuclear horse who devours seven boys while their parents are away. Upon their return, the boys' parents rip open his belly and bring the boys back to life using traditional medicine, the 'juice of the bush john' (*Anancy's Score*, p . 91).[18] However, in a brutal turn of events, the sons decide they want to stay with Anancy and trample their parents to death. Here Salkey warns his readers of the dangers of nuclear weapons, their lure and their ability to corrupt. Like a Trojan horse, these are deceptive, destructive devices, which, once unleashed, will gallop out of control turning existing social and moral structures on their head. In this apocalyptic nuclear world fundamental human relationships are disrupted and children murder their own parents. Salkey's prime concern is the fate of humankind, and his Anancy becomes a lens through which he can examine the fragile and endangered relationships we have with one another and the planet on which we live.

Salkey describes his Anancy as an anarchic force who 'holds no reservations; makes only certain crucial allowances; he knows no boundaries; respects no one, not even himself, at times; and he makes a mockery of everybody's assumptions and value judgments'.[19] When he is not the hero, Anancy does indeed test his people's ways of thinking. Much like his role among the Asante, Salkey's Anancy is used to criticise both the powerful and corrupt and the weak-willed who let themselves become the victims of trickery. In the story 'Political Spider', Anancy plays on his people's greed and leads them away from their lands and homes (*Anancy's Score*, p. 31). Peter Nazareth argues that Salkey's mission is to alert his readers to their clichéd perceptions of the world which are often rooted in colonial ideology; to 'wake them up' and force them to think. Salkey, he states, 'finds it necessary to create a tension in the mind so that individuals may rise from the bondage of myths and half-truths'.[20]

The title of Salkey's first volume, *Anancy's Score*, is aptly ambiguous and open to numerous interpretations. 'Score' alludes to the traditional musical element of the Anancy tales,[21] but also relates to keeping a tally, to procuring drugs or sex (which both feature in the text), to making a mark, to a result, to an unresolved grievance, to a debt or amount due, and to knowledge and understanding (to 'know the score'). Finally, it also refers to a set or grouping of twenty items, and there are indeed twenty tales in this collection. We also learn the 'score' from Anancy as we see the world through his eyes.[22] His grievance, the score he wishes to settle, is the inequality and corruption which he sees all around him. In the final tale the reader is left to ponder if Anancy does in fact 'score' and succeed in improving the world.

Anancy's Score contains vivid and abstract illustrations of Anancy drawn by Jamaican artist Errol Lloyd in black ink. Lloyd, like Salkey, was highly politicised and influenced by the ideas of radical black Caribbean anti-colonialists such as C.L.R. James and John La Rose. Lloyd's illustrations have an unsettling dreamlike quality with Anancy often lurking in the corners of the image, disguised as another object or in his web, surrounded by fragmented forms and shapes. Yet Lloyd's Anancy is also central to the illustration as all the other images on the page absorb the attributes of the spider and his web.

The illustration overleaf accompanies the tale 'Political Spider', in which Anancy is deeply involved in Jamaican politics. He transcends boundaries between rich and poor, leading the poor to complain about his 'bad buckra complex', as he dresses like a dandy and talks to 'those who come from a different class of ideas an' life' (*Anancy's Score*, p. 32). He leads starving crowds of spiders, fleas and leaches to the Great Houses of the rich on North

Hill, promising them wealth, but then steals their belongings, 'making a brazen sale to Brother Tacuma, the world-famous travelling merchant' (*Anancy's Score*, p. 37). They are then appeased by Anancy's music and he teaches them a lesson about greed, showing them the downfalls of coveting wealth and trying to 'get something for nothing'. In Lloyd's illustration we see Anancy addressing crowds of black people. A sinister figure with two faces holds Anancy's head in their hands, perhaps a rich white man by whom the people feel Anancy is being manipulated. The dejected, seemingly pregnant woman in a headscarf to the left of the image is suggestive of the suffering and pain of black Jamaicans, while the mouths of the houses of the rich on North Hill hang open and hungry, wait to devour them.

(illustration by Errol Lloyd, in *Anancy's Score*, p. 30)

Lloyd's illustration focuses on fragmentation and dislocation, as does Salkey's narrative, and one of his recurring themes in *Anancy's Score* is the issue of the construction of a stable identity (Morris, p. 41). This is exemplified in 'How Anancy Became a Spider Individual Person' in which Anancy is depicted as having a dual personality. Based of the story of Adam and Eve in *Genesis*, we find Anancy and his wife 'In the Beginning', before fear is introduced into the world. Anancy's wife is rather troublesome; he has had 'enough [of] her woman back chat', and she insists that Anancy climbs a tree to pick her the 'luscious red fruit growin' on it' (*Anancy's Score*, p. 16). Once Mrs. Anancy eats the apple, Anancy says he feels a 'foreboding, the feelin' is like a ton load pressin' down on me face an' chest' (*Anancy's Score*, p. 21). Fear is thus introduced into 'In The Beginning' and Anancy asks Brother Snake to turn him and his wife into something small. Snake changes them into a 'oneness of a total spider' and thus 'the cunning ways Anancy is famous for are the cunning ways of his wife locked away deep down inside him, and the pretty web you see him spinning so is because of the goodness of the poet-person in Anancy own first ol'-time self' (*Anancy's Score*, p. 27).

Women fare rather badly in Salkey's 1970s collection; in an inadequate defence of Salkey's often sexist portrayals of female characters, Mervyn Morris comments: 'the book appeared in 1973 – we were all chauvinists back then' (Morris, p. 16). Not only is the downfall of spider-kind Mrs. Anancy's fault, as it is Eve's in the story of creation, but she is also to blame for Anancy's cunning ways, while he represents 'the goodness of the poet-person'. In 'Anancy Don't Give Up' the portrayal of the sinful woman is revisited and we find a recurring depiction of women's love, especially mother-love, as suffocating. In a dreamlike narrative sequence, Anancy meets a strange snake-like temptress named Mira, who is described as a 'willing piece of flesh', which echoes Selvon's description of women as 'pieces of skin' in *The Lonely Londoners*.[23] Mira wants to sleep with Anancy, who makes it clear that he 'don' like woman suffocation' and explains that he 'always having mother shadow hanging back o' him head, directing traffic and such like. But he get to know how to dodge it like ace' (*Anancy's Score*, p. 149). He tells Mira he doesn't want the kind of love she offers, which he doesn't consider to be real love. 'Bugguyagga!'[24] Mira bawls out, frustrated, 'Fuck me, I say. Wha' you waitin fo'?' (*Anancy's Score*, p. 152). In 'Seventeen' Anancy kills sixteen of his seventeen mothers and finally, suffocated by mother-love, also kills the seventeenth. Throughout this collection Anancy's inner conflict seems to be epitomised by his fractured and dysfunctional relationships with, and negative attitudes towards, women (Morris, p. 40). Female characters fare a little better in *Anancy, Traveller*, published nearly twenty years later, where we find a slightly more progressive Salkey acknowledging the struggle for women's rights. When Anancy visits the corrupt western 'Land of Super-I' he observes that 'woman not free, here, or nowhere else. Me travelling tell me so. You don't think that woman them should community up themselves and due for change rearrangement' (*Anancy, Traveller*, p. 5).

While liberating women from patriarchal oppression is not high on Salkey's agenda, a strong anti-colonialist theme runs through both volumes. In 'Anancy, the Spider Preacher', a story narrated by 'Brother Oversea', Anancy is an anti-establishment rebel preacher who convinces his congregation to reject the religious teachings of white Christian missionaries. He is described as a 'tall and muscle-up thick' Spiderman who rebukes the white man's god. Anancy is a liminal[25] figure who talks in the 'betwixt and between' and alerts the townspeople to be wary of the

'Spidering Church' as it is 'misleading them too much miles from the deep truth of things' (*Anancy's Score*, p. 71). He encourages his people to return to the African-influenced religious practice of obeah,[26] explaining that Christianity does not represent them: 'F'them tellin [their doctrine] don' belong to we. You ever see colour o' them pictures?' Anancy's 'Anti-Spidering Church' grows quickly giving 'the local spider missionary them heap of worry-head'. He preaches hard that the 'lawd's not no overseas man and spirit at all 'cause He like Anancy self, flesh and blood and natural' (*Anancy's Score*, p.72).

The generation gap, the folly of youth and their lack of interest in history is explored in 'Anancy and the Queen Head'. We find a young Anancy on Emancipation Day 'limin' [hanging out] in the sunshine' by the Walter Rodney memorial in Kingston. He overhears some old folk discuss the history of slavery and emancipation and fails to see the point of their discussion: 'Right there so, Anancy thinking; "Even me 'ear 'bout 1st o' augus' celebration in the ol' capital. So wha' the rass so special 'bout 'membering when freedom grant? Man free, an' that done an' gone"' (*Anancy's Score*, p. 82). As he reaches into his cigarette box 'gangster-style', the old men and women discuss the 'awboltion ack', Wilberforce and Clarkson, and complain about the ills of modern Jamaican society. Anancy feels, like many other youngsters, that he 'ignorant bad about the tune and blind to the beat' of their conversations. Suddenly he is perturbed by the vision of 'plenty foot moving in chains' and decides to walk away. The older generation are cynical, he thinks – why complain when there is enough food and women to go round? He can play dominos, he can go dancing and to the theatre. He wants to tell them 'you days done. You ol' bumpkin, you, you function stop braps.[27] Everybody attitude mus' change, mus' look up an' drif' way from the blasted awbolition ack' (*Anancy's Score*, p. 82). Here Salkey highlights the lethargy and ignorance of youth, but also shows some degree of empathy with the younger generation's desire to celebrate the present and embrace the future, rather than focus on the horrors of the past.

In the final tale in *Anancy's Score*, 'New Man Anancy', Anancy realises that the 'C world', the Caribbean world, is being crushed by the weight of poverty and oppression – it is in a state of 'paralysis' and 'most things looking real ol' and run-down bad, everywhere' (*Anancy's Score*, p. 176, p. 173). Anancy wants to know how to be a 'new man' who can help his country as he figures that '*A world make out o' the riches o' C World; B world make out o' A World an' C world. C World make out o' wha' lef, approx, dregs an' leavin*'' (*Anancy's Score*, p. 175). Sister Cow advises Anancy that a 'new man' must not forget his roots, and Brother Warrior, who 'fight plenty war in foreign', which he now regrets, tells him the new man needs to have fire in his guts. After seeking advice, Anancy looks around the C world with fresh eyes and sees that despite its problems it is green and fertile, beautiful and full of sunshine – a place and a people to be proud of: 'C world is a strong people-world, too, where all the power is people, not matter how them poor, maltreat, and develop under, people with a heap o' invention coil up inside them like watch-spring' (*Anancy's Score*, p. 175). To break out of the 'C world paralysis thing' he thinks of leaving, but the earth, red from the rich resources of bauxite that lie within it, chastises him for thinking of going abroad: 'I make plenty riches under you foot an' you cause all o' it to leave lan' an' go foreign' (*Anancy's Score*, p. 176). The tale ends with image of a little boy, 'who could be Anancy self son', excited by the sight of the big 'A World' ships down at the harbour. An old beggar tells him not to bother with the ships and to go an hear what Anancy has to say, for Anancy has called a 'red dirt meeting' – a political conference – so 'the boy turn him back on the ships, and fix him ears like telescope on the meeting' (*Anancy's Score*, p. 178).

   Despite Salkey's own departure from the 'C World' to the 'A World', this final tale warns against travelling overseas and urges West Indians to stay in the Caribbean in an effort to resolve its problems and take advantage of its resources. Yet, in *Anancy, Traveller*, Anancy abandons his 'red dirt meetings' to travel further afield to aid his homeland. Perhaps this Anancy, like the narrator of Salkey's poem *Away*, is both 'one of those who left the island' and 'one of those few who remained behind' (*Away*, p. 39). Here, in the image of the migrant Anancy with a dual and fragmented identity, we revisit the ambivalence, doubleness and shape-shifting liminality which lie at the heart of the Anancy figure. In *Anancy, Traveller* (1992), Anancy is introduced as a Caribbean migrant traveller, a 'busy universe-citizen with total permission to visit every base', who is summoned by Caribbea and Tacuma to travel the world. With his silver tongue he makes and breaks connections with characters, roaming from the Land of the Super-I to Washing Town, until he comes back to rest in the Caribbean, 'spidering some poetry', 'until Caribbea and Tacuma call him, a next time, to do some necessary travel duty, somewhere, anywhere' (*Anancy, Traveller*, p. 221).

   The stories in *Anancy, Traveller* dwell on the horrors of the history of slavery whilst simultaneously highlighting the destruction of the planet by mankind. Written with a greater sense of anger, injustice and indignation than *Anancy's Score*, each tale centres on a moral message, which Salkey drives home robustly. Salkey's prose leans more heavily towards Standard English and loses some of its Creole inflection; there is less of the subtlety of expression and wit found in his earlier collection. Salkey has an urgent message and takes the moral high ground at the expense of the easy humour found in *Anancy's Score*, with its wonderful turns of phrase such as 'and sure as bauxite get 't'ief [thief] away' as a reference to the draining of resources such as bauxite from the Caribbean by foreign companies (*Anancy's Score*, p. 144). At times the narrative pace lumbers rather awkwardly as Salkey self-consciously moulds Anancy to his political, philosophical and ideological outlook. These stories are aimed at raising awareness and appear to be directed largely at a western, rather than Caribbean, audience, possibly as a result of the twenty years Salkey spent living in the UK and the US between his two collections. While the use of 'in-jokes' and Creole in *Anancy's Score* may at times exclude a non-Caribbean reader, in *Anancy, Traveller* Salkey guides the reader and provides explanations, rather than assuming prior knowledge. Whereas Anancy is depicted as addressing crowds of black people in *Anancy's Score*, in his second collection he explains the history of the Caribbean people, seemingly to an audience of outsiders (*Anancy, Traveller*, p. 11). Creole words are italicised, sentences are less confusing and there is little humour; ridiculously long titles in his first collection ('Anancy not no Pyaa-Pyaa Spider Man come fro Balcarres F'get a Gardener Job from a Brown 'Oman Livin' in a Big Ol'-time Boa'd 'Ouse up a Sain' Andrew Top' (*Anancy's Score*, p. 157)) become short explanatory titles in his second. While it is assumed readers know the places Salkey writes about (Balcarres, Sain' Andrew), the island's race relations (Brown 'Oman[28]) and the comings and goings of Island life in *Anancy's Score*, in his second collection Anancy has travelled away from his homeland and addresses an audience from 'foreign' (*Anancy's Score*, p. 174).

Anancy, Traveller is focused on saving the natural world from imminent disaster; from corruption, greed, 'third-world' poverty, nuclear war, corruption, racism, the hole in the ozone layer, ('ozone have poison speck and crack inside it, and disappearing, and no fuss; we tainting it and draining it, as ever'), and other environmental disasters ('forest emptying. Fish festering. River jamming up') (*Anancy, Traveller*, p. 206, p. 207). Anancy saves the world many times over from the damage done by mankind whose destructive drives are presented as a 'whole complication thing' which 'have root in family, education and power use' (*Anancy, Traveller*, p. 206). Salkey also explores mankind's past sins in tales such as 'Middle Passage Anancy', in which Anancy listens to the voices of the slaves who died during Middle Passage, emanating from the Atlantic Ocean.

The West is a selfish, corrupt 'Land of the Super-I', a place 'full up of free dreamers dreaming a heap of dreams of I-is-I and free-is-free and I-is-the-centre-of-the-world and even more than that I-is-the-world' (*Anancy, Traveller*, p. 3). There is no community, just a place full of 'self moves, self clash, self mash, self melt and free pain' (*Anancy, Traveller*, p. 4). Anancy wants to know what has happened, as 'things was green, one time', but now:

> We start to use the land to rustle up excuse to move and spread weself, to murder, to pocket people property, to pocket other people life, to pocket more and more space so we can spread weself west to the sea as though is yeast we made of. (*Anancy, Traveller*, p. 6)

In the final tale in Salkey's second collection, the apocalypse is nigh. People are dying and 'all round them things collapsing and crashing' (*Anancy,*

Traveller, p. 212). The world's vital substance has gone in a 'thunderstorm of direct loss' (*Anancy, Traveller*, p. 212). Anancy has one final job to do – to find a new substance from which he can rebuild a world devoid of greed and exploitation – so he goes back to the beginning of time to 'Africaland', a place where the 'impossible come as possible' (*Anancy, Traveller*, p. 212). Anancy is successful in his mission and finds a new substance with which he can reform the planet, and this substance is the 'human spirit' – one 'which turn out just as rich and firm as the old land and just as rich and flowing as the old water. But no exploit possible, this time!' (*Anancy, Traveller*, p. 220).

Salkey does not reflect on the process of writing as heavily in *Anancy, Traveller* as he does in his earlier collection. In *Anancy's Score* Salkey seems to revel in adopting an Anancy-like persona, delighting in tricky wordplay and puns and misleading his readers. He utilises Anancy-tactics; meaning is deliberately difficult to access and straightforward interpretations are impossible. Both Mervyn Morris and Peter Nazareth have highlighted Salkey's use of the Anancy persona and Anancy-style narrative in his writing, which Nazareth feels is particularly evident in his first novel, *A Quality of Violence* (1955), that centres on a devastating drought that gripped Jamaica in 1900 and the community's return to traditional African-influenced forms of worship. Several references are made to Anancy in the novel; the character Linda is told that she must understand that 'Anancy and the Lord God son is two different people, entirely. The Lord is no Anancy story', and the central character, Brother Parkin, is described as 'a spider called Anancy'.[29] Wilson Harris has argued that the novel suffers from 'the lack of all meaning, the triumph of all meaninglessness'.[30] However, as Nazareth argues, the apparent 'lack of meaning' is a deliberate attempt by Salkey to make his readers question the narrative:

> [In the prologue to *A Quality of Violence*] Salkey is doing an Anancy on us: giving us a tricky story which we misread if we take it 'straight'. We are being forewarned. And once the story starts, it has twists and turns that leave us going one way while it goes another. (Nazareth, p. 51)

When Salkey writes about Anancy the folk-figure appears to influence him on many levels; Anancy shapes both the content of his stories and his narrative strategies. Salkey implements Anancy tactics to encourage his readers to question his representations and their own worldview, drawing his readers' attention to 'the Anancy way of reading' to 'bring buried contradictions to the surface' (Nazareth, p. 49). Salkey is aware that a good Anancy storyteller must *become* Anancy. To bring Anancy to life the teller must try and convince the reader that fantasy is reality; trick them into a world of make-believe. He aims to control his audience until they become malleable, entranced. The masterful Anancy storyteller revels in Anancy's exploits, celebrates his trickery and attempts to lure his audience like flies into his web as he spins his tale. However, the intelligent reader must question Anancy's worldview, for as Louise Bennett argues, Anancy tales can be implemented to encourage critical thinking and warn people of the pitfalls of leaving themselves exposed to trickery and deceit:

> Anansi is in human nature. Anancy is showing you human traits, pointing out all the human weaknesses. Showing you how you can be tricked, or how somebody can hurt you if you are greedy, thoughtless or stupid.[31]

Through Anancy, Salkey aims to shake people out of their habitualised perceptions of the world around them and initiate change. Salkey's Anancy in *Anancy's Score* may be untrustworthy, but he is a guide, a solver of problems and an emblem of regeneration. He is caught in a web between two worlds, the old and the new, and tries to help his people to come to terms with the past and adapt to the challenges of the present and future. This Anancy promotes resistance to oppression, historical knowledge and the remaking of the self. However, as Salkey reminds us in his poem 'Anancy': 'And always, Anancy changes'.[32] When Salkey decided to revisit Anancy nearly twenty years after the publication of his first collection, he recreated the trickster spider into a figure through which he could express his disillusionment with the modern world. In one of the last texts he wrote before he died, Salkey readapted his 1970s Anancy to suit a new context. Through his reworking of the Anancy figure to address his specific political and social concerns, Salkey thus contributed to the perpetual stream of transformation in which Anancy exists, for the trickster spider continually changes to suit the needs of the people who have narrated his tales across the centuries.

NOTES

1 Andrew Salkey, *Anancy's Score* (London: Bogle-L'Ouverture, 1973) and *Anancy, Traveller* (London: Bogle-L'Ouverture, 1992).

2 See Robert S. Rattray, *Akan-Ashanti Folk-Tales* (Oxford: Clarendon Press, 1930).

3 See Christopher Vecsay, 'The Exception who Proves the Rules: Ananse the Akan Trickster', in *Mythical Trickster Figures: Contours, Contexts, and Criticisms*, ed. by William J. Hynes and William G. Doty (Tuscaloosa: University of Alabama Press, 1993), pp. 106–21; Robert D. Pelton, *The Trickster in West Africa: A Study of Mythic Irony and Sacred Delight* (Berkley: University of California Press, 1989).

4 Aspects of Jamaican plantation life in the Jamaican Anancy tales can be examined in key collections: Walter Jekyll, *Jamaican Song and Story: Annancy Stories, Digging Sings, Dancing Tunes and Ring Tunes* (1966); Martha Beckwith, *Jamaica Anancy Stories* (1924); Philip Sherlock, *Anancy and the Spiderman: Jamaican Folk Tales* (1956) and other collections in 1959, 1966, 1989; Louise Bennett, *Anancy Stories and Poems in Dialect* (1944) and other collections in 1966, 1979; and Laura Tanna, *Jamaican Folktales and Oral Histories* (2000).

5 'Buckra', also spelt 'Backra', meaning white master or boss, is derived from African

Ibo word *mbakáre*, meaning 'white man who governs' (Frederic G. Cassidy and Robert B. Le Page (eds), *Dictionary of Jamaican English* (Cambridge: Cambridge University Press, 2002), p. 18).

6 Mervyn Morris, 'Anancy and Andrew Salkey', *Jamaica Journal*, 19:4 (November 1986), 39–43, p. 29.

7 Bill Carr, 'A Complex Fate: The Novels of Andrew Salkey', in Louis James, *The Islands in Between: Essays on West Indian Literature* (London: Oxford University Press, 1968), pp. 100–08 (p. 101).

8 Andrew Salkey, *Away* (London: Allison & Busby, 1980), p. 39.

9 BBC, 'Black British Literature Since Windrush' <http://:www.bbc.co.uk/history/british/modern/literature> [accessed 10 June 2009].

10 Andrew Salkey, 'Foreword', in *The One: The Story of How the People of Guyana Avenge the Murder of their Pasero with help from Brother Anancy and Sister Buxton* (London: Bogle-L'Ouverture, 1985).

11 Stuart Hall, 'Obituary, Andrew Salkey', *The Independent*, 18 May 1995, n.p. <http://findarticles.com/p/articles/mi_qn4158/is_19950516/ai_n13982680> [accessed 4 June 2009].

12 Edward Kamau Brathwaite, Epigraph to *Folk-culture of the Slaves in Jamaica* (London: New Beacon Books, 1973).

13 Helen Tiffin, 'The Metaphor of Anancy in Caribbean Literature', in *Myth and Metaphor*, ed. by Robert Sellick (Adelaide: Centre for Research in the New Literatures in English, 1982), pp. 3–21 (p. 28); Jean A. Purchas-Tulloch, *Jamaica Anansi: A Survival of the African Oral Tradition* (PhD Thesis, Howard University, 1976), pp. 228–29.

14 Early collections of Anancy tales:

   1816: Lewis, Mathew, *Journal of a West Indian Proprietor 1815–17* (London: George Routledge and Sons, (1929).

   1873: Rampini, Charles, *Letters from Jamaica* (Edinburgh: Edmonston and Douglas, 1873).

   1880: Musgrave.

   1890: Milne-Home, Pamela, *Mama's Black Nurse Stories: West Indian Folklore (Part II)* (Edinburgh: W. Blackwood, 1890).

   1896–1905: Coleman Smith, Pamela, *Annancy Stories* (New York: Russell, 1899).

   1896: Wilson Trowbridge, Ada, 'Negro Folk Customs and Folk-Stories of Jamaica', *Journal of American Folklore*, IX: XXXV (Boston: Houghton-Mifflin, 1896).

   1896: Coleman-Smith, Pamela (1896) *Two Negro Stories From Jamaica* in *Journal of American Folklore* IX, XXXV. Boston: Houghton-Mifflin.

   1899: Jeffery-Smith, Una or 'Wona', *A Selection of Anancy Stories* (Kingston: Aston W. Gardener, 1899).

   1907: Jekyll, Walter, *Jamaican Song and Story: Annancy Stories, Digging Sings, Dancing Tunes and Ring Tunes* (New York: Dover Publications, 1907).

   1907: Harvey Drummond, May, *West Indian Folk-lore Studies*, East & West, 6 (Jan–June 1907), pp. 483–90.

   1924: Beckwith, Martha Warren, *Jamaica Anansi Stories* (New York: American Folk-lore Society, 1924).

   1930–31: Rev Joseph Williams Collection (1930–31), *Anancy Stories of Jamaica* c.5000 items.
   National Library of Jamaica (Mss 1–4897).

   194– Clarke, Dorothy (194– n.d.), *The Adventures of Brer Anansi* (Kingston: Jamaica Social Welfare Commission).
   (n.d.) Carpenter, Zoe.

   1947: Wilson, Una (1947), *Anancy Stories Retold* (Kingston: Jamaica Times).

1953: Griffin, Ella.

1956, 1959, 1989: Sherlock, Philip.

1944, 1950, 1961, 1979: Bennett, Louise.

1967–1969: Grant, Jeannette (1967–1969) Institute of Jamaica Folklore Research Project, National Library of Jamaica (Ref Ms 1947).

1964, 1973: Salkey, Andrew.

1971: Grassussov, Alex.

1910–1977: Lily G. Perkins Collection (1910–1977), National Library of Jamaica (Ms 2019).

1972: Lopez, Vernon.

1984: Tanna, Laura, *Jamaican Folktales and Oral Histories* (Kingston: Institute of Jamaica Publications, (1984).

(Cassidy & Le Page, pp. xxii–xxv; Tanna)

15 Edward Kamau Brathwaite, 'Jazz and the West Indian Novel', in *The Post-Colonial Studies Reader*, ed. by Bill Ashcroft, Gareth Griffiths and Helen Tiffin, (London and New York: Routledge, 1995), pp. 327–32 (p. 328).

16 Nadine Gordimer, 'The Flash of Fireflies', in *The New Short Story Theories*, ed. by Charles E. May (Athens, OH: Ohio University Press, 1994), pp. 263–67 (p. 264).

17 Barry Chevannes, Interview with author on 23 November 2005, Kingston, Jamaica [Mini-disk recording in possession of the author].

18 The wild plant *Hyptis Verticillata*, used medicinally (Cassidy and Le Page, p. 250).

19 Andrew Salkey, 'Author's Note', in *Anancy's Score*.

20 Peter Nazareth, 'The Fiction of Andrew Salkey', *Jamaica Journal*, 19:4 (November 1986), 45–55 (p. 49).

21 Anansi is able to kill, to court, to hypnotise and to lure through playing his fiddle and singing songs. Mathew Lewis records in his journal in 1816: 'the Negros are [...] very fond of what they call Nancy stories, part of which is related, part sung' (Lewis, p. 253). It is often through song that Anansi succeeds in his trick and lures his victims.

22 'The Score' is also a Jamaican expression for 'the story' or 'the news' (Morris, p. 42).

23 Samuel Selvon, *The Lonely Londoners* (London: Penguin Classics, 2006 [1956]), p. 92.

24 The Jamaican Creole 'Bugguyagga' translates most closely to the English word 'Bumpkin' (Carr, p. 101).

25 For more information on the 'liminal' see: Mary Douglas, *Purity and Danger* (1966), Arnold Van Gennep, *The Rites of Passage* (1960) and Victor Turner, *The Forest of Symbols* (1967).

26 Obeah is a Caribbean belief system with West African roots.

27 *Braps*: a sound made to show respect.

28 A 'brown' person: In the Caribbean this term often refers to a person of mixed 'white' and 'black' heritage who has some degree of status or wealth as a result of their dual ethnicity.

29 Andrew Salkey, *A Quality of Violence* (London: New Beacon, 1978 [1955]), pp. 13–14, p. 79.

30 Wilson Harris quoted in Nazareth, p. 55.

31 Interview with Louise Bennett by Paulette Bell, Kingston (n.d.) [Cassette recording in possession of Jamaica Memory Bank, Kingston].

32 Andrew Salkey, 'Anancy', in *Nelson's New West Indian Readers 5* (Cheltenham: Thomas Nelson and Sons Ltd, 1984), pp. 13–14 (p. 14).

BOUNDARY CROSSING AND SHAPE SHIFTING: NALO HOPKINSON'S DIASPORIC, SPECULATIVE SHORT STORIES

GINA WISKER

He listened to my description of my story ['Riding the Red'], then asked, 'What do you think of Audre Lorde's comment that massa's tools will never dismantle massa's house?' I froze [...]. To be a person of colour writing science fiction is to be under suspicion of having internalized one's colonization.

........In my hands, massa's tools don't dismantle massa's house – and in fact, I don't want to destroy it so much as I want to undertake massive renovations – then build me a house of my own.[1]

Here Nalo Hopkinson characterises her own creative take on speculative fiction spliced with traditional folktales not as a mere response to established forms and beliefs but as a complex imaginative challenge. This chapter focuses on the short fictions of Torontonian/Trinidadian/Jamaican Nalo Hopkinson in terms of gender, the postcolonial Gothic and speculative fiction. Hopkinson, a short story writer and novelist, uses strategies of the postcolonial and African diasporan literary Gothic and speculative fiction to explore some of the tensions and potential riches of identity, shape shifting, gender, ageing and cultural hybridity. In her work, experiences and worldviews are often perceived as divisive, dangerous reminders of a troubled past, but they also conjure up culturally intertwined, positive, new futures. This chapter deals, in the main, with three stories, while mentioning others, each of which differently intertwines and develops Caribbean, African diasporan and European myths, oral tales, fairytales, and legends, offering comments on gendered identities and histories, in context. Hopkinson's variations on 'Little Red Riding Hood' in 'Riding the Red' and 'Red Rider', vampirism in 'Greedy Choke Puppy' and the Bluebeard tale in 'The Glass Bottle Trick' are each examples of such new cultural intertwining. She rewrites recognisable European, Western myths, legends and tales, such as the King Midas story in 'Precious' and the Snow Queen in 'Under Glass', transposing them to Caribbean and Caribbean-Canadian contexts, and interlacing them with international issues and polyglossic modes of expression.[2]

Nalo Hopkinson spent sixteen years living in Jamaica, Trinidad and Guyana, with her family. Her father, Abdhur Rahman Slade Hopkinson, the Guyanese actor, poet and playwright, was part of Derek Walcott's

Trinidad Theatre Workshop, and her mother is a library technician. She moved and has to date spent twenty-three years in Toronto, Canada. Hopkinson has started her own mentorship programme for new writers, and her career is notable for awards, mentoring, editing, and sharing the development of her own work (in her blog and on Facebook) and encouraging the work of others both personally and through inviting contributions to edited collections. Nalo Hopkinson has won a variety of awards for new authors including the Warner Aspect First Novel, an Ontario Arts Council Foundation award, the Locus Award, and the John W. Campbell Award. She was Guest of Honour at the 2010 International Conference of the Fantastic in the Arts.

Hopkinson began writing short stories when she and others were unable to afford and could not fill a short story writing class led by science fiction collector and creative writing teacher Judith Merrill.[3] Merrill looked at the work Hopkinson had developed to gain entry into the class and said she and the others did not need a teacher, only a support group of critical friends. They formed one, they wrote stories, the group still supports her, and the habit of using critical friends has continued in the ways in which Hopkinson posts to her blog and discusses on Facebook her development and frustrations, her creative activities, her challenges, her ups and downs, as well as some examples of her work in progress, now predominantly novels rather than short stories. *Skin Folk* (2001), her short story collection, explores metamorphoses. Other stories have appeared in *Tesseracts Nine* (2009) and a number of magazines and collections. She has invited and edited anthologies such as *So Long Been Dreaming: Postcolonial Visions of the Future* (2004), co-edited with Uppinder Mehan, and *Mojo: Conjure Stories* (2003), which contain a mix of African American and postcolonial Gothic, cultural hauntings, revisited myths and speculative fiction.

Influenced by her playwright father and her library technician mother, Hopkinson has recognised the creative and the meticulous, the researcher and the imaginative selves in her own development and work:

> Short story writing demands a particular set of skills in creating a lean, evocative, well-structured story where every sentence is there for a reason, in the same way that every word in a poem is there for a reason. Short story writing is one of my favourite forms in which to work. With every short story I write, I continue to learn more about what makes a good piece of fiction.[4]

Hopkinson works with the story form and myths in new ways, using lively street speech, overturning traditional endings and offering her female characters imaginative alternatives to stereotypical or socially constrained versions of their lives, while emphasising the values of nurturing, self-worth, self-development and social responsibility.

Significant influences on Hopkinson's work include African Americans Toni Morrison, whose *The Bluest Eye* deals with internalised body image hatred, as does Hopkinson's 'A Habit of Waste' (*Skin Folk*), and Octavia Butler, whose speculative fictions influence Hopkinson's forms and concerns. Parallels can be drawn between Hopkinson's replaying of Caribbean and African figures and cautionary tales featuring duppies, Papa Legbara, Anansi, trickster figures, snakes, zombies, soucouyants and werebeasts and their treatment in a wide range of Caribbean writings, including those by Olive Senior and Erna Brodber. Form, derived from the oral folktale, is also important. As Michael Trussler notes, citing Walter Benjamin and Mary Louise Pratt (among others), 'the short story is rooted in the oral tradition'.[5] The popularity and suitability of African American women's use of oral literature is particularly focused on by Lorraine Bethel, whose work deals with a Canadian rather than a Caribbean context:

> Women in this country have defied the dominant sexist society by developing a type of folk culture and oral literature based on the use of gender solidarity and female bonding as self-affirming rituals [...] a distinct Black woman-identified folk culture based on our experiences in this society: symbols, language and modes of expression that specifically reflect the realities of our lives as Black females in a dominant white/male culture.[6]

Rootedness in the oral tradition highlights the gendered and folk cultural nature of African-influenced tales, not least because, historically, many oral storytellers were women, both in African and European culture. The original oral forms of many of the written, collected tales we know from Perrault and the Brothers Grimm initially derived from tales told by women. It is useful to remember that the English-speaking Caribbean has at least as much European as American literary influence. Trinidadian writing is also influenced by the island's Indian population and its proximity to South America, particularly Venezuela, as well as its tradition of carnival, characters from which appear in Hopkinson's short stories and novels (Midnight Robber, for example, is both a Carnival character and the title of one of her novels). Her stories are also influenced by the African practice of voodoo. Hopkinson merges myths, folktales and legends from the Caribbean, Africa and Europe to create new versions, concerns about women's internalised sense of self-worth and how they might challenge and move beyond constraints and social determinants.

Writing about and from her own experience and research into Caribbean contexts and folktales, Hopkinson exemplifies David Punter's note on ways in which colonial histories infuse spaces, haunting and influencing lives. Punter notes the constant presence of histories and lives from the colonial past, explored and expressed in literature, though otherwise hidden, seemingly not present: 'the peculiar condition of the literary will always be to effect a link between the actuality, the presence of such conditions, however powerful and terrifying, and the imaginary, universality [...] in its proper position, in absence'.[7] Literature, and particularly that which uses the fantastic, the haunted, the spectral, can embody such conditions.

In Nalo Hopkinson's work, speculative fiction, the literary Gothic, re-written myths, fairytales and legends, and science fiction enable the exposure of hidden, repressed underlying tensions and contradictions in identity, relationships, and social values. Equally they offer the opportunity to imagine, articulate and embody alternative ways of seeing and being in the world. Hopkinson frequently tackles problematic histories and conditions through the actions of her feisty, increasingly self-aware women.

'Precious', 'Greedy Choke Puppy', 'A Habit of Waste' and 'The Glass Bottle Trick' all engage with cosmeticised versions of beauty developed in the Western world and with the need to recognise alternative versions of beauty and self, the need to adapt myths to other cultural and gender-inflected systems in order to revision female experience and physicality through Caribbean and diasporan eyes.

In 'Riding the Red', Hopkinson specifically engages with the transformations of the European folktale 'Little Red Riding Hood', a tale which aims to manage the sexuality of young women in order to perpetuate title and bloodlines, patriarchal power. She rewrites the tale first as a celebration of female sexual energies, however collusively battened down and hidden, and then in a Caribbean setting, explaining: 'I'm doing more and more research into folkways that operated in the previous century and the beginning of this one. Language, which I talk about more later. Folktales. I love the way they portray archetypes as stories that can resonate on many levels.'[8] Hopkinson creates versions of narratives which differ from those originating in European cultures. In so doing, she develops a continuum which ranges from plots, characters and turning points that are relatively culturally unspecific, found everywhere, to those which are very culturally specific; those which replay established myths and rewrite them, and those which use culturally inflected myths to tell stories in culturally situated and gender-sensitive ways. A strong example of the full range of this is 'Riding the Red', a particularly women-oriented version of 'Little Red Riding Hood', and the culturally specific version, 'Red Rider', which is explicitly Caribbean. In both 'Riding the Red' and the Caribbean Creole 'Red Rider', sexuality and sexual experience with 'wolfie' are seen as natural and necessary rather than to be avoided for the sake of purity, celebrating rather than refusing the danger. If we consider the differences between the European and the Caribbean versions we see Hopkinson making decisions which are culturally constructed – decisions about location, identity, values, behaviour, myth, speech patterns and what kind of 'moral' might be conveyed through a rewritten fairytale, legend, or cautionary tale. Settings and characters change so that underpinning morals or lessons can be modified. Structural changes also modify both message and interpretation. Endings are important in this respect. Trussler notes: 'Story-tellers, entertaining their audiences with folklore, offered their tales as exempla, in which the recitation was dependent upon the ending, since a story's ending offered a means of interpreting the story that had been told' (Trussler, p. 579).

In Hopkinson's work, frequently both challenge and rewriting lie in the endings or in pivotal moments defined in modernist literary criticism as 'epiphanies'. In *Coming to Terms with the Short Story* (1983), Susan Lohafer argues that that the short story is 'the most end-conscious of the literary forms', recognising that 'short story readers are the most end-conscious of all readers'.[9] In the case of well-known legends and fairytales, and local myths, a story's ending is both familiar and socially conventional, underlining threats or reinforcing any socially acceptable behaviour and resolution. For those who reinterpret traditional tales, and problematise their complicity with socially acceptable behaviour, endings are likely to be particularly crucial. In Hopkinson's short stories, endings challenge conventional resolutions, questioning the assumed social complicity behind them and offering, with their new narrative order, a different view of the social order in which they are based.

'GREEDY CHOKE PUPPY'

In 'Greedy Choke Puppy' a woman's selfishness and greed are questioned and problematised through the use of the Soucouyant myth. Originally human, the Soucouyant is metamorphosed into a vampiric ball of flame who preys on babies and young people, draining their blood.[10] Traditionally, the Soucouyant is an old woman.[11] In this story, we have a family of Soucouyants: the nurturing, law enforcing and socially aware grandmother; the now dead, more rebellious mother, and Jacky, the young woman, the grand-daughter whose voice becomes that of the Soucouyant, emphasised in italics. Grandmother has the wisdom to manage her deviant energies. Jacky, however, like many of Hopkinson's women, has internalised cosmeticised versions of women's worth, making her obsessionally intent on catching a man and retaining youthful beauty. Although she is undertaking research, her PhD study seems to offer no alternative sense of identity or worth. Jacky demonstrates society's pressure, thinking: *'I get to find out that when you pass you prime, and you ain't catch no man eye, nothing ain't left for you but to get old and dry-up like cane leaf in the fire'* ('Greedy Choke Puppy', p. 104). This 'voices the socially sanctioned belief that women's worth is determined exclusively by male desire' (Anatol, p. 33). Once she sheds her skin and becomes the Soucouyant she is liberated: *'The skin only confining me* [...] *slip off the nightie, slip off the skin. Oh, God, I does be so free like this'* ('Greedy Choke Puppy', p. 109). But such liberation leads to the death of Jacky's friend's newborn baby, sucked dry by her insatiable need for new blood.

The power to harness, manage and destroy the wayward and selfish Soucouyant, Jacky, is wielded by the wise grandmother, a key feature of women-oriented communities, Caribbean families and much of Hopkinson's work. Indeed, 'Greedy Choke Puppy' is a very Caribbean-flavoured tale, containing features of the trickster narratives found in Anansi stories in Africa, and the Brer Rabbit tales (among others) of African American folklore. Its Caribbean flavour is also infused by Papa Legbara, the Lagahoo, male folk creature and shape-shifter, also sometimes described as a donkey wearing a waistcoat, or a werewolf.[12]

Hopkinson's use of Black vernacular myths, folktales and creatures enables expression freed from dominant, white, often male forms of traditional representations. Whilst the myths and folktales offer an alternative way of looking at the world, making them a liberating force, they can also constrain. 'Greedy Choke Puppy', based on a Caribbean reference to excess, is set in contemporary Trinidad, with references to UWI, the University of the West Indies, where Jacky is a student. The Lagahoo, Papa Legbara or Esu-Elegbara is a trickster from Yoruba culture, which Henry Louis Gates argues exists in several cultures under different names, frequently occurring in vernacular tales and developing into the 'Signifying Monkey' in African American literature:

> Within New World African-informed cultures the presence of this topos, repeated with variations as circumstances apparently dictated, attests to shared belief systems maintained for well over three centuries, remarkably by sustained vernacular traditions.[13]

The trickster appears as 'sole messenger of gods [...] guardian of the crossroads [...] master of style and stylus [...] connecting truth with understanding' (Gates, p. 6). The crossroads can be represented as the physical and spiritual worlds, death and life, or the African and European worlds. Esu Elegbara is figured as limping 'precisely because of his mediating function: his legs are of different lengths because he keeps one anchored in the realm of the gods while the other rests in this, our human world' (Gates, p. 6). The arrival of the Lagahoo, Legbara, is a warning to Granny that Jacky cannot continue the evil ways into which she has fallen. Revealed only towards the end of the short story, this is a turning point in its trajectory, a kind of epiphany.[14] Hopkinson utilises a moment of insight here as she does in other tales, including 'A Habit of Waste'. With 'Greedy Choke Puppy', Hopkinson emphasises resolution and closure. The ending, Jacky's shrieking extradition from her human skin and self, her punishment for collusion with cosmeticised notions of youthfulness and beauty, presents a conundrum rather than a resolution since Granny, guardian of established values, punishes the young woman, a victim to beauty culture (and a baby murderer), for her energy and individualism along with her selfish Soucouyant self.

Nalo Hopkinson also splices her Caribbean-flavoured folkloric tales with speculative fiction and science fiction. The story 'A Habit of Waste' is one such which deals with issues of being Black and female and internalising a historic lack of self-worth in a somewhat more optimistic way than 'Greedy Choke Puppy', and does so using speculative and science fiction locations and actions.

HOPKINSON AND SCIENCE FICTION

Hopkinson is well aware of issues of ethnicity and gender and the challenge offered by being a Black writer of speculative fiction. While the reproducing of tales figuring Tricksters, Lagahoos and Soucouyants are popular among Caribbean women, perhaps science fiction is less so among Black writers.

Elena Clemente Bustamante argues that:

> many speculative tropes appear often in postcolonial fiction, even though they are hardly ever identified as science or utopian fiction. This is because some issues, such as environmental control, cultural clashes and imperialism, are actually relevant to both genres.[15]

Bustamente sees speculative fiction as useful in the creation of what Homi Bhabha identifies as counter-narratives, which allow authors to 'disturb those ideological manoeuvres through which "imagined communities" are given essential identities'.[16] This is particularly relevant in the creation of speculative, positive, alternative futures. Philip E. Wegner comments on this potential of speculative fiction:

> In the narrative utopia, the presentation of an 'ideal world' operates as a kind of lure [...] to draw its readers in and thereby enable the form's educational machinery to go to work – a machinery that enables its readers to perceive the world they occupy in a different way, providing them with some of the skills and dispositions necessary to inhabit an emerging social, political, and cultural environment.[17]

While Hopkinson's more explicit science fiction (sf) work is in her novels, the creation of those alternative speculative futures predominates in her short stories, where endings of traditional myths, fairytales or legends are often refigured to envisage modes of being which refuse materialistic values and patriarchal power, and/or celebrate Black female identity and self-affirmation.

'A HABIT OF WASTE'

'A Habit of Waste' is an example of Hopkinson's gendered sf in its focus on body-swaps. As a short story, it also makes good use of moments of revelation or epiphanies, and the moment of closure.

There are two moments of epiphany or revelation in this story. One comes early. Cynthia, a young Black woman whose job is providing food and support to old and homeless people in a not so distant future Toronto, has saved up to swap her Black body for a white one, chosen from a catalogue. Her rejected self has been replaced by a purchased white body; Cynthia's sense of arrival in society is gained by her simultaneous transformation into a 'Diana' model, with a slim, white, female body and blonde hair. It is a sf scenario, imagining transformations in a future world, and also a cautionary tale. Cynthia's initial questioning of the way in which she has internalised rejection of her homeland and her Black Caribbean female body is suddenly forced on her when she experiences a kind of doppelganger effect – coming face-to-face upon the streetcar with the woman who has been donated her rejected body. So much loathing does she feel for the body she was born in that Cynthia imagines crash victims being given throwaway bodies. It is like staring into the mirror. Its 'same tarty-looking lips; same fat thighs, rubbing together with every step; same outsize ass; same narrow torso that seemed grafted onto a lower body a good three sizes bigger' ('A Habit of Waste', p. 183) disgusts Cynthia, who criticises the back-to-Africa hair, the nappy look: 'Man, I hated that back to Africa nostalgia shit' ('A Habit of Waste', p. 184).

Saving for five years for a body switch is a fantasy only dreamed about for women who loathe their body shape, size, and colour. However, it is ironised as a choice made in response to the internalisation of Western culturally inflected ideals because the woman with Cynthia's body seems to revel in it, much to Cynthia's surprise. Cynthia's troubled position is characterised by her internalisation of white, materialistic consumer values which marginalise her body image, her cultural identity and heritage as waste. Seeing the woman on the bus with her own old body is a wake-up call, an epiphany; the woman's 'proud sexiness' ('A Habit of Waste', p. 185) a challenge to Cynthia's version of her Black body as cast off.

The second epiphany takes place in her interactions with 'Old Man Morris', another example of human marginalisation, who seems little more than a friendly receiver of state handouts in the form of food. His covering up of his specific Caribbean accent both interests Cynthia, who tries to discern his exact origins, and also reminds her of the distance she has travelled from her parents and their island roots. The ones who try to persuade him to eat healthily and accept the appropriate food sigh at his refusal of canned vegetables. Mr Morris is a kind of waste in this society, a society which itself produces excess waste. On the eve of a public holiday, Cynthia takes Mr Morris's food ration to his part of town and finds herself unable to refuse his offer of supper just to keep him company, break his loneliness which follows the death of his wife. However, although he is old, poor and a widower, he is no victim. The waste of other people's lives and the life which springs up in the cracks and corners of this regimented and hierarchised city are the wild and cultivated goods which Mr Morris takes as his own. He uses ornamental cabbage or kale when it would be thrown away and kills wild rabbits with slingshots: 'I aint really stealin, I recyclin! They does pull it all up and throw it away when the weather turn cold' ('A Habit of Waste', p. 194). Mr Morris is stunned by Cynthia's betrayal: 'You mean to tell me, you change from a black woman body into this one? Lord, the things you young people do so for fashion, eh?' ('A Habit of Waste', p. 192). When a mean street youth tries to mug Cynthia, Old Man Morris rescues her with the slingshot he uses on rabbits. He argues that 'you have to learn to make use of what you have' ('A Habit of Waste', p. 199). This example of inventive self-sufficiency, gaining nurture from the waste of an insensitive city, is the catalyst she needs to review and revalue her life.

Shortly after, Cynthia visits her parents for thanksgiving and agrees to eat everything on her plate, even finishing off the cocoa. This acceptance of the food, revaluing it, is a parallel to her own revaluation, so undermining the dominant culturally inflected economy of women's value. Ovid's *Metamorphosis* is as much a source for this tale as contemporary beauty myths or science fiction's body-swaps. Reflecting that '[y]ou've got to work with what you've got, after all' ('A Habit of Waste, p. 201), Cynthia can return to her old ways. For Hopkinson's Cynthia, the decision that she is more comfortable with her own body and self enables her to start to eat her way back into her own body shape, so rejecting the fashionable construction of woman which would have her always thin, androgynous, white. She rejects a society which only values wealth, youth and versions of whiteness. Her metamorphosis returns her to her true self.

SPLICING

Much of Hopkinson's writing is speculative fiction, and is also often defined as science fiction. Importantly, though, it is characterised by what she terms code- or genre-splicing, and for Hopkinson, sf can splice with the use of folktales and other popular cultural forms. To make the most of this variety, she argues, authors need to overcome certain prejudices, such as the expectations of what kind of writing they will engage with. In her blog she discusses conversations she has had with writer and critic, Walter Mosley, arguing that Black writers can claim versions of science fiction, that it offers liberating opportunities to imagine how lives, people and opportunities might be developed in ways that differ from dominant cultural traditions:

> 'Excellence' in the work of black writers is judged by how well we write about 'being black in a white world,' which is obviously only one part of our lived experience. 'A limitation imposed upon a limitation,' he calls it. His words really struck me. They concretized for me some of what I'm trying to do in my writing. I was born in a part of the world where people of African origin are in the majority. Racism most emphatically exists, but my early experience of being made aware that my dark skin, round ass, and tight curled hair made me devalued coin did not come from being part of a minority community. And in fact, being middle-class, I had more access to privilege than many. (http://nalohopkinson.com)

Nalo Hopkinson's is not a history of being marginalised, although she is aware of the ways in which elements of African-originated culture can be so treated. Addressing this, and claiming a rightful lineage of speculative fictions, including science fiction, is a significant force in her work. Such a claim does not denigrate realism:

> The realist work of Caribbean writers must reference the effects of hundreds of years of colonialism. It's there in the work of African writers, too, although my sense is that it's a little less all pervasive, perhaps because it wasn't possible to remove people on the continent from their pre-slavery histories and cultures to the extent that you could when you removed them from their homelands. The experience of slavery is a huge cancer in the collective consciousness of African people all over the diaspora. The ripple effects of it (if you'll bear with a mixed metaphor for a moment) still continue, and they touch the past, the present and the future. (http://nalohopkinson.com)

'THE GLASS BOTTLE TRICK'

'The Glass Bottle Trick' is a Caribbean version of the Bluebeard tale, a favourite of Perrault and Grimm and rewritten in Angela Carter's 'The Bloody Chamber' (1979).[18] Whilst the original is a cautionary tale about patriarchal control of knowledge and the dangers for women who ignore, undercut or usurp male power, Hopkinson's version is specifically Caribbean in its use of duppies or ghosts and revengeful wives, and feminist in its often sexually calculating feisty protagonist. In the traditional tale, Bluebeard, an older, wealthier man, marries a series of wives, offers each the temptation to go against his orders and explore a hidden locked room, and then murders each in turn when they fall prey to temptation, unlock the door, and discover the murdered bodies of his previous wives. The wife whose fate is the subject of the final iteration of the traditional tale is rescued by her brothers and Bluebeard is punished for his evil ways, but the lingering message is that women should avoid the transgressive act of refusing their husbands' wishes, and seeking after forbidden knowledge. It could be read as a version of Eve's trespass into the dangers of banned knowledge, lured by the serpent in the Garden of Eden, which error led to Adam's trusting but foolish complicity and cast mankind into a graceless state, out of the Garden forever. It could also be read as a warning against educating women. In Carter's revision, the young wife is rescued by her warrior mother and marries a blind piano tuner.

Hopkinson rewrites the tale with a Caribbean setting, vernacular language and issues of internalised race and self-worth. Beatrice meets the 'stocious, starchy' bookseller, Samuel, in his bookshop ('The Glass Bottle Trick', p. 87). His flattering comments help her overlook his morose, meticulous, bad tempered and controlling behaviour and her original views of him as 'so boring' ('The Glass Bottle Trick', p. 86). Her mother, however, finds him respectable. Taunted by her ex-friends, 'Leggo beast [...] Loose woman' ('The Glass Bottle Trick', p. 90), Beatrice escapes into marriage with the respectable, 'cultured', 'punctual', 'courteous', 'self deprecating', BMW-driving Samuel ('The Glass Bottle Trick', p. 91), who lacks the fun-loving sensuality of her gold chain-wearing boyfriend, Clifton. The attraction here is not just the wealth but the social conformity Samuel offers, a chance to settle down and so reclaim her respectability. Carter's new bride in 'The Bloody Chamber' recognises her own tendency for eroticism, her secret, now expressed delight at being seen as sexually delicious, and so too Beatrice develops a fulfilling sexual relationship with the ostensibly calmer Samuel. The motif of the glass bottle enters the story early as does that of the egg, the first to keep angry spirits entrapped, the second representing both new life and the preservation of a whole self. As Samuel first asks her mother for Beatrice's hand, she reflects that 'her heart had been trapped in glass, and he'd freed it' ('The Glass Bottle Trick', p. 92), an image which uncannily resembles the two blue glass bottles jammed into the branches of the guava tree in his garden. What might, in one culture, be just a way of identifying a freeing of self-awareness and passion, in Caribbean culture ominously equates her 'rescue' into marriage with the superstition, the management of the previous dead wives' spirits:

'Is just my superstitiousness, darling,' he'd told her. 'You never heard the old people say that if someone dies, you must put a bottle in a tree to hide their spirit, otherwise it will come back as a duppy and haunt you? A blue bottle. To keep the duppy cool, so it won't come at you in hot anger for being dead.' ('The Glass Bottle Trick', p. 86)

If Beatrice knew her Caribbean superstitions and legends she would understand that this imprisonment is that of the earthly soul rather than the heavenly one – but can also refer to a malevolent spirit. The duppy usually stays with the body for three days after death, so separating the duppy from the body is an unusual activity, and probably should indicate that Samuel fears the wrath of his dead wives. Such containment is only for control of the dangerous; those whose anger is pent up, who would like to wreak revenge.

Donald Hill also uses imagery of glass when he tells us that:

> Caribbean folklore is fresh and lacks an ancient history, it is wider than indigenous cultures of the continents from where it came. It holds pieces from all those areas, like a kaleidoscope with bits of glass (but not the entire glass), in ever shifting patterns. It is combinations of ancestral lore, remembered in fragments, and fit and refit to new'. (Hill, p. 6)

Hopkinson's splicing of Western African, Canadian and speculative fiction settings can be viewed in a similar way. It exhibits bricolage, the chance compilation of different traits fused into a new lore for some new purpose. For this reason, it seems to reflect the contemporary world very well, more so than grand old traditions. In this story, Samuel's distaste at his own Black skin leads him to kill his pregnant wives and to rip the foetus and placenta, the whole womb, from their bodies, leaving each dismembered on their beds in the locked room, kept like an icebox by the constantly overworking air conditioner. Samuel's sealing of his house from the warmth outside reflects his sealing of his emotions, his refusal to procreate because of his internalised disgust at his own colour. This self-loathing is articulated through his angry response when Beatrice calls him 'Black Beauty' ('The Glass Bottle Trick', p. 94). When she discovers the frozen bodies, Beatrice realises that her husband's knowledge of her pregnancy will lead not to celebration, the expected response in a marriage, but to her own death. Another scenario of a snake in a tree eating an indignant bird's eggs one by one is replayed in Samuel's destruction of his wives and unborn children, eggs which are not preserved but destroyed. Eve succumbed to Satan in the form of a snake and here Samuel assumes the role of the snake.

Hopkinson plays on versions of guilt, evil, power and gender, rewriting more than the Bluebeard myth, indicating its origins in biblical tales which impressed patriarchal power and obedience, women's guilt. As with Cynthia in 'A Habit of Waste', internalised self-loathing of colour has warped Samuel, in this case to such an extent that he would rather murder than reproduce. The cry of the bird losing its eggs, the Caribbean keskidee replayed round the garden throughout the story, questions the word of patriarchy, of the law, and the meaning of events: 'dit, dit, qu'est-ce qu'il dit!' [say, say, what's he saying!] ('The Glass Bottle Trick', p. 87). Beatrice angrily trying to hit the snake, smashes the glass bottles. She has misjudged Samuel, thinking he will not be as cross as her father used to be with her mother. Though coldly controlled, he has already raised his hand against her and just restrained himself; she is under threat. It is only when she finds the duppy wives waking up in the warming house that she realises Samuel is like the snake, eating the eggs, denying life, an act which is culturally inflected in his case with a desire to prevent reproduction. She remembers him joking that 'no woman should have to give birth to his ugly black babies' ('The Glass Bottle Trick', p. 97), his keeping her out of the sun as she darkened up, no longer 'Beauty. Pale beauty to my Beast.' ('The Glass Bottle Trick', p. 94). Unlike Beauty in 'Beauty and the Beast', Beatrice cannot rescue him from his self-loathing. Entering the room with the bodies, she drops and breaks the egg, and the fertilised bird foetus dies as would her own child if Samuel caught her.

In the original Bluebeard tale, the wives stay dead, but Hopkinson introduces further twists. Warming, the duppy wives feed from their own blood to restore themselves to life, their spirits returning from the broken bottles. Bringing the wives back to life is Hopkinson's own invention, merging the Caribbean tales of duppies with the Bluebeard myth. She does not depend on any myth of feminist sisterhood since Beatrice is not sure whether, when fully restored, they will treat her as fellow victim or rival. 'The duppy wives held their bellies and glared at her, anger flaring hot behind their eyes. Beatrice backed away from the beds. "I didn't know" she said to the wives, "don't vex with me. I didn't know what it is Samuel do to you"' ('The Glass Bottle Trick', p. 100). The mixed Caribbean creolised English and received pronunciation mirrors Hopkinson's newly remixed culturally inflected tales, with her own take. Whether Beatrice can preserve her own egg like the song 'Eggie Law, what a pretty basket' ('The Glass Bottle Trick', p. 101), which her father used to sing to her while hurling her in the air, remains to be seen. One of the twists in this story's ending is our doubts about her safety.

CONCLUSION

Nalo Hopkinson experiments with the short story form as well as with myth, folktale and message, to refocus and rewrite European, white male versions of traditional tales, and splice these with African or Caribbean-originated folktales, producing her blend of gendered speculative fictions. She merges genre characteristics and both uses the epiphany at the centre of many short stories and the message embedded in closure in order to problematise what is being taught or encouraged in more traditional tales. Hopkinson begins by grounding her ideas in a mixture of African-influenced and -originated, and Western, forms of representation, developing narratives influenced by Black vernacular culture, which express social and cultural issues in terms of African-originated folktales, science fiction and speculative fiction as developments, as vehicles for social comment. She agrees with Walter Mosley about the power of speculative fiction to create alternative worlds and realities:

> ...sf makes it possible to create visions which will 'shout down the realism imprisoning us behind a wall of alienating culture.' I don't want to write

mimetic fiction. I like the way that fantastical fiction allows me to use myth, archetype, speculation, and storytelling. I like the way it allows me to imagine the impossible. Mosley also said something to the effect that human beings first imagine a reality, then figure out a way to make it manifest. (http://nalohopkinson.com)

In 'A Habit of Waste' and 'Greedy Choke Puppy' Hopkinson critiques the influences of constraining, racialised and cosmeticised values. In 'The Glass Bottle Trick' she continues to explore issues of race, gender and power, and in 'Riding the Red' and 'Red Rider' she rewrites a favourite European tale used to manage the worth and sexual purity of young girls in order to perpetuate the patriarchal order. Her short fiction is experimental, a fine spliced blend of the speculative and the traditional, her stories focusing on experiences of metamorphosis which themselves are examples of metamorphosis in the short story form.

NOTES

1 Nalo Hopkinson and Mehan Uppinder, *So Long Been Dreaming: Postcolonial Science Fiction & Fantasy* (Vancouver: Arsenal Pulp Press, 2004), pp. 7–8.
2 All of these stories apart from 'Red Rider' were published in Hopkinson's short story collection *Skin Folk* (New York: Warner Aspect, 2001). 'Red Rider', a nation language version of 'Riding the Red' and a monologue for the stage, was published in the anthology *Tellin' It Like It Is* (Toronto: Playwrights' Union of Canada, 2000).
3 Jene Watson-Aifah and Nalo Hopkinson, 'A Conversation with Nalo Hopkinson', *Callaloo*, 26:1 (Winter 2003), 160–69.
4 See: <http://nalohopkinson.com/short_stories_novels_something_else> [accessed 16 August 2010].
5 Michael Trussler, 'Suspended Narratives: The Short Story and Temporality', *Studies in Short Fiction*, 33:4 (Fall 1996), 557–58 (p. 578).
6 Lorraine Bethel, *But Some of Us Are Brave: All the Women Are White, All the Blacks Are Men: Black Women's Studies* (New York: Feminist Press, 1986), p. 179.
7 David Punter, *Postcolonial Imaginings: Fictions of a New World Order* (Edinburgh: Edinburgh University Press, 2000), p. 189.
8 <http://nalohopkinson.com> [accessed 16 August 2010].
9 Susan Lohafer, *Coming to Terms with the Short Story* (Baton Rouge: Louisiana State University Press, 1983), p. 50.
10 Donald Hill, *Caribbean Folklore: A Handbook* (Westport, CT: Greenwood Press, 2007), p. 123.
11 Giselle Liza Anatol, 'A Feminist Reading of Soucouyants in Nalo Hopkinson's *Brown Girl in the Ring* and *Skin Folk*', *Mosaic*, 37:3 (2004), 33–50 (p. 33).
12 'Trinidad and Tobago Folklore', Trinidad and Tobago's *Newsday's Millennium Special* (2000) <http://www.nalis.gov.tt/Folklore/TRINIDAD-AND-TOBAGO-FOLKLORE.htm> [accessed 16 August 2010].
13 Henry Louis Gates, *The Signifying Monkey: Towards a Theory of Afro-American Literary Criticism* (Oxford: Oxford University Press, 1988), p. 4.

14 Epiphany, a Christian festival on January 6th, commemorates the manifestation of Christ to the gentiles. In literature it is a term used by the modernist James Joyce to suggest a symbolic moment of sudden revelation. Short stories often use epiphanies in this way, to suggest moments of realisation, when things must change, as it is used here in Hopkinson's short story.

15 Elena Clemente Bustamante, 'Fragments and Crossroads in Nalo Hopkinson's *Brown Girl in the Ring*', *Spaces of Utopia: An Electronic Journal*, 4 (Spring 2007), 11–30 (p. 12) <http://ler.letras.up.pt> [Accessed June 9 2009].

16 Homi Bhabha, 'Dissemination: Time, Narrative and the Margins of the Modern Nation' (1994), in Homi Bhabha, *The Location of Culture* (London: Routledge, 2004), pp. 199–244 (p. 213).

17 Philip E. Wegner, *Imaginary Communities: Utopia, the Nation, and the Spatial Histories of Modernity* (Berkeley: University of California Press, 2002), p. 2.

18 Angela Carter, 'The Bloody Chamber', in *The Bloody Chamber* (London: Vintage, 1979). See also Jacob and Wilhelm Grimm, 'Fitcher's Bird' and 'The Robber Bridegroom', in Jacob and Wilhelm Grimm, *The Complete Fairy Tales* (London: Routledge, 2002).

THE MARVELLOUS AND THE REAL IN PAULINE MELVILLE'S *THE MIGRATION OF GHOSTS*

PATRICIA MURRAY

Pauline Melville's first collection of short stories, *Shape-shifter*, was published in 1990. This was followed by her novel, *The Ventriloquist's Tale* (1997), and a second collection of short stories, *The Migration of Ghosts*, in 1998. A second novel, *Eating Air* (2009), has just been published. As is clear from her literary awards, reviews and scholarly essays, and speedy integration into university curricula, Melville is widely recognised as an original talent, combining an acute ear for language with a diverse range of topical and intellectual concerns. Two things in particular have appealed to readers and critics alike: the experimental nature of Melville's writing which draws on myth, folktale and orality; and the diasporic locations of her work which point to global affiliations rather than a narrow definition of identity. Nevertheless, at the heart of Melville's ethical worldliness is a cross-cultural Guyanese perspective that is quintessentially Caribbean: bold, rebellious and dynamic. Perhaps unsurprisingly for one born under the influence of Wilson Harris, Melville's work has been keen to emphasise the trickster-like role of the writer and, despite scathing attacks on political and economic injustice, the ability of stories to effect change and transformation.

It is the short story form that has best suited Melville's eclectic investigations so far, its insistence on brevity and condensation forcing her to cut and structure in highly innovative ways. She tells a story typically through a series of condensed scenes, with section breaks or asterisks to mark the multi-layered, often disjunctive, nature of the text. Although there is a chronological thread, the stories are often interspersed with flashbacks or dream visions that work to enact the kind of 'shape-shifting' method indicated in the title of her first collection. These interventions add texture and depth to the narrative by combining different tones and registers, sometimes different generic forms. They are also designed to destabilise the reader who can find that subject matter now begins to fragment, fold and double. In 'A Disguised Land', for instance, it is the overlay of Winsome's strange dreams of sly civility with the social detail of her arrest and treatment by the media that makes for such a devastating critique of English racism. While one sequence identifies clear lines of injustice, the other seems to suggest something larger and more ominous and the reader gets pulled into a haunting, eerie quality of the story. As Mervyn Morris has commented in his analysis of Melville's first collection:

> Though she is adept at satire […] her stories are not content to reinforce
> the settled illusions of realism; they communicate much by indirection,
> by symbolic hints; they traffic in intuition, they travel in dream and myth.[1]

This is particularly true of the final story, 'Eat Labba and Drink Creek
Water', which expands and intertextualises autobiographical material to
explore the anxieties of diaspora and return.[2] The asterisks here mark very
different kinds of text as we cut between fragments of personal history, tales
of discovery and conquest and parodies of travel narrative. As is typical of
Melville's writing, the shifting structure is hinged by arresting images, such
as the narrator's dream of returning to Guyana 'by walking in the manner
of a high-wire artist, arms outstretched, across a frail spider's thread
suspended sixty feet above the Atlantic'[3] or the description of Georgetown
as a 'city of wooden dreams, a city built on stilts, belonging neither to land
nor to sea but to land reclaimed from the sea' (p. 152). The liminal spaces
of desire and transition are reproduced in the short story form which
overlays a series of projected dreams, fantasies and misreadings, so that
Guyana emerges as both a politicised reality and as an unknowable force
that continues to defeat and perplex.

   In this way the short story itself becomes a kind of shifting text,
proceeding as much through gaps and absences as through the power of
cumulative detail. This recalls Joyce's method in *Dubliners* where he uses
the term gnomon[4] to indicate a deliberate strategy of textual evasion, the
writing of a story with key pieces missing. Partly, these are the gaps in our
knowledge, the gaps of colonial history that are still to be fully investigated.
The shortest and most enigmatic section of 'Eat Labba and Drink Creek
Water', for instance, is a barely three-line description of an Amerindian
falling through the air (p. 150) which remains elusive even as other
sections begin to cohere. Although the radically disjunctive, bricolage
effect of the different sections readily suggest postmodernist experimentation, there is something subtly Joycean in the way that Melville uses
silences and absence to create tension and convey ambivalence. Like Joyce,
Melville seems to *hold* tension in the very construction of the story,
unsettling and seducing the reader in the process. But she also adapts and
indigenises the short story form, particularly through her use of oral
traditions. Even in quieter moments it can be her poised use of dialect that
signals an emotional identification. But it is her wider use of dialect in
speech, often witty and dramatic, together with the frequent use of Anancy
and the carnivalesque that uplifts the stories and suggests the possibility of
change and renewal. In stories like 'I Do Not Take Messages from Dead
People' (*Shape-shifter*) or 'Mrs Da Silva's Carnival' (*The Migration of Ghosts*)
the regional folk-hero and the carnival masquerade are not only the subject
matter but also the structuring principle, as the former serves to outwit easy
readings and the latter offers a comedic catharsis. These structuring

principles are evident throughout the stories, particularly with trickster-like narrators who also delight in shape-shifting and making mischief for the reader.

As a collection *The Migration of Ghosts* is more coherent than the eye-catching debut. There seems to be more of a pattern to its design so that there are tensions and ambivalences between, as well as within, the stories and a strategy to their positioning. Whereas Joyce ended where he began, disturbed by the paralysis of his colonial city, Melville celebrates the energy of her communities on the move, though with the same anxiety for the direction of political futures. Partly a comment on migrants and partly a comment on the spirit lives associated with migration, the collection offers an ambitious interweaving of character, place and historical period. Melville uses different literary techniques to explore a range of material and liminal spaces, often with surprising results. Her skill in creating raucous narrators that jostle with all manner of comic and ironic detail is equally matched by quieter moments and subtle changes in pace and tone. Each story succinctly focuses a moral truth but does so through a careful process of deferred meaning that turns on ambivalence and gaps in the record. Melville's narrative voices can be noisy but, as mentioned previously, her writing also knows the value of silence and it is with these spaces that the reader must actively engage. The effect is to suggest a work in progress where the excavation of subaltern perspectives, in the Caribbean and the wider world, is only just under way and where the value of art to sustain understanding is more vital than ever.

In Melville's stories, then, there is no overarching point of view, rather a series of pressure points that build in momentum through cleverly staged dialogic encounters. Some of these are psychological encounters with the self, like 'The President's Exile' or 'The Sparkling Bitch' which tackle head on the corruption and gross indecency of political and economic life. The returning president in the first story is forced to confront the shameful episodes of his past and the abuse of power that characterised his term of office. In the next, the glitzy modernity of the City of London ('a sparkling bitch in glass petticoats'[5]) is punctured by the arrival of the shockingly anorexic wife of an oil-rich businessman. Melville relishes the opportunity to satirise and belittle the grandiose sense of self that afflicts both politician and capitalist and both stories are as funny as they are astute. Indeed, there is a wicked sense of revenge in Susan Hay's arrival at the Guildhall dinner only to crap in the middle of it. We are left in no doubt as to the target of Melville's ire and the callous hypocrisies of government and business are sharply exposed. At the same time as these clear lines are drawn, however, something much more intangible and haunting pervades both stories. The nature of the president's 'exile' is uncertain: he seems to be in a kind of limbo state after his surgery and 'bound by a compulsion to return to the scenes of episodes in his life which had shamed or demeaned him in some way' (p. 9). He worries he may be having a nervous breakdown but on his return home (Guyana is not named, but clearly located) the reader becomes aware of his ghostly status and a more liminal space comes into focus:

> Horse and rider walked through the main doors of the house, down the path, past the unoccupied guard-hut on the left, past the ghostly trunks of the giant royal palms and out into the sleeping city. (p. 20)

Eventually the president rides into the interior, to the Arawak village of Hicuri, where villagers are watching the state funeral of President Hercules[6] who died the week before whilst undergoing minor surgery. The final paragraph is delicately poised with the president about to wake to discover his own status as a 'revenant' (p. 24) and the farcical manner in which his death (and life) have been memorialised. Only as a returning spirit, as a troubled ghost, can he begin to see clearly.

Susan Hay experiences a similar revelation while on a business trip with her husband to Nigeria. Having stopped at a petrol station to use the toilets she stumbles across the figure of a starving child:

> She had not initially recognised that it was a person. The angularity of the black body outlined against the pale concrete forecourt and the faded red gasoline pump made her freeze with shock when she realised. Despite skeletal thinness, the boy's figure resonated with a sort of violent power. The sharp angles made by his arms and legs reminded her of a runic letter she had once seen carved in stone. (p. 120)

Realising the uselessness of offering him a US fifty-dollar note, Susan crouches down beside him and remains transfixed:

> The boy turned his head towards her. The movement pulled the yellow-black skin so tightly over the cheekbones that she could see the cavernous hollow beneath and a faint mocking pulse of life in the neck. [...] His eyelids had been bitten by insects but the eyes beneath were huge and dark and compelling. He said nothing but an exchange had taken place. (p. 121)

Although she returns to England with her husband, Susan remains caught in the liminal space triggered by this encounter. As Charles Hay embraces the gaudy wealth of the financial centre Susan becomes a recluse at their Sussex cottage, welcoming 'this implacable god of starvation, who opposed all fertility, excess and fecundity, as her deliverance' (p. 130). She begins to mirror the foetal crouch of the young Nigerian boy and when she eventually joins her husband at the Guildhall celebration her own spectral figure makes this earlier exchange visible:

> As she moved like a murderous ghost between tables littered with crumbs and half-full wine glasses, people, sensing that something was terribly wrong, gradually turned round to look. Guests shifted their chairs enabling her to pass. Some people recoiled in shock as she approached like some living accusation. (p. 132)

In both stories it could be said that the 'ghost' represents a kind of moral conscience and is the means through which the status quo begins to shift. At the aesthetic level also, the reader moves from the descriptive detail of the material world to the blurred lines of these liminal spaces. Indeed, it is as we follow the 'migration' of a ghost in each story that we apprehend an alterity that is subtly transformative. This is how a collection that focuses so much on death and dying (both individual and cultural) can also be uplifting and inspiring. The ghosts and spirits of these stories are not the strange uncanny of Freudian analysis but part of a spirit world that is held close, though sometimes little understood. What is haunting is not the appearance of spirits per se, but the gaps in our knowledge that limit interaction or cause us to misread these powerful conduits to imagination. Of course, as a creative artist, Melville is aware of the long history of ghosts in literature as metaphors and interlocutors of the human condition and occasionally her secular eye, wary of the dangers of religion, plays with this trope. But the collection is important in the way it also takes seriously a belief in the supernatural and integrates this into the dynamics of the stories. There is a move in this direction in *Shape-shifter*, an interest in local belief systems certainly, but Melville's response is more ambivalent and the supernatural tends to be staged for comic and ironic effect.[7] In *The Migration of Ghosts* Melville immerses herself more deeply in the spirit world of the Caribbean, incorporates more of the myth and ritual of the oral tradition into the structure as well as the subject matter of the stories, but loses none of the wit, politics and scepticism of the earlier collection. In the following analysis I would like to explore this in more detail and show how Melville engages with the spirit world to produce narratives that are both transgressive and deeply historicised.

Melville's writing has coincided with a period of increasing scholarly interest in religion and spirituality in the Caribbean. Work by historians, anthropologists and literary scholars,[8] amongst others, has been invaluable for increasing our knowledge of creole, and especially African Caribbean, religions that were previously outlawed and then neglected as a subject for serious study. The incorporation of this research into the field of literary criticism[9] is still tentative, however, and partly for this reason the work of Alejo Carpentier, especially the prologue to his 1949 novel *The Kingdom of This World*, remains a useful point of reference. Carpentier's early attempt to define a native aesthetic, specifically a style of writing, based on a commitment to the sacred is notoriously slippery, perhaps contradictory in places,[10] but even in this he proves a suitable guide into Melville's work. Inspired by the cultural traditions and spiritual belief systems of the African Caribbean world, and specifically following a visit to Haiti in 1943, Carpentier began to define 'something which might be called the marvellous in the real ("lo real maravilloso")'.[11] In contrast to what he saw as the conjuring tricks of the European avant-garde, poets and artists 'who invoke spirits without believing in spells' (p. 5), Carpentier was impressed by the lived reality of Haitian vodun and argues that the sense of the marvellous first of all 'presupposes a faith' (p. 4), an acceptance of the supernatural. Making links with Cuban Santería and other dance rituals and initiation ceremonies in the wider Caribbean, he is keen to stress the *reality* of the marvellous in the real and its potential resource as a native aesthetic. There is a strong critique of Eurocentric notions of modernity in the prologue and a valorising of the largely untapped creolising cultures of the Caribbean, so that the document has the feel of a manifesto or a call to arms in places.[12] Dismissing the incongruous fantasy of the surrealists, 'the old and fraudulent story of the chance encounter of the umbrella and the sewing machine on an operating table' (p. 2), Carpentier argues for a creative process that is more akin to an intense perception of reality:

> […] the marvellous becomes unequivocally marvellous when it arises from an unexpected alteration of reality (a miracle), a privileged revelation of reality, an unaccustomed or singularly favourable illumination of the previously unremarked riches of reality, an amplification of the measures and categories of reality, perceived with peculiar intensity due to an exaltation of the spirit which elevates it to a kind of 'limit state'. (p. 4)

This 'unexpected alteration of reality' signifying change, rebirth and healing is central to Carpentier's notion of the marvellous in the real and can be compared to the liminal spaces that Melville creates in *The Migration of Ghosts*. In both there is an emphasis on transgression and resistance, of communion with the spirit world as well as the capacity of the spirit that lies within. As Melville indicates in the choice of epigraph to the collection: 'And let thy goste thee lede.'[13]

Two stories in particular can be read as paradigmatic of Carpentier's ideas – 'The *Duende*' and 'The Parrot and Descartes'. Though written in different styles, and with very different narrative voices, both explore the presence of the marvellous in interesting ways. The title of the first story is a Spanish word italicised, already indicating the appearance of something strange.[14] We focus immediately on the main character, Doña Rosita, at a point of transition: 'On the morning of the fiftieth anniversary of her husband's death, Doña Rosita awoke and decided to do things differently' (p. 45). The style is sparse and the pace slow as befitting Doña Rosita's age and extended period of mourning, but the intimations of birth and rebirth continue as the eighty-two-year-old woman examines her bare feet: 'Their appearance was gnarled and twisted like an olive tree. But, she thought, as she wriggled her toes, even the most ancient olive tree still has sap running. That's what gives the touch of greenness to the grey. Her feet felt lively' (p. 46). Interspersed with flashbacks to Rosita's youth, when she frequented the Taberna Verde to listen to the gypsy *siguirya* songs and had a passionate desire to dance flamenco, the story proceeds through the monotony of her day and the memory of her husband's early death until she suddenly decides to travel into town. After a meeting with an old friend, now confined to the shadows of a room suffering from dementia, Rosita determines to discard the black of her mourning attire and buy some coloured material for a new dress. Emboldened by this action she enters the Taberna Verde once again as a dancing competition is taking place. Amidst thoughts of her own death and burial she listens intently to the music and takes to the stage. It is at this point that the play on the silence and stillness of a motionless life and the subtle changes of pace in the story are intertwined as Rosita's life is re-enacted in the ritual of the dance:

> Doña Rosita was clearly waiting. A feeling of anticipation gripped the spectators. She remained utterly still. The musician responded to the challenge of her stillness by making the chords of the guitar scream and slither down the scale until they were vibrating somewhere at the bottom. She did not move a muscle. The guitar tried to shake her into action, writhing, trembling, challenging, enticing her to break into motion. She remained immobile as if she had been there for centuries. Nothing happened [...].
>
> In a split second and too fast for anyone to see, Doña Rosita broke out of the endless expanse of time, raised her arms, threw back her head and stamped her foot on the floor. (pp. 60–61)

The miracle of this 'unexpected alteration of reality' causes pandemonium in the audience with some declaring that they have seen 'the *duende*' which is explained as 'a gust of air, an irrepressible instant; a ghost suddenly appears and vanishes and the world is re-born' (p. 61). Closely resembling Carpentier's description of the marvellous in the real, it is interesting that Melville stages this moment so that it can be interpreted as either a visitation by a spirit *or* the capacity of the spirit within. In either case, a threshold is crossed and in the liminal space of the dance Rosita's life is celebrated.[15]

The focus broadens considerably in 'The Parrot and Descartes' which cleverly combines myth and history. The story opens dramatically with a first person narrator recounting a myth from the oral tradition:

> I had better tell you about the parrot.
>
> In the Orinoco region, it is said, everything began with a wish and a smell. A hand stuck up out of the earth. An arm. The earth opened. A woman who was watching turned into a male parrot and began to scream a warning. Then all sorts of things happened. A man dropped a gourd of urine, scorching his wife's flesh with it. Her skin was roasted. Her bones fell apart. Night burst over the world and something white like a capuchin monkey went running into the forest. That's what they say. I wasn't there myself. (p. 101)

There is a comic undercurrent here with Melville both using and playing with the flexibility of myth and creating a narrator who employs Anancy-like tactics of wit, parody, laughter and play. The South American parrot – 'a natural representative of the oral tradition' (p. 112) – is later captured and brought to Europe where he also represents the earthiness and unpretentious humour of the Americas.[16] At first he enjoys the intellectual stimulus of places like Heidelberg and Prague:

> [...] the wondrous city of Prague was host to every sort of Cabbalist, alchemist and astronomer and housed the most up-to-date artistic and scientific collections. The Parrot inspected the paintings of Arcimboldo the Marvellous (who had also been the Master of Masquerade) which showed men made of vegetables, tin pots and books. Tycho Brahe had discovered the fixed position of seven hundred stars and Johann Kepler raced to discover the periodic laws of planets. [...] Ideas were propounded which made men's mouths dry with excitement and fear, giving them palpitations and erections, often at the same time. (p. 105)

These are centres of scientific learning but Melville is keen to emphasise how they co-exist with the marvellous and applauds 'the unity of magic and science' (p. 109) as it developed in Bohemia. Of course, the comic hyperbole reminiscent of García Márquez also reminds us of the absurdity as well as the wonder of all learning, with man's place in the universe always vulnerable and unstable in the eyes of the parrot and the ebullient narrator.

The story presents momentous histories and great icons through apparently inconsequential and ridiculous moments, such as the arrival of René Descartes as a foot soldier in the Hapsburg army 'thoughtfully chewing on a piece of dried beef' (p. 109). In this way, Melville creates a carnivalesque version of the world turned upside down with the privileged (Descartes) brought down to earth and the epic quality of the repressed and marginalised (the parrot) reinstated. Accidentally, and for a brief moment, the parrot and Descartes come face to face in Prague, thus staging the dialogic encounter between the Americas and enlightenment modernity that the story is concerned to explore. The parrot intuitively recognises the danger of a man 'who contributed to the rout of a certain sort of imagination' (p. 110) and is not surprised when 'mind and matter started to divide, body and soul to separate and science and magic to march in opposite directions' (p. 111). It is not that Melville rejects scientific-rational ideas. On the contrary: the narrator carefully engages in systematic debate and the parrot is seen to be sceptical and informed. Rather, the story critiques the privileging of the scientific method and the written word over the powerful storehouse of the oral tradition:

> Books had become the truth. The written word had become proof. Laws were built on books which contained precedent. People were killed in their name. Confession, word of mouth, rumour, gossip, chattiness and oratory had all lost their place in the hierarchy of power. Passports verified. Documents condemned. Signatures empowered. Books were the storage place of memory. Books were written to contradict other books. (p. 111)

The parrot escapes back to Guyana only to find this shift in perspective already taking place with the arrival of the early colonists. With the priests and the traders comes a theatre troupe performing a version of *The Tempest*. The parrot is captured once again and this time chained to a cardboard tree as part of the set. The manacling of the parrot (the spirit of the Americas) to two-dimensional representations of his world is an apt signifier of the colonial process to come. Despite a history of invasion and appropriation, though, the long-lived parrot has a gifted memory and as he migrates once more at the end of the story we are left in no doubt that mythical time is longer than historical time.

With these two stories, then, Melville encapsulates the key elements of Carpentier's native aesthetic: the necessary critique of Eurocentric notions of modernity and the connection to a spirit world that might be described as the marvellous in the real. More explicitly comedic than Carpentier, Melville's focus on migration also means that she is more open to diaspora identities and less caught up in the notion that the sense of the marvellous is specific to the Caribbean or the Americas.[17] Though her stories express a strong sense of regional identity, and a desire to validate subaltern perspectives, she is also careful to trace the complexity, indeed the messiness, of Europe and to explore those landscapes that still have much in common with the Americas. This is why a story like 'The *Duende*', which is set in Andalucía, can have so much the feel of an early García Márquez short story. Melville is aware of the spirit worlds that were carried to and then adapted in the wider Caribbean and the way in which travelling cultures continue to interact.

The title story, 'The Migration of Ghosts', explores these ideas specifically in terms of migration and diaspora and presents a variety of spirit worlds on the move. In the characters of Vincent Dawes (an Englishman living in Brazil) and his Macusi wife Loretta (whose family are from the Guyanese/Brazilian border) the story sets up a dialogue about the nature of identity and the attachment to landscape and spirits that we carry within. Although there are moments of reconciliation and healing, the story is also structured around the gaps and misreadings of cultural difference and there are no easy resolutions, rather the tension of different perspectives. On tour in Europe for the first time together (visiting London and Prague) we first encounter Vincent's enthusiasm for the scenes and political affiliations of his youth. But Vincent's stories alienate Loretta and turn her into a kind of ghost, disassociated from events around her. Melville sets up a tension here between Vincent as a Eurocentric male who wants to educate Loretta into his treasured memories and her more intuitive way of seeing. Vincent operates on a material plane, full of detail and information, but blind to the clues of marital breakdown and political corruption in Prague. His voice dominates the first half of the story but this sense of clarity is undermined by Loretta's flashbacks and dream visions – the bride fleeing into the woods 'like a white capuchin monkey' (p. 180), the tale of Irakaru the mischief-maker (pp. 188–89) or the charming seducer who turns out be a river dolphin (p. 190) – that seem opaque at first but gradually throw light on events around them. Loretta lives a more liminal existence and through her mythical/dreamlike visions intuits a reality of foreboding and trickery that Vincent cannot see.

Their disjunctive ways of looking at the world are interrupted by two moments of genuine connection: firstly when Loretta recognises a common ancestry with the drummer of a local band – 'the same jet-black straight hair, the same brown face and flat features and fat brown eyelids over black pebble eyes' (p. 186). His parents turn out to be migrants from Mongolia, possibly the starting point for her own people who may have travelled to the Americas via the Bering Straits, and the narrative pauses to acknowledge a moment of reconciliation:

> The boy with the drum slung over his shoulder looked towards Loretta with curiosity. He nodded acknowledgement and gave a little bow. They faced each other across tens of thousands of years. She smiled back at him. (p. 187)

And later on when Vincent and Loretta enter a small courtyard to find murals of water spirits:

> Rotund, naked women rolled in and under the blue waves, an aqueous erotica in pale blues and yellows, gentle and playful. The sight was entirely unexpected. Its mood belonged to a warmer climate. They stood still in the secluded courtyard as if treading water in the warm centre of the city. The heart of Prague, despite the Czech Republic being a land-locked country, seemed to belong to water spirits. (p. 190)

Loretta feels that she has been sent a message from home and, reminded of her own water spirits and the myths attached to them, she is inspired to think about whether spirits can migrate. Vincent feels the connection but his response is more limited: as he had not seen Anne Boleyn walking around Roraima he concludes that 'spirits are quite conservative. They stick around the same place' (p. 190). Missing the point of the story that the spirit lives associated with migration are constantly on the move and need to be integrated and adapted, Vincent becomes detached and alienated.

Despite his love of life, his worthy political convictions and genuine feel for the spirit of the English landscape, Vincent does not experience that sense of the marvellous that frees Loretta to talk about her past and her fears for the future. The violence that Loretta has witnessed is still very real for the Amerindians in her village and the story does not underestimate, indeed brings into focus, the nature of radically different worlds. In parallel with Vincent's and Loretta's journey to Europe, Melville also traces the collapse of communism in the Eastern bloc (now reduced to slogans and

souvenirs in the market place) and its resurgence amongst the destitute in
Brazil. Loretta recalls a young communist who came banging on her door
with his pregnant girlfriend, both having escaped a massacre of the Sem
Terra people (the landless ones) by pretending to be dead amongst the
other bodies:

> In his hand he grasped a cheaply printed copy of the Communist Manifesto
> and some other tattered texts with pictures of Lenin on the front. Even
> in these circumstances, immediately after witnessing a massacre, his
> description and analysis of the events were illuminated by ideas and
> sayings gleaned from these books which he studied every night. (p. 183)

In Melville's fiction there is always more than one kind of ghost, and as
communism is extinguished in one part of the world she wonders if its
spirit may rise to empower in another.

   This interweaving of the spirit world with a sharp focus on contemporary politics, indeed a harnessing of the spirits to *intervene* in political life,
is key to Melville's strategy in this collection and brilliantly executed in the
wonderfully cathartic story entitled 'Erzulie'. Set in Guyana at a time of a
national crisis[18] the story draws on myth and ritual as well as the tactics of
crime and detective fiction to engage the reader in solving an intriguing
puzzle. We are first introduced to Mr and Mrs Jenkins who recently moved
from Canada to Guyana – Armand Jenkins to supervise the operations of
Omai Gold Mining Ltd and Rita Jenkins to catch up with her native
Georgetown and show off her status and wealth. They rent an enormous
old-style house but only use the second floor and engage a number of staff,
one of whom is Margot, a sixty-year-old deaf mute. Rita Jenkins is now
bored and wants to return to Canada, fed up of the blackouts and water cuts
and disconcerted by 'that awful Shallow-Grave case' (p. 139). Eight dead
bodies have been discovered along the main river and a woman has recently
been charged with their murder: 'The woman was known as Shallow-
Grave because that was the way she disposed of her victims, or alleged
victims, along the banks of the Essequibo River' (p. 139). But there is
something different about this woman, as is immediately evident to those
in the courtroom:

> People strained forward, not only to get a better look, but as if, by reaching
> closer, they might be able to dip into one of the blackwater creeks of
> the Essequibo region and escape the broiling heat. The air surrounding
> her seemed to be of a considerably lower temperature than the air in
> the rest of the courtroom. When Shallow-Grave leaned forward, the
> crowd leaned forward. When Shallow-Grave left the room at lunchtime,
> the atmosphere returned to one of habble and babble and clatter, everyday
> business and heat, the black radiance of a dark lake having moved elsewhere.
> (p. 140)

Elegant and dignified, and with an inexhaustible supply of water, when she
is found caressing a huge snake in her cell people start to believe that she

is in fact 'a water mumma' (p. 148). This reference to the water mumma spirit – historically one of the most powerful spirits in Guyana and related to the West African worship of river gods – at first seems to indicate a motive for her acts. If all the men have been involved in exploitation of the river, is this a modern water mumma taking retribution? In fact this turns out to be a red herring. As becomes clear later in the story,[19] the Omai Gold Mining Company has been discharging cyanide into the rivers as part of its shoddy operations. It is more likely that this woman has been retrieving the bodies and giving them a proper burial.

Margot is particularly fascinated by Shallow-Grave. Having met her in prison after being arrested for a minor misdemeanour, she decides to serve her as an acolyte. Previously, Margot had 'felt like a ghost in her own city. A jumbie. Nobody seemed to notice her. She could have been invisible' (p. 143). Serving Shallow-Grave gives her a purpose in life and, in turn, Margot starts to be healed. She regains her hearing as Shallow-Grave sings and, like the other inmates, is inspired by her presence. One scene in the jail is particularly relevant. As a strong wind blows through the dormitory Miss Vinny suddenly 'felt released' (p. 151) to do something her Surinamese grandmother had taught her: The Winti Dance:[20]

> No sooner had she begun to move around the room than her tongue became empowered with a host of sounds, an extraordinary range of noises. Each new one took her by delighted surprise and affected the movements of her body. Each one flung her into a different position to a subtly changed rhythm. She had tapped into a stream of energy. Sometimes the noise turned her into a tall, powerful man with a limp and sometimes into an undulating, hip-winding woman. At the age of sixty-seven, Miss Vinny opened herself up joyously to the whole pantheon of creation. (p. 152)

Like the dance rituals that inspired Carpentier, this is a call to the gods and acts as an initiation ceremony for the other women who also experience a spirit possession like Miss Vinny. The guards are moved from Shallow-Grave's cell to protect the dormitory from any further 'outbreak' (p. 153) and in a clever move from the liminal back to the material space, this is the opportunity for Shallow-Grave to escape. As in 'The Migration of Ghosts' the presence of the marvellous in the real – the 'unexpected alteration of reality' via water spirits in the courtyard or spirit possession of the Winti – structures the story and initiates change. Margot hides Shallow-Grave in one of the many unused rooms of the Jenkins's rented house and it is here that the significance of her real name becomes apparent. As she has told us previously when declaring her innocence in the jail: 'I know what every-body does call me. But my name is Erzulie' (p. 144). Inside the house, Margot opens old trunks and panels and discovers luxurious items of clothes and jewellery in which to dress her mistress. In remarkably sensuous prose, we are reminded that Erzulie is the Haitian goddess of love, often associated with luxury, sensuality and female love, and the bond between these two women becomes one of spiritual regeneration.

Melville combines and adapts various myths and rituals in this story and Shallow-Grave/Erzulie emerges with the powerful force of a hybridised African Caribbean spirit. When she overhears Armand Jenkins trying to cover up a massive cyanide spill into the rivers: 'her hair lost its healthy spring and her body broke out in a riot of sores that gathered in groups, sent out messengers, erupted in angry outbursts, opened their mouths and yelled. A revolution broke out all over her skin' (p. 161). Her reaction to the pollution of the rivers confirms her role as a water mumma and in a vivid realisation of the myth she (with Margot) follows Armand to the Brazilian border where he is killed and buried in a shallow grave. Retribution having finally taken place, the two women cross into Brazil where they rent a small room and Margot prepares a cleansing bath for her mistress:

> The aroma, combined with the melodious voice that mingled with the steam and issued from the scabby window on that hypnotically warm evening, stuck in the memories of local people. It was an evening when peace unexpectedly burst over the poorest quarter of Boa Vista. (p. 166)

This capacity to heal, to effect change and transformation, is central to Melville's engagement with the spirit world in *The Migration of Ghosts*. Although she is careful to combine myth and ritual with realistically drawn social and political scenarios – to emphasise, like Carpentier, the *reality* of the marvellous in the real – she also takes seriously a belief in the supernatural and incorporates local belief systems into the dynamics of the stories. On the one hand, Guyana is a rich resource in this respect and Melville draws on native Amerindian as well as African Caribbean spiritual beliefs as they exist both within Guyana and on the borders of South America and the wider Caribbean. On the other hand, Guyana remains one of the poorest and under-researched areas in the Caribbean, its people often elided in discussions of the region.[21] In my reading of the final story of the collection – 'English Table Wuk' – I will show how Melville focuses on these hidden lives and the religious ceremonies that are still to be fully understood.

The story is structured as a journey from the centre to the periphery – the centre being Auntie May's sitting room in Georgetown where Adriana is watching the funeral of Princess Diana with her friends and Auntie May is preparing for a flight to Miami. Middle-class and educated, Adriana and her friends bring a sociological eye to the discussion of funerals (both Diana's and Cheddi Jagan's), dismiss the spectacle and reassure themselves of the 'superiority of their own rational politics' (p. 200). This is contrasted with the lower-class space of the kitchen where the servants Barbara and Gita are discussing the funeral of Barbara's father – 'It was nice. We did sit up and sing hymns and march about. My brother did call out de words'

(p. 201) – as well as various rituals that they observe with respect to the dead. In between, Gita has told Auntie May that she must leave early 'to do some English Table Wuk' which Auntie May imagines 'involved embroidering a pretty tablecloth or something of the sort' (p. 199).

English Table Work is in fact a ceremony that forms part of the Comfa religion[22] in Guyana, though this is not named specifically and remains one of the crucial gaps in the story. Melville constructs the narrative around a series of misreadings and points to the ambivalence, as well as the diversity, of the nation in action. The two social worlds first collide when Adriana comes downstairs to see Gita packing up Auntie May's best china and silver. Assuming she is stealing but unsure what to do, Adriana follows Gita out of the house then confronts her at the bus-stands. In a richly comic scene, with Adriana completely misreading the nature of Gita's transgression and Gita too flustered to explain her purpose, Adriana is bundled onto a bus to Mahaica and then follows Gita further out of town to the grounds of an old plantation. In this remote and unfamiliar terrain Adriana 'wondered anxiously whether she had fallen amongst a gang of thieves' (p. 205) but eventually observes Gita and a group of others put together an elaborate dinner:

> Under the open sky, they struggled to set ten chairs in place, four on each side of the table and one at each end. Baskets of food were unpacked. Gita laid out the silverware that glinted in the sunshine. Pride of place in the centre of the table was given to a rich dark plum fruit-cake with plenty of whisky in it, resplendent on its tall, silver-plated cake-stand. (p. 206)

Seen through the eyes of the uninitiated (Adriana and the detached narrator) it is the incongruousness of the scene that is first described, especially in relation to the status of the people involved:

> The wealth of the display was in the greatest possible contrast to the appearance of the people who carried out the tasks, each one of whom was poorly dressed in faded, skimpy, stained and ill-fitting clothes and shoes. (pp. 206–207)

Though this may imply a criticism, a concern about the economic burden and exploitative nature of the offering, it is important to note that their care and attention to detail is also highlighted and their own feelings taken into account: 'The group looked back with pride at the fine display. There was a palpable feeling of satisfaction amongst them' (p. 207). When the table is finished the group mark the occasion with the singing of hymns accompanied by a drum and Gita later explains to Adriana:

> 'Every year we does conduct a ceremony in order to appease the spirits of the English dead who bury across de road right here. We does leave de table piled with food for dem jus' so. Whoever arrive first in the morning gathers together de crockery and silverware. It is always de same story. Nothing ever stolen. Silverware, dishes and tablecloth always

remain intact, jus' how we leave dem. But de food has always been attacked, gnawed and scattered, whether by animals or ravenous English spirits we ain' too sure. Abdul will bring back your Aunt's property early tomorrow. It will be safe. That is de English Table Wuk. You see it now?' (p. 208)

The reader, like Adriana, experiences a journey of discovery but Melville leaves many questions unanswered. In terms of the extended meditation on how we relate to the dead that the story enacts, there is no doubt that Gita's ceremony is as valid as the televised spectacle with which we began. English Table Work is only a small part of Guyanese Comfa which honours spirits from seven ethnic groups – African, Amerindian, Chinese, Dutch, East Indian and Spanish as well as the English.[23] But the reference to the English is the most ironic considering the history of colonialism and Melville is being deliberately provocative here. Are Gita's efforts a waste of time, as Adriana's friends might say, merely a colonial hangover? Or is Gita's connection to the spirit world a more inclusive and hybridised response to Guyanese reality? The use of dialect in the title – English Table *Wuk* – points up the creolised nature of the practice and validates the subaltern perspective. In terms of the collection as a whole, it is interesting that the spirits have already migrated to form the Comfa pantheon, which may itself be a liminal space in which practitioners can access the marvellous in the real.

As Gita and Adriana drive away into the night it is clear that insights have been gained and two more pieces of the puzzle have been brought into dialogue. The social hierarchy has shifted and Gita's voice and world-view brought into focus. Melville's use of dialect and dramatic comedy are perfectly timed interventions here and create much of the intimacy for the reader. But Melville also reminds us of the distance between these worlds, of the tension between material and spiritual world-views and the political realities of Guyana that constantly hinder progress. Gita's explanation of the 'English Table Wuk' is the deferred piece of information on which the story turns, but other gaps – such as the link to the wider religion of Comfa – remain. In the description of the 'unpractised chorus which petered out towards the end' (p. 207) Melville also seems to be deferring that experience of the marvellous that is so intensely realised in some of the other stories. This may be because we are not seeing the bigger picture yet, like Adriana and the narrator we do not *hear* the ceremony fully, or the ceremony itself may not have developed the necessary energy and momentum. Comfa is connected to but does not yet have the status of the Haitian Vodun that so inspired Carpentier and with Gita's enigmatic reference to the 'unappeasable' Dutch spirits (p. 209), the story ends on a humorous and ambivalent note.

The migrating ghosts of Melville's title are, on the one hand, a very real reflection of the journeys of the deprived and the dispossessed. During the

Burnham era Guyana suffered mass emigration and internal implosion and became known as the land of ghosts. Melville's stories expose the dysfunctional nature of Guyanese society and in revenge dramas such as 'Erzulie' and 'The President's Exile' there is a distinct settling of old scores. Where political corruption has been allowed to, quite literally, get away with murder the short story imagines a moral catharsis. But Melville also sees through any narrow caricature of victimhood. Through a particular use of the marvellous real and an interrogation of global political failure Melville gathers the spirits of the diaspora in a powerful and emotional tour de force. She extends and adapts Carpentier by unsettling the notion of the fixed location of the marvellous and foregrounding diasporic connections rather than the familiar disconnect. Her method of writing through gaps and silences means that tensions and ambivalence are also subtly foregrounded. For Melville these are the aesthetic and psychological gaps that allow her to proceed, trickster-like, through the dialogic encounters and competing points of view that form the basis of her stories. There is no straightforward belief in the supernatural and no spiritual or religious worldview is allowed to dominate, rather these are integrated into the dynamics of the stories and brought to bear on the capacity of the spirit in art and literature. From *Shape-shifter* to *The Migration of Ghosts* Melville has drawn on a variety of indigenous sources – the South American shaman, the carnival masquerade, Anancy – to indicate her method as a writer and the need for the reader to be alert. In this way she adapts and indigenises the short story form and encourages the reader to look again at the marvellous and the real.

NOTES

1 Mervyn Morris, 'Cross-Cultural Impersonations: Pauline Melville's *Shape-shifter*', *Ariel*, 24:1 (1993), 79–89 (p. 88).
2 For the autobiographical antecedents of this story see Melville's discussion in 'Beyond the Pale' which is collected in Margaret Busby (ed.), *Daughters of Africa* (New York: Pantheon, 1992), pp.739-43.
3 Pauline Melville, *Shape-shifter* (London: Picador, 1991 [1990]), pp. 148–49. All future references are to this edition.
4 Gnomon refers to a parallelogram with a part missing and is introduced by Joyce in 'The Sisters', the opening story of *Dubliners* (London: Penguin, 2000 [1914]) p. 1. See also Terence Brown's useful introduction and notes to this edition.
5 Pauline Melville, *The Migration of Ghosts* (London: Bloomsbury, 1999 [1998]), p. 124. All future references are to this edition.
6 Many of the details in this story relate to the life and infamous career of Guyana's first president, Linden Forbes Sampson Burnham (leader of Guyana 1964–1985), which Melville transposes into Baldwin Hercules. See James W. Ramsahoye, *A Mouldy Destiny: Visiting Guyana's Forbes Burnham* (London: Minerva Press, 1996) in which Ramsahoye imagines confronting the ghost of Burnham in the underworld.

7 As she states in 'The Truth is in the Clothes' Melville is keen to distinguish between '[t]he gifts of the genuine shaman' and 'the psychological wizardry of the charlatan' (p. 99). Shakespeare McNab is also a confidence trickster in 'I Do Not Take Messages from Dead People' though his appropriating the role of Anancy to outwit the bullying Vice-President is treated sympathetically. The detached narrator also casts doubt on the powers of the obeah man in 'The Conversion of Millicent Vernon' where the 'conversion' as such is treated ironically. Interestingly, the overall effect of this story (which begins with the sounding bells of the established churches) is to *include* obeah in the pantheon of multiple religious faiths.

8 See for instance Barry Chevannes, ed., *Rastafari and other African-Caribbean Worldviews* (London: Macmillan, 1995), Dale Bisnauth, *A History of Religions in the Caribbean* (Trenton, NJ: Africa World Press, 1996), Patrick Taylor, ed., *Nation Dance: Religion, Identity and Cultural Difference in the Caribbean* (Bloomington: Indiana University Press, 2001), Lizabeth Paravisini-Gebert and Margarite Fernández Olmos, *Creole Religions of the Caribbean: An Introduction from Vodou and Santería to Obeah and Espiritismo* (New York: New York University Press, 2003).

9 Work in the hispanic Caribbean, and especially Cuban criticism, is more developed in this respect. See for instance Antonio Benítez-Rojo's application of the work of Fernando Ortiz in *The Repeating Island: The Caribbean and the Postmodern Perspective*, trans. by James E. Maraniss, 2nd edn (Durham, NC: Duke University Press, 1996 [1989]). The ideas outlined in 'Between voodoo and ideology' (pp. 159–166) as well as his interesting chapter on Alejo Carpentier and Wilson Harris (pp. 177–96) could usefully be applied to Melville's stories. Postcolonial theory, which has only recently taken questions of religion and spirituality seriously, has tended to dominate anglophone literary criticism. Fiona Darroch's new book *Memory and Myth: Postcolonial Religion in Contemporary Guyanese Fiction and Poetry* (Amsterdam and New York: Rodopi, 2009) is a welcome addition here, though does not look specifically at Melville's writing.

10 For instance, critics often draw a contradiction between the declared faith in the spirit world in the 'Prologue' and Ti Noël's decision to remain in the kingdom of *this* world in the novel though as in Melville's writing I prefer to read this as a fruitful tension.

11 Alejo Carpentier, 'Prologue' to *The Kingdom of this World*, trans. by Harriet de Onís (London: André Deutsch, 1990 [1949]), p. 5; all future references are to this edition. For the Spanish see the extended essay, 'De lo real maravilloso americano' in *Tientos y diferencias* (Montevideo: Arca, 1967), pp.102–20.

12 See also Shalini Puri's interesting discussion of this in 'Manifestos of Desire: Hybridity as Forced Poetics', in *The Caribbean Postcolonial: Social Equality, Post-Nationalism and Cultural Hybridity* (Basingstoke: Palgrave Macmillan, 2004), pp. 83–105.

13 'Balade de Bone Conseyl', Chaucer.

14 The meaning of this word is deferred in the story until after Doña Rosita's performance, which is itself an example of duende. In Andalucía people say of certain toreros and flamenco artists that they *have* duende – an intense power to move an audience as if they are possessed by a spirit. Lorca developed this in terms of Arabic and gypsy inheritances in his 'Play and Theory of the Duende' which also provides the source material for this story: a brief mention of an eighty-year-old woman who won first prize in a dance contest in Jerez de la Frontera. See Federico García Lorca, 'Play and Theory of the Duende' (1933) in *In Search of Duende* ed. and trans. by Christopher Maurer (New York: New Directions Bibelot, 1998), p. 54. There are interesting overlaps between Lorca and Carpentier who are both developing a theory of the creative process in opposition to a dominant European mentality,

    though Lorca's untimely death means that he was not able to fully elaborate his ideas.

15 This could be compared to 'Lucifer's Shank', the story which immediately follows 'The *Duende*', in which Melville takes a more secular approach to illuminating the ghost/spirit within. The emotional response to music/dance is transferred here to literature and art as a young woman dying of cancer and her first-person narrator friend look for guidance at a traumatic time. It is interesting that the text which provides consolation and support – Dante's *Divine Comedy* – is itself a vision of the Christian afterlife and in quoting both Dante and Rushdie in the story Melville sets up a dialogue between different worldviews.

16 The parrot in this story reminds us of the trickster-narrator in *The Ventriloquist's Tale* (London: Bloomsbury, 1997) who also has parrot-like qualities. See especially the novel's 'Prologue' (pp. 1–9) for the kind of witty, anarchic sense of humour that also characterises this story. See also Kathleen Renk's analysis of the subversive mockery of the parrot and her lively discussion of the Rosicrucian background to this story in '"Magic that Battles Death": Pauline Melville's Marvellous Realism', *Journal of Commonwealth Literature*, 44:1 (2009), 106–08, an article that otherwise develops a different reading to my own.

17 Carpentier's nativist manifesto has been critiqued as overly-essentialist in its claims of authenticity and for 'othering' that which it seeks to connect with. See the classic reading by Roberto González Echevarría in *Alejo Carpentier: The Pilgrim at Home* (New York: Cornell University Press, 1977), pp. 126–28. Puri, on the other hand, reads this as part of the 'aesthetic of excess' (p. 88) and the 'rhetorical energy' (p. 89) of the hybridist manifesto, in which she includes Carpentier's 'Prologue'.

18 The historical backdrop is the massive cyanide spill at the Omai Gold Mining Company in 1995, though this is not specified in the story. Cyanide compounds are used in the chemical process at the mines. See Desiree Kissoon Jodah, 'Courting Disaster in Guyana', *The Multinational Monitor*, 16:11 (1995) <http://multinationalmonitor.org/hyper/mm1195.04.html> [accessed 14 August 2010].

19 Again, the process of deferment is important. As in 'The Migration of Ghosts' the full extent of political corruption and exploitation only emerges as we piece the scenes together, by which point the more liminal figures (Loretta and Erzulie/Margot) have also emerged and their perspectives validated.

20 Winti, meaning wind or spirits and referring to the African Caribbean religion of Surinam which borders Guyana. See Jan Voorhoeven and Ursy M. Lichtveld, eds, *Creole Drum: An Anthology of Creole Literature in Surinam*, trans. by Vernie A. February (New Haven: Yale University Press, 1975). The Winti song to the snake god that Miss Vinny sings in the story (p. 152) is recorded and translated in this classic text (p. 56 and p. 58). See also Petronella Breinburg, 'Communicating with Our Gods: the Language of Winti' in Taylor, *Nation Dance*, pp. 32–39 where she contextualises the work of Voorhoeven and others.

21 Guyana is often absent, for instance, from discussions of religion and spirituality in the region. Of the scholarly works mentioned above, only Bisnauth and Taylor have a specific entry on Guyana. Compared to the many works on Santería, Vodun and Rastafari there is only one book on the African Caribbean Guyanese religion of Comfa (by Gibson, see details below).

22 See Keane Gibson's *Comfa Religion and Creole Language in a Caribbean Community* (New York: SUNY Press, 2001).

23 These categories are also somewhat fluid. Note the reference to the Scottish doctor (p. 207) who would also be included in the 'English' ethnic group.

CROSS-CULTURAL READINGS OF THE CARIBBEAN SHORT STORY

SANDRA COURTMAN

In 1960, buoyed by the promise of a newly independent Caribbean, C.L.R. James suggested that only a great artist would have the ability to 'sum up the past' and open out 'the way to the future'.[1] In this public lecture, James spoke as a visionary historian who also happened to be a supreme artist of the short story: he had published his celebrated short story 'La Divina Pastora' in Trinidad's *Saturday Review* more than thirty years earlier.[2] A rigorous colonial education equipped pioneers like James to intervene in a long tradition of short fiction which continues to flourish. The international appeal of the short story canon is exemplified by recent collections such as James Daley's *The World's Greatest Short Stories* (2006). Daley includes in his 'small and idiosyncratic distillation' the work of Leo Tolstoy, Franz Kafka, Virginia Woolf, Raymond Carver, Ernest Hemingway, Katherine Mansfield, Chinua Achebe and Jorge Luis Borges, amongst others.[3] Daley's stories are selected for their ability to deliver narrative pleasure to a global readership with differing backgrounds and tastes; therefore their achievements in storytelling might be regarded as aesthetic rather than partisan. In a humanist plea for their universal truths, Daley asserts that they have 'the greatness that transcends the author, the time, and the place of its initial creation' (Daley, p. vi).

Significantly, regardless of the disclaimer of a 'small and idiosyncratic' selection of twenty stories, Daley does not include a Caribbean exemplar. Even the prestigious collection of forty-one stories in the *Oxford Book of Short Stories*, edited by V.S. Pritchett and in print since 1981, does not include a Caribbean-authored story. There are many single-authored collections but in terms of the anthology, the Caribbean is still largely contained in a literary ghetto of specialist publications. Hence, the stories discussed here are published in influential Caribbean anthologies, such as Stewart Brown's and John Wickham's *The Oxford Book of Caribbean Short Stories* (1999), and are highly valued by a particular constituency of readers. It is the availability of these rich and comprehensive anthologies that has enabled me to teach a course on the Caribbean short story to British literary competent students, with little or no knowledge of the Caribbean. Based on this experience, this essay will argue that the stories seem able to meet both Daley's (humanist) and James's (materialist) criteria in that they deliver a type of transcultural narrative pleasure (to readers from very different constituencies) but that they do this by reworking the specific content of a colonial past and a creolised present in a very compact way. This essay selects stories from Caribbean anthologies enabling us to access the fictional worlds of different periods, regions and diasporas: John Figueroa (Jamaica, 1960), Stuart Hall (Jamaica/UK, 1960), Rosario Ferré (Puerto Rico, 1991) and Willi Chen (Trinidad, 1988). My aim is to explore how these very different Caribbean authors exploit the accessibility and immediate pleasure of the short story to enable a transnational readership to understand the history and politics that have shaped their modern societies.

The stories have their provenance in the cultural crossings that have formed the modern Caribbean region and their writers seem able to use the process and experience of creolisation to bridge cultural boundaries for a wide readership. The stories discussed here have been selected not only for their ability to cross cultural boundaries but because they each advance the creolisation of a highly wrought form which exists in a literary space somewhere between the poem and the novel. John Figueroa's 1960s story of a Jamaican party captures a range of distinctive satirical Caribbean voices as metaphorical agents in an ideological battle over cultural sovereignty. Stuart Hall's early story of the lonely West Indian migrant hints at a type of narrative-linguistic inventiveness that is fully realised in novel form by Sam Selvon. Rosario Ferré's bold structural experimentalism eschews Western rationalism to explore the pain of Puerto Rican cultural schizo-phrenia. In a micro form made all the more effective because of its brevity, Willi Chen creolises the short story in his comic depiction of a Trinidadian multiracial community and its generational conflicts.

In the 1960s, artists questioned how a nationalist imperative could represent the sheer diversity to be found in the 'high' and 'grass-roots' culture of a Caribbean population with different origins and interests in the business of slavery and indenture. This is one of the motifs of John Figueroa's short story set at a scotch- and rum-soaked Jamaican party. The story has the Latin title 'Ars Longa; Vita Brevis [Art Remains; Life is Short]' and ends with the narrator musing on loneliness, death and what endures.[4] The characters debate, cajole and compete for women in a series of surreal arguments which are interrupted by the calypsonian's ironic interventions. These lyrics disrupt the multi-vocal flow of the arguments and Figueroa sets them aside in the form of italics. In this way the story enacts structurally the debates about the value of high and low culture explored through the juxtaposition of, for example, the closing lines of T.S. Eliot's 'Preludes' alongside such calypsonian wisdom as 'Six feet of earth/ And we gone to eternity/ Death is so compulsory'. Early in the story, during an argument about the value of local art versus Old-World culture, one ironic voice claims to be 'beyond the West Indian pale by various acts of indiscretion' (*West Indian Stories*, p. 209). These transgressions include the following:

I have thought our cricket umpires wrong on occasion; I have dipped my headlights; and I have, no doubt when alcohol had dissolved my entire super-ego, thought the History of the Romans more important to our young children than that of the Arawaks and Caribs. (*West Indian Stories*, p. 209)

On the other side of the argument is Freddy, an Englishman who 'would hardly accept the free gift of a Turner but he pays ten guineas [...] for almost any ill-drawn local painting' (*West Indian Stories*, p. 214). The story suggests that such widely different value judgements are inevitable with guests who include black, brown and white, and a mix of 'artists, intelligentsia, athletic men, gay-time girls [...] confused and lonesome people, all seeking their Lethe water' (*West Indian Stories* p. 220). Lethe water is literally a potent fruit cocktail with a classical Greek name which invokes the obvious use of alcohol as a means of inducing forgetfulness. The name also suggests how the guest list is made up of a metaphorical 'cocktail' of class, race and gender that may be attempting to blot out aspects of Jamaica's colonial inheritance which conflict with a nationalist agenda. Values are shifting to the extent that the narrator observes that 'when I was young the thing to have was a degree, now one does better to have an artist, or at least a friend who is the friend of an artist' (*West Indian Stories* p. 207). Figueroa satirises the debate about the value of art and whether this should transcend the partisan view of '*West Indian culture* [Figueroa's italics]'. At the end of the story the narrator observes how the calypso infects all the dancers to the extent that 'the artists are forgetting their Art, intelligentsia their Reason, and the cricket enthusiasts their cricket' (*West Indian Stories* p. 221). It is the undertow of the calypso which seems to unite the guests with 'empirical and pragmatic [...] dancing [...] adapted to the necessities of the music' (*West Indian Stories*, p. 213). In this response 'a Jamaican will now be dancing more like a Trinidadian' (*West Indian Stories,* p. 209). Figueroa's story shows Jamaicans literally acting under the influence of the musical traditions of Trinidad and suggests that it is impossible to separate out the cocktail of 'pragmatic' cross-cultural transformations that have inflected the lives of different peoples in the Caribbean.

Figueroa's story articulates a cultural dichotomy for Jamaicans on the brink of a political independence which foregrounds the tension between residual and emergent cultures. In his story he represents an inclusive meeting place which ultimately accommodates the different cultural origins and values of T.S. Eliot and calypso. He shows how calypsos and folk art are emerging as important creolised forms but the story also suggests that they need not be valorised as complete replacements for T.S. Eliot's poetry, for Turner's paintings, or any other part of the 'culture of the foreign overlord' (*West Indian Stories* p. 208).

Figueroa's story negotiates the local, as it was first published in *Bim* for a Caribbean audience with a vested interest in these important debates, and the transcultural when it was subsequently published in London by Faber and Faber. As Hyacinth Simpson suggests, the trajectory of the story's publication, beginning with a home-grown readership in Barbados and transferring to a metropolitan readership, also warns that emerging indigenous cultural formations will be judged by traditional critical standards. Caribbean authors were all too aware that their work would have to make this transfer and have the ability 'to cross generic, cultural and temporal limits and still retain its power for all readers'.[5]

Figueroa's short story is a creative response to a fight over form, language and culture that he plays out through the views expressed by his argumentative guests. For artists like Figueroa working on the cusp of independence, this debate is crucial to their development. It features in the plea that Walcott issues in his much quoted poem, 'A Far Cry from Africa', where he rails against the futility of imposing a choice: '...I who have cursed/ The drunken officer of British rule, how choose/ Between this Africa and the English tongue I love?'[6] This battle ground would prove to be an intensely creative space involving political and aesthetic choices along a language continuum offered by the polyphonic Caribbean. Kenneth Ramchand argues that 'In the twentieth century, we have to give up the notion of separate languages (Creole English and Standard English) and we have to envisage a scale'.[7] The language dialectic would inspire some of the richest linguistic experiments in representation, involving a decision by the artist about how accessible the voice depicted should be to a non-Caribbean reader. At one end of the scale is action, thought, and speech represented through Standard English prose, but the continuum also contains the hardcore Jamaican Creole of Louise Bennett and the lyrical verisimilitude of Sam Selvon's fictive voices.

The desire to hear these voices, on or off the page, is caught in a short story by Stuart Hall entitled 'Crossroads Nowhere' which appeared in Salkey's 1960 anthology, *West Indian Stories*. As one of our most important postcolonial cultural critics, Hall is not usually thought of as a writer of short stories, but in this example he displays a nascent talent. He describes the impact of a chance encounter with a fellow West Indian who interrupts the gloomy thoughts of the narrator with 'A'right, sagga boy' as he weaves his way through dismal London streets.[8] The narrator races after the unknown West Indian and self-consciously approaches him: 'What could I say? That I hadn't heard words slip off the tongue like that, like a cascade of minted pennies, for months, that we should go somewhere and talk...' (*West Indian Stories*, p. 187). The potent sound / word image of 'a cascade of minted pennies' evokes the colour, music, freshness and sparkle of the West Indian voice that stands in for a deeper, and routinely repressed, longing for its tropical home. The voice is so distinctive and delectable that

'Out of a thousand mocking murmurs in a thousand foreign tongues, his had caught my ear, as the single call of a fisherman across a harbour brings the pasteboard canoes dancing and jigging together from the darkness' (*West Indian Stories*, p. 188).

Hall's use of a West Indian vernacular idiom is a small intervention in a story narrated entirely in eloquent Standard English prose but it still suggests the importance of representing both types of voices. Writers are sometimes expected to make a choice between the language of the colo-niser (T.S. Eliot in Figueroa's story) and what is seen as the 'authentic' Creole voice of the dispossessed (the 'sagga boy' in Hall's story). Language choice still remains a controversial issue for contemporary Caribbean writers, including Puerto Ricans Rosario Ferré and Judith Ortiz Cofer. Ortiz Cofer responds to criticism with the comment: 'I really resent the prevalent attitude that if you really care about the Island you have to write in Spanish. It is not my fault that 95% of my education was in English in American schools.'[9] Yet the very nature of this debate about what consti-tutes a West Indian language and culture, however divisive, evidences the sense of historical and cultural responsibility operating in the creative output of Caribbean writers. The need to invent a new fictional represen-tation of code-switching has led to a creolisation in form. In order for different groups to survive together, new languages had to be formed in the everyday violence of the colonised Caribbean and this is a difficult process to represent. In former colonies, language choice is politically symbolic of the need to represent the voices of many people who have historically been occluded. Postcolonial writers must gather up the shrapnel of embittered histories and make it cohere into a story which opens up the way to a better understanding, or James's 'way to the future'.

Nadine Gordimer asserts that 'the short story is the form for our age, being well suited to representing the fragmentary nature of much contem-porary experience'.[10] Frank Birbalsingh also observes that the 'shorter literary form is better capable of expressing the fragmentary nature of West Indian experience that is produced by the displacement and mixing of different cultures'.[11] The fragmentary nature of experience in the Carib-bean and its diasporas, its linguistic differences and inventiveness, its pragmatic origins in oral and newsprint traditions, are all important reasons why the short story has been so firmly rooted in cultural practice. Carib-bean writers are from a region which is characterised both by its very diversity and by the number of its practitioners whose work was/is pro-duced in the diaspora. The short story form has inevitably developed as a transnational configuration with roots in a Caribbean populated from the Indian, Chinese, Syrian, African, and European diasporas and whose population has since dispersed across the world. Migration is not the only challenge to nationalism, as Stephano Harney explains when he writes

about Trinidad. How does a 'search for a national identity', which is so
often characterised from the outside as African-Trinidadian, take account
of a multiracial population of 'two and half thousand Chinese, a thousand
Portuguese, a thousand Syrians and Lebanese, and 144,000 East Indians
who made the journey to Trinidad in the post emancipation era' (Harney,
p. 74)?[12] And as E.A. Markham reminds us, it may seem perverse to return
'to the question of defining a national literature when its practitioners seem
permanently encamped on all five continents'.[13]

Many pioneering Caribbean short story writers were recognised first in
the US or Europe; an early example would be Jamaican Claude Mckay's
1932 collection *Gingertown* which was first published in New York.[14] One
way of addressing the complexity of defining 'a national literature', which
seems so often to have been both written and recognised in its diasporas, is
to return key developments to their cultural contexts. Scholars such as Frank
Birbalsingh have attended to developments in the Indo-Caribbean short
story.[15] Hyacinth Simpson has meticulously traced the history of the
Jamaican short story to find publications in Jamaica as early as 1855
(Simpson, p. 219). In the post-war boom, Jean Rhys, C.L.R. James, V.S.
Naipaul, George Lamming and Samuel Selvon developed their reputations
abroad but there were always practitioners who chose to stay in the Caribbean and there was sometimes a tension expressed by those who stayed to
create/maintain a literary space for a home-grown writer and audience, and
those who sought transnational attention for their work. For example, one
of the stories discussed below is by Willi Chen, who has chosen to stay in the
Caribbean to work. Even though he is increasingly the subject of Euro-
American critical attention, Chen is widely recognised as one of Trinidad's
supreme artists whose practice stays firmly rooted in the Caribbean.

In any case, the successful 'export' of the Caribbean short story would
not have been possible without a history of storytelling in the region. Louis
James explains that there are practical reasons for its development: 'It was
the shorter pieces that could be ensconced in the columns of local newspapers and magazines that, from the eighteenth century onwards, created
the beginnings of an indigenous literature.'[16] This long valued tradition of
indigenous stories contributed to the tension between the nationalist
political agendas of early twentieth-century Caribbean literary magazines
and opportunities presented abroad. Both are illustrated by the acknowl-
edgements listed at the end of Andrew Salkey's 1960 collection *West Indian
Stories*. Original places of publication seem equally divided between home-
grown magazines *Bim* (Barbados, first issue 1942), *Focus* (Jamaica, first
issue 1943), and US and European sources including *The Atlantic Monthly*
(US) and the BBC (through its Caribbean and Colonial Service in the
UK). Salkey suggests that the 'problem' of fragmentation has been partly
resolved by the metropole:

> To the West Indies, with its uncertain roots and highly original racial mixtures, with its scattered islands and its doubtful yet enthusiastic claims to nationhood, with its turgid colonial history, part rejected and part subconsciously absorbed, England has been a sort of necessary common denominator, a link holding all of its constituent parts together.[17]

The idea of England as socially adhesive for emerging post-imperial artistic identities, with enormously diverse cultural traditions, is a controversial one which only applies to ex-British colonies. The work discussed here is by authors from a much wider Caribbean region and what unifies their disparate output would seem to be their commitment to a type of creative decolonisation of their histories, their cultures, their languages and their bodies. As Harney asserts: 'The Beacon group of the 1930s, led by C.L.R. James and Alfred Mendes, sought specifically – as Mendes has maintained in recent interviews – to ground their literary discourse in indigenous language and culture, taking on an overt nationalist project' (Harney, p. 72).[18] Even given the nature of its many regional divisions and nationalist agendas, there is a common experience of disenfranchisement through colonisation. Colonisation induces a creative project to imagine a different future where new identities can be forged in the reclamation of troubled histories.

Puerto Rico's troubled history has resulted in an often literally divided society with many of its peoples living in the US. Up to one third of the island's population left for the US between 1940 and 1960.[19] By 1990 a staggering seventy-five per cent of the home population lived in the US metropolis.[20] Puerto Rico has a creolised language and culture inflected by indigenous Taíno Indians, imported African slaves and successive Spanish and US ownership. Language choice in literature is often metonymic for Spanish and Anglo-American domination. Whilst the US superpower attempted to impose English as the official language, four hundred years of Hispanic rule had already invested Spanish as the language of preference for many Puerto Ricans.[21]

A writer like Rosario Ferré works within the crucible of conflicted languages and cultures and she has expressed a sense that Puerto Ricans often feel that '[we] have no language of our own' (Santos-Phillips, p. 118). Ferré was born to the Governor of the Commonwealth in Ponce in 1938 and has been criticised both for being privileged and for importing US feminist politics. However, James Ferguson asserts that she is the writer who 'best conveys the complex Puerto Rican cultural inheritance' (Ferguson, p. 151). Suzanne Bost explains how Ferré uses this complexity to her advantage:

> ...Ferré's ability to speak as a feminist about Puerto Rican women, to write in two languages, and to explore the convergence of African and European lineage in Puerto Rico fuses different codes of gendered, linguistic, and racial identity.[22]

At the heart of these linguistic and cultural convergences is a recognisably macho society and Ferré also uses patriarchal power as a metaphor for colonial power structures.

Ferré's linguistic style offers her a highly inventive and effective way of representing cultural schizophrenia as the psychological consequence of colonisation. Exemplary is her feminist-inspired short story, originally written in Spanish as 'Cuando las mujeres quieren a los hombres' ('When Women Love Men') which was published in 1991 in a collection of short stories entitled *The Youngest Doll*. Ferré explores the melding of (pure/ impure) identities through multiple female voices which reveal the most intimate aspects of a relationship with the same powerful man, Ambrosio. Ferré advances the story and our understanding of the women's identity crises almost entirely through the free indirect discourse of a pious wife, Isabel Luberza, and Ambrosio's black prostitute/mistress Isabel la Negra.[23] It is a narrative technique which fragments a linear account of their lives with Ambrosio and does not privilege either experience. As Elizabeth Black explains, generally the use of free indirect discourse (FID) is a 'potent source of complexity and irony in discourse'.[24] Ferré's use of FID problematises and blurs their identities, offering a reading of the two Isabels as the split psyche of a Madonna and a whore who can speak both to and for each other: 'We, your lover and your wife, have always known that a prostitute hides beneath the skin of every lady.' (*OBCSS*, p. 258)

Ferré's complex narrative structure separates and sometimes interlaces their idiolect. Her prostitute even engages in an ongoing argument about the Puerto Rican 'authenticity' of island-based versus New York residents. Isabel La Negra has provided sex for both types of clients and is well placed to deny their essential difference: '... affirming from her platform that she is the proof in flesh and blood that there was no difference between those of Puerto Rico and those of New York because they had all been united in her flesh...' (*OBCSS*, p. 258).

These two characters represent conflicting elements of a fluid identity which have to be faced and, eventually, equally loved. There is clear symbolism operating in the women's relationship which is understand-ably bitter. Each of them held a very different type of power over their husband/lover and when he dies they are thrown together. Like Puerto Rico itself, both are left with half of his inheritance and their economic power becomes interdependent. Years after Ambrosio's death, Isabel la Negra visits Isabel Luberza in the house they jointly own with the idea of taking her brothel out of the slum and paying the wife rent to operate from the family home. At the meeting, they are forced to confront their jealousy and begin to exchange aspects of their identities, which eventually fuse as in the following: '...purifying ourselves of everything that defined us, one as a prostitute and the other as a lady. So that in the end, when one of us won over the other, it was our most sublime act of love' (*OBCSS*, p. 258).

The story interweaves the Catholic/pagan, black/white, and sexual/virginal so that they cannot be regarded as distinct. These strands have an historical resonance which goes back to slavery and colonisation. Towards the end of the story, the wife's memory ranges over her self-sacrifice, a different type of slavery that articulates what was necessary to maintain the persona of whiteness, of duty, of fertility and Catholic respectability:

> I imagined her eyes, soft and bulging like hicaco seeds, placed inside that yellowish egg white that always surrounds Negroes' eyes, and I thought of mine, restless and hard like emerald marbles, enslaved from day to day, coming and going, measuring the level of flour and sugar in the jars in the pantry... [...] the body where you scrubbed your penis quickly to have an almost pure orgasm, as clean as a butterfly's, so different from those you have with her when the two of you wallow in the mud of a slum... (*OBCSS*, p. 267)

Sharing Ambrosio has only brought pain to both women. Their relationship with him has meant equally repressive constructions of femininity: masochism or sexual commodification. Their story is a forensic examination of an identity crisis which results from a long history of different ownership. Since men were the colonisers, this is overlaid by sacrificial attempts to service conflicting male desires. Symbolically in this black/white, colonial/postcolonial opposition, Ferré shifts a considerable amount of power to the black whore; she even substitutes for the wife at important social events with Ambrosio:

> I knew from the very beginning why she had come. She had already succeeded in replacing me in all the town activities that I had presided over with you, holding on to your arm like a sprouted jasmine clinging to the wall. (*OBCSS*, p. 268)

By the end of the story Isabel la Negra may be in control but by then both identities are inseparable, having become, like modern Puerto Rican society, an undeniable part of each other. As Bost puts it:

> Both [Ana Lydia] Vega and Ferré thus share an interest in the ways in which black and white are intertwined in Puerto Rican mestizaje [an inclusive concept which offers a paradigm for the internal contradictions within identity]. Their depictions expose the hypocrisy of pretensions to racial purity, and they ultimately envision the defeat of white separatists. Both depict empowered biracial heroes who get the better of light-skinned characters. (Bost, p. 193)

It would be far too simplistic to read this story as a victory for the disenfranchised black mistress over the bourgeois wife because it is clear that, in spite of race and class determinants, they can operate more holistically together. As Augustus C. Puleo puts it: 'when the paternal signature is erased from the text, the two Isabels are left, paradoxically with more, not less'.[25]

The idea that cultural exchange produces more and not less for its participants is also the theme of Willi Chen's short story 'Trotters'. Shin Yamamoto argues that Chen is characteristic of the few well-known Chinese writers in the Caribbean diaspora who have developed a unique perspective on 'the social and historical conditions of race'. He argues:

> This stance seems related to the 'neutrality' of Chinese in the Caribbean because as latecomers to the area they have had to exist between other races to survive, especially in commerce. Sitting in the far corners of shops or giving a glance from behind the counter, Chinese eyes have observed the multi-ethnic society of the Caribbean since their arrival.[26]

Chen is a second-generation Chinese Jamaican born in Trinidad in 1934 of parents from the village of Tien Tsien in the Guandang Province of China. As a playwright, mas-maker, sculptor, visual artist and business-man, he has all the qualities of a Renaissance man. In his short stories, Chen applies the extraordinary insight described by Shin Yamamoto into the rural East Indian community into which his family settled. Harney agrees that Chen's unique perspective facilitates 'the resistance of identity to disarm the will to nationalism. And, in the process, he defeats the metadiscourse of race embedded in that will' (Harney p. 72).

Chen's short stories were originally published in *King of the Carnival* in 1988 and, along with Jan Lowe Shineborne's Guyanese novel *Timepiece* (1986), were one of the first literary productions by a Caribbean writer of Chinese origin. 'Trotters' reflects the author's observations on notions of racial purity in a playful exchange of identity politics. The story provides a superlative creative challenge to the maintenance of 'authentic' racial identities which have so often divided the poor people of his native Trinidad. As Shalini Puri explains:

> It is one of the great ironies of decolonization in Trinidad that racial tensions have taken the form of horizontal hostility between blacks and Indians (the two largest ethnic groups, each with its own related histories of exploitation – slavery for blacks and indentureship for Indians), rather than the vertical hostility directed by blacks and Indians *together* against the economically privileged French Creole elite, the white ex-plantocracy.[27]

Although racial division in Trinidad is necessarily a serious subject, Chen uses irony to confront culturally significant conflicts over African and Indian food rituals. He exploits the brevity of the short story form to reveal the absurdity of cultural separatism in a family struggling to feed itself. Muslims Azard, an East Indian sugar estate worker, and his ancient and exhausted mother represent a generational split. The story opens with an image of Ma Abdool still struggling to carry 'bundles of yellowing chive and pale ochroes which like her dry self had long passed the age of slime'. Ma still attempts to maintain crops which, like some of her rigid beliefs, are no longer sustainable and '[y]et, she planted the only way she knew of…'.[28]

Muslim and African 'differences' are symbolised by squabbles over Zobida, Azard's new wife, and the food she prepares for her mother-in-law. These arguments contribute to the suspicion that Zobida is part-African 'dougla'. Although strongly denied by Zobida's parents, there are signs enough to warrant a boycott of the wedding by the groom's best friends. As Zobida attempts to settle in and cook for the household, we are entertained by arguments which rumble on about what her food might signify. Chen is using the motif of food to symbolise how tradition and transformation are carried in the rituals of a diasporan diet. As Vijay Mishra writes: 'a large Pan-Indian plantation diaspora is linked to cuisine. [...] Food links the old Indian diaspora from Surinam to Mauritius to Fiji.'[29] Mishra explains that there are practical reasons for uniformity associated with the routine of plantation rations, but so pervasive are certain dishes of Indian origin that they have become the 'standard cuisine of indenture' (Mishra, p. 92). 'Trotters' illuminates how a taste for different foodstuffs, whether Indian, African or Creole, breaches ethnic boundaries. Many dishes with clear origins in the Pan-Indian diaspora have had a cross-cultural impact on the creolised food preferences of the diversely populated Caribbean.

Whilst the ancient Ma Abdool is skeletal and finicky, Zobida is easy-going, bright-eyed and plump. We see the markings of racial ambiguity through the adoring eyes of husband Azard, who finds Zobida's physical differences 'dizzying', especially 'her waist – rounded and moulded – rotating in that flawless rhythm as she walked' (*OBCSS*, p. 289). The story explores the futility of policing interracial relationships, particularly love matches, which will always breach the irony of an African/Indian divide. Chen uses food as one of the most recognisable markers of religious difference to explore what Puri has described as the 'dougla poetics' of Trinidad. Puri has traced the genesis of the idea of the 'dougla', a person of mixed Indian and African descent, in an attempt to rescue the pejorative term from its origins and reinstate the interracial identity as a symbol of growth:

> ... contemporary Indian disavowals of the dougla [are traced] back to the highly skewed sex ratios within the Indian population during the period of indentureship, as well as to Hindu notions of caste endogamy. It is in this context that the pejorative Hindi term 'dougla' or bastard was applied to people of mixed Indian and African descent. (Puri, p. 127)

Without suggesting a resolution to the conflicts between Indian and African communities and their religious beliefs, Chen's highly individual characters eventually enjoy the possibility of a healthy cultural exchange. The story invites a literal re-evaluation of separatism when Zobida hides the blasphemous 'pig foot' in a multi-ethnic soup. Whilst Azard guesses that Zobida has added pigs' trotters to the pot, when she is quizzed by Ma, an amused husband and wife corroborate insisting that it contains 'Nothing. Is beef bone' (*OBCSS*, p. 291). Hence, a huge row is avoided by an act of deception. Eventually Ma gives in to the sensual pleasure of Zobida's cooking and in the final line of the story even asks 'Beta, yuh haveam any more chotters?' The trotters are satisfying, enjoyable and have been rendered socially harmless as but one ingredient amongst many. Even the word for 'trotters', a term usually collocated with pig, has mutated via Ma's new pronunciation as she repeats her question: 'Chotters is beef bone. Beta?' Azard has to avoid the question as he and Zobida are becoming hysterical. In answer, he can only manage to turn away from her and give out 'a throttled, piggy grunt' (*OBCSS*, p. 291). The humour lies in the suggestion that all three characters are complicit in the deception but choose not to reveal the 'truth' and jeopardise their pleasure in the creolised food. Ma disregards Zobida's 'dougla' identity because she is reliant on her skills.

In the story Ma Abdool demands that her food is prepared in ways that have survived the journey from India to the Caribbean diaspora. The inventiveness of the following dialogue, its word order and vocabulary, is central to the story's humour about this survival. This routine spat is between Ma and Zobida:

> Late one afternoon, Ma returned from selling.
> 'You na cookam yet, gul. And night done come.'
> 'Mai, ah done put water to boil.'
> 'Wata.... wata.... what you make am?'
> 'Mai, Azard say he goh take some soup tonight.'
> 'Soop... soop. We is creoni? Only creoni does drinkam soup.'
> 'But Ma, it still have a piece of sada roti.'
> 'Bete, I wantam choka too. See you have am damadol and chonkay it.' (*OBCSS*, p. 288)

Interestingly, when Ma demands 'choka', it is literally untranslatable as a single term since she is demanding a cooking method passed down through indentured labourers. 'Choka' is an Indian-style preparation derived from the Hindi word 'Chhownk'; this is similar in meaning to 'chonkay' from the Hindi word 'chaumkna'. These terms mean 'to give a dish extra piquancy by adding a blistering hot mixture of oil in preparation' and poured over at the end of the cooking (Mishra, p. 92). Ma also asks for 'damadol', meaning tomato, 'sada roti', a plain flat bread like a Chapatti and 'dry bagee', dry vegetables. Chen has creolised these Hindi words, retaining their meaning and significance but losing their 'authentic' spellings, just as his characters have inevitably changed in the diaspora. In conflict with the 'purity' of the Indian food that Ma demands, Azard enjoys Zobida's 'flair for cooking exotic, greasy dishes' of Afro-Creole origin including 'chocolate tea', 'fry fish' and 'salt beef' (*OBCSS*, p. 289). The pragmatism and resourcefulness of this cross-cultural food exchange is typical of how different groups of settlers have had to be open to alternatives in the immigrant society that is Trinidad.

If exposed, the trotters would be strictly forbidden and Chen parallels this conflict with Ma's disavowal of Zobida's 'dougla' identity. Whilst Chen's depiction of linguistic verisimilitude is convincing, he juxtaposes his characters' speech with a Standard English narration. Azard struggles with his divided loyalty, so Chen's external narrator intervenes to offer a philosophical take on the difference between wife and mother and what they each represent:

> Azard knew of the mild bickerings at home. That clash between old world philosophy and the challenging horizons of anticipated resistance. The strong-willed hard-core precepts clashing against the liberal exuberance of new world ethics. Yet he loved them both: the caring mother and the loving wife. (*OBCSS*, p. 289)

Ultimately, in spite of Ma's disapproval, it is Azard and Zobida who have to bridge the race, class, religious and caste divisions. Whilst Azard is hurt by his friends' rejection of Zobida, he chooses love over conformity:

> To hell with them [...] He loved Zobida and that was that. After all she was his wife and if she wanted to eat pig foot at times, why not? That was her own business. And who cared if she was Dougla, part Creoni, or even full blooded Creole. (*OBCSS*, p. 291)

The final message is clear. Azard will take Zobida as she is and as he 'probed the murky depths of his own bowl' we are left wondering what 'ingredients' make up any gene pool (*OBCSS*, p. 291). The metaphorical soup of humankind in Chen's story may be indeterminate but can be rich enough to nourish all.

Chen shows a superb mastery of technique in 'Trotters' and achieves a great deal in a very compact form. In a three-page story, there is no space for preaching about the origins of his generational split and therefore the importance of finding a way to 'sum up the past' and see a way to a less troubled future is conveyed entirely through characterisation. The story resists didacticism by allowing the characters themselves to carry the past, the present and the future in their interaction. Chen represents these likeable characters and their conflicts vividly through dialogue and description. The style is polyphonic as the reader moves along the language continuum from Standard English to his characters' idiomatic speech. Chen uses local terms in the arguments because they encode historical and cultural resonances associated both with the history of settlement and the cross-cultural influences of creolised cuisine. Although Chen represents a specific Trinidadian context and uses an idiolect and vocabulary particular to his fictive East Indian community, most of the story is intelligible and pleasurable for readers without knowledge of its cultural referents.

It is Chen's compact rendering of Trinidadian languages and complex cultural contexts which creolises the short story form. His skill in story-telling means that potentially any reader can recognise the significance of these conflicts over food without prior knowledge of their specific cultural origins. In my experience, British students find the words and trying to find out what the dishes might look or taste like hugely enjoyable. We return, as in Stuart Hall's story, to an inherent pleasure to be found in literature's ability to evoke the sound of a language, strange or familiar. The success of Chen's deceptively simple three-page story is that without fixing the meaning or suggesting a solution, it recognises that arguing over food, as a universal symbol of sustenance and pleasure, is a good way to understand the history of apparently irreconcilable differences. The story explains the pressure and the risks involved in attempting to retain religious and cultural practices that have had to survive the trauma of collective migra-tion. Chen explains, without judgement, why Ma Abdool is so rooted in the past and why Azard and Zobida are open to a different vision of the future.

This essay is founded on the idea that the Caribbean short story is able to explain history and culture more effectively than some of the most rigorous postcolonial theorists. As in some of the most critically acclaimed short stories, for example those of Ernest Hemingway and Raymond Carver, effects and ideas are illuminated by the use of a very compact form of storytelling. Arguably, the important insights provided by these stories would lose some of their power in a longer form of fiction.

Harney agrees that theorists are rarely able to compete with writers like Willi Chen in their 'understanding of the diasporic, tentative nature of the nation, nor in their attention to the ethnogenesis and repluralization that diaspora implies' (Harney, p. 6). Pioneering writers and intellectuals like John Figueroa, C.L.R. James and Stuart Hall reinforce literature as a site of ideological conflict and evidence its ability to illuminate contradictory elements of their fictive colonial/postcolonial regions and diasporas. All the short stories discussed in this essay engage readers through character, and their struggles over language and identity contain important lessons about history and culture.

The essay has argued that, in a unique way, the genre of the Caribbean short story has consistently engendered aesthetic experimentation as a form of resistance. Whilst entertaining us with the undeniable pleasure of their stories, all the writers here induce the reader to question notions of 'truth' and 'reality' generated by patriarchy, successive colonisers and political regimes. The stories discussed are historically located, linguisti-cally challenging and yet one of their achievements is that they are accessible to readers who have little or no experience of the Caribbean. In that sense, if we return to Daley's prime criterion for his 'best short stories' of the world, we might conclude that they indeed display 'the greatness that transcends the author, the time, and the place of its initial creation'. If Caribbean short story writers achieve this transcendent universality, then they do so by means of the paradox that their concerns are far from generic. They also respond to James's call for an artist who can sum up the past in the present and open up the way to a future.

NOTES

1 C.L.R. James, 'The Artist in the Caribbean' was delivered as part of Open Lecture series at the University College of the West Indies, Mona (1959–1960), in C.L.R. James, 'Two Lectures by C.L.R. James', *Caribbean Quarterly*, 54:1 (March–June 2008) 179–87 (p. 179).
2 C.L.R. James, 'La Divina Pastora' was first published in Trinidad in October 1927 in *The Saturday Review*. Reprinted in C.L.R. James, *Spheres of Existence: Selected Writings* (London: Allison and Busby, 1980), pp. 5–8.
3 James Daley, ed., *The World's Greatest Short Stories* (Mineola, New York: Dover Publications, 2006), pp. v–vii (p. v).
4 John Figueroa, 'Ars Longa; Vita Brevis', in *West Indian Stories*, ed. by Andrew Salkey (London: Faber & Faber, 1960) pp. 207–21.
5 Hyacinth M. Simpson, 'Patterns and periods: Oral Aesthetics and a Century of Jamaican Short Story Writing', *Journal of West Indian Literature*, 12:1 (2004), 1–30 (p. 9).
6 Derek Walcott, 'A Far Cry from Africa', in *The Penguin Book of Caribbean Verse in English*, ed. by Paula Burnett (London: Penguin Books, 1986), p. 243.
7 Kenneth Ramchand, *The West Indian Novel and its Background*, 2nd edn (Kingston: Ian Randle Publishers, 2004), p. 68.
8 Stuart Hall, 'Crossroads Nowhere', in *West Indian Stories*, ed. by Salkey, pp. 186–88 (p. 188).
9 Edna Acosta-Bellen, 'A MELUS interview: Judith Ortiz Cofer', *MELUS*, 18 (1993), 83–97, cited in Suzanne Bost, 'Transgressing Borders: Puerto Rican and Latina Mestizaje', *MELUS*, 25:2 (2000), 187–211 (p. 189).
10 Nadine Gordimer, 'The International Symposium on the Short Story', *Kenyon Review*, 30 (1968), 457–63, cited in Lynda Prescott, ed., *A World of Difference: An Anthology of Short Stories from Five Continents* (Basingstoke: Palgrave Macmillan, 2008), p. 3.
11 Frank Birbalsingh, 'The Indo-Caribbean Short Story', *Journal of West Indian Literature*, 12 (Nov 2004), 118–36 (p. 122).
12 Stefano Harney, *Nationalism and Identity: Culture and the Imagination in the Caribbean Diaspora* (London and New Jersey: Zed Books; Kingston: University of the West Indies, 1996), p. 74.
13 E.A. Markham, 'Introduction', in *The Penguin Book of Caribbean Short Stories* (London: Penguin, 1996), pp. xi–xlv (p. xiii).
14 *Gingertown* is the subject of Dave Gunning's essay in this volume.
15 Birbalsingh, 'The Indo-Caribbean Short Story'.
16 Louis James, 'Writing the Ballad: The Short Fiction of Samuel Selvon and Earl Lovelace', in *Telling Stories: Postcolonial Short Fiction in English*, ed. by Jacqueline Bardolph (Amsterdam and Atlanta: Rodopi, 2001), pp. 103–108 (p. 104).

17 Andrew Salkey, 'Introduction', in *West Indian Stories*, ed. by Salkey, pp. 9–12 (p. 10).

18 The Beacon group is discussed in depth in Raymond Ramcharitar's essay in this volume.

19 James Ferguson, *Traveller's Literary Companion to the Caribbean* (Chicago: Passport Books, 1997), p. 150.

20 David Baronov and Kelvin A. Yelvington, 'Ethnicity, Race, Class and Nationality', in *Understanding the Contemporary Caribbean*, ed. by Richard S. Hillman & Thomas J. D'Agostino (Kingston: Ian Randle Publishers, 2003), pp. 209–38 (p. 232).

21 Eva L. Santos-Phillips, 'Abrogation and Appropriation in Rosario Ferré's *Amalia*', *Studies in Short Fiction*, 35:2 (Spring 1998),117–29 (p. 118).

22 Suzanne Bost, 'Transgressing Borders: Puerto Rican and Latina Mestizaje', *MELUS*, 25:2 (Summer 2000), 187–211 (p. 189).

23 Rosario Ferré, 'When Women Love Men', trans. by Cynthia Ventura, in *The Oxford Book of Caribbean Short Stories*, ed. by Brown and Wickham, pp. 257–69.

24 Elizabeth Black, *Pragmatic Stylistics* (Edinburgh: Edinburgh University Press, 2006), p. 68.

25 Augustus C. Puleo, 'The Intersection of Race, Sex, Gender and Class in a Short Story of Rosario Ferré', *Studies in Short Fiction*, 32:1 (Spring 1995), 227–34 (p. 230).

26 Shin Yamamoto, 'Swaying in Time and Space: The Chinese Diaspora in the Caribbean and Its Literary Perspectives', *Asian Ethnicity*, 9:3 (2008), 171–77 (p. 174).

27 Shalini Puri 'Race, Rape and Representation: Indo-Caribbean Women and Cultural Nationalism', *Cultural Critique*, 36 (1997), 119–63 (p. 120).

28 Willi Chen, 'Trotters', in *The Oxford Book of Caribbean Short Stories*, ed. by Brown and Wickham, pp. 288–91 (p. 288).

29 Vijay Mishra, *The Literature of the Indian Diaspora: Theorizing the Diasporic Imaginary* (London: Routledge, 2007), p. 91.

PART FIVE

GENERIC BOUNDARIES AND TRANSGRESSIONS

INTERTWININGS: THE 'AMAZING FECUNDITY' OF OLIVE SENIOR

SHIRLEY CHEW

> Gardening in the Tropics,
> you'll find things that don't
> belong together often intertwine
> all mixed up in this amazing fecundity.
> 'The Knot Garden'[1]

'Not belonging' and 'intertwining': these are some of the dominant notes sounded in Olive Senior's accounts of herself as 'racially and socially a child of mixed worlds'.[2] Born in 1941 to poor farmers in 'a small, very backward village' in the province of Trelawney in western Jamaica, Senior was, from the age of four, sent to stay for periods of time with her mother's well-to-do relatives on their big 'cattle and citrus' property in Westmoreland.[3] Economically the two worlds were at opposite ends of colonial society in Jamaica in the 1940s and 1950s. Culturally, too, they were very different. At the village, which was 'largely black and strongly African in character' (Rutherford, p. 12), Senior grew up with a robust folk and oral tradition and, her mother being a fervent Christian, with Bible stories, church hymns, '"hot" preaching, praying and testifying' (Rowell, p. 480). At the estate of her landed relatives with their gentrified and European values, she was introduced to 'broughtupcy',[4] that is, social manners and education, became an avid reader with a passion for 'words well crafted' (Rowell, p. 480), and studied to gain admittance to high school.

For the subjects and themes of her short stories, Senior has often relied upon her memories of those early years when she was shuttled between polarised worlds, at home in neither.

> [A]s a child I felt totally at the mercy of forces outside my control. I never felt secure, had no sense of belonging or any real identity with adults, including my own family. [...] People wanted me to conform to their notion of what the 'good child' was, and I don't think that is what I was at all. (Rutherford, p. 15)[5]

But, if the alienation of her protagonists is one of the preoccupations of Senior's work,[6] another is their struggle to find a space for themselves amid the different social and cultural contexts, and to know who they are and where they belong. Discoursing on our attempts to 'make sense of our lives', Frank Kermode comments: 'fictions are for finding things out', and 'it is ourselves we are encountering whenever we invent fictions'.[7] In Senior's attempts at 'sense-making', her recourse to the short story form has a double-edged significance: first, it situates her among women writers and postcolonial writers for whom – as 'a form of the margins, a form which is in some sense ex-centric, not part of official or "high" cultural hegemony' – it is a chief means of expression;[8] second, it roots her at the heart of an indigenous cultural tradition from which she speaks and writes as a Caribbean writer – '[W]e all come out of a society in which storytelling is very important [...] I know I grew up hearing stories and of course these are short stories' (Dubois and Devoize, p. 291).

To read Senior's short stories and poems is to come upon 'things [...] all mixed up' in unexpected and imaginative ways. It is to find the 'intertwinings' of the garden landscape reconceived and reworked in her writing as a vital, organising principle, one that, with its capacity for new, strange, and even disturbing unions and alliances, holds out certain correspondences with Édouard Glissant's 'rhizomatic thought'.[9] Glissant borrows the concept of the rhizome as developed by Gilles Deleuze and Felix Guattari – 'an enmeshed root system, a network spreading either in the ground or in the air, with no predatory rootstock taking over permanently' (Glissant, p. 11) – and sounds, in elaborate, subtle, and at times elusive fashion, its constituent ideas of 'errantry' and 'rootedness', and the dynamics which galvanise and sustain them.[10] The outcome is a poetics that situates 'Relation' centrally, enabling explorations where 'identity is no longer completely within the root' but 'extended through a relationship with the Other'; form is 'the thing relayed as well as the thing related'; and language is at its most inventive when, against 'the totalitarianism of any monolingual intent', it is spoken and written 'multilingually' (Glissant, p. 18, p. 11, p. 27, p. 19). It is in the light of these several inflections of 'Relation' in Glissant's disquisition, and the 'intertwinings' they resonate, that I read below Senior's short story 'Ballad',[11] and the sequence of poems, 'Gardening in the Tropics',[12] paying attention to their fecund engagements with identity, narrative form, and language.

★★★

> But big people have a habit of not telling children anything and if they su-suing together as soon as you get near they stop and change the subject or else they send you down to spring for water or to shop to get something they don't need and all of it is to get rid of you. But I learn from long time that what big people talking is sweeter than any other talking and though I never used to understand plenty of what they say I learn plenty so what I do now is I dont let them see me when they talking so they cant send me away and I hide under house and listen. And that is how I come to learn so much about Miss Rilla though nobody know I know. ('Ballad', p. 129)

In the above passage from the eighth and last section of 'Ballad', Leonora's complaint functions in several ways. It locates her in a community where everyday talk is the main source of news, information, entertainment, and wisdom. It makes clear her devotion to Miss Rilla, even though the latter is generally stigmatised, alive and after her death, as a licentious woman who had been nothing but trouble to her lovers, had lived shameless and unwed with Poppa D, and been punished for her bad ways with childlessness.[13] It reflects on Leonora's solitariness with much of her time spent eavesdropping 'under house' or 'bout the yard' ('Ballad', p. 114), or on the edge of groups of women washing by the river. Finally, it touches implicitly upon the kind of story Leonora has ended up telling, one that is marked both by her keenness to speak what she 'knows' at first-hand of Miss Rilla and by her perplexity over what she has 'come to learn' from listening to 'big people'.

Leonora remembers Miss Rilla for her kindness, laughter, and freedom of spirit – qualities which had made her different from the rest of the village of Springville and are the more important to Leonora because of her own sense of apartness. Her father's 'outside child',[14] she is raised by his wife, MeMa, to avoid the disgrace among her church sisters of having 'a Barstard round the place' ('Ballad', p. 102). Then there is Leonora's appearance – with her head 'so natty and red' ('Ballad', p. 111) and her darker 'coloration', she is cast as inferior to girls with 'good colour and straight hair' ('Ballad', p. 109). Having to put up with MeMa's heavy hand, harsh words, and intolerance of people and things beyond the confines of a narrow religion and hard existence, Leonora sees school as a means of escape. But colonial education is itself a closed system. That it, too, has no room for difference becomes clear when she is forbidden to write on Miss Rilla as 'The Most Unforgettable Character I Ever Meet' in her school composition.

One other character, likewise out-of-place and Leonora's friend, is Blue Boy. In contrast to Springville's macho males (Pa, for one, brawls, drinks, and terrifies even MeMa with his acts of violence), Blue Boy 'don't talk much' and spends his time playing 'music on one fife he did make himself and this music tall and pale and thin just like him' ('Ballad', p. 100). Not surprisingly, he is the butt of MeMa's torrents of contempt, delivered with unflagging pace, and a heady admixture of biblical phrases, familiar sayings, rhetorical questions, snappy abuse, and well-turned concatenations of blame.

> 'Look at that wutless good-fe-nutten a gwan there nuh. Whoever hear bout a big man a-play on a half-ass piece of bamboo all day long, tell me nuh? But what you expect no Laplands he come from? An' let me tell you that nutten good ever come out of that backward place and that is the Lord own truth. [...] He might be yu cousin out of wedlock that yu father brother Rennis did have on the side with that Coromantee woman and blood thicker than water but I still don't see why you have to mix yuself up with that trash because everybody trying hard to bring

yu up in a good Christian home with decent people children. Anyway bird of a feather flock together and everybody know your pedigree not so hot so if is that class of people yu want to mix up wid dog nyam yu supper.' ('Ballad', pp. 101–02)

Prevented from writing on Miss Rilla at school, Leonora thinks of composing a ballad for her, 'like they do for famous people in the old days' ('Ballad', p. 100). She is acquainted with some of the features of the genre. The traditional ballad is associated with love, death, and heroic deeds, with romance and tragedy. An oral form consisting almost always of two- or four-line stanzas that are interspersed in some cases with a refrain, it is meant to be sung with the verses and refrain alternating between leader and chorus.[15] Finally there is the ballad's distinctive manner of telling its story which is to 'deal with one situation and deal with it dramatically', allowing the action and emotional burden to reveal themselves in event and dialogue without intrusion from the storyteller (Hodgart, *The Ballads*, pp. 10–11). With Blue Boy disappearing from the village after Miss Rilla's death, 'and nobody make music round here since that Blue Boy gone away' ('Ballad', p. 100), producing a ballad to be sung has to be out of the question. Leonora settles instead for a 'ballad story' ('Ballad', p. 109) and, in the style of the oral performers she has come across, she will speak directly to her listeners[16] and improvise as needed:

> I will *just tell you* the story of Miss Rilla and Poppa D, Blue Boy and me *though is really about* Miss Rilla. And when we come to the sad part we can have *something like* a chorus because they have that in all the ballad song they sing but *I dont think bout the chorus yet*. ('Ballad', p. 100, my emphases)

Given her hesitancies, Leonora soon discovers that taking control of her story is less easy than anticipated. In the first place, it has a tendency to ramify, in contrast to the strict lines of the traditional ballad. For, although the story is 'really about Miss Rilla', it is also, as it turns out, about the identity of the storyteller herself; and for Leonora to celebrate her friend, Miss Rilla's difference has to be recalled by comparing her with some of the village's representative figures, such as MeMa, Teacher, and Teacher's wife. Furthermore, with her original cast expanding in unforeseen ways, Leonora's storytelling is constantly broken into by the voices of other tale-bearers, all insisting on having their say. From Big Mout Doris' report of the fateful trip to Kingston market, Leonora learns of the circumstances of Miss Rilla's death; from her father, she picks up the dark history of the fight between Miss Rilla's lovers, Jiveman and Bigger; and from Miss Rilla herself, she hears of Poppa D's loyalty, of how he had stood by her amid widespread condemnation of the 'scarlet woman' ('Ballad', p. 118).

With so much information, all pointing to the contradictions in a woman who had once seemed 'free and easy and happy' ('Ballad', p. 126),

'I know' in Leonora's experience becomes coupled with 'I confuse'. To compound her dilemma, there are her own suspicions regarding her two friends who, shortly before Miss Rilla's death, had seemed to enjoy an intimacy from which she was excluded – 'I wonder if Miss Rilla and Blue Boy deceive me and in there doing it' ('Ballad', p. 127). If Leonora's suspicions are correct, are the villagers justified in branding Miss Rilla as wickedly promiscuous? Should Miss Rilla be held responsible for the sad fates of Jiveman and Bigger? Yet was she not also the woman who, having found love, chose to live faithfully with Poppa D? Was her teasing behaviour in the presence of Blue Boy innocent displays of playfulness or seductive ploys? How dangerous is the sexuality that is so attractively accented in, say, the big gold earring she wears and her infectious laughter?

Telling her 'ballad story' stirs up many of Leonora's doubts relating to Miss Rilla. It also raises questions about Leonora herself. And, since a key aspect of Olive Senior's narrative strategy is 'to leave a lot of my work open-ended' (Rowell, p. 483), it is up to the reader to find the answers, having once entered the world of the story/work. Should Leonora take the part of the villagers and see in Miss Rilla's friendship with Blue Boy a sign of her untrustworthiness? Can she be said to be jealous of that friendship in view of her own awakening sexuality? Clinging to her sense of loss, to what extent is she shying away from the prospect of growing up and the problems awaiting her? Should she ignore gossip and remember instead the care and affection Miss Rilla showed her, and be guided by her courage and freedom of spirit?

From the start, Leonora has felt that 'This whole thing too deep and wide for a little thing like a Ballad' ('Ballad', p. 100). Indeed, a key concern in Senior's fiction with its self-consciously ironical title is the dismantling of the form of the English ballad and its reinvention as a Caribbean 'ballad story'. As elaborated above, this is enacted in the several ways in which 'Ballad' intertwines Leonora's story and the stories of the village personalities, the oral narrative and the written, a tale told 'in the moment of performance'[17] and the writer's craft realised on the page (Rowell, p. 483). That broader reworking of genre aside, I go on to address below Senior's handling of a formal property which distinguishes the traditional ballad, and which is the music that accompanies its verses and refrain or 'chorus' as Leonora terms it.

Even with no one to provide the music, Leonora's chorus communicates an artful and characteristic plangency. 'O Lord. No more laughing. No more big gold earring. No more Miss Rilla gizada to cool down me temper when MeMa beat me. All the sweetness done' ('Ballad', p. 104). In all, there are five variations of the lament – 'no more' – each appearing at the close of the first five sections of the story. The question then arises as to why, as a formal device, the chorus is missing from the last three sections.

Is one to assume that, with Leonora's attention directed towards Miss Rilla's interest in Blue Boy, mourning for her friend in these final sections is displaced by feelings of mistrust? Or that, despite being pulled one way and then another in her confusion, Leonora's re-emerging faith in Miss Rilla – 'I believe it is better to be someone that can laugh and make other people laugh and be happy too' ('Ballad', p. 134) – has rendered the sad cadences of the chorus no longer appropriate? There is finally the matter of form, and I would suggest that, in the course of reinventing the traditional ballad, the music of Leonora's 'ballad story', rather than being limited to the chorus, has passed into the diverse creole speaking voices of her characters, and hence the sounds, movements, and textures of Senior's prose. The insistent rhythms and dissonances of MeMa's tirade have been noted above and have a musicality all their own. On a different register, there is Miss Rilla's account of the day love found her:

> 'Leonora,' she tell me, 'The Lord did cast me down bad bad. O God is when yu in trouble that you really know who your friend is. [...] And the only friend I have in the world at the time was Poppa D. ... And is so love bloom for me Leonora, love bloom on my doorstep just like so. Poppa D ugly like sin eh? – but he have a heart of gold and he so brave. He brave just like Daniel in the lion den for he never care at all how them ignorant people badmouthing him. No sah. Poppa D would use them up like blotting paper if they bother him. He don't fraid of no man. So chile is fifteen year now I living with Poppa D and that man never lift a hand or give me a harsh word. A tell you Child, that day Poppa D came to me in my sorrow I feel just like love light up the whole world.' ('Ballad', p. 125)

The genuineness of Miss Rilla's utterance is unmistakable, conveyed as it is in the repeated words ('love', 'brave'), the quietly affirmative phrases ('and is so', 'just like so', 'just like love light up the whole world'), and, oddly yet persuasively, in the mismatches of imagery (low and elevated, romantic and prosaic, biblical and secular, the full notes of a woman's happiness and the grim realities of a male-dominant society).

Finally, there is Leonora's version of the fight between Jiveman and Bigger:

> Well, nobody who was there that day can give a full account of what happen next for all they see is Bigger come up fast with a machete flashing in his hand, flashing and flashing at Jiveman. The women start scream and the men they try to get at Bigger but is like the boy gone mad for he slashing away at Jiveman even after he drop to the ground and the blood just flowing away from him into the sunhot. O God. Never before such a thing happen in this district. ('Ballad', p. 133)

In the retelling, the excitement and shock of the incident come alive with the verbal echoes ('flashing', 'slashing', 'flowing'), the rhythmic patterns of the prose ('Bigger come up fast', 'the boy gone mad', Jiveman 'drop to the

ground', 'the blood just flowing away'), and the dual and opposite movements of the action (the rushing up to attack, the drifting away in death),
the whole account ending in the creole usage, 'the sunhot', an image that,
rooted in the everyday, yet lends, paradoxically, strangeness and beauty to
a scene of violence.

In 'Ballad', a borrowed form is remade in narrating the experiences of a
young girl growing up within the confines of her community. A short
story, it reconfigures many of the features of the poetic genre; an oral tale
it is also a written text; a young girl's tribute to her friend, it is besides a
social critique of life in mid-twentieth-century rural Jamaica. As well as
collections of short stories, Olive Senior has published several books of
poems. While she is inclined to be wary when questioned about the
different creative impulses that might be supposed to lie behind her poetry
and fiction, she evidently sees the border between the two genres as a
relaxed one:

> I am in both forms telling stories, exploring consciousness. I can't always
> decide on what form what I want to say will take. I have started out to
> write stories that have ended up as poems and had ideas for poems that
> have ended up as stories. If there is a difference it is that in my poems I
> am more explicitly political than in my stories. (Rowell, p. 482)

Taking a cue from Senior's comments, I discuss below 'Gardening in the
Tropics', a sequence, and its 'explicitly political' engagement with pastoral.

A 'voracious reader' (McClean and Bishop, p. 12), a writer who,
growing up in a colonial society, was exposed to the whole canon of English
literature (Dubois and Devoize, p. 292), Senior is naturally familiar with
different forms of pastoral (poems, romances, drama), its characteristic
features (the idyllic landscape whether rustic spaces or seclusive garden,
the simple and innocent life, the natural scene as setting for song, the
shepherd as singer/poet), and the variety of ways in which historically the
genre has been rewritten (examples are Sidney's *Arcadia*, Shakespeare's *As
You Like It*, Milton's 'Lycidas'). Earlier, I quoted in part from Frank
Kermode on 'fictions' and 'sense-making'. Transcribed in full, the statement reads as follows: 'Fictions are for finding things out and they change
as the needs of sense-making change' (Kermode, p. 39). With these words
in mind, the questions addressed in speaking to 'Gardening in the Tropics'
are: What must be the implications for 'sense-making' when pastoral is
carried across to the Caribbean? How are its conventions, motifs, and
forms of expression remade and transformed under the pressures of 'sense-
making' in the work of a Caribbean writer such as Olive Senior? What
significant part do the formal properties of the sequence play in Senior's
revisioning of pastoral?

Gardening in the Tropics,
You'll find things that don't

belong together often intertwine
all mixed up in this amazing fecundity.
                    'The Knot Garden' ('Gardening', pp. 86–87)

In place of the landscapes of traditional pastoral, the tropical garden as topos and its 'amazing fecundity' of growth evoke feelings of wonder and not a little fear.[18] This is due to the negative senses of 'to amaze' ('to fill with consternation, terrify, alarm'), and 'amazing' ('stupefying, terrifying, dreadful') which, although obsolete after the eighteenth century according to the *OED*, can be felt to hover still over the words. Senior's apprehension of nature's inbuilt energies and resourcefulness is evident in the sequence; so, too, is her acute historical consciousness. To garden in the tropics, in her native Caribbean, is to do so in the haunting knowledge of 'slave gardens' and their place in the plantation system. Jill Casid calls attention to their dominant aspects in her critical study.[19] Found on poor and difficult terrain, 'slave gardens' consisted of individual plots and common provision grounds known as 'polincks' where the slaves were expected to grow crops to feed themselves. While colonial records exist of 'slave ingenuity and labor', and of stubborn ground yielding a variety of produce to the extent in some instances of dominating the local markets in eighteenth-century Jamaica (Casid, p. 199), the bitter realities are rooted in the very name itself. Tellingly ambivalent, 'slave gardens' calls up a space that is at once alien and domesticated, part of the 'order' of colonial rule and plantation system yet potential ground for revolt and marronage, tied to European technologies of production and also steeped in indigenous practices and skills transported from Africa and/or gleaned locally from the native peoples (Casid, pp. 197–98). A dominant strand of interest in Casid's work deals with the narrative strategies by means of which 'slave gardens' were written into colonial texts of the eighteenth century. One of her examples is an engraving of Agostino Brunias' *A Negro Festival Drawn from Nature in the Island of St Vincent* (1794) which was reproduced in Bryan Edwards' *The History, Civil and Commercial, of the British Colonies in the West Indies* (1807).[20] Adapting pastoral conventions, and so belying the 'drawn from nature' in its title, the visual text produces a mimic version of Arcadia with its images of fruit in abundance and well-attired slaves happily dancing, music making, and feasting – in brief, a representation of 'slavery as a system of joy and plenty' and, implicitly, 'slave labor as the natural order' (Casid, p. 201).

Not surprisingly, there are no indications of pastoral innocence, leisure, and harmony in the garden landscape of Senior's 'Gardening in the Tropics'. There is, however, the unavoidable presence of death.[21]

Gardening in the Tropics, you never know
what you'll turn up. Quite often, bones.
                    'Brief Lives' ('Gardening', p. 83)

And, as the colloquial yet exact phrase 'turn up' in the opening lines of the sequence makes clear, in contrast to the commemorations of exceptional loss in works such as 'Lycidas' and 'The Ruined Cottage', death within the projected Caribbean world of the poem is liable to be too commonplace an occurrence to be deemed significant. In his critical investigation of the many attempts at reinventing the literary pastoral, and the continuity and diversification of the genre, Paul Alpers notes:

> representations of nature or of landscape are not all of a piece; they answer to and express various human needs and concerns; *pastoral* landscapes are those of which the human centers are herdsmen or their equivalents.[22]

In Senior's sequence, the topos of the garden, which intermixes luxuriant growth and bare bones, figures forth the Caribbean region's violent history as well as its natural vitality. Contracting within its small compass temporal and spatial extensiveness, the formal device of 'garden' also enables the 'coming together' (Alpers, p. 81)[23] of a range of pastoral speakers. 'I like to write in the first person,' Senior informs her interviewers. 'I like to inhabit somebody else's body and tell the story through that person' (Dubois and Devoize, p. 294). In 'Gardening in the Tropics', she is gardener/ poet and diverse other personae besides – raconteur, historian, entrepreneur, gossip, wise woman. That Senior is highly skilful in her impersonations[24] is evident in the ways the narrating voices with their play of tonalities perform the many roles, addressing the listener/reader on a range of subjects – slavery, legendary women, higglers and drug barons, colour prejudice, corrupt politicians, deforestation, mixed and single-crop farming.

Unlike the herdsmen of Virgil's *Eclogues* or the shepherds in Spenser's *Shepherds Calendar*, Senior's pastoral speakers do not make up a homogenous social group. What they do have in common is little or no power. In the 'fictions' they speak, two aspirations are sounded repeatedly: first, the right to a small portion of the earth as one's own; and second, the opportunity to fulfil one's obligation to respect external nature, and make the earth 'a fit habitation for human beings' (Alpers, p. 267). Both aspirations are liable to prove elusive, as the maroon in 'Gardening on the Run' discovered.

> Gardening in the Tropics for us
> meant a plot hatched quickly,
> hidden deep in forest or jungle,
> run to ground behind palisade or
> *palenque*, found in cockpit, in
> *quilombe* or *cumbe*.
>
> 'Gardening on the Run' ('Gardening', p. 105)

Hunted, tortured, and killed when he had wanted 'nothing more than to be/ left alone, to live in peace,/ to garden' ('Gardening', p. 108), the maroon speaks here for himself and for a people – the slave whose exploits will

'forever' be 'interleaved with the stories' of his enemy's soldiers ('Gardening', p. 107), the Other who will always be, for the white man, 'out there
as your own unguarded/self, running free' ('Gardening', p. 108), a presence ineradicable in the Caribbean landscape.

While 'plot' in the passage quoted above may suggest that gardening and
insurgency are not necessarily distinct in the life of the maroon, the
preoccupation of the Amerindian gardener/farmer is with his native ground
and the activities, practical as well as cultural, which connect him to his
world.

> We cleared just enough for our huts
> and our pathways, opened a pinpoint in the canopy
> to let the sun through. We made the tiniest scratch
> on Mother Earth (begging her pardon). When we moved
> on, the jungle easily closed over that scar again.
> We never took more than we needed. Always gave back
> (to Earth) our thanks and our praises ...
> 'Seeing the Light' ('Gardening', pp. 93–94)

To attempt to retrace the path leading back, however, is to come up against
a terrible impasse – the severance of the native peoples from land, community, history. 'Only our bones', it is said, 'will remain as testament' to the
crimes committed in the name of '*Conquista*? *Evangelismo*? *Civilizacion?*'
('Gardening', p. 93). And yet, was an alternative to the destruction and
death altogether impossible?

> There was enough
> in the jungle to provide gardens for everyone.
> All over these green and tropical lands there
> could have been pinpricks of light filtering
> through the leaves to mirror the stars of Heaven,
> invert the Pleiades.
> 'Seeing the Light' ('Gardening', pp. 93–94)

The poem's movement, however, is against that dream of wholeness, and
unfolds steadily from present tense report in the first verse paragraph
('Gardening in the Tropics nowadays means [...] they've brought in
machines') to recollection in the next ('Before you came ...') to an elegiac
contemplation of the future in the closing lines ('Maybe many more trees
must die [...] many leaves/ must fall to cover up our dying').

Diaries, letters, court records and law books – all part of a colonial
archive – are mentioned in 'Gardening on the Run'; 'leaves' – of books, it
is suggested, as well as trees – conceal the widespread decimation of the
Arawaks, Caribs and Tainos in 'Seeing the Light'. How then does one
retell/rewrite the past given the accretions of representation over time? The
noisily defensive storyteller of 'Amazon Women' is aware that she is
exploiting the exotic and sensational elements in the accounts of Toeyza of
Guiana which have appeared since 'the missionary Brett and Sir Walter

Raleigh wrote' of the warrior woman ('Gardening', p. 95). Would she tell her stories differently if her subject were the noble women of history?

> like Nanny the Maroon queen mother
> or the fair Anacaona, Taino
> chieftainess who was brutally
> slain by the colonists, or of
> the Carib women whom the said Colón
> relied on for navigation
> throught the islands.
>
> 'Amazon Women' ('Gardening', p. 97)

Very likely not. A professional storyteller, she is of the opinion 'there's no gain in telling stories/about ordinary men and women' ('Gardening', p. 97). Yet even she is compelled momentarily by the realities of existence to bring her narrative to its close with a powerful image of unexceptional women, transformed and made extraordinary by hard labour and sheer determination to survive.

> gardening
> in the Tropics, every time you lift
> your eyes from the ground
> you see sights that strain your
> credulity – like those strong
> Amazon women striding daily across
> our lands carrying bundles of wood
> on their heads and babies strapped
> to their breasts and calabashes of
> water in both hands.
>
> 'Amazon Women' ('Gardening', p. 97)

The gardener/storyteller is removed from the lives of the women she sees passing by. It is her eyes that are lifted, and her credulity that is strained. In the women's case, it is the material burdens – the 'bundles', 'babies', 'calabashes', made emphatic by the half rhymes and alliterations – which necessitate the feats of lifting, carrying, and straining. These burdens, 'strapped' and commonplace, cannot lend themselves to sensationalising nor exoticising. What they can do is to revise the notion of 'Amazon women' to include 'ordinary' women of flesh and blood as well as the personages of legend and history. One of these women speaks for herself in 'Tropic Love' which, rewriting Marlowe's pastoral song 'Come live with me and be my love', makes plain it is not the imagined pleasures ('sweet words') she needs but a sharing of the 'heavy responsibilities' that come with 'love'. They, in her view, constitute the subject for poetry.

> Love me and my family or leave me
> to sit by the roadside to sell,
> by the riverside taking in washing,
> by milady's fire cooking for my living.
> I am a woman with heavy responsibilities.

With my lot I'm prepared to be contented.
With your sweet words, Lover, tempt me
not, if you've come empty-handed.
                    'Tropic Love' ('Gardening', p. 98)

Historically literary pastoral, as noted above, has undergone diverse
changes while maintaining continuity with many features of the form
(Alpers, p. 25). One of these changes relates to pastoral's capacity to
represent contemporary realities 'without losing its character as pastoral'.
In approaching this issue, Alpers points out, with reference to Virgil's
Eclogue 1, that 'the poem *limits* its representation of social forces [...] to what
can be accommodated to pastoral utterance'. In addition, the pastoral
character of Virgil's speakers – Tityrus and Meliboeus – is 'particularly
apparent in their consciousness of *boundaries*'. In Tityrus' case, for example,
his awareness of Rome 'revolves around its difference and *distance* from the
world he knows' (Alpers, p. 163, my emphases).[25] In contrast, crucial to
Senior's 'Gardening in the Tropics', as demonstrated above, is the constant
subjection of pastoral to the scrutiny of history, and of the realities of
existence in the Caribbean region. Her remaking of the genre, therefore,
takes radical forms – the idea of the garden as idyllic landscape is over-
turned, the homogeneity of pastoral characters is dispersed, and the
subject-matter of song is expanded to comprehend the crimes of empire
and contemporary issues such as land utilisation – even while pastoralism
continues to be exemplified in her engagement with the stories of ordinary
men and women, the delineation of work, the articulation of loss and
suffering, and the evocation however tentative of a sense of community.

Senior's creativity lies in particular in her handling of the formal properties of the sequence. Consisting of twelve discrete items (as in a book of
eclogues), 'Gardening in the Tropics' is held together as one entity by means
of an accentual verse pattern of either four or three stresses, language that
moves with ease and agility across several different registers, and a structure
of images and symbols continually reworked as same and different –
'garden' and 'bones' among them. Each of the items is a story and each is a
complete poem in itself. Each is part of the pastoral landscape of the garden
and each is made distinct as a space to include kitchen garden, banana
plantation, a cleared patch of ground in the jungle, the *palenque, quilombo*, and
cumbe that the enslaved carved out for themselves. Each represents a
moment of narrative and each is a segment of an extensive history.

Within the discontinuous structure of 'Gardening in the Tropics', in
other words, boundaries are transgressed and this is nowhere more evident
than in Senior's treatment of time. With a temporal span stretching back to
Conquest (Nicholás de Ovando's arrival in 1502 in Hispaniola is noted)
and forward to post-independence (presidential jets are said to fly off to
IMF meetings), Senior's sequence 'operates by juxtaposition without the

inhibition of surface continuity'.[26] The result is that, told as independent items, disparate moments and events in the passage of Caribbean history are also synchronically linked. Coexisting and viewed on the same plane, the stories/poems – relating the plight of Amerindians whose world was lost to them or the victims of land forcibly cleared to make room for 'tourists, investors and/extractors' ('Gardening', p. 101); slaves murdered or the 'disappeared ones' of recent times ('Gardening', p. 83); the banana grower with lungs corroded by pesticides which had to be used under government order or the old woman coerced by property developers to vacate her basement home or the young man who lost his way and was killed in 'rival political territory' ('Gardening', p. 83) – unsettle the listener/reader with the question as to what has changed, if anything, across the centuries.

★★★

I began this essay by drawing attention to the feelings of alienation Olive Senior experienced as a young person and which she has referred to in interviews. Senior left high school at the age of nineteen, and her subsequent career and experiences were to contribute actively to her confidence in herself. She joined the *Jamaica Gleaner* in Kingston, and later won a scholarship to study journalism at Carleton University, Ottawa, graduating in 1967. The 1960s were an exciting and significant time to begin adult life in Jamaica, as Senior recalled.[27]

> You know, independence was really a wonderful time because we were engaged in a dialogue then, the whole *society*. People were talking about things we'd never talked about before [...] For a while we were really trying to come to grips with who we were, with questions of identity. (McLean and Bishop, p. 9)

A good deal of that newfound energy, intellectual and social, was to be converted into publications on Jamaican politics and culture, such as *The Message Is Change: A Perspective on the 1972 General Elections* (1972), *A-Z of Jamaican Heritage* (1984), and *Working Miracles: Women's Life in the English-Speaking Caribbean* (1991). It was while studying in Canada that Senior began to write short stories and poetry. Some of the fiction later appeared in her first book of stories, *Summer Lightning* (1986), which won the Commonwealth Writers' Prize for 1987, while some of the poetry was included in *Talking of Trees* (1986). Together with the non-fiction work, the imaginative attempts at recounting her early life, and at relating to the different cultures she inhabited and the people she came across – the intertwinings that are all part of the process of creolisation – have resulted in a firm sense of knowing where she belongs and her identity: 'I represent many different races [as a Jamaican] and I'm not rejecting any of them to please anybody. I'm just who I am.'[28]

NOTES

1 Olive Senior, *Gardening in the Tropics* (Newcastle upon Tyne: Bloodaxe Books, 1995), p. 86.
2 Charles H. Rowell, 'An Interview with Olive Senior', *Callaloo*, 36 (Summer, 1988), 480–90 (p. 481).
3 Anna Rutherford, 'Olive Senior: Interview', *Kunapipi*, 8:2 (1986), 11–20 (p.11).
4 Senior's parents very likely looked to the adoptive family to give their daughter the opportunities which would lead to social advancement. See 'broughtupcy' and 'child-shifting' in Olive Senior, *Working Miracles: Women's Lives in the English-Speaking Caribbean* (Cave Hill, Barbados/London: University of the West Indies/James Currey, 1991).
5 See also Rowell, p. 482; Dolace McLean and Jacqueline Bishop, 'On Hearts Revealed: An Interview with Olive Senior', *Calabash: A Journal of Caribbean Arts and Letters*, 2:2 (Summer/Fall 2003), 3–13 (p. 5–6); Dominique Dubois and Jeanne Devoize, 'Olive Senior – b. 1941', *Journal of the Short Story in English*, 41 (Autumn 2003), 287–98 (p. 295). [Editor's note: 'first published in *JSSE*, 26 (1996)'.] <http://jsse.revues.org/index337.html> [accessed 25 October 2009].
6 Examples are 'Bright Thursdays', in *Summer Lightning and Other Stories* (Harlow: Longman, 1992 [1986]), and 'The Two Grandmothers', in *Arrival of the Snake-Woman and Other Stories* (Harlow: Longman, 1989).
7 Frank Kermode, *The Sense of an Ending: Studies in the Theory of Fiction* (Oxford: Oxford University Press, 1981 [1966]), pp. 39, 2.
8 Clare Hanson, 'Introduction', in *Re-reading the Short Story*, ed. by Clare Hanson (Basingstoke: Macmillan, 1989), pp. 1–9 (p. 2).
9 Édouard Glissant, *Poetics of Relation*, trans. by Betsy Wing (Ann Arbor: University of Michigan Press, 1997), p. 11.
10 See statements such as 'the notion of the rhizome maintains [...] the idea of rootedness but challenges that of a totalitarian root', and '[w]hereas exile may erode one's sense of identity, the thought of errantry – the thought of that which relates – usually reinforces this sense of identity' (Glissant, p. 11, p. 20).
11 Olive Senior, *Summer Lightning and Other Stories*, pp. 100–34. All subsequent page references, entered under 'Ballad', are to the 1992 edition and included in the text of the essay.
12 Olive Senior, *Gardening in the Tropics*, pp. 83–112. All subsequent page references, entered under 'Gardening', are to the 1995 edition and included in the text of the essay.
13 For the view that 'the real vocation' for Caribbean women is motherhood, and that 'the greatest social condemnation' a Caribbean woman can receive is that of being a 'mule' or childless woman, see Olive Senior, *Working Miracles*, pp. 66–76.
14 An 'outside child' is one 'born outside [the man's] stable residential union'. See Senior, *Working Miracles*, pp. 20–24.
15 M.J.C. Hodgart, *The Ballads* (London: Hutchinson University Library, 1964 [1950]), pp. 80–84.
16 Senior has remarked that 'The need always to imagine a listener is basic to the origins of the short story.' Here the bond between audience and storyteller having been initiated, the oral narrative can begin. See Olive Senior, 'Lessons from the Fruit Stand: Or, Writing for the Listener', *Journal of Modern Literature*, XX:1 (Summer 1996), 39–44 (p. 40).
17 See Hyacinth M. Simpson, '"Voicing the Text": The Making of an Oral Poetics in Olive Senior's Short Fiction', *Callaloo*, 27:3 (Summer 2004), 829–33 (p. 831).

18 Compare Marvell's use of the word in 'The Garden' (1681): 'How vainly men themselves amaze/to win the palm, the oak, or bays'.

19 Jill H. Casid, *Sowing Empire: Landscape and Colonization* (Minneapolis/London: University of Minnesota Press, 2005).

20 Brunias' painting for a plantation owner, Sir William Young, as engraved for Bryan Edwards' *The History, Civil and Commercial, of the British Colonies in the West Indies* (London, 1807), vol 2, 185, is reproduced in Casid, *Sowing Empire: Landscape and Colonization*, p. 200.

21 The Latin tag, 'Et in Arcadia ego' ('Even in Arcadia I exist'), calls to mind the shadow of death amid the idle lives and pleasures of the shepherds and shepherdesses in Arcadia. It is the title of two pastoral paintings by Nicolas Poussin. See also the pastoral laments in Virgil's *Eclogue* 5 and Milton's 'Lycidas'.

22 Paul Alpers, *What is Pastoral?* (Chicago & London: University of Chicago Press, 1996), p. 28. Alpers refers to pastoral settings as different as those represented in Theocritus' first idyll and Marvell's 'The Garden'; the respective concerns of the shepherds/poets in Virgil's *Eclogue* 1 and 'Lycidas'; pastoral speakers as various as Colin Clout in Spenser's *Shepherds Calendar*, the rogue Autolycus in *The Winter's Tale*, and the Pedlar in Wordsworth's 'The Ruined Cottage'.

23 Referring to the root meaning of 'convention', that is, to come together (from Latin *convenire*), Alpers elaborates on the 'coming together' of songs and colloquies in pastoral, of literary herdsmen who need to sing for others and hear others sing, of the pastoral poet and the work of his predecessors.

24 See, for example, my discussion of 'Ballad' above.

25 For a similar view of *Eclogue* 1, see R.O.A.M. Lyne, 'Introduction', in *Virgil, The Eclogues. The Georgics*, trans. by C. Day Lewis (Oxford: Oxford University Press (World's Classics), 1983), pp. xiii–xxxii (p. xix): 'Virgil wants to probe the moral and political issues of his day, but declines to tie his poetry to such a tedious and perhaps imprudent thing as a poetical history or allegory'. Instead he chooses to write '*ambiguously*' and the poem oscillates between 'an allegory of contemporary events' and 'an entertaining fiction based on (Theocritean) slave shepherds'.

26 I borrow the phrase from M.L. Rosenthal and Sally M. Gall, *The Modern Poetic Sequence: The Genius of Modern Poetry* (Oxford: Oxford University Press, 1983), p. 14.

27 Jamaica became independent in August 1962. The Federation of the West Indies had collapsed in May that year.

28 Laura Tanna, 'One_on_One with Olive Senior (Pt III)', *Jamaica Gleaner*, 31 October 2004, n.p. <http://www.jamaica-gleaner.com/gleaner/20041017/arts/arts3.html> [accessed 25 October 2009].

'A KIND OF CHAIN': REWORKING THE SHORT STORY SEQUENCE IN V.S. NAIPAUL'S *A WAY IN THE WORLD*

LUCY EVANS

In his essays, V.S. Naipaul has stressed the need for writers and critics to recognise the cultural specificity of form. Writing in 1998, he describes the novel as an 'extraordinary tool' with which European writers in the nineteenth century were able to give 'industrialising or modern society a very clear idea of itself'.[1] He considers, however, that the novel form may not be so useful a mode of expression for contemporary Caribbean writers. In an interview, he discusses the problems of adopting a form inappropriate to the subject matter: 'What happens when you pour your content into [a] borrowed form you ever so slightly distort the material. Different cultures have different ways of feeling, seeing, different visions'.[2] Naipaul's observations on *A Way in the World* (1994) suggest that in structuring the text as a sequence of linked episodes, he hoped to avoid such distortions:

> This book is a way of dealing with all the various strands of the Caribbean or New World background, the place, and all the different stages of learning about it, as well. [...] My story does have connections; they are associations. They are inseparable from the background.[3]

Subtitled 'A Sequence' in the Minerva edition, *A Way in the World* consists of nine separate narratives. Shifting between Trinidad and Venezuela, England, and Africa, these narratives are geographically wide-ranging. They also extend through time from the experiences of a seventeenth-century English explorer to the struggles of a post-independence African Trinidadian political leader. Furthermore, as an eclectic assortment of short fiction, autobiographical fragments, literary criticism, travel writing, and dramatised historical reconstruction, these narratives move between diverse generic frameworks. In temporal, spatial and formal terms, then, Naipaul's text locates itself in movement. Despite this, his comment on the text firmly situates it within a 'Caribbean or New World background'. The 'associations' connecting the narratives across space, time and style are emphatically *not* translatable to any other social or cultural context; they are 'inseparable from the background'.

Critics have regarded *A Way in the World* and Naipaul's earlier sequence, *The Enigma of Arrival* (1987), as marking a shift in the style and tone of his writing. Salman Rushdie explains how in *The Enigma of Arrival*, characters' lives are 'observed from a distance', the main events of their lives 'taking place off-stage'. He goes on to suggest that '[a]s a result of this emptying, the writer becomes the subject; the story-teller becomes the tale'.[4] In Rushdie's view, then, Naipaul's intensified focus on his own life and work involves an 'emptying' of his resources as a writer; the self-conscious elements of his more recent work are achieved at the cost of character and plot. Naipaul's subject matter in *The Enigma of Arrival* may be 'illness' and 'exhaustion' (Rushdie, p. 149), but I would argue that to align this with the idea of an exhausted and defunct literary practice is to ignore the formally energetic aspects of Naipaul's sequences of the late 1980s and early 90s. *A Way in the World* does begin and end with death; the 'Prelude' features Parry's Funeral Parlour, and the concluding episode deals with the brutal murder of a Trinidadian politician in Africa. Nevertheless, in its revised approach to the concept of a Caribbean community and its reinvention of the sequence as a literary form, this text is equally concerned with renewal.

While Edward Said finds 'an increasingly bitter and obsessive strain in Naipaul's writing since the early 1970s',[5] my reading of *A Way in the World* identifies a movement on Naipaul's part away from bitterness and towards compassion. It is true that within certain episodes of *A Way in the World* the 'story-teller becomes the tale'. However, by combining autobiography with fiction, travel writing and historical study, Naipaul presents himself in relation to others. The construction of his writing self therefore becomes enmeshed with the writing of community. By foregrounding the movement of his various semi-autobiographical narrators, intersecting with the journeys of fictional and historical figures, Naipaul positions himself within a Caribbean community of global scope.

Focusing on the second, fourth, sixth and seventh episodes of *A Way in the World*, this essay considers how the figure of the chain provides a way of reading both the structural dynamics of this sequence of interlinked narratives and Naipaul's intertextual references to his earlier work. I offer a reading of *A Way in the World* in relation to Naipaul's travel narrative, *The Middle Passage* (1962), and his historical study, *The Loss of El Dorado* (1969), situating his multigeneric sequence within a longer chain of texts which extends through his oeuvre. I argue that *A Way in the World* breaks the chain of external constructions of the region set in motion by nineteenth-century travel writers, and suggest further that in returning critically to his earlier ways of seeing, Naipaul breaks the chain of continuity within his own body of work. I conclude by positioning *A Way in the World* alongside Naipaul's much earlier story sequence, *Miguel Street* (1959), in order to clarify the ways in which both the form of the sequence, and the idea of community, are renegotiated in his later text.

Wilson Harris evokes the image of a chain in his attempt to explain the 'native and phenomenal environment of the West Indies', claiming that 'the longest chain of sovereign territories one sees is ultimately no stronger than its weakest and most obscure connecting link'. For Harris, the idea of a chain's 'connecting links' offers a way of visualising the creative possibilities latent within a physical, social and cultural environment made up of 'broken parts'.[6] In Naipaul's writing, the recurring motif of the chain operates more ambiguously. In the second episode of *A Way in the World*, 'History: A Smell of Fish Glue', Naipaul's semi-autobiographical narrator describes how five Amerindian chiefs tortured by conquering Spaniards were 'held together on one chain'.[7] This image illustrates the dual action of a chain which simultaneously connects and confines. In *A Way in the World*, the image of the chain is figured both positively and negatively, inviting us to consider both its associative and its constrictive power.

According to Paula Burnett, 'the figure of the chain is used repeatedly' by Naipaul as a means of 'posit[ing] a continuity from pre-Columbian Trinidad to slavery and modernity'.[8] However, the trajectory identified by Burnett is not the only line of continuity traced by Naipaul in *A Way in the World*. The idea of a chain is first introduced in 'History', when the narrator returns to Trinidad aged twenty-four with a heightened awareness of the violence and power struggles underlying the Port of Spain streets he used to find so 'calm and quiet':

> I saw that there was an immense chain of events. You could start with the sacrament of the square and work back: to the black madmen on the benches, the Indian destitutes, the plantations, the wilderness, the aboriginal settlements, the discovery. And you could move forward from that exaltation and mood of rejection to the nihilism of the moment. (p. 40)

The 'chain of events' described here links a sequence of occurrences in a chronological order. Yet the narrator's repeated use of the conditional – 'you could' – indicates the provisional nature of these connections. Moreover, this historical 'chain of events' is overlaid in 'Passenger: A Figure from the Thirties' with a succession of travel writers whose work forms 'the great chain of changing outside vision' (p. 102) of Trinidad. This second chain erases much of the first chain's sociocultural content, blocking out the unsightly details of 'black madmen' and 'Indian destitutes', and offering instead a series of 'discoveries'. In these two moments, and in their juxtaposition, Naipaul makes it clear that any continuity derived from the chain image is only one of many possible configurations.

In 'Passenger', the narrator charts a course through the 'great chain of changing outside vision' of Trinidad (p. 102), examining the particular motivations of each era of European travellers:

> The tourists at the turn of the century [...] came for the history. They wanted to be in the waters of the great naval battles of the eighteenth century, when the powers of Europe fought over these small, rich sugar islands of the Caribbean. After the First World War, that idea of glory vanished. [...] The tourists came [...] to be in places that were unspoilt,

places that time had passed by, places, it might be said, that had never
been discovered. So history was set on its head; the islands were
refashioned. (p. 73)

Both sets of travellers impose a false temporality on the island. The
Edwardians inscribe the kind of narrative of colonial history which Derek
Walcott dismisses as an absurd 'vision of progress'.[9] Conversely, the 1930s
cruise ship tourists render it ahistorical, reinventing it as an 'unspoilt'
aboriginal island, and thus re-enacting Columbus's initial 'discovery'. In
this way, Trinidad's local community is repeatedly erased. This 'great
chain' of external vision is 'changing' in that the Caribbean islands are
continually 'refashioned' (p. 73) according to the needs and concerns of
each generation of travellers. However, these visions also form a 'tiring
cycle', to borrow Walcott's words, in their repetition of the myths which
have fuelled a series of European conquests of New World locations
(Walcott, p. 39).[10] They therefore obstruct any real change in external
perceptions of Trinidad.

Critics have argued that Naipaul's work contributes to this constrictive
chain of 'outside vision' of Trinidad, reinforcing the values and assumptions of European travel writers. For example, Ian Gregory Strachan
discusses Naipaul's admiration for the work of the nineteenth-century
writers James Anthony Froude and Anthony Trollope, arguing that Naipaul
has 'internalized' their imperialist discourse,[11] and Rob Nixon sees the
postcolonial elements of Naipaul's work as discordantly set against an
identification with nineteenth-century travel writers.[12] Both critics view
Naipaul's affiliation with the European tradition of travel writing as closely
related to his dissociation from the Caribbean. Some of Naipaul's earlier
work, particularly *The Middle Passage*, can certainly be read in this way.
However, in the writing of *A Way in the World* Naipaul negotiates a different
kind of relationship both with colonial travel narratives and with the
Caribbean region. Both *The Middle Passage* and *A Way in the World* reference
Froude, Trollope and Charles Kingsley, but the two books deal with their
legacy differently.

In *The Middle Passage*, Naipaul often draws on the work of Trollope,
Froude and Kingsley to support his own statements about Trinidad. For
example, when discussing Trinidadian people's rejection of local food in
favour of foreign goods, he quotes Trollope at length, and follows this
immediately with an anecdote from Kingsley. This leads him directly into
his own assertion that '[m]odernity in Trinidad, then, turns out to be the
extreme susceptibility of people who are unsure of themselves and, having
no taste or style of their own, are eager for instruction'.[13] Naipaul's use of
the word 'then' suggests a causal link between these nineteenth-century
travel writers' constructions of Trinidad and his own.

In *A Way in the World*, allusions to these writers are more oblique. The narrator of 'Passenger' discusses 'cruise books' which were 'descended in form from Victorian travel journals', but 'not like the books of Trollope or Charles Kingsley or Froude of fifty or sixty years before' (p. 74). As this casual aside indicates, their work is no longer central to Naipaul's representation of Trinidad, but is rather set awkwardly at an angle from his own narrative. The narrator makes the following point:

> Like people of small or far-off communities, we liked the idea of being visited. And though I distrusted tourist-board ideas of glamour, I feel that without those ideas (if only as things to reject or react against), without the witness of our visitors, we would have been floating people, like the aborigines first come upon below Point Galera, living instinctive, unobserved lives. (p. 73)

In *The Middle Passage*, Victorian travel writers' accounts of the Caribbean serve to authorise Naipaul's own observations. Here, he does not entirely reject that earlier position, since he continues to emphasise the role of foreign 'witness' in enabling Caribbean communities to locate themselves globally. However, the phrase 'as things to reject or react against' marks a shift in Naipaul's treatment of colonial travel discourse. In this later text, he raises the possibility of using earlier representations of New World societies as ideas to be challenged rather than uncritically replicated. 'Passenger' opens with the statement: 'I thought that before I settled into the writing of this book I should go and look at old scenes' (p. 69). The narrator means this partly in a literal sense; in preparation for a book which engages closely with New World landscapes, he returns to the places he had known earlier in his life. However, this idea of looking at 'old scenes' also refers to the way in which this episode revisits foreign travellers' depictions of the Caribbean, ranging from Christopher Columbus to contemporary tourists, in order to question their ways of seeing. At the same time, I suggest, Naipaul's return to 'old scenes' involves critical reflection on his own previous account of Trinidad in *The Middle Passage*.

In a discussion of *A Way in the World*, Naipaul comments: 'The chain just goes on and on. You have to break the chain at some stage' (Hussein, p. 160). With this in mind, it could be argued that *A Way in the World* breaks the chain of external constructions of the island to which Naipaul as writer of *The Middle Passage* had contributed. The narrator of 'Passenger' describes how his father found inspiration for an entire article in a line from a book about Trinidad by the English travel writer Owen Rutter: 'The trains are all right, but the buses are a joke' (p. 75). He considers that were it not for Rutter's derogatory comment, his father might 'not have seen that the local buses were something he could write about', and concludes from this: 'So there is a kind of chain' (p. 76). In 'Prologue to an Autobiography' (1982), Naipaul identifies his father's work as an inspiration for his own writing, despite the fact that the enclosed East Indian community of his father's stories is very distant from the Trinidad of his own experience.[14] By tracing his father's story back to 1930s European travel writing, Naipaul's semi-autobiographical narrator plots an alternative continuity of cultural influence to the 'great chain of changing outside vision' which links the accounts of Raleigh and John Hawkins to contemporary British travel writers, via the work of Trollope, Kingsley and Froude (p. 102). In putting forward this other 'kind of chain', which charts the inception and development of a Caribbean literary tradition, Naipaul revises his earlier censure of Trinidad as an 'uncreative' society which has 'produced nothing' and lives happily unaware of its own 'buried past' (*The Middle Passage*, p. 34, p. 35, p. 36).

Bearing in mind this self-critical element of *A Way in the World*, I want to suggest further that the idea of a broken chain offers us a way of reading Naipaul's engagement in this text with his earlier writing. A chain of self-affirming continuity can be identified running through his work prior to *A Way in the World*. For example, comments made in 'Prologue to an Autobiography' serve to explicate and justify the approach of his earlier historical study, *The Loss of El Dorado*, which is written almost exclusively in the third person. In that text Naipaul makes a conscious effort to abstract himself from his writing, leaving us with what appears to be a straightforward, expressionless account of events. This distancing in narrative mode coincides with the writer's geographic distance from the Caribbean region at the time of writing; as he informs us in 'Prologue to an Autobiography', the book was researched over two years spent 'reading in the British museum, the Public Record Office, the London Library', a period where he 'lived with the documents of our region' in order to develop '[t]rue knowledge of geography, and with it a sense of historical wonder' ('Prologue', p. 80). This explanation of his own writing process serves to emphasise the importance of *The Loss of El Dorado* as part of Naipaul's developing understanding of the Caribbean region. The physical and emotional distance from his subject matter achieved in the writing of this book, he implies, was necessary in order to appreciate the 'truth' of his cultural background.

Naipaul's methodology in *The Loss of El Dorado* is also confirmed in his 1970s fictional writing. The first of the two 'forgotten stories' explored in his historical study is Sir Walter Raleigh's fruitless quest for gold in the Americas in the seventeenth century.[15] Naipaul examines in detail the trials and frustrations experienced by Raleigh, placing his psychological deterioration at the heart of the narrative. He acknowledges the partiality of a story reliant on colonial documents, but sees no alternative:

> History was a fairy-tale about Columbus and a fairytale about the strange customs of the aboriginal Caribs and Arawaks; it was impossible now to set them in the landscape. History was the Trinidad five-cent stamp:

Ralegh [*sic*] discovering the Pitch Lake. History was also a fairytale not so much about slavery as about its abolition, the good defeating the bad. It was the only way the tale could be told. (*El Dorado*, p. 353)

Here Naipaul attempts to account for the fact that the voices of Trinidad's almost completely eradicated Amerindian communities and enslaved African communities are absent from his narrative, despite their central role in the island's history. He suggests that representations of these communities can never be more than 'fabulous' since their lives can only be accessed indirectly through the written records of European colonisers. As a result, a full understanding of these people and their experiences is 'impossible'. This claim is borne out in his fiction of the 1970s, none of which touches upon the Caribbean region's vanished past. In this way, Naipaul's work across a range of generic modes is linked together in a mutually supportive relationship.

In *A Way in the World*, Naipaul returns to material covered in *The Loss of El Dorado*, but this return serves to disrupt rather than reinforce the continuity linking his earlier works. In 'A Parcel of Papers, A Roll of Tobacco, a Tortoise: *An Unwritten Story*', he challenges the idea of restricted vision in the writing of Caribbean history put forward in his historical study. His conclusive statement that an account written from the point of view of European explorers was 'the only way the tale could be told' is replaced with alternative ways of seeing and telling. Whereas *The Loss of El Dorado* traces a repetitive sequence of 'changing outside vision' of the New World, from Christopher Columbus to Antonio de Berrio to Captain Wyatt to Raleigh, 'A Parcel of Papers' is structured as a cinematic sequence in which the 'camera's eye' (p. 181) alternates between insider and outsider perspectives. Although Naipaul returns at length to material covered in *The Loss of El Dorado*, he enters new stylistic territory in this 'unwritten story', stepping away from his earlier reliance on written records.

In *The Loss of El Dorado*, Naipaul regrets how when seen through colonial documents, '[t]he slave was never real. Like the extinct aboriginal, he had to be reconstructed from his daily routine. [...] In the records the slave is faceless, silent, with an identification rather than a name. He has no story' (*El Dorado*, pp. 353–54). In 'A Parcel of Papers', an Amerindian figure previously 'faceless' and 'silent' in Naipaul's work is given a name, a voice and a story. The first scene focuses on a conversation between Raleigh and his surgeon, and ends by introducing the half-Amerindian character Don José, dressed in Spanish clothes, seen from their perspective hoisted up to the ship's deck from the river. After a section break, the camera cuts to a room in New Granada, a year later, where a priest, Fray Simón, is questioning Don José in order to write 'a history of the Spanish New World' (p. 181). After another section break, the narrator tells us:

'Here we begin to fit pictures to the words of Don José. The narrative is now his' (p. 181). At first, the flow of Don José's story is frequently broken by the voice of Fray Simón, who questions its validity and makes corrections; for example, he amends Don José's 'Don Palmita' to 'Don Diego Palomeque' (p. 182), and 'Captain Erenetta' to 'Arias Nieto' (p. 183). However, this is followed by an uninterrupted stretch where the mispronounced names return (p. 185), implying that the priest's mediation has diminished.

At the end of Don José's story, he describes his experience of being dressed up in 'pretty clothes' which were 'too big for me' (p. 188), returning us to the moment explored in the first scene from the point of view of Raleigh and the surgeon. This repetition of the initial sighting of Don José from the opposite point of view creates a layering of perspectives, illustrating that a story centred on Raleigh's inner struggle is not in fact 'the only way the tale could be told'. Naipaul's statement in *The Loss of El Dorado* that the region's past is 'many-sided and ambiguous' (*El Dorado*, p. 352), an idea which in his historical study receives no more than a comment, serves as the organising principle of this cinematic reconstruction. Naipaul's shift to a fictional mode of writing in his treatment of Raleigh's story enables him to extend empathy towards those figures formerly absent from his writing, or present only in a shadowy, indistinct form. In breaking the chain of continuity within his own writing, then, Naipaul forges new connections unprecedented in his work.

Both Naipaul's reflections on nineteenth-century travel writing and his revisiting of Raleigh's story in *A Way in the World* exemplify how the disruption of continuity can generate alternative associations. The same idea is suggested in the text's structure. While the 'immense chain of events' offered by the narrator of 'History' connects chronologically a series of moments in Trinidad's history, from 'the discovery' to 'the nihilism of the moment' (p. 40), Naipaul's multiple self-figuring in the various semi-autobiographical fragments laced around his 'unwritten stories' forms another kind of chain. Linking Naipaul's perceptions of Trinidad at various points in his life, this alternative chain is associative rather than chronologi-cal; the sequence of visions built up through the 'Prelude', 'History' and 'A New Man' binds together the narrator's response to the island as a child, adolescent, young adult and older man in a productive tension, generating a more complex and dynamic impression of the place and its history than the twenty-four-year-old narrator's 'immense chain of events'. To con-sider the various 'I's of *A Way in the World* in relation to those of *The Middle Passage* further complicates this picture. As I will show, *A Way in the World*'s associative sequence of semi-autobiographical sketches contributes to Naipaul's re-envisioning of community.

In *The Middle Passage* we are presented with an interplay between insider and outsider perspectives, and between the narrator's adolescent and adult

responses to Port of Spain. At the end of the opening paragraph to the
Trinidad chapter, Naipaul's narrator makes the following observation:

> And the city throbbed with steel bands. A good opening line for a novelist
> or a travel-writer; but the steel band used to be regarded as a high
> manifestation of West Indian Culture, and it was a sound I detested.
> (*The Middle Passage*, p. 34)

Here Naipaul initially sets up the role of the travel writer exploring
Trinidad for the first time, and then proceeds to set himself apart from this
role by demonstrating his insider knowledge of the place, knowledge
which serves to authorise his rejection of it. Here and elsewhere in the text,
his negative statements are backed up by the way in which he positions his
adolescent self within the society he denigrates. For example, his assertion
that 'there was no community' is followed by the explanation: 'We were of
various races, religions, sets and cliques; and we had somehow found
ourselves on the same small island. Nothing bound us together except this
common residence. There was no nationalist feeling; there could be none'
(*The Middle Passage*, p. 36). Naipaul includes his younger self in his
depiction of colonial Trinidad in order to license the extreme pessimism of
a passage punctuated with the words 'no', 'nothing', and 'none'.

In *A Way in the World*, insider and outsider perspectives are again
combined, but to different effect. The Trinidad chapter of *The Middle
Passage* opens with an outright rejection of the island: 'I did not want to stay'
(*The Middle Passage*, p. 33). In contrast, 'History' initially casts us back to
the period of the narrator's first encounter with Port of Spain, which he
refers to as 'one of the most hopeful times in my life' (p. 11). As in the
corresponding chapter in *The Middle Passage*, the narrator launches into a
detailed description of the town's architecture. However, this time a more
affirmative tone is generated by a series of sentences beginning with the
words 'I liked': 'I liked the paved cambered streets [...] I liked the
pavements [...] I liked the way the pavements dipped outside the big side
gates [...] I liked the street lamps' (p. 12). The passage ends: 'Port of Spain
was small, really, with less than a hundred thousand people. But to me it
was a big town, and quite complete' (p. 12). Whereas in *The Middle Passage*,
the first person plural is used to present Naipaul's adolescent self as
complicit with the narrator's belittling statements, here a town which
appears small and incomplete to the well-travelled and older narrator
remains 'big' and 'quite complete' in his memory. The two sentences
present us with two opposing ways of seeing the town, putting into play a
tension which is not resolved either within this episode or in the later
autobiographical pieces of *A Way in the World*. As we have seen, Naipaul as
writer of *The Middle Passage* deploys his childhood memories as a means of
authorising his disparaging observations of Trinidadian society. The narrator of 'History' reaches back through this phase of rejection, figured in

the twenty-four-year-old version of himself, to an earlier period of hopefulness.

The modified dynamic between insider and outsider perceptions of Trinidad enables Naipaul to critically examine his previous responses to Trinidad as a child and as a returning migrant. In 'A New Man', the seventh episode of *A Way in the World*, an older narrator visiting Trinidad and Venezuela reflects upon his impressions of Trinidad at two earlier stages in his life. He describes his childhood enjoyment of the cocoa woods northwest of Port of Spain, which 'fixed for [him] the idea of the perfect tropical landscape' (p. 213). This 'idea' of natural beauty, persisting in the narrator's mind during his absence from Trinidad, is shattered on his return, aged twenty-four, when he is confronted by a landscape rendered 'crowded and noisy and confused' by immigration from other islands (p. 213). Neither the narrator's eight-year-old self nor his twenty-four-year-old self acknowledge that the idyllic cocoa woods, as a remnant of the plantation economy, are themselves the product of the import of people and vegetation, and are therefore no more 'natural' than the 'hillside slums' which appear to 'damage' the woodland (p. 213). Neither of these younger selves recognise movement and change as the basis of, rather than a threat to, the Trinidadian landscapes he has known and 'cherished' (p. 213).

The older narrator's critical reflections on his early attachment to, and later disconnection from, rural Trinidad, generate a new way of seeing appropriate to an episode entitled 'A New Man'. When describing the changing landscape, he considers how '[w]e ourselves had been there at a moment of change. We had been part of the change, and this change speeded up after we left' (p. 213). As immigrants moving from town to country, the narrator's family is as involved in the increase of Port of Spain's urban sprawl as the illegal workers from other islands. In identifying the upheavals of his personal migrations within as well as beyond Trinidad with the continuing 'insurrection' (p. 33) of the island's social and natural landscapes, the narrator works towards an acceptance of changes which had once deeply disturbed him.

The older narrator's renewed connection with Trinidad is therefore developed through an awareness of the Caribbean region's complex history of multiple migration, in which his own journeys are implicated. In an interview, Naipaul reflects on his attempt, in his fiction and travel writing, 'to express the movement of one's soul and of the world'.[16] These two movements, of the traveller and the site traversed, are presented in *A Way in the World* as interrelated. Furthermore, the notion of a region characterised by movement forms the basis of Naipaul's reinvestment in the idea of community in *A Way in the World*. The text's reworking of the 'I' of *The Middle Passage* involves a revision not only of his earlier responses to Trinidad, but also of his uncompromising statement: 'there was no community'. The narrator's insistence in *The Middle Passage* that '[n]othing bound us together except this common residence' is doubly undermined in *A Way in the World*, where interconnected episodes generate associations between a geographically extensive network of fictional, historical and semi-autobiographical figures who do not share island space, but whose various trajectories overlap in a number of ways.

These connections between Naipaul's various narrators and a range of partially identifiable figures produce yet another 'kind of chain'. Don José, the seventeenth-century half-Amerindian boy in the second 'unwritten story', has 'crossed the ocean twice' (p. 204). His path therefore converges – spatially, if not temporally – with that of the narrator's twenty-four-year-old self, who has returned to visit Trinidad after six years in England. However, while the narrator's migration is optional, Don José's is compulsory. Sir Walter Raleigh, his expedition having failed, takes the boy to England as 'a remnant or proof of the kingdom of gold in his head' (p. 200). Don José is therefore the object which validates Raleigh's quest, rather than the subject of his own. As discussed above, Naipaul's semi-autobiographical narrator is presented as a viewing subject in an associative chain of perspectives. In comparison, Don José describes himself as 'moving on in a chain of death from one man to his enemy' (p. 204). While the narrator's journeys are motivated by his own ambition to develop as a writer, Don José's movement is precipitated by the desires and antagonisms of others. Naipaul's narrator is free to move in any direction he chooses, but Don José is constrained by his economic dependency.

In her analysis of *A Way in the World*, Fawzia Mustafa describes the 'narrative meeting' in Africa of 'three Caribbean players': Naipaul's narrator and the characters Lebrun and Phyllis, both originally from the Caribbean.[17] In her view, the relationship between the trajectories of fictional, historical and semi-autobiographical figures allows Naipaul to demonstrate how '[o]nly Naipaul as narrator survives, thus reiterating one of the earliest obsessions of his writing life: the escape, release, that writing has granted him' (Mustafa, p. 212). According to Mustafa, Naipaul's text privileges one way in the world: that of an internationally renowned writer. In light of my own reading of *A Way in the World*, I would argue that travel in this text becomes the common practice of a community which exceeds the limits of a literary elite. The text offers an assortment of 'Caribbean players' who are comparable but not identical to Naipaul, and not all of whom are literate or materially privileged. The associative links between the episodes do not, as Mustafa implies, serve to emphasise the success of Naipaul's life course. Instead they enable Naipaul to broaden his textual terrain and extend his attention from the individual to the collective.

Naipaul's writing since the late 1960s has become increasingly detached from both the urban creole community of *Miguel Street* and the insular East

Indian community of *A House for Mr Biswas* (1961). However, this movement away from his earlier depictions of Trinidadian communities has involved a rearticulation rather than a rejection of communal identifications. In *A Way in the World*, Naipaul writes himself into a wider picture of migrants and displaced people who may not share a 'common residence', but who move within the sociocultural context of a 'Caribbean or New World background'. In its portrayal of a mobile network of travellers, *A Way in the World* returns to the idea of community without attempting to recapture the more concrete and geographically localised communities depicted in Naipaul's work of the 1950s and 60s.

Naipaul's new approach to the notion of a Caribbean community in *A Way in the World* is tightly bound up with his reworking of the sequence as a literary form. He claims that in the writing of his first short story sequence, *Miguel Street*, his suppression of 'the setting, the historical time, the racial and social complexities of the people concerned' was part of a 'wish to simplify' in order to fit the material to the 'rhythm' and 'speed' of the narrative which the opening sentences had instigated ('Prologue', p. 58). This movement towards simplicity directly opposes the ramifying effect of *A Way in the World*, a 'form where the material is linked by associations – that begin very simply and then radiate through the text' (Hussein, p. 159). Equally, the brief and one-dimensional character sketches making up *Miguel Street* differ stylistically from *A Way in the World*'s lengthier episodes which are not only optically plural, combining the perspectives of a series of semi-autobiographical narrators, but are also often split into shorter sequences.[18]

The formal modifications of this later text coincide with a change in setting. Naipaul describes how in *Miguel Street*, he attempted to 'establish the idea of the street as a kind of club' ('Prologue', p. 59). Each episode focuses on a different inhabitant of the street, and this – along with the reappearance of earlier protagonists in later stories – builds up a sense of community. There is also a feeling of solidarity in the characters' attitudes and behaviour towards each other; for example, in the way that Hat quietly explains Bogart's unheroic actions to his adopted son, without laughter or derision, and in the narrator's attachment to, and esteem for, the fraudulent poet B. Wordsworth. Naipaul's affirmation of community in *Miguel Street* jars with his later comment, in *The Middle Passage*, that in Trinidad 'there was no community. […] Nothing bound us together except this common residence'. In *A Way in the World* Naipaul returns to the possibility of communal identifications glimpsed in *Miguel Street*, but reinscribes community within a more complex 'world picture',[19] widened both by his travels and through his exploration of a range of literary forms.

Significantly, *Miguel Street* ends with the narrator's departure from Trinidad, whereas *A Way in the World* begins with the return of another semi-autobiographical narrator to his place of birth. As we progress through *Miguel Street*, the narrator becomes increasingly detached from, and critical of, the community he depicts, and more aware of the need to escape, until eventually he leaves 'not looking back', aware only of his own shadow, 'a dancing dwarf on the tarmac'.[20] Conversely, the concept of looking back – of return to earlier places, earlier writing, and earlier ways of seeing – is, as I have shown, a dominant theme and structuring principle in *A Way in the World*. If we read *Miguel Street* as charting a developing dissociation from Trinidad and the Caribbean, *A Way in the World* could be seen to explore a developing re-association, or a 'fresh association', to borrow the words of the book's epigraph. Naipaul cannot, with the knowledge and experience he has gained in the interim, return to an atmosphere where 'historical time' and 'racial and social complexities' are submerged. However, the mutual sympathy and conviviality of the multi-ethnic and socially uneven Miguel Street inhabitants are echoed in *A Way in the World* within a more extensive spatial, temporal and formal framework, in the fleeting moments of connection between semi-autobiographical, semi-historical and fictional figures.

NOTES

1 V.S. Naipaul, 'Reading and Writing: a Personal Account', in *Literary Occasions: Essays* (London: Picador, 2004 [2003]), pp. 3–31 (p. 27).
2 Ahmed Rashid, 'The Last Lion', *Far Eastern Economic Review*, 30 (1995), 49–50. Reprinted in *Conversations with V.S. Naipaul*, ed. by Feroza Jussawalla (Jackson, MS: University Press of Mississippi, 1997), pp. 135–53 (p. 167).
3 Aamer Hussein, 'Delivering the Truth: An Interview with V.S. Naipaul', *Times Literary Supplement*, 2 September 1994, 3–4. Reprinted in *Conversations with V.S. Naipaul*, ed. by Jussawalla, pp. 154–61 (pp. 154–55).
4 Salman Rushdie, 'V.S. Naipaul', in *Imaginary Homelands: Essays and Criticism 1981–91* (London: Granta, 1991), pp. 148–51 (p. 148).
5 Edward Said, *Reflections on Exile* (London: Granta, 2000), p. 99.
6 Wilson Harris, 'Tradition and the West Indian Novel', in *Selected Essays of Wilson Harris: The Unfinished Genesis of the Imagination*, ed. by Andrew Bundy (London and New York: Routledge, 1999), pp. 140–51 (p. 142).
7 V.S. Naipaul, *A Way in the World* (London: Vintage, 2001 [1994]), p. 41. Subsequent references will be to this edition and will appear in parentheses in the main body of the essay.
8 Paula Burnett, '"Where else to row, but backward?" Addressing Caribbean Futures Through Re-visions of the Past', *Ariel*, 30:1 (1999), 11–37 (p. 14).
9 Derek Walcott, 'The Muse of History', in *What the Twilight Says: Essays* (London: Faber & Faber, 1998), pp. 36–64 (p. 41).
10 For Walcott, the history of the New World is characterised by 'tiring cycles of stupidity and greed' (Walcott, p. 39).

11 Ian Gregory Strachan, *Paradise and Plantation: Tourism and Culture in the Anglophone Caribbean* (Charlottesville, VA: University Press of Virginia, 2002), pp. 179–80.

12 Rob Nixon, *London Calling: V.S. Naipaul, Postcolonial Mandarin* (New York and Oxford: Oxford University Press, 1992), p. 65.

13 V.S. Naipaul, *The Middle Passage: Impressions of five colonial societies* (London: Picador, 2001 [1962]), p. 41.

14 V.S. Naipaul, 'Prologue to an Autobiography', in *Literary Occasions,* pp. 53–111 (p. 71).

15 V.S. Naipaul, *The Loss of El Dorado: A Colonial History* (London: Picador, 2001 [1969]), p. 3.

16 Alastair Niven, 'V.S. Naipaul Talks to Alastair Niven', *Wasafiri*, 21 (1995), 5–6. Reprinted in *Conversations with V.S. Naipaul*, ed. by Jussawalla, pp. 162–65 (p. 163).

17 Fawzia Mustafa, *V.S. Naipaul* (Cambridge: Cambridge University Press, 1995), p. 211.

18 See for example, 'On the Run', where the narrator's account of Lebrun is divided into episodes each marked by the consumption of a different meal. See also the cinematic sequence in 'A Parcel of Papers', discussed above.

19 In his 2001 essay, 'Two Worlds', Naipaul explains how his 'aim has always been to fill out [his] world picture'. See *Literary Occasions*, pp. 181–95 (p. 191).

20 V.S. Naipaul, *Miguel Street* (London: Heinemann, 2000 [1959]), p. 176.

LIMINALITY AND THE POETICS OF SPACE IN MARK MCWATT'S *SUSPENDED SENTENCES* AND KWAME DAWES'S *A PLACE TO HIDE*

ANDREW H. ARMSTRONG

I begin this essay by stating the obvious, namely that storytelling is both a temporal and spatial process. It is a journey without a definitive closure or resolution. Yet, stories must begin and end. Stories therefore have both roots and routes: both sites of origin or dwelling, and modes of travel or dispersal. Just as there are specific modes of dwelling and travel, there are specific modes of storytelling or representation. My discussion in this essay brings me into contact with one such specific or distinctive mode of storytelling, the short story collection. I consider the spatial and temporal processes that make up the short story. More specifically, I look at what I call the poetics of space, the compressed space of the short story, in analysing the work of two new practitioners of the short story in Caribbean fiction: Mark McWatt (*Suspended Sentences*, 2005) and Kwame Dawes (*A Place to Hide*, 2002). As a central part of my argument, I discuss liminality and the poetics of space specifically as these refer to the process of framing in these two collections. This paper is therefore in two parts: first, there is a theoretical discussion of framing, liminality and the threshold, referring to the writings of both writers, followed by a closer analysis of selected stories.

To this end, it is helpful to consider what Malashri Lal identifies in *The Law of the Threshold* as the three spaces which 'a text may be seen to inhabit':[1] these are interior space, the threshold itself, and the world beyond the domestic or 'home' (Lal, p. 19). These three spaces are essential to the argument sustained by Lal, and call into question the whole matter of space in the text – of form and content and how they challenge each other. They may also call to mind Gaston Bachelard's conception of space in *The Poetics of Space* (1964), specifically his construction of interior space (the house, drawers, chests, wardrobes, nests, shells); corners (as thresholds); and the dialectics of outside and inside. For the law of the threshold as I employ it in this essay does not refer only to thematic issues related to crossings, journeyings and borders, but also to the ways in which the form of the short story collection impacts upon the reading experience. In other words, I am examining here the liminality of the frame and its capacity to direct interpretation. This latter point can be strengthened by turning to some observations made by John Matthews in his essay on framing in *Wuthering Heights*. Matthews states:

As in paintings, the literary frame appears as little more than a preliminary passage: pre-liminary literally, in the sense of being before the threshold, before the liminal division of introduction and story proper [...]. The frame is always that which is first to be passed through or beyond. The literary frame exists as a function which enables a relation between differentiated realms (the reader and author, the world and the artwork, the reality and imagination, and so on).[3]

This can certainly be seen in McWatt's preface to *Suspended Sentences*, where he begins by stating that:

The idea of writing a book of short stories, purportedly by different authors and within a narrative frame, first occurred to me in 1989, when I remember discussing it briefly with David Dabydeen, who thought that it would prove too difficult to maintain distinctions between the styles/voices of the storytellers. He was (is) probably right, but I wasn't concerned too much with that, I just wanted to try it if/when I got the chance.[4]

This may be seen as the first threshold in the collection, a preliminary or pre-liminal statement that directs the reader to the form and content of the collection. The preface here, even before the reader gets to the fictional 'Introduction', serves as a border that marks our entry into the aesthetic world of the text. Here, we are in the liminal area between the real and the represented. In the case of Dawes's *A Place to Hide*, however, the framing device passes through the entire collection, in the form of five 'Vershans' which function, in the language of Gérard Genette's narratological formulations, more like 'paratexts': in-between zones or 'privileged place[s]' that help to 'frame', or influence, readings or interpretations.[5] Hence, what we encounter, first of all, are the spatial arrangements of the texts and how these arrangements may affect the experience of reading and meaning-making. In addition, it is important to note, in keeping with my concerns here, that the fundamental structuring device in both collections is the journey, or movement from one place to another, one experiential level to another. This will be discussed further as I proceed.

Since both McWatt's and Dawes's texts are short story cycles or sequences – that is, collections of stories deliberately placed together to form a longer narrative, and connected with frame stories (in Dawes's text the frame narrative runs through the collection) – they offer a very distinctive use of the short story. My own reading of the short story cycle here is guided by three interrelated definitions from short story theorists over the span of thirty years. Firstly, Forrest Ingram (1971) sees the cycle as 'a set of stories so linked to one another that the reader's experience of each is modified by his experience of the other'.[6] Though this may be more true of Dawes's collection than of McWatt's, it can nevertheless be seen more loosely in the latter. Secondly, Susan Garland Mann (1989) describes the short story cycle as unified by a 'framing device' which can be 'the prologue, epilogue or transitional paragraphs'.[7] Thirdly, James Nagel, in his work on the contemporary American short story cycle, observes that:

> a central point is that in the short-story cycle each component work must stand alone [...] yet be enriched in the context of the interrelated stories [...]. The cycle lends itself to diegetical discontinuities, to the resolution of a series of conflicts, to the exploration of a variety of characters, to the use of a family or even a community as protagonist, to the exploration of the mores of a region or religion or ethnic group, each story revealing another aspect of the local culture.[8]

The short story cycle, in keeping with my focus on liminality, may be seen as exploring that grey area between the short story and the novel. Two other examples within recent Caribbean fiction are Colin Channer's *Passing Through* (2004), a collection of stories linked by letters to a fictional 'editor' and which follow each other in chronological order (more novel-istic in style), and Kevin Baldeosingh's novel, *The Ten Incarnations of Adam Avatar* (2004), where each chapter narrates a distinctive, yet linked, 'incar-nation' of the protagonist, Adam, while being linked by the session notes of a psychiatrist (more in the manner of the short story cycle).[9] The formal and creative qualities of the short story cycle can be briefly summed up by citing Rachel Lister's opening statement in her essay on selected short story cycles of Eudora Welty and Joyce Carol Oates, where she states: 'As a versatile, provisional form, the short story cycle privileges plurality and openness. It contests boundaries and enacts the possibility of multiple beginnings and renewable identities.'[10] With this in mind, I will consider in my textual analysis not only the structure of individual stories but also the dynamics of the collection. In addition, I wish to explore both Dawes's and McWatt's use of the ideas of liminality, journeying and boundary-crossing as a means of articulating not only the themes, but also the form of connected stories, where the commonly cited idea of short stories as compressed space is challenged. This challenge is most evident in McWatt's case in 'Afternoon without Tears', 'The Tyranny of Influence', 'Sky' and 'Two Boys Named Basil'. In Dawes's collection, it is manifested in his crossings and journeying across the landscape of Jamaica in 'Flight', 'A Place to Hide', 'Foreplay' and even 'Marley's Ghost'. But Dawes also crosses generic boundaries in his 'Vershans', where the poetic impulse threads through and throbs within the collection. For both writers, the turn from poetry to short story writing coincides with their articulation of late twentieth-century Caribbean identities in transition both within the Car-ibbean and abroad, and the concerns and problems of their particular nation states at this turn-of-the-century moment.

My principal argument is that these writers have shown an 'urge to find better words for the complex condition in which new literatures are written'[11] *in* the Caribbean and *about* the Caribbean *by* Caribbean writers.

Thus, I consider the role that the short story plays in contemporary discourses of Caribbean identities. In Caribbean storytelling, the short story collection provides or allows for the digressions and many tales-within-a-tale which are features of Caribbean oral or folk storytelling. Both writers' fictive spaces are not only geographical, but also imaginative and mythic. McWatt and Dawes narrate the empty spaces and ambiguities of postcolonial, post-independence history – a recent history of disillusionment and loss, of violence and scarcity, yet of struggle for survival for a better life (as seen in the struggles of many of Dawes's characters, who work to construct meaning and purpose). The collections not only offer a very distinctive use of the short story, but also open up the geographical, cultural and imaginary spaces of the postcolonial to interrogate notions of history and time, being and knowing, often demonstrating the changing forces at work within Caribbean postcolonial societies – the dynamic (and at times destructive) forces of politics, money, religion and power. The latter is particularly true of Dawes's stories.

Both McWatt and Dawes bring to their short story writing the influences of their earlier work as poets; poetry's spare use of language, and its focus on imagery, symbol and metaphor, is transferred or transposed onto the short story genre, which too requires a minimalist, at times liminal, use of language and imagery within its small space. This bears out Charles May's observation that, from its beginning 'as a separately recognized literary form, the short story has always been more closely associated with lyric poetry than with its overgrown narrative neighbour, the novel'.[12] Because of its 'compactness', the use of symbol and metaphor is intense in the short story, serving 'to transform mere objects and events into significance'.[13] The body of the short form is at times strained to contain the concerns of the stories. For example, McWatt's 'Afternoon without Tears' takes place at the edges of consciousness and unconsciousness and expands existential space into the limitless realms of dream and imagination. This is seen in the dreamlike language of the story and the dream/reveries that Victor undergoes while lying in the armchair in the hotel foyer. 'The Tyranny of Influence', in which the artist falls into a painting of 'The Dead Christ, Supported by an Angel', enters the liminal worlds of history, myth and fable, where the artist, in the language of Wilson Harris, 'acquires phantom limbs' in his encounter with versions of the dead Christ (another phantom). The artist in 'Tyranny' resembles the 'traveller coincident in time' in McWatt's poem 'Suspension Bridge': 'All travel beyond that moment/has been charged with the weight/of a country's misfortune;/all departures are uncertain,/each arrival seems too late'.[14] McWatt's artist figure in 'Tyranny' extends or expands space even as he moves in time, straddling temporalities from present to recent past to ancient past and back to the present, even as he projects a 'redeemed' future for the unfortunate country. The expanded,

interconnective space of the short story cycle gives these otherwise compressed stories room to breathe – the small space opens out.

These collections present challenges to the generic boundaries of the
short story form even as they thematise crisis, crossings and thresholds in
the lives of the various characters. In *A Place to Hide*, Dawes constructs a
violence-filled society in crisis showing the poverty and harshness of daily
life in Kingston and other places. Dawes's concern with and thematisation
of recent Jamaican socioeconomic and political history – the crisis of the
1970s – recurs in the narrative as a raison d'être for the violence and
disorder in the current society. But his writing explores the border between
cruelty and beauty: we come face to face with the 'anger and oppression, the
cruelties of life, the beauty of sexuality, the humour of human existence –
all at the same time',[15] and we also come into contact with 'the inherent
creativity of the erotic' (*Natural Mysticism*, p. 149) as a means of countering
the harshness and desolation of the society. I interpret the erotic as a close
space, an intimate space, or to borrow from Gaston Bachelard, as both 'nest'
and 'corner'. I see the erotic as nest in the way that it speaks to those 'primal
images; images that bring out the primitiveness in us' (Bachelard, p. 91),
and as corner because of its solitude and seclusion, its tendency to foster
withdrawal into the self or into the recesses of the imagination (Bachelard,
p. 136). For the erotic involves the imagination at its most primal, yet at its
most creative. It is within the erotic imagination in 'At the Lighthouse', for
example, where the narrative creates a primal space, a nest, a space of
seclusion for Joan away from the religious chauvinism that governs the
public space of the small church community.

Dawes's inter-generic poetics in this collection, his slippage from
poetry to prose, the use of what may be seen as poetic prose, resonates with
much of his earlier poetry. I am thinking here of many of the poems in
Shook Foil (1997) which not only thematise the same concerns dramatised
in the stories (violence, urban survival, faith, redemption, music, the soul),
but also beat with the familiar rhythms of ska, reggae, dub that thread
through *A Place to Hide*. For example, the poem 'I Am a Stranger on Earth'
draws both thematic and rhythmic comparisons with the title story 'A
Place to Hide', 'Tending Rosebuds', 'Flight' and 'Foreplay'. The speaking
voice in the poem speaks many of the concerns expressed in the short story
collection. The sordid and harsh realities narrated in many of the stories
are also spoken of in the poem: 'The spilling of blood /leaves me drained
and tender /like the soft place of a lanced boil' (*Shook Foil*, p. 176). The
voice says: 'I stand before the language of this storm /again an alien, a
sojourner, waiting for a clue /to lead me homeward – a place of quiet rest'.[16]
The speaker's 'place of quiet rest' calls to mind the place to hide or to escape
to that the protagonists of Dawes's stories seek. The choice of language
signals a refuge or a secret place from the harshness of life, or, in keeping

with the biblical and religious imagery that proliferates within the stories, invokes a quest for 'the secret place of the Most High' of the ninety-first Psalm of the Bible. We note, therefore, the ways that Dawes's use of language allows for creative linguistic responses to the violence and oppression of the society. There is much of the linguistic potency of poetry in his stories, and at the same time a network of links weaving between the stories and extending out beyond the book, creating further resonances with much of his other writing.

One of the ideas connecting the stories in *A Place to Hide* is that, through their searches for safety, rest and redemption, these protagonists are engaged in 'making [their] own myths to cope with [their] own tragedies' (*Place*, p. 58). One of Dawes's damaged characters, Sarah, the 'fallen angel' of the title story, 'A Place to Hide', embarks on a quest for God as a search for selfhood and for redemption. Sarah does not fit into the 'neat' spaces of her Mona Heights district. As a 'fallen angel', she is in search of a place of refuge. Her desire is for God and for good from her backslidden life. Sarah's need for redemption, for atonement for her loss, is foremost in her quest; hence the final act in the story of her redemption is her return to the baptismal place, the ritual space of cleansing and renewal. 'A Place to Hide' ends with Sarah's journey to the hills for the baptism – her own baptism this time, performed not for her father, not to appease an angry God, but for her own self-worth. The story fittingly ends with Sarah 'holding on' (*Place*, p. 26). In this story the depiction of interior space – the apartment – as limiting and oppressive often mirrors internal space – Sarah's conscious-ness, her memories, thoughts and dreams. Thus, her final act of atonement occurs in exterior space, within the boundless world of the outside in her journey to the hills. Here, the expansive landscape mirrors or represents the opening-out of her consciousness. The same is true of Sandra, the protagonist of 'Tending Rosebuds', who, after suffering a miscarriage, leaves Kingston to seek cleansing and renewal in a journey to the hills. Again, the cleansing or bath ritual leads to regeneration and hope. Hence, we note the final scene of wholeness: 'The hill was whole. Away from the sordid fragmentation of the city she could think clearly. From the porch she stared into the Caribbean Sea, stretching out in multiple shades of blue. She began to regroup, pull together the scatterings of her mind' (*Place*, p. 97). The narrative trajectory or itinerary of 'Tending Rosebuds' is fittingly summed up in its conclusion:

> That night, Sandra drove home, travelling westward, the long way around the island. As she drove she counted the impossible hopes she had, tasted the sweetness and comfort of contentment, and then imagined the texture of grace, her fingers feeling the soft petals. Her body was stronger now. [...] [S]he could sense that the restlessness that had consumed her for months and months had been replaced by a calm, as incomprehensible and impossible as an answered prayer. (*Place*, p. 98)

Sandra's return home to Kingston is not in actuality to the physical place of the house or apartment, but more importantly to a space of well-being, to a place where she could experience 'the texture of grace' and the true rhythms and cadences of home amidst the cacophony of the city.

In their complex play of narrative and imaginative spaces, these two stories, like others in the collection, *exceed* the idea of the short story as compressed space. The collection highlights the tension between form and content, between tidy generic categorisation and the open spaces of the imagination. Just as many of the protagonists struggle against the restrictiveness of their ordered worlds – not only Sarah, but also Joan in 'At the Lighthouse', Mona in 'Foreplay', the young girl in 'Evening Song' and Hugh in 'Flight' – so too do the stories themselves spill over into the untidy, wild spaces of his poetry.

The collection's relationship to poetry can be linked both to the rhythmic 'vershans' that intercut the stories and to the cadences and rhythms of language in the stories themselves. In 'Marley's Ghost' Dawes brings to the reader the rhythms of Kingston as 'a city determined to pursue its Third World rituals of laughter, dubwise, gunshot, car crash, screwing, hallelujahs, praise and the telling of stories' (*Place*, p. 253). This is a unique city in some ways, but in others is not unlike any other in the First World (New York, London, Toronto). The violence, the cacophony of voices and city rituals, the journeying, all stretch the limits (boundaries) of genre and form in this story. This is the story of Joseph, a man locked in a room for six days feeding on oranges, surrounded by orange peels. Born in 1962, the year of his nation's independence, his growth is coterminous with the nation, and Dawes uses the changing forms of Jamaican music to trace the progress of Joseph's own development. He is seen as a child of hope: 'When he was born, ska was jumping around the city. In that year, someone said that he was a child of the future. An old man touched his forehead and said "As your future go, so go the nation"' (*Place*, p. 260). Later we are told that 'he would live his life wondering whether he was guiding the fate of the nation or whether he was simply reflecting a nation bent on its own self-destruction' (*Place*, p. 260). Dawes paints a vivid picture of the violence and chaos of postcolonial Jamaica, showing the depths it has sunk to by the end of the twentieth century:

> With it came the frenzy of cars crashing, bodies mutilated, flesh exposed – the coked-up madness of a city coming of age, hungry to remind itself of its own strength. This was a country in trauma as it struggled to show that it still had possibilities, a country caught up in a mid-life crisis, looking back at the hopeful years, the years of promise and prophecy [...]. His journey passed through the fearful, hopeful millenarian years of the 1970s [...] the chaos and sexual wildness of those 1980s [and] in the 1990s he was trying to beat back the gruff voice of Capleton chanting another apocalypse, but this time with blood in his eyes. (*Place*, p. 260–61)

Journeying from Kingston, to New York, to Miami, to London, to Germany, and narrated in sixteen sections, mixing mundane prose with poetic diction, with ska and dub rhythms, with reggae and psalmody – this story, the last full story in the collection, at times appears too large, too weighty, for the compressed space of the short story. Blending myth, legend, fable, memory and dream with sociopolitical and cultural history, the spectral narrative of 'Marley's Ghost' reads like a culmination of the five 'Vershans' that Dawes has inserted as a thread through the collection. After representing the grim, harsh realities of contemporary Jamaican life in these stories, Dawes concludes the collection with the hopeful and positive vision of Bob Marley's 'Three Little Birds' in the final 'Vershan: Scratch Madness': 'Rise up this morning /Smiled with the rising sun'. And concludes with the narrator's own observation: 'And for a moment, everything shimmered' (*Place*, p. 310).

Like Dawes, McWatt is concerned with the themes of atonement and regeneration. McWatt's work (his poetry and prose and, at times, even his critical work) is rooted in and routed through his place of origin, Guyana. The fact that he has lived in Barbados for over thirty years has not diminished this. In fact, I wish to suggest, borrowing from Dermot McCarthy's views on the poetry of Ralph Gustafson, that living away from Guyana has resulted not only in the richness of his work but also 'in a viewpoint which sees the local both in itself and as part of a rich network of association and memory'.[17] His construction of the Guyanese landscape is partly informed by this. According to James Fox, '"Landscape" is [...] variously represented as a topographic vista, as an intimate emplacement of local experience, or as the "interanimation" of sense, speech and memory'.[18] In 'Afternoon Without Tears' and 'The Tyranny of Influence', the narrators work with hidden legacies that animate their stories and augment their artistic vision of history, time and place. I am thinking here of the ghostly Amerindian presences in both stories, and the conquistadorial presence that fills them, especially the skulls in the river in 'Tyranny'. In the short stories in this collection the landscape is encoded as both a geographic and narrated or linguistic text that speaks to forms of social behaviour, rights, responsibilities and relations (Fox, p. 7). Here, stories create itineraries or social ways of moving through the spatial and cultural landscape,[19] and thus involve the crossing of thresholds from place to place, from one way of seeing to the next, from youth to adulthood, dream to reality. Thresholds are everywhere in the stories in this collection: from its title, *Suspended Sentences*, which speaks to provisionality and contingency, to the eleven 'authors' of the stories, 'the gang', young people on the cusp of adulthood and adult awareness, to the young nation of Guyana itself on the verge of moving towards maturation, to the language of the stories which invites the reader into protean worlds and experiences.

In most of the stories, the protagonists/characters are on the threshold of self-discovery. In 'Two Boys Named Basil' there is an unveiling of personality, a change in Basil Ross's behaviour after a trip to the bush (another liminal space) where he assumes the persona of his friend, the long lost Basil Raatgever: 'Behind the veil of falling water next to the vertical edge of one of the boulders, Basil Ross thought he saw a face [...] that of Basil Raatgever [...] smiling' (*Suspended Sentences*, p. 48). In the delightfully erotic 'A Lovesong for Miss Lillian', which plays on some Oedipal strains (the young man desiring his father's former lover), Raymond Rose discovers a sexual awakening in meeting the older 'courtesan' Lillian de Cunha who herself undergoes a re-awakening with Raymond. 'Still Life: Bougainvilla and Body Parts' narrates the unfolding of a daughter's artistic potential and a revelation of other dimensions of knowledge and knowing, while the painful awareness of love and betrayal is encountered in 'The Bats of Love'. A journey beyond the mundane into the magical folkloric is experienced in 'Alma Fordyce and the Bakoo' and in 'The Visitor' the story narrates a journey across the threshold of the present real into the future fantastic in a dramatisation of the dystopian nature of a Guyanese society masquerading as socialist utopian. Finally, in 'The Tyranny of Influence' the narrative takes on the transhistorical and multi-dimensional by dramatising an artist's crossing of boundaries into a conquistadorial past, to a genocidal moment perhaps, on to a present that points to a future of hope and rebirth. Hence, the idea of itineraries and crossings is crucial to the workings of McWatt's poetics in *Suspended Sentences*.

Because his collection purports to comprise stories authored by different characters, McWatt's stories contain compressed time in their various imaginative spaces. In 'Tyranny', the poetic imagination compresses almost two millenia into the small space of the short story. Story space and imaginative space become one through the deft narration of the teller, as the artist journeys back in time from late twentieth-century (postcolonial) Guyana to a Guyana five hundred years earlier, to the Palestine of the 'Dead Christ'. The law of the threshold here allows for this slippage across temporal and spatial boundaries, from the postcolonial to the Renaissance to the classical, thereby demonstrating the artificiality of all periodisation and the porousness of borders. A similar narrative feat is performed in 'Afternoon without Tears' and 'The Visitor'. Compressed time is represented in the protagonists' movements into the past and future respectively, demonstrating Bachelard's statement that 'in its countless alveoli space contains compressed time' (Bachelard, p. 8). The image of the alveolus seems ideally suited to McWatt's stories, as a recess or space that contains sources of life. In this case, the stories provide little cavities from which we look out over a large space or span of time. In 'Tyranny', the small, bounded space of the framed portrait of 'The Dead Christ, Supported by an Angel' reveals an expansion of space and time that challenges the limits of generic specifications (both that of painting and of the short story). Similarly, it is from the small, comfortable, housed space of the armchair in the lobby of the Purple Heart Hotel that Victor dream-journeys into a conquistadorial world beyond the present. Time is compressed at the same time that it is imaginatively expanded through the dream structure of the story. Here, the poet's use of the small structure to contain large, unbounded images and symbols is revealed. The poet/artist utilises the image of the alveoli, with its recesses, for the containing of time and concerns beyond the size of the form.

In turning to McWatt's use of the frame as structuring and thematic device, I begin with Mae Henderson's observation that 'the frame generates meaning through its internal arrangement of space as well as through its definition of the boundary between images'.[20] In addition, the use of the frame underscores the fact that the text, to draw again on Henderson, is 'a strategic designation [that] recognize[es] that the content cannot be fully contained within its borders' (Henderson, p. 2). Frames also allow for an examination of the tension between outside and inside and of conceptual boundary-crossings. In this collection McWatt utilises the structure of the framed-novelle[21] – an assemblage of stories linked by a frame narrative – to express formally concerns explored within his stories. One such concern is the social interaction between his storytellers, as in Boccaccio's *Decameron*. The title of the collection is indicative of an organising concept that acquires depth and resonance as the collection unfolds. While McWatt's 'Celebration' holds the inside stories together by giving the story behind the sentence that occasioned the writing of the stories, it is the framing pieces 'Introduction' and 'Remainders' that hold the collection together. Thus we can identify a frame within a frame.

But there is also a structural counterpoint between the frame or framing device and the stories themselves that is inherently dialogical. In its structural counterpointing, 'the frame perspective open[s] up the possibility for ironi[s]ing the stories' (Donovan, p. 32). This is particularly so in McWatt's collection, where the irony of stories written by a single author that feature stories purportedly written by many surrogate authors is the controlling structural and formal device. McWatt's 'Introduction' acts as a narrative occasion for the telling of the other stories, the journey of storytelling. The final piece, 'Remainders', serves a similar purpose of telling the stories or brief biographies of how the gang turned out. The stated purpose of this conclusion is 'to close the book by bringing any reader who is still interested up-to-date on the lives and fortunes of the members of the "gang" – the story-tellers' (*Suspended Sentences*, p. 245). In short then, both the 'Introduction' and 'Remainders' may be seen as stories in themselves, framing the eleven inside stories. These two framing narratives serve the rhetorical roles of introducing and closing the ceremony or itinerary of storytelling.

The final story, 'Celebration', points to the ceremonial nature of the stories in this collection, offering a forum within which its fictional authors commemorate, commiserate, communicate, and talk about, independent Guyana. 'Celebration' is really the beginning in the sense that it is here that we 'unearth' the reasons for the stories. What brought the 'gang' together? What brought the stories about? We meet the 'authors' as young people, early school leavers, budding just like their young nation. In a sense, the young people's growth is coterminous with that of their nation. There is thus a hint of the bildungsroman here. Like their nation, they are on the cusp of creativity, maturity, setting out. Each story therefore, speaks to some aspect of Guyanese history, culture and society, without being didactic. We should also note the confessional mode in this story which, in a sense, holds the other 'suspended' stories together. The 'gang' stands at a crisis-laden moment in the sense of taking on the new challenges of their new lives and in the sense that they are members of a newly independent nation trying to make its way in the world. These young people are both aware and unaware of their potentialities. (Crisis is also a moment of suspense, racked by tension and possibility.) They stand on the threshold of the new, where the new in itself is partly that of 'meaning on the way to its own self-knowledge'.[22] All of the stories in this collection draw attention to boundaries and border-crossings, journeys (whether physical or psychological), itineraries of initiation, rites of passage.

In 'The Tyranny of Influence', newness emerges in a moment of suspense or suspension (a pregnant moment filled with potentialities and possibilities) where the meeting between the postcolonial subject and the classical/neoclassical creates a heightened moment of rupture, chaos, revolution and creativity in the birth of the 'miracle' son, but also in the artistic vision in the re/turn to an ancient moment, stripped of its prior influence and invested with the power of recreation. Hence, newness may emerge at a moment of disruption, clatterings, uncertainty, chaos, movements and traffic-flows; but also in serene moments of contemplation as in Victor's dream/vision in 'Afternoon Without Tears' and in the epiphanic moment in 'Still Life: Bougainvilla and Body Parts'. In addition, 'Tyranny' narrates an event taken out of his/story by using the device of a representation of a representation – Antonello's painting of 'The Dead Christ, Supported by an Angel' creating a tension between the visual and the verbal, story and referent. This is further emphasised in the author's use of four prints of Antonello's paintings at the end of the story under the caption: 'Antonello Da Messina: Italian painter, Southern Italy school'. The prints are of: 'The Dead Christ, Supported by an Angel', 1475–78; San

Cassiano Altar, 1475–76; St Sebastian, 1476–77; and St Jerome in his Study, c. 1460. These paratexts occupy both a physical and imaginative part of the text and may be said to be liminal in this regard.

Additionally, to borrow from Michael Dash on Alejo Carpentier's writing, it may be said that in this story McWatt 'dramati[s]es the dilemma of the Caribbean artist: the fact [...] that the very need to record an image points to an absence of the real thing'.[23] The artist here faces the challenge of creating a New World epistemology – a New World way of knowing in the face of the conquistadorial violence and absences that have confronted Caribbean peoples. When he enters the world of the painting the artist not only enters 'the fallenness of history' (Dash, p. 85) – the skulls in the river, the skeletons of the Amerindian people – he also 'journeys backward toward a primal innocence' (Dash, p. 85); the birth of the man-child and the resulting naming ceremony. In a sense, then, 'Tyranny' plays on Carpentier's *The Lost Steps* (1953), but eschews the search for a utopian heartland, seen in Carpentier's protagonist. McWatt's artist is no mere copy of Carpentier's musicologist; he is less innocent, more aware of his world. Hence, there is no need here to 'mock the idea of new beginnings' that is evident in Carpentier's work (Dash, p. 84). This story also interrogates issues of representation, reception, spectatorship and reading, and suggests that for peoples of the Caribbean the new literatures may also point to new ways of reading place and identity in twenty-first-century cultural praxis. But I would suggest that McWatt's story, his entire collection perhaps, under-lines the work of art/literature as a journey, not in the linear sense, but a reversible journey, even one that spirals, towards a Caribbean aesthetics, a way of representing the worlds and experiences of the peoples of the region.

Despite the serious social commentary on post-independence Guyana, McWatt manages to cast an amused/amusing and even satirical glance at his country and its people, as in 'Uncle Umberto's Slippers', 'Alma Fordyce and the Bakoo' and 'The Visitor.' Yet, in all these stories Guyana is portrayed with intimacy where the prose more often than not reveals its most secret and mysterious side. Again in Victor's 'Afternoon without Tears' and Desmond Arthur's 'Sky' we encounter this intimacy in the journeys into the interior (as both place and imagination) where the narrator treats us to a moving description of landscape and people. McWatt's collection invites a fresh look at his native land in light of its post-independence devastation.

If, as Margaret Cohen has observed, the 'poetic function' of space in prose fiction is 'narrative – to help advance the action – as well as to convey theme and content',[24] then in the compressed aesthetics of these short stories the production of space has seen not only a wide engagement with the various issues affecting the diverse nature of Caribbean identities and epistemologies, but also the differing techniques of the writers in traversing and transgressing this restricted space. Both Dawes and McWatt thematise the destructive forces that haunt their societies – the violence of 1970s/80s Jamaica and that of the Burnham years in Guyana. But both writers have also created voices that articulate an earlier violence that, perhaps, inaugurated a chain of violence within these countries. While Dawes's collection is linked by a threnody found in his 'vershans' and by the theme of healing or recovery seen in the collection's title, McWatt's is brought together by an event and by the whole process of storytelling or storymaking, where 'the process of creating fiction becomes the focus and cohering technique of the collection'.[25] Both collections may be said to be framed within post-independence settings and to have collective protagonists. If Dawes has utilised the lyrical nature of poetry more effectively in his collection than McWatt, this may be due to his commitment to what he sees as a reggae aesthetics. McWatt, meanwhile, has drawn from wider sources and influences that include a Latin American strain found in the work of someone like Borges, for instance, whose stories also transgress the boundary between poetry and fiction. Perhaps it is the nature of the short story, more so than other literary genres, to transgress generic boundaries and display the diversity of its form. And indeed, it has been in what Gyssels and Hoving, cited at the beginning of this essay, call that '"pent-up force of Diversity", that complex concept marking our times', that we have encountered, in our twenty-first-century short fiction, the continued diversity and complex nature of Caribbean literature as it writes the new spaces into the future.

NOTES

1 Malashri Lal, *The Law of the Threshold: Women Writers in Indian English* (Shimla: Indian Institute of Advanced Study, 1995), p. 14.

2 Gaston Bachelard, *The Poetics of Space*, trans. by Maria Jolas (Boston: Beacon Press, 1969 [1964]).

3 John T. Matthews, 'Framing in Wuthering Heights', *Texas Studies in Literature and Language*, 27 (1985), pp. 25–61 (p. 26).

4 Mark McWatt, 'Preface', in *Suspended Sentences: Fictions of Atonement* (Leeds: Peepal Tree, 2005), p. v.

5 Gérard Genette, *Paratexts: Thresholds of Interpretation*, trans. by Jane E. Lewin (Cambridge: Cambridge University Press, 1997), p. 2.

6 Forrest L. Ingram, *Representative Short Story Cycles of the Twentieth Century* (The Hague: Mouton, 1971), p. 13.

7 Susan Garland Mann, *The Short Story Cycle: A Genre Companion and Reference Guide* (New York and London: Greenwood Press, 1989), p. 2.

8 James Nagel, *The Contemporary American Short Story Cycle: The Ethnic Resonance of Genre* (Baton Rouge: Louisiana State University Press, 2001), p. 15.

9 Kevin Baldeosingh, *The Ten Incarnations of Adam Avatar* (Leeds: Peepal Tree, 2004);

Colin Channer, *Passing Through* (New York: Random House, 2004).

10 Rachel Lister, 'Female expansion and Masculine Immobilization in the Short Story Cycle', *Journal of the Short Story in English*, 48 (2007), 43–58 (p. 43).

11 Kathleen Gyssels and Isabel Hoving, 'Introduction', in *Convergences and Interferences: Newness in Intercultural Practices*, ed. by Kathleen Gyssels, Isabel Hoving and Maggie Ann Bowers (Amsterdam: Rodopi, 2001), pp. 11–18 (p. 11).

12 See Charles E. May, 'Chekhov and the Modern Short Story', in *The New Short Story Theories*, ed. by Charles E. May (Athens: Ohio University Press, 1994), pp. 199–217 (p. 214).

13 Charles E. May, 'Why Short Stories are Essential and Why They are Seldom Read', in *The Art of Brevity: Excursions in Short Fiction Theory and Analysis*, ed. by Per Winther, Jakob Lothe, and Hans H. Skei (Columbia: University of South Carolina Press, 2004), pp. 14–25 (p. 18).

14 Mark McWatt, 'Suspension Bridge', in *The Language of El Dorado* (Sydney: Dangaroo Press, 1994), pp. 71–72 (p. 72).

15 Kwame Dawes, *Natural Mysticism: Towards a New Reggae Aesthetic in Caribbean Writing* (Leeds: Peepal Tree, 1999), p. 150.

16 See Kwame Dawes, *Shook Foil: A Collection of Reggae Poetry* (Leeds: Peepal Tree, 1997), p. 176.

17 Dermot McCarthy, *A Poetics of Place: The Poetry of Ralph Gustafson* (Montreal: McGill Queen's University Press, 1990), p. 3.

18 James T. Fox, 'Place and Landscape in Comparative Austronesian Perspectives', in *The Poetic Power of Place: Comparative Perspectives on Austronesian Ideas of Locality*, ed. by James T. Fox (Canberra: ANU Press, 2006), pp. 1–21 (p. 2).

19 See Sandra Pannell, 'From the Poetics of Place to the Politics of Space: Redefining Cultural Landscapes on Damer, Maluka Tenggara', in *The Poetic Power of Place: Comparative Perspectives on Austronesian Ideas of Locality,* ed. by James T. Fox (Canberra: ANU Press, 2006), pp. 163–172 (p. 165).

20 Mae Henderson, 'Introduction: Borders, Boundaries, and Frame(work)s', in *Borders, Boundaries, and Frames: Cultural Criticism and Cultural Studies* (London: Routledge, 1994), pp. 1–30 (p. 21).

21 Josephine Donovan, *Women and the Rise of the Novel, 1405–1726* (New York: St. Martin's Press, 1999), p. 29.

22 Andreas Gailus, 'Form and Chance: The German Novella', trans. by W. Martin, in *The Novel, Vol. 2: Forms and Themes,* ed. by Franco Moretti (Princeton: Princeton University Press, 2006), pp. 739–76 (p. 751).

23 J. Michael Dash, *The Other America: Caribbean Literature in a New World Context* (Charlottesville: University Press of Virginia, 1998), p. 85. He is commenting on Alejo Carpentier, *The Lost Steps*, trans. by Harriet De Onis (New York: Farrar, Straus and Giroux, 1953).

24 Margaret Cohen, 'The Chronotopes of the Sea', in *The Novel Vol. 1: History, Geography, and Culture*, ed. by Franco Moretti (Princeton: Princeton University Press, 2006, pp. 647–66 (p. 647).

25 Michael L. Storey, 'The Composite Novel: The Short Story Cycle In Transition – A Review', *Studies in Short Fiction* (1997) <http://findarticles.com/p/articles/mi_m2455/is_2_34/ai_57564381/> [accessed 19 Nov 2009].

'ANCIENT AND VERY *MODEM*': READING KAMAU BRATHWAITE'S *DREAMSTORIES*

ELAINE SAVORY

The work of Kamau Brathwaite has continually evolved, and therefore his readers have to evolve also. There are elements of his later style in even his earliest work, and of his earlier work in his most recent. His more recent poetry and poetic prose (proems) are particularly challenging, even for informed readers who have long read Brathwaite. Opal Palmer Adisa, for example, in a recently published interview with him, says of reading *Barabajan Poems* (1994): 'I have to admit [...] I'm [...] trying to *decipher* [...] I'm trying just to find the path of my way into'.[1] Brathwaite's short fiction is particularly demanding, but key to understanding his work as a whole. But these stories are key for another reason: in them Brathwaite reinvents the story. Reading Brathwaite is most successfully done with awareness of individual texts, groups of closely interrelated texts, and his work as a whole. This essay focuses most on a group of interrelated texts, but mindful of the two other levels at which we should read Brathwaite.

He began writing and publishing short fiction in the 1950s, during the period of the early *Bim*, using conventions for short fiction of the time.[2] However even these stories are unusual in that a dreamlike or non-linear quality informs them. Brathwaite went on to use poetic prose (the proem) as a major element in *Sun Poem* (1982), demonstrating that he sees no real boundaries between poetry and fiction.[3] Just as he has constantly reinvented his poetic style, especially since he adopted video style, he has constantly rethought the story.[4] There is always a story, no matter what the form it takes: what changes is that form. For example, 'The Black Angel' has been published three times, in 1955, 1994 and 2007, and each iteration is markedly different in style and tone.[5] Firstly a conventional story in form if not in content, it changes into a richly dreamlike narrative: a dreamstorie. To understand how to interpret such texts, we must consider Brathwaite's own explanation of the role and nature of his dreamstories in his creative process, as well as his remarkable conjugation of magical realism into a tool entirely suited to his own particular creative needs.

NOT FRAGMENT BUT FRACTAL

Stewart Brown remarks in his introduction to *The Oxford Book of Caribbean Short Stories* (1999) that Brathwaite's 'fractured poetic-prose in some ways serves as a kind of bridge between the anglophone and the wider Caribbean traditions'.[6] In Derek Walcott's essay, 'The Antilles: Fragments of Epic Memory', Caribbean culture is a finite object, a shattered vase needing to be glued slowly back to a whole: 'the love that reassembles the fragments is stronger than the love which took its symmetry for granted when it was whole [...]. Antillean art is this restoration of our shattered histories'.[7] But Brathwaite's apprehension of Caribbean culture has been increasingly conveyed by images of water, the most fluid of elements, most importantly through his term 'tidelect' (or 'tidalect' or 'tidelectic'), its variant iterations conveying that Caribbean culture is constantly shape-shifting, separating, recombining and reinventing its many elements.[8] It is the sea which delivers the old African gods to the shores of Caribbean islands, following the slaves whose collective spiritual imagination calls them. In Walcott's image, the vase becomes whole by loving restoration, fragments reassembled, whereas for Brathwaite, new shapes are always happening, generated out of the old.

Brathwaite has explained his progress from more conventional language to his more recent video style, an explanation which is critical for understanding the dreamstories. Of great importance are the enormous traumas he suffered between the second half of the 1980s and the first half of the 1990s. Doris, his beloved first wife and muse (whom he called Zea Mexican), died in 1986. Then Hurricane Gilbert caused great damage to his house, archives and library in Jamaica. Lastly, he had a terrifying near-death experience at the hands of thugs in Kingston, which he describes as being 'shot through my imagination' (Adisa, p. 205).

The combined effects were devastating, and prevented him from writing: 'my writing hand turn to a granite hand of silence tone' (Adisa, p. 205). He describes realising that his immediate options were '**death**, (suicide), **dumb/ness** (alzheimers or autistic), **catatonic switch-off** // (stroke or (**im**)passionate despair)'.[9] But there was one other outcome: 'I cd begin to dream. dream journey. dream serpent. dream memory. dream history. Dreamstorie...' (*MR*, p. 408).

Critical to realising this possibility was the computer, with which he began to experiment, discovering that the cursor, on an early Mac, could reinvent language through font changes. This restored his creative energies. He would come to see this new language and style (the video style) as an emanation of Sycorax, the mother of Caliban, Shakespeare's character revisioned in Brathwaite's work. Though she has been dispossessed and marginalised by colonial and racist power, for Brathwaite she is still powerful. Like another female spirit, Namsetoura (a slave woman long-buried in Barbados), she inspires the connection of the poet's creative energies to the world of the *lwa*, gods of the African diaspora.

Sycorax and Namsetoura are very important figures who represent the mother tongues of Africa suppressed during colonialism and slavery.

Sycorax appeared mysteriously in a poem in *X/Self* (1987), and has been the explicit 'muse' in the computer since.[10] Namsetoura is much more threatening: an angry spirit of a slave woman who speaks out of a bush in the poet's Barbadian yard, furious about the denial of proper burial and lack of respect from her descendants, and scornful of the poet's mixed race: *'buckra broni half-white back.site bwoy. eatin de buckra culcha.'*[11] She takes the poet back to a nation language which is born of the forced union of African languages and English in the time of the plantation.[12]

So they are *lwa*, New World African spirits: Brathwaite has long extended the term which is most closely associated with Haitian voudoun. Brathwaite sees himself led and informed by the need to find a language capable of Xpressing African diaspora history, facing the trauma of history without being oppressed by it, rather coming through to the celebration of life. That the newer work is 'ital', borrowing the Rastafarian word for proper nutritious food, 'native and community-based' (Adisa, p. 206), reminds us that he has more sustainedly employed Caribbean demotic in recent years (it was always present in some poems from the beginning). This is very evident in the dreamstories. Brathwaite explains: 'So that out of the computer itself comes this figure which begins to influence the way I actually write and form words on the page; and since sycoraX and Namsetoura are conneXed if not the same *lwa*, the new so-call experimental work is also very ital, native and community-based' (Adisa, p. 206).

Brathwaite's use of X, as in Malcolm X, makes these two powerful female spirits not only connected but conneXed through a common African diaspora experience or Xperience. The term 'experimental' bothers Brathwaite, with its vaguely scientific associations, perhaps signifying change for the sake of change. The new work is profoundly grounded in the voices of ordinary people. It is also 'the new world of dream & dreamstorie and fractal not fragment & magical realism' (Adisa, p. 206).

This choice of fractal over fragment is of major importance. Though fractal as a term derives from the Latin word fractus which means broken (fragmented), it is understood as signifying the mathematical conception of structures which vary in size but remain closely similar in structure (such as clouds). They are, however, too irregular to be described in Euclidean terms. Visual art which utilises repeating but not quite identical motifs or shapes might also be seen as fractal: strong reiterated designs in much African art and architecture could perhaps be said to be fractal also, highly relevant to Brathwaite's African-inspired work. He has employed repetition, especially of a syllable followed by a word containing that syllable, since his first trilogy, *The Arrivants* (1973),[13] echoing Akan drum language, but we can also understand this as a verbal equivalence of the fractal, as in 'fe/fe/feared' (*Dreamstories*, p. 107).

MAGICAL REALISM

Stewart Brown sees the employment of folktales, spiritual traditions and myths in Caribbean stories as a liberation from the norm of realistic narrative. He links Brathwaite and Gabriel García Márquez: both are, he says, 'magic-realist' (Brown, p. xxiii).

However, magical realism is notoriously hard to define in general, and Brathwaite revisions everything he employs in his work. Fortunately, we have his *MR*, in two volumes, in which he explores his own understanding and employment of the term, along with offering examples of its use by other writers. Like Brown, he sees it of course as an alternative to the mainly 'social realist' Caribbean literary tradition (*MR*, p. 407), and also stresses that it is often used by anglophone Caribbean writers. He lists Jamaica Kincaid, Robert Antoni, Erna Brodber, Fred D'Aguiar and Wilson Harris (*MR*, p. 407).[14] He is wisely cautious about inferring their reasons for turning to magical realism but in a key passage, he says that for him this came as a result of 'certain significant personal central disrupt/ions of cosmos, powerful enough to be catastrophe' (*MR*, p. 407).

1994, the year *Dreamstories* appeared, saw an outpouring of a new voice: including a memoir, *The Zea Mexican Diary*, a radical witness of post-traumatic writing, *Trench Town Rock*, and a poetic autobiography, *Barabajan Poems*.[15] In his introduction to the 1994 version of *Dreamstories*, Gordon Rohlehr quotes from a letter Brathwaite sent him in November 1993, in which he described the stories as 'a kind of RIFT VALLEY in my senscape after the psychic disaster slippages of Mexican (86), Shar (88) and TTR (90)'.[16] *Shar: Hurricane Poem* was written after Hurricane Gilbert, but also for the death of Brathwaite's niece, Sharon, a further traumatic loss.[17] As Rohlehr puts it, the disasters which struck seemed to Brathwaite 'the microcosmic equivalent of the geological faulting and subsidence whose result is the formation of rift valleys' (Rohlehr, p. iii). Thus the voice which emerges for this cluster of important new works is a post-catastrophe survivor's voice, changed, but still vibrantly alive.

Brathwaite has said that three dreamstories were especially critically important in his recovery from those multiple traumas: 'And so i able to etch upon that screen "4th Traveller" and "Dream Chad" and the terrible "Salvages" (which as you kno is what Shakespeare and Salt Eliot call us...)' (Adisa, p. 206).[18] '4th Traveller' (first created 1988) and 'Dream Chad' (also first created 1988) both appear in *Dreamstories* (1994). '4th Traveller' reappears in *DS (2)* (2007). It was first published in 1989 and then revised in 1993, 2003, 2004 and 2005.[19] Brathwaite notes that he worked for three days on this in July 2003. He worked all night (writing dreams without sleep) not only in July 2003, but in June 2004 and October 2005. Thus the story is a shape-shifter, and the reader needs to expect to have a different experience in reading each version, even if the actual story remains the same. By changing the presentation of the words on the page, Brathwaite simulates the way oral performance revises and recreates a known story or text. 'Salvages' appears in both the 1994 and the 2007 collections, in the latter as 'Salvage(s)'. It was first written in 1991 and revised in 1993, during what Brathwaite has called his 'time of salt'.[20] New Directions (2007) gave Brathwaite more leeway for the Xpression of the video style, and so differences lie in the visual presentation of the text, not of course a superficial or unimportant aspect of its meaning. For example, at the beginning of Part Two, in the 2004 version, we find 'The boat speed south of mankind for days' (*Dreamstories*, p. 152) and in the 2007 version, 'The lighter speed south of man//-kind for days...' (*DS (2)*, p. 228). The second version marks the separation of man and kind (kindness) which is the subject of the story, whereas the first has a poetic flow. The shift from boat to lighter provides both a practical description of a kind of boat and a sense of floating above the real world.

The changes reinforce the subject matter, which is deeply disturbing and extremely violent. This is clearly related to the torture and 'death' enacted on Brathwaite, in mid-July 1990, when he was attacked by several men who entered his apartment and tied and gagged him. One of the men pushed his gun into Brathwaite's neck and seemed to press the trigger – then he experienced the 'forever of nothing happening',[21] but he still thought he had been killed in a certain way: 'I *feel* it go through my mind, right?... I'm not the same person after this experience' (*ConVERsations*, p. 246). This is the 'ghost bullet', which severs past from future, and is one of the causes of the new way of apprehending reality, for it allows him to dream (as a member of the audience for his conversation with Nathaniel Mackey puts it) (*ConVERsations*, p. 288). The dreaming is key to the creative process continuing, for Brathwaite says if he had only written *Trench Town Rock*, which was brutally realistic, but not as he says, 'creative writing' (*ConVERsations*, p. 288), he could not have gone forward: it was the dreaming which made it possible to evade silence, and prevent the ghost bullet from being real and killing the poet (*ConVERsations*, p. 289). Thus Brathwaite's aesthetic in his dreamstories is directly related to post-traumatic recovery – not the suppression of memory, individual or collective, but the insistence of articulating what happened, however disturbing and painful.

The only vehicle suitable for this lifeline, the chance to return to creative health, was a highly inventive new style fashioned by means of the computer's particular resources, and thus literally 'postmodem'. Though video style had begun to develop in Brathwaite's work by the late 1980s in his poetry, the 'postmodem' version represents a very different aesthetic, appropriate to express what he calls the 'time of salt', the painful time of these great traumas and griefs. He almost died as a writer, and came back to life only because of the possibility of dream. Brathwaite says in *ConVERsations* that his 'very concept of writing' has changed, related to his 'revolution' into 'surrealism, if you like, or magical realism' (*ConVERsations*, p. 166):

> it's as if I'm
> gone back to the Middle Ages…and I'm trying to cre-
> create those things that they did- …Scro-
> lls? that kind of tone. And the computer gives me that oppor-
> tunity. To release the pen from the fist of my broeken hand
> and begin what I call my **'video style'**, in which I tr
> (y) to make the words themselves live off –away from– the 'pa-
> ge'…
>
> (*ConVERsations*, p. 166)

In illuminated manuscripts, the 'written word /could still *hear itself speak*', even to the extent of hieroglyphics (*ConVERsations*, p. 167). Thus the very construction of the book must change: much of Brathwaite's more recent work has been presented in large volumes, which do resemble, by size and weight, very old books monks compiled. This is a fascinating reconnection of the very ancient and the contemporary, reflecting Brathwaite's strong sense of the interrelation of the far past to the immediate present, through spiritual apprehension: old gods reappear, in new forms, and old lives inform new ones. The reference to illuminated books reminds the reader that for Brathwaite, words have magical powers, powers drawn from the *lwa* in this case. The old illustrated manuscripts, laboriously and brilliantly made into complex and lovely art works by devoted and gifted monks in Christian monasteries, are fundamentally logocentric. Brathwaite's post-modem is as contemporary as postmodernism but is not the same, any more than fractal is fragment, or tidelectic/tidalectic is dialectic.[22] Postmodem can utilise the computer to harness the energies of people oppressed by centuries of European thought and practice, without losing the power of the spiritual which brought them through unspeakable atrocities and losses.

In *MR*, Brathwaite speaks of the '**MR principle**' as '**where the surface of the txt reflexts the "magical"** (catastrophic or serene) **underground or submerged fracture of "reality" in order to catch/xpress its wound & heel/its wound and healing nature**' (*MR*, p. 431). Thus the text's appearance on the page discloses its inner actuality, whether wound (catastrophe) or healing (serene). 'Heel' seems to evoke 'wheel' or cycle, as well as 'heel', agent of motion.

This is strongly related to Brathwaite's description of magical realism as a series of stages: disruption of the cosmos, appearance of new spirits (*lwa*), to heal or redeem the catastrophe, reconstitution of fragments of catastrophe into new shapes, the invention of new artistic techniques to map all this, and finally, a '**a muse/ic of the future/culture continuum**' (*MR*, p. 452). He further makes a wonderful connection of Einstein's reading of the cosmos, the computer which enables Brathwaite's video style, and the role of the old but still powerful gods of voudoun, the *lwa*. By connecting Einstein and *MR*, Brathwaite brings together science, magic and religion, defining magical realism as the literary counterpart to Einstein's realisation of new realities in the laws of physics (certainly to lesser minds than Einstein's appearing to be remarkably magical ideas, reflecting a logic not available outside outstanding mathematical abilities). Brathwaite argues it is the *lwa* who actually teach how to read a text so that its way of seeing is understood: thus those who refuse to open themselves to these spiritual guides will not succeed in reading rightly.

Even publishers of this work have failed, he says, by baulking at producing it as he wishes. The 1994 Longman version of *Dreamstories* he refers to as 'short-cut, short-circuited' (*ConVERsations*, p. 176). *Dreamstories* is for Brathwaite 'a collection which, as I've said, you really have to *see* rather than read aloud', which has 'visual hearing', but is 'not graphics' (*ConVERsations*, p. 177). The very physical presentation of the work, then, expresses Brathwaite's post-trauma vision, 'obscured by a landslide of awesome proportions out of which it's necessary to travail' (*ConVERsations*, p. 177). But the travail is also travelling, both 'underground' and 'implosive' (*ConVERsations*, p. 177): it is work and it is journey, a kinetic process in which change occurs as the creative process goes forward.

THE EVOLUTION OF *DREAMSTORIES*

Some stories have been evolving for a very long time, such as 'The Professor', 'The Black Angel' and 'Law and Order', all originally written in the mid-1950s.[23] Brathwaite acknowledged that seven of the nine stories in the 2007 collection had been previously published (in earlier versions). Five of them appeared in the 1994 edition. The first, fourth, fifth, sixth and seventh story in the 1994 collection reappear (in revised form) as the second, seventh, fifth, eighth and ninth in the second. Two stories appear only in the first collection and four only in the second. What all this means is that the stories are not discrete entities, but happenings in language which evolve, and have previously evolved out of his poetic style. He describes his poem collection *X/Self* as the entry or 'the omen or magnet' to *Dreamstories* (*ConVERsations*, p. 165). It is not only syntax and the visual appearance of words on the page which are important in *Dreamstories*: symbols are key, both in the sense of hieroglyph, the visual mark which must be translated into concept, and as entrance to the 'underground' world of the imagination. It is also vital to remember that each story is both discrete and collective: even those which appear only once are related to the evolution of the whole in terms of style and tone, as if they were a carefully arranged poem collection.

The three versions of 'The Black Angel' (1955, 1994, 2007) provide insight into the evolution of Brathwaite's dreamstorie voice.[24] He says the germ of the story comes from a dream his mother had in the 1950s (*Dreamstories*, p. 5). Published first in *Bim* (1955), it was first an unsettling obeah story about strange negative spiritual powers associated with the leather jacket known as the 'Black Angel'. In 1955, the story was told in expected linear narrative, presented in conventional type. The language was accessible: 'Now that I think back, the first time I thought The Black Angel unusual, to say the least of it, was when I went to call on Bee' ('The Black Angel' (1955), p. 79). Brathwaite retells the story in markedly different voice, its increasing demotic tone reinforced by the type he uses. In 1994, the story ends 'But high & low/although I looked and looked/I couldn't find/poor Kappo/anywhere to tell/him what had/happened to his/ jacket' (*Dreamstories*, p. 44). But this becomes, in 2007, 'But high or low. altho I look I look/I can't find Kapp/o anywhere to tell im what had happen /to im jacket' (*DS (2)*, p. 41). In 1994, the ending of the story is in large, bold font, whereas in 2007, though the font is still bold, the type is small and the ending consists of three lines in a verse paragraph, of medium, long and short lengths, respectively. These differences are like jazz improvisations or extempore calypso, where the story is the main melody but the perform-ance is in the new phrasings and inventive musical innovations. In this way, Brathwaite moves towards words as a symbolic language, close to hieroglyph, or 'visual hearing', something he has used frequently in his recent work.[25]

READING *DREAMSTORIES*: STRATEGIES

The reader can experience a dreamstorie in one version or several. The latter is no more demanding in fact than, say, listening to three versions of a piece played by Miles Davis or John Coltrane, but we are not used to thinking of published text as such a kinetic entity. Sometimes, frustrated readers of Brathwaite ask why he couldn't simply publish on the computer, with the advantage of simultaneous visual, aural and textual resource. But to do so would destroy the ancient/modem connection: the book as sacred illuminated text.

Reading the individual text means approaching it as a proem. What it does as a text on the page, the ways in which it enacts language, are as with poetry more important than its plot or story (though that strongly contrib-utes to the emotional tone of a given text). The reader needs to enter a series of powerful allegories, metaphors and dream-images. In all these cases, meaning is strongly layered and may be contradictory. It is unstable at best, but not in the way postmodern language is unstable: rather ancient/ postmodern, full of old beliefs and ancestral connections and at the same time in a bewildering and often traumatising now, where language and people are both unnervingly mysterious.

Brathwaite's 'Dream Haiti' has appeared in whole or in part in several publications.[26] It is dedicated to David Rudder, the Trinidadian calypsonian, whose song for Haiti paid tribute to Toussaint L'Ouverture, marked the price Haiti has paid since his victory over the imperial French, and hauntingly apologised for the marginalisation and misunderstanding of Haiti in Caribbean consciousness now.[27] In 1995 and 2007, Brathwaite included a couple of verses from Rudder's song at the beginning of the story.

Brathwaite offers the idea that his first apprehension of magical realism was a visit to Haiti in 1943 (he would have been thirteen if this had happened) (MR, p. 77). Thus he constructs Haiti and voudoun and what is now his MR voice as foundational to his task as a poet/writer. The story represents the suffering of the so-called 'Haitian boat people', trying desperate means of escape from poverty in overcrowded and unseaworthy boats, often interdicted by the US coastguard. This dream is nightmare, a nightmare from which it is very hard to awaken, and in the 2007 version, Brathwaite indicates his awareness that his writing about the suffering of peoples of African descent is hard for some readers to accept: he specifically cites an English critic. Gordon Rohlehr points out the parallel in the story (2004 version) between the fate of modern-day Haitian refugees and slaves who leapt overboard to their deaths from the ships which carried them to servitude on the plantation (Rohlehr, p. xv). Thus people are turned into fish or sea creatures, asking to be fished out of the water (Dreamstories, p. 104). Brathwaite's changes in subsequent versions of this story intensify the visual and therefore also oral effect, making it more horrifying, suitable for representing a national and regional series of tragedies over a long period of time. In this, he joins other writers on Haiti. Joan Dayan says that the novels of Jacques Roumain, Jacques-Stéphen Alexis, and Marie Chauvet 'examine the causes and effects of a misery unalleviated and brutal', and in a 'landscape of loss'. She goes on to say that they mark 'the one thing that remains', namely 'the heritage of Guinea preserved in services for the gods'.[28] These gods are the lwa, which Brathwaite makes the gateway into understanding his dreamstories: at the centre of relation between the lwa and their devotees, who bring them to life, is powerful transformation through ritual. His work has always reinforced awareness of the spiritual, still such a central part of even postmodern Caribbean experience.

All the versions of 'Dream Haiti' are in first person narrative (I shall refer to the 1994 version here). A poet on the Coastguard cutter (called 'Gutter', a place which is designed to alleviate the spreading of dirt and flood by containing it in more density), experiences many confusing and painful scenes. The plot is sketchy and confusing, and needs to be read for its allegorical significance. There are other writers on board but none of them know how or why they are there and they are 'strangers/to each other': this terrible place is isolating (*Dreamstories*, p. 101). Madame Margaret Eugenia Azuchar is described by Rohlehr as signifying 'the politicians of the region' in a 'composite imperialist/colonialist allegorical figure' (*Dreamstories*, p. xv). She is equally impotent in the face of trauma, only talking in clichés (commanding heights, level playing field, light at the end of the tunnel). Brathwaite's description of a floating 'black head' is a deeply disturbing image, suggesting that living human beings are turned into fish or sea creatures, needing to be 'fished out' of the water.

When Christophe (Henri Christophe, the Haitian revolutionary leader) and Toussaint (Toussaint L'Ouverture, who led the revolution in its early success) are mentioned, they are gods, walking on water (Christophe) or a manifestation of Legba (Toussaint), but curiously ineffective, because separated from their worshippers, who are drowning. Even if some of the refugees survive, they will face more rejection in the US, from Judge Thomas (Clarence Thomas of the Supreme Court), among others. Thus the story tells of a static trauma, of being caught in a terribly painful place without the ability to help (sometimes we dream so near to consciousness that we feel paralysed from action in the dream, because our brain activity relating to motion is turned off, but we desire to move, to literally move our limbs).

'4th Traveller' was first published in 1989. It was first written in 1988, not long after Doris Brathwaite's death, and appears in both the 1994 and 2007 collections, and once again, the 2007 version is more demotic. The story opens in 2004 with 'About four weeks after Mexican died, four of us was delivering canes in a cart into the depths of the black country. Everything went well until we reach like this village of the dead' (*Dreamstories*, p. 80). In 2007, this has changed to 'About four weeks after Zea Mexican dead. Three of us was delivering canes in a cart into the depths of the black country. Evvathing went well until we reach like this village of the dead' (*DS (2)*, p. 132). Zea Mexican was the name Brathwaite gave to his first wife, Doris, who died in 1986. That he gives the full name in the 2007 version makes the connection between this story and *The Zea Mexican Diary* more definite and manifest to the reader. Changing the number of people from four to three makes the numerical symbolism of the Chinese divination, I Ching, to which the title refers, also more explicit, for it works with both four and three.[29] The ideogram is first displayed in the opening of *The Zea Mexican Diary* (1993). Brathwaite's version of the explanation of the ideogram is interesting: he 'reads' it more starkly, and with less balance between yin and yang. However the details are decoded, it is helpful to read this story in conjunction with the I Ching as well as *Zea Mexican*, for whilst the details are different (the strong theme of guilt and repentance of the I Ching passages in *Zea Mexican* is absent), the story, like both of these texts, reflects an arduous journey through testing and often painful obstacles. But whereas both the I Ching and *Zea Mexican* conclude with cautious optimism, in '4th Traveller', the narrator becomes foreman of the dead village, digging 'yr graves in the game of yr luck or yr **warri**' (*Dreamstories*, p. 92), in short an ominous figure who has joined the deathliness he once fled. The I Ching is also important in another sense: reading it demands the suspension of logic and linear thinking, much as reading Brathwaite's dreamstories requires.

The travellers come across a sinister group of men playing draughts and dominoes, games popular among men in the Caribbean, and sense they are not welcome. But (as in a dream, where things change shape and meaning) they realise the game being played is warri, the ancient strategic combat played by moving seeds and capturing those of the opponent. The travellers feel threatened. Indeed, three 'atts' sound in the narrator's head, recalling the two 'shatts' which announce the violence at Marley Manor in *Trench Town Rock* (p. 9). This is the village of the dead and wants no contact with the living. Rohlehr identifies the threatening figures as a combination of Brathwaite's colleagues, neighbours and friends after the loss of Doris, when grief was intensely alienating (Rohlehr, p. xiv). Rohlehr tries to explain the autobiographical backstory of the dream, enduring intensely painful self-immolating grief, and when one of the travellers dies as they flee, he says this may be the death of the old persona Edward Brathwaite, who is henceforth only Kamau Brathwaite (Rohlehr, p. xv). But much as Rohlehr is always insightful, this seems a move to interpret which is not sufficiently multilayered and tempts the unwary reader to make direct equivalences between Brathwaite's life and his text. The travellers flee. Then the scene changes to Zea Mexican's dying, and to the death of the 4th traveller, who is male. As the story closes, he is sitting in the village of the dead, 'digging yr graves in the game of luck or yr **warri**' (*Dreamstories*, p. 92). In 2007, the last passage makes clear that the 4th traveller is of indeterminate gender and the reference to 'his dreams' (2004), turns into 'her dreams', so that the missing 4th person might be Mexican. Once more, we realise the dreamstorie, in its progress through versions, teaches us to read for the changes and transformations which gradually make the dreaming fathomable if not rational.

'Dream Chad' and 'Dream Crabs' are only in the 1994 collection and 'The Professor', 'Law and Order', 'Meridiam' and 'My funny Valentine' only in 2007. Dream Chad is the female muse and love of the poet in his period of deepest trauma, and as Rohlehr points out, is by her name recognised as 'the highly idealised essence of African womanhood' (Rohlehr, p. xi). She draws the poet back to life and writing from the catatonic state of grief and fear. The story begins with a letter to the reader, 'DearReader+' (*Dreamstories*, p. 47). This explains that the poet was at Harvard, and that this was the third dreamstorie to be written. His first attempt, written on a Harvard computer, vanishes. Eventually, he discovers that the computer knows someone else is using the dream, so he must cease to work on it. His response is to get another computer by means of which he succeeds in completing and printing his story. But then Hurricane Gilbert, like some perverse god, rises up out of the sea and moves towards Jamaica. After the storm, Chad healingly salvages much of his work and possessions.

The actual story is about Chad appearing in Harvard Yard, or at least a woman who resembles her, rousing the poet from his trauma by her sensual and gracious presence. He sees her walking beyond 'the rail/ings' (*Dreamstories*, p. 53). Railings have an important role in 'The Black Angel', and in the 2007 story, the narrator says 'I am to see these same railings taller in a storie call "Dream<<Chad". But that's past in another storie' (*DS (2)*, p. 19), signifying that readers are to see the boundaries between different stories and collections as porous. Brathwaite's stories are not hermetically sealed from each other so can be read as one continuous text in some ways. 'Dream Chad' is in the 1994 collection (right after 'The Black Angel'), but not in the 2007 one, therefore 'past'. It is a love story, about the struggle to recover from loss and pain.

'Dream Crabs' is very short, and describes River Bay, an actual place in Barbados where the sea crashes through a channel it has made between high coral rock walls and finally settles into a narrow rush of water, a small river leading away from the sea. In the dream, crabs are everywhere, and then Bessie Smith appears to keep company with the narrator, though since the narrator has never seen her face, she may be someone else, just as Barbados is confused with St. Lucia. Reading these stories requires resisting the impulse to have them 'make sense', rather approaching them as poems or proems, through their play with language and their vivid images.

The ordering of the stories is also an interesting aspect of their interpretation.

The 2007 contents page groups the nine stories into three sections, with 'The Professor', 'The Black Angel' and 'Law and Order' first. 'The Professor' represents an interaction between the famous literary couple, F.R. and Queenie Leavis, and the narrator, in Cambridge; and in 'Law and Order' a young couple, the woman local and the man foreign, try to find a space for a love tryst in Ghana, running up against local custom. Brathwaite went to Cambridge for his first degree, and lived in Ghana for the best part of a decade.

In the second section are 'Meridiam', 'Grease' and 'My funny Valentine'.

'Meridiam' is about a lovely moonlit night in Harvard, Boston, as the narrator listens to a programme on BBC radio, and sees two planes seemingly flying together towards Logan airport, which is his dream-state seem like 'planetary bodies' (DS (2), p. 91). The night is a place where dreams are available, but as morning comes, the narrator must try to 'wrestle these words back to dream' (DS (2), p. 101). 'Grease' is a disturbing story about domestic abuse and infidelity. It begins with a menacing image, of dark green 'water of the mirror in the room', in the shape of an island, perhaps Trinidad or Virgin Gorda (DS (2), p. 105). When one of the characters, a plumber, recognises 'so much pollution' in his heart, it is 'darkening frills of water' (DS (2), p. 112). He exploits his wife physically, without love, and she sees their sexual life as a 'yellow and entangling vine' (there is a common Caribbean plant called a 'love vine'), and her husband as 'contaminating' (DS (2), p. 115). She encourages a lover in the same room she shares with her husband, with its 'map of green lake on the wall' (DS (2), p. 119). 'My funny Valentine' represents sexual arousal, in a dream state, where it is impossible to find sexual fulfillment, perhaps because the woman dreamed of is dead, 'the brown daemon eyes of the once/was my di./was my die./ was my di/-amond darling' (DS (2), p. 127).

The third and final section of DS (2) contains '4th Traveller', 'Dream Haiti' and what is now titled 'Salvage(s)' (in 1994, it was titled 'Salvages'). These are all about extremely traumatic, deathly situations, in which the narrators both witness and directly experience threats, or violence or the after effects of violence. 'Dream Haiti' begins with an image of the sea as 'slake grey', as the narrator says, 'of what was left of my body' (DS (2), p. 159). Those who die in the attempt to escape Haiti in our times recall those who died when thrown from slave ships. Thus this trio of stories are the most difficult in the whole volume, representing the trauma they depict in the degree of their impenetrability and nightmarish illogicality.

But once again, they respond to a patient and careful reading which explores their vivid, often arresting images, their hieroglyphics and their emotional tension. They are heartbreakingly elegiac and tormented. In '4th Traveller', a group of characters are pursued, fearful of the sound of dogs and of 'the plot against us' and 'those threshers try/-ing to destroy us' (DS (2), p. 143). In 'Dream Haiti', the narrator is on a ship, where 'there was rapes neatly coiled' (DS (2), p. 175), a reference to the sexual violence inflicted on slaves. In 'Salvage(s)', a character called Gareth, the narrator's 'twin', tears the penis off a man, bites it, swallows some of it and throws the head away, 'the way you wd toss /-way a dead eel or fish head' (DS (2), p. 236). These stories enter a hellish place where the cruelty and destruction which humankind practise on one another and the world is all encompassing and brutalises language itself in the telling.

Brathwaite's dreamstories are highly surreal, told in an intensely kinetic style. The dreamstories, often thought of as an aside from his poetry or cultural essays, are a key entry into his work, for learning to read them effectively provides tools for reading the whole of Brathwaite's work, which is best approached both on the level of the single text and as a body of strongly intertextual texts. Caribbean (creole) cultures and languages are constantly being reinvented to meet new challenges and new times, without destroying long held words and phrases, linking to the past, and Brathwaite's style in the dreamstories heightens this familiar process. They are therefore also a key way of understanding the Caribbean through his innovative reinvention of the ancient art of storytelling in postmodern style.

WORKS BY KAMAU BRATHWAITE

Please note that Brathwaite published as Edward Brathwaite for his first trilogy and Edward Kamau Brathwaite for his second, but since he has published as Kamau Brathwaite, and that is the name listed below.

Brathwaite, Kamau, 'Ancestories', *Caribbean Quarterly*, n.d., 32–78
____ *Barabajan Poems* (New York: Savacou North, 1994)
____ 'The Black Angel', *Bim*, 6:22 (1955), 79–87; *Dreamstories* pp. 4–45; *DS (2)* pp. 14–42
____ *Born to Slow Horses* (Middletown: Wesleyan University Press, 2005)
____ *ConVERsations with Nathaniel Mackey* (New York: We Press, 1999)
____ 'Dream Chad', in *Dreamstories*, pp. 46–73
____ 'Dream Crabs', in *Dreamstories*, pp. 74–77
____ 'Dream Haiti', in *Dreamstories*, pp. 94–111; *DS (2)*, pp. 155–202
____ *Dream Haiti* (New York: Savacou North, 1995)
____ *Dreamstories* (Burnt Mill: Longman, 1994)
____ *DS (2) Dreamstories* (New York: New Directions, 2007)
____ '4th Traveller', in *Dreamstories*, pp. 78–93; *DS (2)*, pp. 131–54.
____ *Golokwati 2000* (New York: Savacou North, 2002)
____ 'Grease', in *Dreamstories* (Burnt Mill: Longman, 1994), pp. 112–33; *DS (2)*, pp. 103–21
____ 'History of the Voice', in *Roots* (Ann Arbor: University of Michigan Press, 1993), pp. 259–304
____ 'Law and Order', in *DS (2)*, pp. 43–81
____ 'Meridiam', *DS (2)*, pp. 85–102.
____ *MR* (New York: Savacou North, 2002)
____ 'My funny Valentine', *DS (2)*, pp. 122–27
____ 'Namsetoura', in *Born to Slow Horses*, pp. 118–22
____ 'Salvages', *DS (2)*, pp. 134–76; as 'Salvage(s)', *DS (2)*, pp. 203–65
____ *Shar: The Hurricane Poem* (Mona: Savacou, 1990)
____ *Sun Poem* (Oxford: Oxford University Press, 1982)
____ 'The Professor', in *DS (2)*, pp. 3–13
____ *The Zea Mexican Diary* (Madison: University of Wisconsin Press, 1993)
____ *Trench Town Rock* (Providence: Lost Roads, 1994)
____ *X/Self* (Oxford: Oxford University Press, 1987)

NOTES

1 Opal Palmer Adisa, 'Walking on Water: A ConVERsation with Kamau Brathwaite', *The Caribbean Writer*, 23 (2009), 92–216 (p. 209); *Barabajan Poems* (New York: Savacou North, 1994).

2 The famous literary journal founded in 1942 in Barbados, which gave Caribbean writers a publishing outlet (including Brathwaite, George Lamming, Samuel Selvon and many others). It has recently been brought back to life, publishing new work but also reprinting some of the most important pieces from its early days (*Bim* (revived series) November 2007–, Barbados: University of the West Indies).

3 *Sun Poem* (Oxford: Oxford University Press, 1982) reads in part like a highly poetic novel, but at the time when Brathwaite began to publish, social realist fiction was the dominant mode in the anglophone Caribbean. Some anglophone Caribbean novelists of his generation, such as George Lamming and Wilson Harris, began as poets, and their fiction should be read with an awareness of poetics. Both have been less popularly read than more socially realist writers such as V.S. Naipaul, Samuel Selvon or Paule Marshall.

4 I have mostly not attempted to reproduce video style with its wonderfully meaningful fonts, despite the importance of this in reading the stories. In effect, the fonts deliver a score for the voice, and the reader aware of this (willing to read aloud, for example), will apprehend the stories on this level without trouble. I recommend that the reader of this essay return to Brathwaite's original score/text whenever I quote from his work.

5 *Bim*, 6:22 (June 1955), 79–87; *Dreamstories* (Burnt Mill: Longman, 1994), 4–45; *DS (2) Dreamstories* (New York: New Directions, 2007), 14–42.

6 Stewart Brown, 'Introduction', in *The Oxford Book of Caribbean Short Stories*, ed. by Stewart Brown and John Wickham (Oxford: Oxford University Press, 1999), pp. xiii–xxxiii (p. xxv).

7 Derek Walcott, 'The Antilles: Fragments of Epic Memory', in *What the Twilight Says* (New York: Farrar, Straus and Giroux, 1998), pp. 65–84 (p. 69).

8 *Barabajan Poems* (p. 114) builds on a lovely passage in *Sun Poem* (p. 3), adding the concept of tidelect, which shifts into tidelectic, reflecting the complex interaction of waves at the water's edge, continuously fusing and separating, opposing and combining. This is Brathwaite's answer to 'dialectic'.

9 Kamau Brathwaite, *MR* (New York: Savacou North, 2002), p. 408.

10 Edward Kamau Brathwaite, *X/Self* (Oxford: Oxford University Press, 1987).

11 Kamau Brathwaite, 'Namsetoura', in *Born to Slow Horses* (Middletown: Wesleyan University Press, 2005), pp. 118–22 (p. 120).

12 Brathwaite heard that the land where his house stands at Cow Pastor in Barbados was once a slave graveyard. There were so many slaves in Barbados over such a long time that there ought to be many large graveyards, at least after slaves were allowed to become Christian. We have to assume that since hardly any have been found, they were deliberately or thoughtlessly built over, or slaves were not buried in collective spaces, but perhaps under the floors of slave houses, a tradition known in West Africa. What this means is that a home today might very well be standing on the bones of slaves and Brathwaite's powerful poem dramatises this very well.

13 Kamau Brathwaite, *The Arrivants* (Oxford: Oxford University Press, 1973.

14 The odd one out here is Jamaica Kincaid, who is often thought poetic but not usually magical realist. But bringing an expectation of the non-linear and fantastical helps avoid the mistaken reductiveness of a closely biographical reading of her fiction.

15 Kamau Brathwaite, *The Zea Mexican Diary* (Madison: University of Wisconsin Press, 1993); *Trench Town Rock* (Providence: Lost Roads, 1994).

16 Gordon Rohlehr, 'Dream Journeys', in *Dreamstories* (Burnt Mill: Longman, 1994), pp. iii–xvi (p. iii).

17 Kamau Brathwaite, *Shar: The Hurricane Poem* (Mona: Savacou, 1990).
18 Kamau Brathwaite, '4ᵗʰ Traveller', 'Dream Chad', and 'Salvages', in *Dreamstories*,
   pp. 78–93; 46–73; 134–76. Kamau Brathwaite has informed me that some versions
   of *The Tempest* term Caliban a 'salvage' (avoiding 'savage'). Stephen Orgel, in his
   introduction to the play, notes that 'salvage' was a variant form of spelling for
   'savage', and the former was the usual version used by Ralph Crane who prepared
   the text of the play for the press (William Shakespeare, *The Tempest*, ed. by Stephen
   Orgel (Oxford: Oxford University Press, 1994), p. 26). Brathwaite terms T.S.
   Eliot 'salt' Eliot because of the strong presence of the sea: he points out that both
   Eliot and Robert Lowell had a strong connection with the North Atlantic coast,
   and the sea permeates their work. Eliot's 'The Dry Salvages' from *Four Quartets*
   begins with the note that the small group of rocks called 'The Dry Salvages', off
   Cape Ann, Massachussetts, was presumably first called 'Les Trois Salvages' (T.S.
   Eliot, 'Dry Salvages' [1936], in *Collected Poems* (London: Faber & Faber, 1974),
   pp. 205–13). Brathwaite's practice in linking words of similar sound but highly
   different meanings draws attention to the very arbitrariness of language, and also
   to the importance of the voice in making interpretation possible. Before written
   texts became dominant, spelling was not consistent. Brathwaite's orality makes
   us sensitive to the power of the human voice as a key cognitive tool, as in his essay,
   'History of the Voice' (*Roots* (Ann Arbor: University of Michigan Press, 1993),
   pp. 259–04). Brathwaite's recent titling of 'Salvages' as 'Salvage(s)' (2007) marks
   emphasis on eruptions of human brutality through the very splitting of the word.
19 Brathwaite includes publication and revision details for each story in *DS (2)*.
20 Kamau Brathwaite, *Golokwati 2000* (New York: Savacou North, 2002), p. 200.
21 Kamau Brathwaite, *ConVERsations with Nathaniel Mackey* (New York: We Press,
   1999), p. 246.
22 Brathwaite employs variant spellings, 'tidelect'(ic) and tidalect(ic), the first bringing
   the Caribbean Sea to mind and the second Hegel's dialectic.
23 'The Professor', 'The Black Angel' and 'Law and Order' are all included in *DS
   (2)*, but in revised form (pp. 3–13, pp. 14–42, pp. 43–81).
24 See note 5 for publication history for 'The Black Angel'.
25 Brathwaite points out that the oral tradition is not only heard but witnessed in
   terms of its performance (*Barabajan Poems*, p. 224). This is 'visual hearing' also.
26 This is particularly poignant in this moment after the catastrophic earthquake
   (January 2010), which has brought a pan-Caribbean humanitarian response marking
   hopefully the dawning of a new unity of purpose across the Caribbean.
27 David Rudder, 'Haiti', *The Gilded Collection 1986–1989*.
28 Joan Dayan, *Haiti, History and the Gods* (Berkeley: University of California Press,
   1998), p. 79.
29 Thomas Cleary's translation of the three-thousand-year-old I Ching, eventually
   annotated by Confucius centuries later, begins with his advice that there are two
   modes, the yin and the yang. The former signifies flexibility, weakness, stillness,
   passivity, sadness, depression and the latter, firmness, strength, movement, activity,
   happiness and elation (Thomas Cleary (trans.), *I Ching: The Book of Change* (Boston:
   Shambhala, 1992), p. xii), but whereas the former is feminine and the latter masculine,
   these are not to be associated with gender, or simplistically with good or bad. Yin
   and Yang each have a major and minor mode, and as trigrams (3 lines), major
   yang is associated with sky and lake, and yin with thunder and fire, and minor
   yin with earth and mountain, minor yang with water and wind (*I Ching*, p. xiii).
   Each of these have symbolic attributes (lake is strength or creativity, for example).
   But the application of the hexagrams is individual and personal. It is clear that
   Brathwaite has interpreted the hexagram as a poem.

BIBLIOGRAPHY

This is by no means a comprehensive bibliography of the Caribbean short story and its criticism, but rather a list of stories and critical texts referred to in this volume. For an excellent and more extensive resource, see Hyacinth M. Simpson, 'Bibliography of Anglophone Caribbean Short Stories', Journal of West Indian Literature, *12 (2004): 204-213.*

SELECTED SHORT STORIES AND COLLECTIONS (SINGLE-AUTHOR)

Aarons, R.L.C., 'The Cow That Laughed', *Life and Letters*, 57 (1948), pp. 50–57
____ 'The Road from St. Thomas', in *The Cow That Laughed and Other Stories* (Kingston, Jamaica: Kingston Printers, 1944)
Antoni, Robert, *My Grandmother's Erotic Folktales* (London: Faber & Faber, 2000)
Anthony, Michael, *Cricket in the Road* (London: Heinemann, 1973)
Baksh, Elahi, 'The Propagandist', in *Jahaji: An Anthology of Indo-Caribbean Fiction*, ed. by Birbalsingh (Toronto: TSAR, 2000), pp. 15–30
Baldeosingh, Kevin, *The Ten Incarnations of Adam Avatar* (Leeds: Peepal Tree, 2004)
Brathwaite, Kamau, *Born to Slow Horses* (Middletown: Wesleyan University Press, 2005)
____ *Dream Haiti* (New York: Savacou North, 1995)
____ *Dreamstories* (Burnt Mill: Longman, 1994)
____ *DS (2) Dreamstories* (New York: New Directions, 2007)
____ 'The Black Angel', *Bim*, 6:22 (1955), 79–87
Channer, Colin, *Passing Through* (New York: Random House, 2004)
Chen, Willi, 'Trotters', in *The Oxford Book of Caribbean Short Stories*, ed. by Stewart Brown and John Wickham (Oxford: Oxford University Press, 1999), pp. 288–91
Crichlow, Marina, 'Cane Harvest Barren', BBC *Caribbean Voices* manuscript broadcast 19 May 1957
Danticat, Edwidge, *The Dew Breaker* (New York: Knopf, 2004)
Dawes, Kwame, *A Place to Hide and Other Stories* (Leeds: Peepal Tree, 2003)
Deonandan, Raywat, *Sweet Like Saltwater* (Toronto: TSAR, 1999)
Ferré, Rosario, 'When Women Love Men', trans. by Cynthia Ventura, in *The Oxford Book of Caribbean Short Stories*, ed. by Brown and Wickham, pp. 257–69
Figueroa, John, 'Ars Longa; Vita Brevis', in *West Indian Stories*, ed. by Andrew Salkey (London: Faber & Faber, 1960), pp. 207–21
Gilroy, Beryl, *Sunlight on Sweet Water* (Leeds: Peepal Tree, 1994)
Hall, Stuart, 'Crossroads Nowhere', in *West Indian Stories*, ed. by Salkey, pp. 186–88
Hill, Frank A, 'Toss Away the Old', *Public Opinion*, 27 December 1937, p. 5
Hopkinson, Nalo, *Skin Folk* (New York: Warner Aspect, 2001)
Howland, Cicely, *The Long Run* (London: Victor Gollancz, 1961)
James, C.L.R., 'La Divina Pastora', *The Saturday Review* [Trinidad] (1927). Reprinted in C.L.R. James, *Spheres of Existence: Selected Writings* (London: Allison and Busby, 1980), pp. 5–8
____ 'Triumph', in *The Oxford Book of Caribbean Short Stories*, ed. by Brown and Wickham, pp. 35–49
Keens-Douglas, Paul, *Is Town Say So!* (Port of Spain: Keensdee Productions, 1981)
____ *Role Call: Poetry and Short Stories by Paul Keens-Douglas* (Port of Spain: Keensdee Productions, 1997)
Khan, Ismith, *A Day in the Country: And Other Stories* (Leeds: Peepal Tree, 1994)
Lahens, Yanick, *La folie était venue avec la pluie* (Port-au-Prince: Presses Nationales d'Haïti, 2006)
____ *La petite corruption* (Port-au-Prince: Mémoire, 1999)

____ *Tante Résia et les Dieux, nouvelles d'Haïti* (Paris: L'Harmattan, 1994)

Lindo, Archie, *Bronze* (Jamaica: College Press, 1945)

____ *My Heart Was Singing* (Jamaica: College Press, 1945)

Lovelace, Earl, *A Brief Conversion and Other Stories* (Oxford: Heinemann, 1988)

Mais, Roger, *Listen, the Wind and Other Stories* (Harlow: Longman, 1986)

____ 'Tig', *Public Opinion*, 12 April 1941, pp. 8–10

____ 'You've Gotta Go Home', *Public Opinion*, 10 September 1949, p. 6

Markham, E.A., *Taking the Drawing Room through Customs: Selected Stories 1972–2002* (Leeds: Peepal Tree, 2002)

McKay, Claude, *Gingertown* (Freeport, NY: Books for Libraries, 1972 [1932])

McKenzie, Earl, 'Cricket Season', in *A Boy Named Ossie – A Jamaican Childhood* (Oxford: Heinemann, 1991), pp. 19–24

McWatt, Mark, *Suspended Sentences: Fictions of Atonement* (Leeds: Peepal Tree, 2005)

Melville, Edwina, 'Fishing in the Rupununi Savannah, British Guiana', BBC *Caribbean Voices* manuscript broadcast Sunday 9 August 1953

____ 'The Voice', BBC *Caribbean Voices* manuscript broadcast Sunday 20 June 1954

____ 'Tikerish-Din, The Fire Tiger', BBC *Caribbean Voices* manuscript broadcast Sunday 18 September 1955

Melville, Pauline, *Shape-shifter* (London: Picador, 1991 [1990])

____ *The Migration of Ghosts* (London: Bloomsbury, 1999 [1998])

Monar, Rooplall, *Backdam People* (Leeds: Peepal Tree, 1987)

Naipaul, Seepersad, *Gurudeva and other Indian Tales* (Port of Spain: Trinidad Publications, 1943)

____ *The Adventures of Gurudeva and Other Stories* (London: Andre Deutsch, 1976)

Naipaul, V.S., *A Way in the World* (London: Vintage, 2001 [1994])

____ *Miguel Street* (London: Heinemann, 2000 [1959])

Ogilvie, W.G., 'The Cottage Concert', *Life and Letters*, 57 (1948), pp. 144–48

____ 'The Great Kranjie', in *14 Jamaican Short Stories* (Kingston: Pioneer Press, 1950)

Reid, Victor, 'Dead Drunk', *Focus* (1948), 61–67

____ 'Digging Match', *Focus* (1948), 48–51

____ 'Pattern', *Focus* (1948), 52–56

____ 'Waterfront Bar', *Focus* (1948), 56–61

Rhys, Jean, *The Collected Short Stories* (New York and London: W.W. Norton, 1992)

____ *The Left Bank and Other Stories* (New York: Books for Libraries Press, 1970 [1927])

Salkey, Andrew, *Anancy's Score* (London: Bogle-L'Ouverture, 1973)

____ *Anancy, Traveller* (London: Bogle-L'Ouverture, 1992)

____ *The One: The Story of How the People of Guyana Avenge the Murder of their Pasero with help from Brother Anancy and Sister Buxton* (London: Bogle-L'Ouverture, 1985)

Scott, Lawrence, *Ballad for the New World and Other Stories* (Oxford, UK and Portsmouth, NH: Heinemann, 1994)

Senior, Olive, *Arrival of the Snake-Woman and Other Stories* (Harlow: Longman, 1989)

____ *Summer Lightning and Other Stories* (Harlow: Longman, 1992 [1986])

Shirley, Maureen, 'The Thirteenth Step', *Daily Gleaner*, 5 September 1951, p. 8

____ 'Thou Fool', *Daily Gleaner*, 10 July 1951, p. 6

Sibley, Inez K., 'A Case in Court', *Daily Gleaner*, 25 February 1939, p. 35

____ *Quashie's Reflections in Jamaican Creole* (Jamaica: Bolívar Press, 1968)

____ 'The Terror Bull and Taunt Song', *Focus* (1956), pp. 60–67

Thompson, Claude, *These My People* (Kingston, Jamaica: The Herald Printers, 1943)

Walrond, Eric, 'On Being Black' [1922], in *'Winds Can Wake Up the Dead': An Eric Walrond Reader*, ed. by Louis J. Parascondola (Detroit: Wayne State University Press, 1998), pp. 76–80

____ 'The Voodoo's Revenge' [1925], in *'Winds Can Wake Up the Dead': An Eric Walrond Reader*, ed. by Parascandola, pp. 94–103

____ *Tropic Death* [1926] (New York: Collier, 1972)

____ 'Vignettes of the Dusk' [1924], in *'Winds Can Wake Up the Dead': An Eric Walrond Reader*, ed. by Parascandola, pp. 90–93

Wynter, Sylvia, 'Paramour', BBC *Caribbean Voices* manuscript broadcast 25 November 1956

Selected Anthologies (multi-author)

Beckwith, Martha Warren, *Jamaica Anansi Stories* (New York: American Folk-lore Society, 1924)

Behar, Ruth, and Mirta Yáñez, eds, *Cubana: Contemporary Fiction by Cuban Women* (Boston: Beacon Press, 1998)

Bennett, Louise, *Anancy Stories and Poems in Dialect* (Kingston, Jamaica: Gleaner, 1944)

Berg, Mary, ed., *Open Your Eyes and Soar: Cuban Women Writing Now* (Buffalo, NY: White Pine Press, 2003)

Birbalsingh, Frank, ed., *Jahaji: An Anthology of Indo-Caribbean Fiction* (Toronto: TSAR, 2000)

Bobes, Marilyn, ed., *Cuentistas cubanas de hoy* (Mexico: Océano, 2002)

Brown, Stewart, ed., *Caribbean New Wave: Contemporary Short Stories* (London: Heinemann, 1990)

Brown, Stewart, and John Wickham, eds, *The Oxford Book of Caribbean Short Stories* (Oxford: Oxford University Press, 1999)

Cámara, Madeline, ed., *La memoria hechizada: Escritoras cubanas* (Barcelona: Icaria, 2003)

del Llano, Eduardo, ed., *Voces cubanas: Jóvenes cuentistas de la isla* (Madrid: Editorial Popular, 2005)

Esteves, Carmen C., and Lizabeth Paravisini-Gebert, eds, *Green Cane and Juicy Flotsam: Short Stories by Caribbean Women* (New Brunswick: Rutgers University Press, 1991)

Fornet, Jorge, and Carlos Espinosa, eds, *Cuento cubano del siglo XX* (Mexico: Fondo de Cultura Económica, 2002)

Glave, Thomas, ed., *Our Caribbean: A Gathering of Lesbian and Gay Writing from the Antilles* (Durham, NC: Duke University Press, 2008)

Hernández Miyares, Julio E., ed., *Narrativa y libertad: Cuentos cubanos de la diáspora* (Miami: Ediciones Universal, 1996)

Hopkinson, Nalo, ed., *Whispers from the Cotton Tree Root: Caribbean Fabulist Fiction* (Montpelier, VT: Invisible Cities Press, 2000)

López Sacha, Francisco, ed., *La isla contada: El cuento contemporáneo en Cuba* (Donostia: Tercera Prensa, 1996)

Markham, E.A., ed., *The Penguin Book of Caribbean Short Stories* (London: Penguin, 1996)

Mordecai, Pamela, and Betty Wilson, eds, *Her True-True Name: An Anthology of Women's Writing from the Caribbean* (London: Heinemann, 1990)

Obejas, Achy, ed., *Havana Noir* (New York: Akashic, 2007)

Prescott, Lynda, ed., *A World of Difference: An Anthology of Short Stories from Five Continents* (Basingstoke: Palgrave Macmillan, 2008)

Ramchand, Kenneth, ed., *Best West Indian Stories* (Kingston: Nelson Caribbean, 1982)

____ *West Indian Narrative: An Introductory Anthology* (London: Nelson Caribbean, 1966)

Redonet, Salvador, ed., *El ánfora del diablo: novísimos cuentistas cubanos* (Veracruz: Instituto Veracruzano de Cultura, 1996)

____ *Para el siglo que viene: (post)novísmos narradores cubanos* (Zaragoza: Prensas Universitarias, 1999)

Reid, Vic, et al, *14 Jamaican Short Stories* (Kingston, Jamaica: Pioneer Press, 1950)

Riverón, Rogelio M., ed., *Cuentos cubanos contemporáneos: La línea que cruza el agua* (Caracas: Monte Avila Ediciones Latinoamericana, 2006)

Salkey, Andrew, ed., *Caribbean Prose: An Anthology for Secondary Schools* (London: Evan Brothers, 1967)

____ *Stories from the Caribbean* (London: Paul Elek, 1965)

____ *West Indian Stories* (London: Faber & Faber, 1960)

Sander, Reinhard, and Peter K. Ayers, eds, *From Trinidad: An Anthology of Early West Indian Writing* (New York: Africana Pub. Co., 1978)

Shor, Jacqueline, ed., *Nueva narrativa cubana* (Santiago: RIL Editores, 2003)

Strausfeld, Michi, ed., *Nuevos narradores cubanos* (Madrid: Ediciones Siruela, 2000)

Tanna, Laura, ed., *Jamaican Folktales and Oral Histories* (Miami: DLT Associates, 2000 [1984])

Valle, Amir, ed., *Caminos de Eva: Voces desde la isla: Cuentistas cubanas de hoy* (Puerto Rico: Editorial Plaza Mayor, 2002)

Waters, Erika J., ed., *New Writing from the Caribbean: Selections from the* Caribbean Writer (London: Macmillan Caribbean, 1994)

Whitfield, Esther, and Jacqueline Loss, eds, *New Short Fiction From Cuba* (Evanston, IL: Northwestern University Press, 2007)

SELECTED SHORT STORY CRITICISM

Alvarez IV, José B., 'El cuento cubano de 1959 a 1990: Un movimiento pendular', *Southeastern Latin Americanist*, 43:3 (2000), 21–36

____ '(Re)escritura de la violencia: El individuo frente a la historia en la cuentística novísima cubana', *Chasqui*, 26:2 (1997), 84–93

Balogun, F. Odun, *Tradition and Modernity in the African Short Story: An Introduction to a Literature in Search of Critics* (New York: Greenwood, 1991)

Bardolph, Jacqueline, ed., *Telling Stories: Postcolonial Short Fiction in English* (Amsterdam and Atlanta, GA: Rodopi, 2001)

Bennett, Bruce, *Australian Short Fiction: A History* (Santa Lucia: University of Queensland Press, 2002)

Birbalsingh, Frank, 'The Indo-Caribbean Short Story', *Journal of West Indian Literature* 12:1&2 (2004), 118–35

Bone, Robert, *Down Home: A History of Afro-American Short Fiction from its Beginning to the End of the Harlem Renaissance* (New York: Putnam, 1975)

Brown, Stewart, 'Introduction', in *The Oxford Book of Caribbean Short Stories*, ed. by Brown and Wickham, pp. xiii–xxxiii

Davidson, Jeremy H.C.S., and Helen Cordell, eds, *The Short Story in South East Asia: Aspects of a Genre* (London: SOAS, 1982)

Dubois, Dominique, and Jeanne Devoize, 'Olive Senior – b. 1941', *Journal of the Short Story in English*, 41 (Autumn 2003), 287–98

Dunn, Maggie, and Ann Morris, *The Composite Novel: The Short Story Cycle in Transition* (New York: Twayne, 1995)

Evans, Lucy, 'Questioning Black Identity: Strategies of Digression in E.A. Markham's *Meet Me in Mozambique*', *Moving Worlds*, 9:2 (2009), 125–36

Fallon, Erin C., Rick. A. Feddersen, James Kurtzleben and Maurice A. Lee, eds, *A Reader's Companion to the Short Story in English* (Westport, CT: Greenwood, 2000)

Ferguson, Suzanne C., 'Defining the Short Story: Impressionism and Form', *Modern Fiction Studies*, 28:1 (1982), 13–24

Fernández Marcané, Leonardo, 'Panorama del cuento en las Antillas', *Baquiana*, 5 (2003), 254–62

García, Luis Manuel, 'Crónica de la inocencia perdida: La cuentística cubana contemporánea', *Encuentro*, 140–141 (1995), 121–27

Garland Mann, Susan, *The Short Story Cycle: A Genre Companion and Reference Guide* (New York and London: Greenwood Press, 1989)

Gordimer, Nadine, 'The Flash of Fireflies', in *The New Short Story Theories*, ed. by May, pp. 263–67

Hanson, Clare, *Short Stories and Short Fictions, 1880–1980* (London: Macmillan, 1985)

Hanson, Clare, ed., *Re-Reading the Short Story* (Basingstoke: Macmillan, 1989)

Head, Dominic, *The Modernist Short Story* (Cambridge: Cambridge University Press, 1992)

Hopkinson, Nalo, http://nalohopkinson.com/short_stories_novels_something_else

Hunter, Adrian, *The Cambridge Introduction to the Short Story in English* (Cambridge: Cambridge University Press, 2007)

Iftekharrudin, Farhat, Joseph Boyden, Mary Rohrberger, and Jaie Claudet, eds, *The Postmodern Short Story: Forms and Issues*, (Westport, CT and London: Praeger, 2003)

Iftekharrudin, Farhat, Joseph Boyden, Joseph Longo, and Mary Rohrberger, eds, *Postmodern Approaches to the Short Story* (Westport, CT and London: Praeger, 2003)

Ingram, Forrest L., *Representative Short Story Cycles of the Twentieth Century* (The Hague: Mouton, 1971)

James, Louis, 'Writing the Ballad: The Short Fiction of Samuel Selvon and Earl Lovelace' in *Telling Stories: Postcolonial Short Fiction in English*, ed. by Jacqueline Bardolph (Amsterdam and Atlanta, GA: Rodopi, 2001), pp. 103–08

Kotrodimos, Paul, 'Jean Rhys', in A *Reader's Companion to the Short Story in English*, ed. by Erin C. Fallon, Rick. A. Feddersen, James Kurtzleben And Maurice A. Lee (Westport, CT: Greenwood, 2000), pp. 357–63

Lee, Maurice A., ed., *Writers on Writing: The Art of the Short Story* (Westport, CN and London: Praeger, 2005)

Lister, Rachel, 'Female Expansion and Masculine Immobilization in the Short Story Cycle', *Journal of the Short Story in English*, 48 (2007), 43–58

Lohafer, Susan, *Coming to Terms with the Short Story* (Baton Rouge: Louisiana State University Press, 1983)

Lohafer, Susan and Jo Ellyn Clarey, eds, *Short Story Theory at a Crossroads* (Baton Rouge: Louisiana State University Press, 1989)

López Sacha, Francisco, 'Current Tendencies in the Cuban Short Story', *The South Atlantic Quarterly*, 96:1 (1997), 181–98

Lounsberry, Barbara, Susan Lohafer, Mary Rohrberger, Stephen Pett, and R.C. Fedderson, eds, *The Tales We Tell: Perspectives on the Short Story* (Westport, CT and London: Praeger, 1998)

Luis, William, 'The Short Story in the Hispanic Antilles', in A *History of Literature in the Caribbean: Hispanic and Francophone Regions*, ed. by A. James Arnold, Julio Rodríguez-Luis, and J. Michael Dash (Philadelphia: John Benjamins, 1994), pp. 101–208

Mais, Roger, 'The Short Story', *Public Opinion*, 27 March 1943, p. 4

Malcolm, Cheryl Alexander and David Malcolm, *Jean Rhys: A Study of the Short Fiction* (New York: Twayne, 1996)

March-Russell, Paul, *The Short Story: An Introduction* (Edinburgh: Edinburgh University Press, 2009)

Matthews, Brander, 'The Philosophy of the Short-Story', in *The New Short Story Theories*, ed. by May, pp. 73–80

May, Charles E., ed., *The New Short Story Theories* (Athens, OH: Ohio University Press, 1994)

____ *The Short Story: The Reality of Artifice* (New York and London: Routledge, 2002 [1995])

____ 'Why Short Stories Are Essential and Why They Are Seldom Read', in *The Art of Brevity: Excursions in Short Fiction Theory and Analysis*, ed. by Per Winther et al (Columbia: University of South Carolina Press, 2004), pp. 14–25

Mentón, Seymour, 'El cuento de la revolución cubana: Una visión antológica y algo más', in *El cuento hispanoamericano ante la crítica*, ed. by Enrique Pupo-Walker (Madrid: Castalia, 1973), pp. 338–55

Morrell, A.C., 'The World of Jean Rhys's Short Stories', in *Critical Perspectives on Jean Rhys*, ed. by Pierrette Frickey (Boulder, CO: Three Continents, 1990), pp. 95–102

Nagel, James, *The Contemporary American Short Story Cycle: The Ethnic Resonance of Genre* (Baton Rouge: Louisiana State University Press, 2001)

New, W.H., *Dreams of Speech and Violence: The Art of the Short Story in Canada and New Zealand* (Toronto: University of Toronto Press, 1987)

Nischik, Reingard M., *The Canadian Short Story: Interpretations* (Rochester, NY: Camden House, 2008)

O'Connor, Frank, *The Lonely Voice: A Study of the Short Story* (London: Macmillan, 1963)

Poe, Edgar Allan, 'Nathaniel Hawthorne', in *The Works of Edgar Allan Poe*, Vol. 3 (New York: Widdleton, 1849), pp. 188–202

____ 'Review of *Twice-Told Tales*', *Graham's Magazine*, May 1842. Reprinted in *The New Short Story Theories*, ed. by May, pp. 45–51

Pratt, Mary Louise, 'The Short Story: The Long and Short of It', in *The New Short Story Theories*, ed. by May, pp. 91–113.

Ramchand, Kenneth, 'The Short Story – An Introduction', in *Best West Indian Stories* (Kingston: Nelson Caribbean, 1982), pp. 1–5

____ 'The West Indian Short Story', *Journal of Caribbean Literatures*, 1:1 (1997), 21–30

Ramraj, Victor, 'Short Fiction', in *A History of Literature in the Caribbean, Vol. 2*, ed. by James A. Arnold et al (Amsterdam: John Benjamins, 2001), pp. 199–223

Reid, Ian, *The Short Story* (London: Methuen, 1977)

Rohrberger, Mary, 'The Short Story: A Proposed Definition' [1966], in *Short Story Theories*, ed. by May, pp. 80–82

Senior, Olive, 'The Story as Su-Su, the Writer as Gossip', in *Writers on Writing: The Art of the Short Story*, ed. by Lee, pp. 41–50

Shaw, Valerie, *The Short Story: A Critical Introduction* (London: Longman, 1983)

Simpson, Hyacinth M., ed., *Journal of West Indian Literature*, 12 (2004) [Special double issue on the Caribbean short story]

____ 'Patterns and periods: Oral Aesthetics and a Century of Jamaican Short Story Writing', *Journal of West Indian Literature*, 12:1 (2004), 1–30

____ '"Voicing the Text": The Making of an Oral Poetics in Olive Senior's Short Fiction', *Callaloo*, 27:3 (Summer 2004), 829–33

Trussler, Michael, 'Suspended Narratives: The Short Story and Temporality', *Studies in Short Fiction*, 33:4 (Fall 1996), 557–58

Yáñez, Mirta, 'Introduction', in *Making a Scene: Cuban Women's Stories* (London: Mango, 2004), pp. 5–13

General Sources on Caribbean Literature, Culture, History

Adisa, Opal Palmer, 'Walking on Water: A ConVERsation with Kamau Brathwaite', *The Caribbean Writer*, 23 (2009), 92–216

Alexander, K.J., 'Review: *Face and Other Stories*', *Public Opinion*, 9 May 1942, p. 6

Anatol, Giselle Liza, 'A Feminist Reading of Soucouyants in Nalo Hopkinson's *Brown Girl in the Ring* and *Skin Folk*', *Mosaic*, 37: 3 (2004), 33–50

Añel, Armando, 'Censura y autocensura en la literatura cubana de los noventa: una observación y algunos apuntes', *Revista Hispano Cubana*, 13 (2002), 71–78

Angier, Carole, *Jean Rhys: Life and Work* (London: Penguin, 1992)

Arnold, Albert, Julio Rodriguez-Luis, Vera Kutzinki, Ineke Phaf-Rheinberger and J. Michael Dash, eds, *A History of Literature in the Caribbean – Volume 2* (Amsterdam, Philadelphia: John Benjamins Publishing Company, 2001)

Arnold, James A., et al, eds, *A History of Literature in the Caribbean Vol. II: English- and Dutch-Speaking Regions* (Amsterdam: John Benjamins, 2001)

Arzola, Jorge Luis, 'La moda de la literatura cubana en el exterior es un gran mito', Interview with Aymara Aymerich, *La Jiribilla: Revista Digital de la Cultura Cubana*, 10 (2001) <http://www.lajiribilla.cu/2001/n10_julio/264_10.html>

Athill, Diana, 'Introduction', in Jean Rhys, *The Collected Short Stories* (New York and London: W.W. Norton, 1987), pp. vii–x

Baronov, David, and Kelvin A. Yelvington, 'Ethnicity, Race, Class and Nationality', in *Understanding the Contemporary Caribbean*, ed. by Richard S. Hillman and Thomas J. D'Agostino (Kingston: Ian Randle, 2003), pp. 209–38

Beckles, Hilary McD., *The Development of West Indies Cricket: Volume 1. The Age of Nationalism* (London: Pluto, 1998)

Benítez-Rojo, Antonio, *The Repeating Island: The Caribbean and the Postmodern Perspective*, trans. by James E. Maraniss, 2nd edn (Durham, NC: Duke University Press, 1996 [1989])

_____ 'Three Words toward Creolization', trans. by James Maraniss, in *Caribbean Creolization: Reflections on the Cultural Dynamics of Language, Literature and Identity*, ed. by Kathleen M. Balutansky and Marie-Agnès Sourieau (Gainesville, FL: University Press of Florida, 1998), pp. 53–61

Benn, Dennis, *The Caribbean, an Intellectual History* (Kingston: Ian Randle, 2004)

Bennett, Louise (n.d.), Interview with Louise Bennett by Paulette Bell, Kingston, Jamaica [Cassette recording in possession of Jamaica Memory Bank, Kingston]

Birbalsingh, Frank, ed., *Frontiers of Caribbean Literature* (London and Basingstoke: Macmillan, 1996)

Birbalsingh, Frank, and Clem Seecharan, *Indo-West Indian Cricket* (London: Hansib, 1988)

Bisnauth, Dale, *A History of Religions in the Caribbean* (Trenton, NJ: Africa World Press, 1996)

Blackman, Peter, 'Is There A West Indian Literature?', *Life and Letters*, 59, (1948) pp. 96–102

Bost, Suzanne, 'Transgressing Borders: Puerto Rican and Latina Mestizaje', *MELUS*, 25:2 (Summer 2000), 187–211

Brathwaite, Edward Kamau, *ConVERsations with Nathaniel Mackey* (New York: We Press, 1999)

_____ *Folk-culture of the Slaves in Jamaica* (London: New Beacon, 1970)

_____ *History of the Voice* (London: New Beacon, 1984)

_____ *MR* (New York: Savacou North, 2002)

Braithwaite, Lloyd, *Social Stratification in Trinidad* (Mona, Kingston, Jamaica: Institute of Social and Economic Research, University of the West Indies, 1975)

Brown, Mariel, 'Finding Her Own Way Home', interview with Edwidge Danticat, *Caribbean Beat*, 64 (Nov–Dec 2003), 55–60

Bundy, Andrew J.M., 'Introduction', in *Selected Essays of Wilson Harris: The Unfinished Genesis of the Imagination*, ed. by Andrew Bundy (London: Routledge, 1999), pp. 1–33

Burnett, Paula, '"Where else to row, but backward?" Addressing Caribbean Futures through Re-visions of the Past', *Ariel*, 30:1 (1999), 11–37

Busby, Margaret, ed., *Daughters of Africa* (New York: Pantheon, 1992)

Bustamante, Elena Clemente, 'Fragments and Crossroads in Nalo Hopkinson's *Brown Girl in the Ring*', *Spaces of Utopia: An Electronic Journal*, 4 (Spring 2007), 11–30 <http://ler.letras.up.pt>

Campbell, Carl, *Colony and Nation: A Short History of Education in Trinidad and Tobago* (Kingston: Ian Randle, 1992)

Carpentier, Alejo, 'Prologue', in *The Kingdom of this World*, trans. by Harriet de Onís (London: André Deutsch, 1990 [1949])

———— *Tientos y diferencias* (Montevideo: Arca, 1967)

Carr, Bill, 'A Complex Fate: The Novels of Andrew Salkey', in *The Islands in Between: Essays on West Indian Literature*, ed. by Louis James (Oxford: Oxford University Press, 1968), pp. 100–108

Carr, Helen, *Jean Rhys* (Plymouth: Northcote House, 1996)

Carter, Marina, and Khal Torabully, *Coolitude: An Anthology of the Indian Labour Diaspora* (London: Anthem, 2002)

Chancy, Myriam, *Framing Silence: Revolutionary Novels by Haitian Women* (New Brunswick, NJ: Rutgers University Press, 1997)

Chapman, Esther, 'Negro's "Public Enemy Number 1": Editor is a Woman', *Daily Gleaner*, 2 August 1939, p. 6

Chevannes, Barry, ed., *Rastafari and Other African-Caribbean Worldviews* (London: Macmillan, 1995)

Cobham, Rhonda, 'Introduction', in Alfred Mendes, *Black Fauns* (London: New Beacon, 1984), pp. i–xvi

———— 'The Background', in *West Indian Literature*, ed. by King, pp. 11–26

Condé, Mary, 'Unlikely Stories: Children's Invented Worlds in Caribbean Women's Fiction', *Commonwealth Essays and Studies*, 15:1 (1992), 69–75

Conroy, Mary, 'The Vagabond Motif in the Writings of Claude McKay', *Negro American Literature Forum*, 5:1 (1971), 15–23

Cooper, Wayne F., *Claude McKay: Rebel Sojourner in the Harlem Renaissance: A Biography* (Baton Rouge: Louisiana State University Press, 1987)

Dabydeen, David, and Brinsley Samaroo, eds, *India in the Caribbean* (London: Hansib: 1987)

Dalleo, Raphael, 'Bita Plant as Literary Intellectual: The Anticolonial Public Sphere and *Banana Bottom*', *Journal of West Indian Literature*, 17:1 (2008), 54–67

Dance, Daryl Cumber, *New World Adams: Conversations with Contemporary West Indian Writers* (Leeds: Peepal Tree, 1992)

Darroch, Fiona, *Memory and Myth: Postcolonial Religion in Contemporary Guyanese Fiction and Poetry* (Amsterdam and New York: Rodopi, 2009)

Dash, J. Michael, *Literature and Ideology in Haiti* (London: Macmillan, 1981)

———— *Édouard Glissant* (Cambridge: Cambridge University Press, 1995)

———— *Haiti and the United States: National Stereotypes and the Literary Imagination*, 2nd edn (Basingstoke and New York: Palgrave Macmillan, 1997)

———— *The Other America: Caribbean Literature in a New World Context* (Charlottesville: University Press of Virginia, 1998)

Dawes, Kwame, *Natural Mysticism: Towards a New Reggae Aesthetic in Caribbean Writing* (Leeds: Peepal Tree, 1999)

Dayan, Joan, *Haiti, History and the Gods* (Berkeley: University of California Press, 1998)

Donnell, Alison, *Twentieth-Century Caribbean Literature: Critical Moments in Anglophone Literary History* (London: Routledge, 2006)

Donnell, Alison, and Sarah Lawson Welsh, eds, *The Routledge Reader in Caribbean Literature* (London: Routledge, 1996)

Edwards, Brent Hayes, *The Practice of Diaspora: Literature, Translation, and the Rise of Black Internationalism* (Cambridge, MA and London: Harvard University Press, 2003)

Emery, Mary Lou, *Modernism, the Visual and Caribbean Literature* (Cambridge: Cambridge University Press, 2007)

Evans, Lucy, 'Local and Global Reading Communities in Robert Antoni's *My Grandmother's Erotic Folktales*', in *Postcolonial Audiences: Readers, Viewers and Reception*, ed. by Bethan Benwell, James Procter and Gemma Robinson (London and New York: Routledge, 2011)

Ferguson, James, *Traveller's Literary Companion to the Caribbean* (Chicago: Passport Books, 1997)

Figueroa, John, 'The Flaming Faith of those First Years: Caribbean Voices', in *Tibisiri*, ed. by Maggie Butcher (Sydney: Dangaroo Press, 1989) pp. 59–80

Ford, Ford Madox, Preface to Jean Rhys, *The Left Bank and Other Stories* (New York: Books for Libraries Press, 1970 [1927]), pp. 7–27

Fowler, Henry, 'Foreword', *Focus* (1956)

Frederick, Rhonda D., *Colón Man a Come: Mythographies of Panamá Canal Migration* (Lanham, MD: Lexington, 2005)

Frickey, Pierrette, ed., *Critical Perspectives on Jean Rhys* (Boulder: Three Continents, 1990)

García Hernández, Arturo, 'Literatura en la Isla, hoy', *La Jornada* <http://www.jornada.unam.mx/ultimas/2002/09/24/literatura-en-la-isla-hoy/>

Gibson, Keane, *Comfa Religion and Creole Language in a Caribbean Community* (New York: State University of New York Press, 2001)

Gikandi, Simon, *Writing in Limbo: Modernism and Caribbean Literature* (Ithaca and London: Cornell University Press, 1992)

Glissant, Édouard, *Caribbean Discourse: Selected Essays*. trans. by J. Michael Dash (Charlottesville: University of Virginia Press, 1989 [1981])

____ *Poetics of Relation*, trans. by Betsy Wing (Ann Arbor: University of Michigan Press, 1997 [1990])

González Echevarría, Roberto, *Alejo Carpentier: The Pilgrim at Home* (New York: Cornell University Press, 1977)

Green, William A., 'Emancipation to Indenture: A Question of Imperial Morality', *The Journal of British Studies*, 22:2 (1983), 98–121

Gregg, Veronica Marie, 'Jean Rhys and Modernism: A Different Voice', *The Jean Rhys Review*, 1:2 (1987), 30–46

Griffith, Glyne, 'Deconstructing Nationalisms: Henry Swanzy, *Caribbean Voices* and the Development of West Indian Literature', *Small Axe*, 10 (September 2001), 1–20

____ 'This Is London Calling the West Indies', in *West Indian Intellectuals in Britain*, ed. by Schwarz, pp. 196–208

Gunning, Dave, 'Caribbean Modernism', in *The Oxford Handbook of Modernisms*, ed. by Peter Brooker et al (Oxford and New York: Oxford University Press, 2010), pp. 910–925

Gyssels, Kathleen, 'Haitians in the City: Two Modern-Day Trickster Tales'
    <http://social.chass.ncsu.edu/jouvert/v7isl/gyss.htm>
Harney, Steve, 'Nation Time: Earl Lovelace and Michael Anthony Nationfy Trinidad',
    Commonwealth Essays and Studies, 13:2 (1991), 31–41
Harney, Stefano, *Nationalism and Identity: Culture and the Imagination in a Caribbean
    Diaspora* (London and New Jersey: University of the West Indies, 1996)
Harris, Wilson, *Selected Essays of Wilson Harris: The Unfinished Genesis of the Imagination*,
    ed. by Andrew Bundy (London: Routledge, 1999), pp. 1–33
Hayward, Helen, *The Enigma of V.S. Naipaul: Sources and Contexts* (Basingstoke: Palgrave
    Macmillan, 2002)
Hernandez-Reguant, Ariana, 'Writing the Special Period: An Introduction', in *Cuba
    in the Special Period: Culture and Ideology in the 1990s* (New York: Palgrave Macmillan,
    2009), pp. 1–18
Herring, Robert, 'What I Look For in West Indian Literature', *Life and Letters*, 57
    (1948), pp. 1–3
Hill, Donald, *Caribbean Folklore: A Handbook* (Westport, CT: Greenwood Press, 2007)
Howe, Linda S., *Transgression and Conformity: Cuban Writers and Artists After the Revolution*
    (Madison, Wisconsin: University of Wisconsin, 2004)
Howland, Cicely, 'Review: *Face and Other Stories*', *Public Opinion*, 9 May, 1942, p. 6
James, C.L.R., *Beyond a Boundary* (London: Serpent's Tail, 2000)
____ 'Interview', in Ian Munro and Reinhard Sander, eds, *Kas Kas: Interviews with
    Three Caribbean Writers in Texas*, pp. 23–41
____ *Spheres of Existence: Selected Writings* (London: Allison and Busby, 1980)
____ 'Two Lectures by C.L.R. James', *Caribbean Quarterly*, 54:1 (Mar–Jun 2008), 179–87
James, C.L.R., and Michael Anthony, 'Discovering Literature in Trinidad: Two
    Experiences', *Journal of Commonwealth Literature*, 7 (1967), 73-87
James, Cynthia, 'From Orature to Literature in Jamaican and Trinidadian Children's
    Folk Traditions', *Children's Literature Association Quarterly*, 30:2 (2005), 164–78
James, Louis, ed., *The Islands in Between: Essays on West Indian Literature* (London:
    Oxford University Press, 1968)
Jussawalla, Feroza, ed., *Conversations with V.S. Naipaul* (Jackson, MS: University Press
    of Mississippi, 1997)
Kale, Madhavi, *Fragments of Empire: Capital, Slavery, and Indian Indentured Labor Migration
    in the British Caribbean* (Philadelphia: University of Pennsylvania Press, 1998)
King, Bruce, ed., *West Indian Literature*, 2nd edn (London: Macmillan, 1995)
King, Nicole, 'Performance and Tradition in Earl Lovelace', in *Caribbean Literature
    After Independence: The Case of Earl Lovelace*, ed. by Bill Schwarz (London: Institute
    for the Study of the Americas, 2008), pp. 111–129
Kissoon Jodah, Desiree, 'Courting Disaster in Guyana' in *The Multinational Monitor*,
    16:11 (1995) <http://multinationalmonitor.org/hyper/mm1195.04.html>
Krise, Thomas W., 'Introduction', in *Caribbeana, An Anthology of British Literature of
    the West Indies, 1657–1777*, ed. by Thomas Krise (Chicago: The University of
    Chicago Press, 1999), pp. 1–15
Korom, Frank, *Hosay Trinidad* (Philadelphia: University of Pennsylvania Press, 2003)
Lahens, Yanick, *L'Exil: entre l'anchrage et la fuite, l'écrivain haïtien* (Port-au-Prince: Éditions
    Deschamps, 1990)
Lamming, George, *The Pleasures of Exile* (London: Allison and Busby, 1960)
'Literatura cubana finisecular: un balance posible', *Inter Press Service*, 2004
    <http://ips.org/cuba/enflitcu.htm>
Lovelace, Earl, and George Lamming, 'Interview with George Lamming', *Caribbean
    Writer's Summer Institute Archival Video Collection* (University of Miami, 1992)

Lutz, Tom, 'Claude McKay: Music, Sexuality and Literary Cosmopolitanism', in *Black Orpheus: Music in African American Fiction from the Harlem Renaissance to Toni Morrison*, ed. by Saadi A. Simawe (New York: Garland, 2000), pp. 41–64

Mais, Roger, 'Why Local Colour?', *Public Opinion*, 8 January 1944, p. 3

____ 'Words and So Forth', *Public Opinion*, 30 May 1942, p. 6, p. 8

Marson, Una, 'Wanted: Writers and Publishers', *Public Opinion*, 22 May 1937, p. 6

____ 'Unsung Heroes', *Public Opinion*, 30 October 1937, p. 12

____ 'Problems of Coloured People in Britain', Una Marson Papers box 1944C, 1

Martin, Tony, *Literary Garveyism: Garvey, Black Arts and the Harlem Renaissance* (Dover, MA: Majority, 1983)

Marty, Anne, *Haïti en littérature* (Paris: Maisonneuve & Larose, 2000)

Más Zabala, Carlos, 'Las nuevas del libro en Cuba', *La Revista del Libro Cubano*, 3:1 (2000), 49–52

McFarlane, J.E.C., *A Literature in the Making* (Kingston, Jamaica: Pioneer Press, 1956)

McKay, Claude, *Trial by Lynching: Stories about Negro Life in North America*, trans. by Robert Winter; ed. by A.L. McLeod (Mysore: Centre for Commonwealth Literature and Research, University of Mysore, 1977)

____ *A Long Way from Home: An Autobiography* [1937] (London and Sydney: Pluto, 1985)

McKenzie, Earl, 'C.L.R. James on Cricket as Art', *Caribbean Quarterly*, 40:3&4 (1994), 92–98

McLaughlin, Joan, 'Jamaican Creole', in Sibley, *Quashie's Reflections in Jamaican Creole*, pp. iii–ix

McLean, Dolace, and Jacqueline Bishop, 'On Hearts Revealed: An Interview with Olive Senior', *Calabash: A Journal of Caribbean Arts and Letters*, 2:2 (Summer/Fall 2003), 3–13

Meighoo, Kirk Peter, *Politics in a 'Half Made Society': Trinidad and Tobago, 1925–2002* (Kingston; Oxford; Princeton: Ian Randle Publishers; J. Currey Publishers; M. Wiener Publishers, 2003)

Mendes, Alfred Hubert, and Reinhard Sander, 'The Turbulent Thirties in Trinidad: an Interview with Alfred H. Mendes', *World Literature Written in English*, 12:1 (1973), 66–79

Miller, Daniel, *Modernity: An Ethnographic Approach: Dualism and Mass Consumption in Trinidad* (Oxford and New York: Berg, 1994)

Mishra, Vijay, *The Literature of the Indian Diaspora: Theorizing the Diasporic Imaginary* (London: Routledge, 2007)

Misrahi-Barak, Judith, 'The Detours of Narrative Voice: a Precondition of Self-Narration in Caribbean Literature', *Commonwealth Essays and Studies*, 19:1 (1996), 71–79

Montes Huidobro, Matías, 'Transgresiones y transgresores', *Encuentro*, 28–29 (2003), 273–85

Morris, Mervyn, 'Anancy and Andrew Salkey', *Jamaica Journal*, 19:4 (November 1986), pp. 39–43

____ 'Cross-Cultural Impersonations in Pauline Melville's *Shape-shifter*', *Ariel*, 24:1 (1993), 79–89

Munro, Ian, and Reinhard Sander, eds, *Kas-kas: Interviews with Three Caribbean Writers in Texas* (Austin: African and Afro-American Research Institute, University of Texas at Austin, 1972)

Murray, Patricia, 'Writing Trinidad: Nation and Hybridity in *The Dragon Can't Dance* and *Witchbroom*', in *Caribbean Literature After Independence*, ed. by Schwarz, pp. 94–110

Mustafa, Fawzia, *V.S. Naipaul* (Cambridge: Cambridge University Press, 1995)

Naipaul, V.S., *Finding the Centre: Two Narratives* (London: Andre Deutsch, 1984)

____ *Literary Occasions: Essays* (London: Picador, 2004 [2003])

____ *The Loss of El Dorado: A Colonial History* (London: Picador, 2001 [1969])

____ *The Middle Passage: Impressions of Five Societies – British, French and Dutch – in the West Indies and South America* (Harmondsworth: Penguin, 1985 [1962])

Nanton, Philip, 'What does Mr. Swanzy want? Shaping or reflecting? An assessment of Henry Swanzy's contribution to the development of Caribbean literature', *Kunapipi: Journal of Post-Colonial Writing*, 20:1 (1998), 11–20

____ 'London Calling', *Caribbean Beat*, 63 (September–October 2003), 66–71

Nazareth, Peter, 'The Fiction of Andrew Salkey', *Jamaica Journal*, 19:4 (1986), pp. 45–55

Neptune, Harvey, Jr., *Caliban and the Yankees: Trinidad and the United States Occupation* (Chapel Hill: University of North Carolina Press, 2007)

Nicholls, David G., 'The Folk as Alternative Modernity: Claude McKay's *Banana Bottom* and the Romance of Nature', *Journal of Modern Literature*, 23 (1999), 79–94

Nixon, Rob, *London Calling: V.S. Naipaul, Postcolonial Mandarin* (New York and Oxford: Oxford University Press, 1992)

Northrup, David, *Indentured Labor in the Age of Imperialism, 1834–1922* (Cambridge, New York and Melbourne: Cambridge University Press, 1955)

O'Callaghan, Evelyn, 'The Modernization of the Trinidadian Landscape in the Novels of Earl Lovelace', *Ariel*, 20:1 (1989), 41–54

Paravisini-Gebert, Lizabeth and Margarite Fernández Olmos, *Creole Religions of the Caribbean: An Introduction from Vodou and Santería to Obeah and Espiritismo* (New York: New York University Press, 2003)

Patterson, Tiffany Ruby, and Robin D.G. Kelley, 'Unfinished Migrations: Reflections on the African Diaspora and the Making of the Modern World', *African Studies Review*, 43:1 (2000), 11–45

Pouchet Paquet, Sandra, 'The Fifties', in *West Indian Literature*, ed. by King, pp. 51–62

____ *Caribbean Autobiography: Cultural Identity and Self-Representation* (Madison: University of Wisconsin Press, 2002)

Pouchet Paquet, Sandra et al, eds, *Music, Memory, Resistance: Calypso and the Caribbean Literary Imagination* (Kingston: Ian Randle, 2007)

Price-Mars, Jean, *De Saint-Domingue à Haïti* (Paris: Présence Africaine, 1959)

Procter, James, 'A "Limited Situation": Brevity and Lovelace's *A Brief Conversion*', in *Caribbean Literature After Independence*, ed. by Schwarz, pp. 130–45

Puleo, Augustus C., 'The Intersection of race, sex, gender and class in a short story of Rosario Ferré', *Studies in Short Fiction*, 32:1 (Spring 1995), 227–34

Purchas-Tulloch, Jean A., *Jamaica Anansi: A Survival of the African Oral Tradition* (PhD Thesis, Howard University, 1976)

Puri, Shalini, 'Beyond Resistance: Notes Toward a New Caribbean Cultural Studies', *Small Axe*, 7:2 (2003), 23–38

____ 'Race, Rape and Representation: Indo-Caribbean Women and Cultural Nationalism', *Cultural Critique*, 36 (1997), 119–63

____ *The Caribbean Postcolonial: Social Equality, Post-Nationalism and Cultural Hybridity* (New York and Basingstoke: Palgrave Macmillan, 2004)

Ramchand, Kenneth, 'Introduction', in Roger Mais, *Listen, the Wind and Other Stories* (Harlow: Longman, 1986) pp. vi–xxx

____ *The West Indian Novel and Its Background* (Kingston: Ian Randle, 2004 [1970])

____ 'The Writer Who Ran Away: Eric Walrond and *Tropic Death*', *Savacou*, 2 (1970), 67–75

Ramdin, Ron, *Arising From Bondage: A History of the Indo-Caribbean People* (London: I.B. Taurus, 2000)

Ramesh, Kotti Sree, and Kandula Nirupa Rani, *Claude McKay: The Literary Identity from Jamaica to Harlem and Beyond* (Jefferson, NC: McFarland, 2006)

Ramsahoye, James W., *A Mouldy Destiny: Visiting Guyana's Forbes Burnham* (London: Minerva Press, 1996)

Redonet, Salvador, 'Para ser lo más breve posible', in *Los últimos serán los primeros* (Havana: Letras Cubanas, 1993), pp. 5–31

Renk, Kathleen, '"Magic that Battles Death": Pauline Melville's Marvellous Realism' *Journal of Commonwealth Literature*, 44:1 (2009), 101–15

Rohlehr, Gordon, *The Shape of That Hurt and Other Essays* (Port of Spain: Longman, 1992)

____ 'Dream Journeys', in Kamau Brathwaite, *DS (2) Dreamstories* (New York: New Directions, 2007), pp. iii–xvi

Rosenberg, Leah, *Nationalism and the Formation of Caribbean Literature* (New York: Palgrave Macmillan, 2007)

Rowell, Charles H., 'An Interview with Olive Senior', *Callaloo*, 36 (Summer 1988), 480–90

Rubio Cuevas, Iván, 'Lo marginal en los narradores novísimos narradores cubanos: estrategia subversión y moda', in *Todas las islas la isla*, ed. by Janette Reinstädler and Omar Ette (Madrid and Frankfurt: Iberoamericana & Vervuert, 2000), pp. 79–90

Rutherford, Anna, 'Olive Senior: Interview', *Kunapipi*, 8:2 (1986), 11–20

Sander, Reinhard W., *The Trinidad Awakening: West Indian Literature of the Nineteen-Thirties* (New York: Greenwood Press, 1988)

____ 'The Thirties and Forties', in *West Indian Literature*, ed. by King, pp. 38–49

Santos-Phillips, Eva L., 'Abrogation and appropriation in Rosario Ferré's *Amalia*', *Studies in Short Fiction*, 35:2 (Spring 1998), 117–29

Savory, Elaine, *Jean Rhys* (Cambridge: Cambridge University Press, 1998)

Schwarz, Bill, ed., *Caribbean Literature After Independence: The Case of Earl Lovelace* (London: Institute for the Study of the Americas, 2008)

Seecharan, Clem, 'The Shaping of the Indo-Caribbean People: Guyana and Trinidad to the 1940s', *Journal of Caribbean Studies*, 14:1&2 (1999/2000), 61–92

Senior, Olive, 'Lessons from the Fruit Stand: Or, Writing for the Listener', *Journal of Modern Literature*, XX:1 (Summer 1996), 39–44

____ *Working Miracles: Women's Lives in the English-Speaking Caribbean* (Cave Hill, Barbados/London: University of the West Indies/James Currey, 1991)

Sherlock, Philip, 'Foreword', in Sibley, *Quashie's Reflections in Jamaican Creole*, pp. i–ii

Singh, Sherry Ann, 'The Ramayana Tradition and Socio-Religious Change in Trinidad, 1917–1990' (UWI, St Augustine: Unpublished PhD Thesis, 2005)

SookDeo, A. Neil, 'Involuntary Globalization: How Britain Revived Indenture and Made it Largely Brown and East Indian (Trinidad 1806–1921)', *Man in India*, 88:1 (2008), 5–28

Stephens, Michelle Ann, *Black Empire: The Masculine Global Imaginary of Caribbean Intellectuals in the United States, 1914–1962* (Durham, NC: Duke University Press, 2005)

____ 'Disarticulating Black Internationalisms: West Indian Radicals and *The Practice of Diaspora*', *Small Axe*, 17 (2005), 100–11

____ 'Eric Walrond's *Tropic Death* and the Discontents of American Modernity', in *Prospero's Isles: The Presence of the Caribbean in the American Imaginary*, ed. by Diana Accaria-Zavala and Rodolfo Popelnik (Oxford: Macmillan Education, 2004), pp. 167–78

Stephens, Michelle A., 'Black Transnationalism and the Politics of National Identity: West Indian Intellectuals in Harlem in the Age of War and Revolution', *American Quarterly*, 50:3 (1998), 592–608

Strachan, Ian Gregory, *Paradise and Plantation: Tourism and Culture in the Anglophone Caribbean* (Charlottesville and London: University of Virginia Press, 2002)

Swanzy, Henry, 'Caribbean Voices – A Review of the Last Six Months', *Public Opinion*, 15 October 1949, p. 6

____ 'Caribbean Voices – A Review of The Last Six Months', *Public Opinion*, 10 October 1953, p. 5

____ 'Caribbean Voices – Prolegomena to a West Indian Culture', *Caribbean Quarterly*, 1.1 (1949), 21–28

____ 'The Literary Situation in the Contemporary Caribbean', in *The Routledge Reader in Caribbean Literature*, ed. by Donnell and Lawson Welsh, pp. 249–52

Tanna, Laura, 'One_on_One with Olive Senior (Pt III)', *Jamaica Gleaner*, 31 October 2004 <http://www.jamaica-gleaner.com/gleaner/20041017/arts/arts3.html>

Taylor, Patrick, ed., *Nation Dance: Religion, Identity and Cultural Difference in the Caribbean* (Bloomington: Indiana University Press, 2001)

Thieme, John, *The Web of Tradition: Uses of Allusion in V.S. Naipaul's Fiction* (London: Hansib Publishing, 1987)

Thomas, Sue, *The Worlding of Jean Rhys* (Westport, CT: Greenwood Press, 1999)

Tiffin, Helen, 'The Metaphor of Anancy in Caribbean Literature', in *Myth and Metaphor*, ed. by R. Sellick (Adelaide: Centre for Research in the New Literatures in English, 1982), pp. 3–21

Tillery, Tyrone, *Claude McKay: A Black Poet's Struggle for Identity* (Amherst: University of Massachusetts Press, 1992)

Valladares Ruiz, Patricia, 'Lo especial del período: Políticas editoriales y movimiento generacional en la literatura cubana contemporánea', *Neophilologus*, 89 (2005), 383–402

Valle, Amir, '"No soy un bestseller": Conversación franca y abierta con Leonardo Padura', *Librusa*, August 2000 <http://www.librusa.com/entrevista4.htm>

Vertovec, Steven, 'East Indians and Anthropologists: A Critical Review', *Social and Economic Studies*, 40:1 (1991), 133–69

Walcott, Derek, 'The Antilles: Fragments of Epic Memory', in *What the Twilight Says* (New York: Farrar, Straus and Giroux, 1998), pp. 65–84

____ 'The Muse of History', in *What the Twilight Says: Essays* (London: Faber & Faber, 1998), pp. 36–64

Walmsley, Anne, *The Caribbean Artists Movement 1966–1972: A Literary and Cultural History* (London and Port of Spain: New Beacon Books, 1992)

Walvin, James, *Making the Black Atlantic: Britain and the African Diaspora* (London and New York: Cassell, 2000)

Watson-Aifah, Jene, and Nalo Hopkinson, 'A Conversation with Nalo Hopkinson', *Callaloo*, 26:1 (Winter 2003), 160–69

Whitfield, Esther, *Cuban Currency: The Dollar and 'Special Period' Fiction* (Minneapolis: University of Minneapolis Press, 2008)

Wyndham, Francis, 'Introduction', *Jean Rhys Letters, 1931–1966* (London: André Deutsch, 1984), pp. 9–12

Yamamoto, Shin, 'Swaying in Time and Space: The Chinese Diaspora in the Caribbean and Its Literary Perspectives', *Asian Ethnicity*, 9:3 (2008), 171–77

Yelvington, Kevin A., *Producing Power: Ethnicity, Gender, and Class in a Caribbean Workplace* (Philadelphia: Temple University Press, 1995)

____ 'Trinidad and Tobago, 1988–89', *Latin American and Caribbean Contemporary Record*, 8 (1991), B459–77

Zimra, Clarisse, 'Haitian Literature after Duvalier: An Interview with Yanick Lahens', *Callaloo*, 16:1 (1993), 77–93

343

NOTES ON CONTRIBUTORS

Andrew Armstrong is Lecturer in Literatures in English in the Department of Language, Linguistics and Literature at the University of the West Indies, Cave Hill. His PhD dissertation was on narrative strategies in contemporary African fiction and film. He currently teaches African Literature, African Film as well as West Indian Literature and The Novel. His recent publications focus on African and Caribbean literature since the mid-1980s with emphasis on the writing of Ben Okri, Moses Isegawa, Goretti Kyomuhendo, Caryl Phillips and Mark McWatt. He has had articles published in *Journal of African Cultural Studies*; *Journal of International Women's Studies*; *Journal of West Indian Literature*; *Shibboleths: a Journal of Comparative Theory*, among others.

Patricia Catoira is Associate Professor of Spanish and Latin American Studies at Montana State University in Bozeman. She is also the Chair of the Women's and Gender Studies Program at this university. Her recent publications in journals such *Confluencia* and *Letras Hispanas* focus on Cuban literature since the 1990s and the representation and cultural production of Latin American immigrants in contemporary Spain. Her most recent article in the collection *Literatura y Cultura Cubana del Siglo XXI* (Iberoamericana/Vervuert, 2010) analyzes sex tourism and prostitution in recent Cuban literature. She is presently writing *Sexuality, Postmodernism, and Globalization: The Prostitute in Recent Latin American Fiction*.

Shirley Chew is Emeritus Professor of Commonwealth and Postcolonial Literatures at the University of Leeds. She has published widely in the field of literatures from Commonwealth countries. She is a co-editor of *Unbecoming Daughters of the Empire* (1993), *Translating Life: Studies in Transpositional Aesthetics* (1999), *Reconstructing the Book: Literary Texts in Transmission* (2001), and the *Blackwell Concise Companion to Postcolonial Literature* (2010). She is the founding and general editor of *Moving Worlds: A Journal of Transcultural Writings* (2001–). Her work in progress includes the *Blackwell History of Postcolonial Literature*.

Sandra Courtman teaches literature and creative writing at the University of Sheffield, UK. Her work on women writers of the Windrush generation led to a 1969 Jamaican autobiography, Joyce Gladwell's *Brown Face, Big Master*, being reprinted as a Macmillan Caribbean Classic in 2003. She has published work on women and the black British canon and Birmingham's photographic collections and edited *Beyond the Blood, the Beach and The Banana: New Perspectives in Caribbean Studies* (Kingston, Jamaica: Ian Randle, 2004).

Alison Donnell is a Reader in the Department of English and American Literature at the University of Reading, UK. She has published widely on Caribbean and black British writings, including a book-length revision of literary history: *Twentieth-Century Caribbean Literature: Critical Moments in Anglophone*

Literary History (Routledge, 2006). She is currently completing a monograph on the work of Una Marson and Louise Bennett and co-editing, with Michael Bucknor, a major new *Companion on Caribbean Literature* to be published by Routledge in 2011. She is a Founding and Joint Editor of *Interventions: International Journal of Postcolonial Studies* and on the editorial boards of *Journal of West Indian Literature* and *MaComère*.

Lucy Evans is Lecturer in Postcolonial Literature at the University of Leicester, UK. She has published articles on Caribbean and black British writing in the *Journal of Commonwealth Literature, Moving Worlds: A Journal of Transcultural Writings*, the *Caribbean Quarterly* and *Atlantic Studies*, and has book chapters forthcoming in *Postcolonial Audiences: Readers, Viewers and Reception* (Routledge, 2011) and *Constructing Crime: Discourse and Cultural Representations of Crime and 'Deviance'* (Palgrave, forthcoming 2012). She is currently completing a monograph entitled *Communities in Contemporary Caribbean Short Stories*.

Dave Gunning lectures in English literature at the University of Birmingham, UK. His first book, *Race and Antiracism in Black British and British Asian Literatures* (Liverpool University Press) was published in Autumn 2010; his second, *Postcolonial Literature* (Edinburgh University Press), should follow soon.

Joanna Johnson is Senior Lecturer in the Department of English at the University of Miami, where she is also a member of the Caribbean Literary Studies group. She is currently writing her PhD thesis, in which she examines representations of the English countryside in Caribbean writing.

Patricia Murray is a fellow of the Institute for the Study of the Americas [ISA], London University. She was previously Senior Lecturer and Director of the MA in Postcolonial Cultures at London Metropolitan University. She has published on a range of pan-Caribbean and Black British writers and co-edited *Comparing Postcolonial Literatures: Dislocations* (2000). She is currently co-ordinating a research project to investigate the literary forms of magical realism in the wider Caribbean and is completing a book-length study on the work of Wilson Harris and Gabriel García Márquez.

Jak Peake is a PhD student in the Department of Literature, Film, and Theatre Studies at the University of Essex, UK. He is currently completing his thesis on the literary geography of western Trinidad, which forms part of a collaborative AHRC-funded project, 'American Tropics' (see http://www.essex.ac.uk/lifts/American_Tropics/index.htm). He has articles and book reviews on Trinidadian and Caribbean literature due to be published in *Sargasso, Moving Worlds* and *Wasafiri*. He has had articles published in national newspapers and an excerpt of his creative writing anthologised in *Bedford Square 2*.

James Procter is Reader in Modern English and Postcolonial Literature at Newcastle University, UK. He is the editor of *Writing Black Britain* (MUP, 2000) and (with Keown and Murphy) *Comparing Postcolonial Diasporas* (Palgrave, 2008), and the author of *Dwelling Places* (MUP, 2003) and *Stuart Hall* (Routledge, 2004). He is currently Principal Investigator on a collaborative AHRC project looking at the relationship between reading, location and migration. <http://www.devolvingdiasporas.com/>

Raymond Ramcharitar is a Trinidadian poet, fiction writer and cultural critic. His books include *American Fall* (poems, 2007), *The Island Quintet* (fiction, 2009), and *Breaking the News* (media, 2005). He has degrees in Economics, Literature and History from the University of the West Indies, and has written highly polemical and revisionist articles on art and literary history and criticism, media theory and practice, and cultural nationalism in Trinidad and the West Indies. *The Island Quintet* was the only book by a West Indian writer to be shortlisted for the 2010 Commonwealth Writers Prize for Best First Book.

Elaine Savory has published many essays on Caribbean and African literature, especially on poetry and drama and theatre and women's writing. She has written *Jean Rhys* (1998) and *The Cambridge Introduction to Jean Rhys* (2009) (both for Cambridge University Press), as well as *flame tree time* (poetry, Sandberry Press, 1993). She co-edited *Out of the Kumbla: Women and Caribbean Literature* (Africa World Press, 1990). She is presently completing *The Quarrel with Death: Elegiac Poetry in the Shadow of Empire*, and editing the MLA *Teaching Approaches to the Work of Kamau Brathwaite*. She has also written the essay on the Caribbean for the forthcoming *Cambridge History of Postcolonial Literatures*. She teaches at the New School University (New York) in the Literary Studies Department.

Suzanne Scafe is a Senior Lecturer in English Studies at London South Bank University. She has published several essays on Black British writing and culture and Caribbean women's fiction. Her recent work includes two essays on Black British women's autobiographical writing, published in the journals *Changing English* and *Women: A Cultural Review*. She is the co-editor of a collection of essays, *I Am Black/White/Yellow: The Black Body in Europe* (2007), which includes her own chapter on the drama of Roy Williams, and she has written the introduction to Courttia Newland's play, *B is for Black*, published in the collection *Hidden Gems* (2008). Her essay '"Gruesome and Yet Fascinating": Hidden, Disgraced and Disregarded Cultural Forms in Jamaican Short Fiction 1938–50' will be published in the *Journal of Caribbean Literatures* (2011).

Emma Smith was awarded her PhD in narrative theory and contemporary women's writing from the University of Leeds in 2008. She has lectured in post/colonial literature and history at Leeds, Leeds Metropolitan and Newcastle Universities, and her interests in British and Caribbean diasporic fiction have resulted in publications in *Contemporary Women's Writing*, *Moving Worlds*, and *Canadian Studies in Europe*. She currently works in the editorial department at Peepal Tree Press, and is particularly interested in the role of publishing in postcolonial cultures.

THE CARIBBEAN SHORT STORY: CRITICAL PERSPECTIVES

Elizabeth Walcott-Hackshaw is a Senior Lecturer of Francophone Caribbean Literature and Nineteenth-century French poetry at the University of the West Indies, St. Augustine. Her academic research has focused on the Caribbean cultural landscape as presented in the works of Gisèle Pineau, Yanick Lahens, and Edwidge Danticat. Her most recent scholarly publication has been a co-edited collection of essays entitled, *Echoes of the Haitian Revolution: 1804–2004* published in 2008. *Reinterpreting the Haitian Revolution and Its Cultural Aftershocks*, the first in the series, was published in 2006. As a short story writer her work has appeared in several journals including *Callaloo* and *Small Axe*. *Four Taxis Facing North*, her first collection of short stories, was published in 2007.

Abigail Ward is Lecturer in Postcolonial Studies at Nottingham Trent University, UK. Her monograph, *Caryl Phillips, David Dabydeen and Fred D'Aguiar: Representations of Slavery*, is forthcoming in 2011 with Manchester University Press (Contemporary World Writers Series) and she has published essays in a range of edited books and journals, including *The Journal of Commonwealth Literature*, *Journal of Postcolonial Writing* and *Moving Worlds*.

Claire Westall is the Modern Literature Teaching Fellow in the Department of English and Related Literature at the University of York, UK. She previously taught in the Department of English and Comparative Literary Studies at Warwick University where she also completed her doctoral research on cricket's place in English and Caribbean literatures. Alongside a sustained research interest in Caribbean and postcolonial literature, her work is concerned with literary and cultural negotiations with national identities, the intersection of postcolonialism and postcolonial theory with questions of Englishness and Britishness, and the economic, cultural and literary consequences of globalisation. She has published a range of essays, book chapters and review pieces, including work in *Anthurium: A Caribbean Studies Journal*, *New Formations*, *Race & Class* and *Sport in Society*.

Gina Wisker is Professor of Higher Education and Contemporary Literature and Head of the Centre for Learning and Teaching at the University of Brighton, UK. Gina co-edits online magazines *Spokes* and *Dissections*, and her publications include *Teaching African American Women's Writing* (ed., 2010); *Atwood's Handmaid's Tale* (2010); *Rites of Passages* (ed. with Pauline Dodgson Katiyo, 2010); *Key Concepts in Postcolonial Literature* (2007); *Postcolonial and African American Women's Writing* (2000). She has written several essays on Nalo Hopkinson in *Femspec*, *Diagesis* and other journals and her own short stories have appeared in *Femspec* and *Dissections*. Gina's poetry has appeared in *Ambit*.

Emily Zobel Marshall is a Senior Lecturer in the School of Cultural Studies at Leeds Metropolitan University. She teaches courses on African-American, Caribbean, African and Black British literature. Her PhD thesis was entitled 'The Journey of Anancy: An Exploration of Jamaican Cultural Resistance'. She has had articles published in *World Literatures Written in English*, *Caribbean Beat*, *Jamaica Journal*, *Caribbean Quarterly* and *Wadabagei: A Journal of the Caribbean and Its Diaspora*.

Aarons, R.L.C. 52–53, 58n
Adisa, Opal Palmer 312
aesthetic, defining a Caribbean literary
    11–13, 15–17, 19, 29, 45, 56, 237–
    38, 241, 309–310
Africa: 284, 285; Cuban presence in 87;
    cultural forms, 24n, 202, 220;
    diaspora 142–45, 218; influence of
    7, 17, 56, 78–79, 223, 230, 276, 314;
    in the colonial imaginary 61–62, 64;
    in Latin America 79; language 314;
    pan-Africanism 142 (see also Asante-
    Akan culture, Black internationalism,
    diaspora, slavery)
African Caribbean: culture 46–49, 225,
    256, 257; people 20, 78, 95, 97–98,
    227, 269, 290; 320; relation to Indian
    Caribbean, 104–107, 125, 131, 135,
    160, 260–61; religions 211, 214, 217n,
    237, 244, 245, 249–50n, 313–4;
    stories 127
African American literature 48, 52, 142,
    219, 220, 223 (see also Harlem
    Renaissance)
Aguiar, Raúl 85
Alexis, Jacques-Stéphen 113, 123n, 320
alienation 19, 56, 97–100, 103, 107, 109,
    114, 119, 120, 126, 128, 136, 143, 147,
    162, 241–42, 269 (see also isolation)
allegory 36, 50, 56, 78, 283n, 319, 321;
    'national allegory' 128, 189, 194
All Jamaica Library project 30
Alpers, Paul 277, 280, 283n
ambivalence 164, 166, 212, 234, 235, 246,
    248
America, United States (see USA)
Americas 148, 183, 191–95, 240–42, 289
    (see also Canada, Latin America, South
    America, USA)
Amerindian: characters 37, 39, 234, 242,
    278, 281, 305; culture 17, 245;
    peoples 33, 38, 39, 106, 290
Anancy tales 197n, 201–217, 220, 223,
    234, 240, 248, 249n
Añel, Armando 87
Angier, Carol 178, 181n
anglophone 16, 23, 24n, 29, 124, 155,
    249n, 257, 313, 315, 326n
anthologies 7, 17, 23, 81, 86–90, 92n,
    124, 197n, 203, 251–52, 331–32
Anthony, Michael, **127–28**
anti-colonialism 17, 44, 67, 131, 134,
    155, 183, 201–202, 205, 208, 210

Antoni, Robert 18, 315
Arango, Arturo 82
Archibald, Kathleen 67
Arenal, Humberto 80
Argos, Trinidad 63
Arrufat, Antón 88
art 46, 54, 68, 253, 276, 308, 314, 317
Arzola, Jorge Luis 85
Asante-Akan culture 201–202, 206, 314
Athill, Diana 166, 170, 171, 173, 179–
    80, 182n
Auguste, Rose 33
'authenticity' 66, 151, 162, 164, 255, 260,
    262
authorship, as profession 30–31, 34, 42,
    88, 219
autobiographical references 37, 96, 112,
    125, 126, 129, 142, 146, 152, 156,
    162, 166, 184, 234, 248n, 284–85,
    289, 291, 294, 322, 326n
awakening 45, 46, 60, 128, 160, 168n,
    204

Bachelard, Gaston 298, 302, 306
Bahr, Aída 85
Baker, Houston A. 48
Baksh, Elahi, 124, **134–36**
Baldeosingh, Kevin 300
ballad form 272–75, 282n
Barbados 16, 30, 31, 68, 69, 131, 148,
    150, 152, 160, 254, 256, 305, 312–
    314, 323, 326n
Bardolph, Jacqueline 14
Barnet, Miguel 85–86, 87
barrack-yard stories 17, 65, 67, 70–73,
    125, 160, 183–86, 191
Batista, Fulgencio 79–80
BBC 16, 29–43, 127, 156, 157, 203,
    216n, 256, 324 (see also *Caribbean
    Voices*)
Beacon, The 16, 59–75, 77n, 96, 125, 163
Beacon Group 59–75, 160, 163, 183–
    85, 191, 195, 197n, 257
Benn, Dennis 75n
beauty, female: manipulated 115–116;
    Western myths revised 221–22, 226
belonging 42, 48, 107, 142, 269, 281
Benítez-Rojo, Antonio 19, 80, 81, 249n
Bennett, Louise 30–31, 35, 215, 217n,
    254
Bethel, Lorraine 220
Bhabha, Homi 60, 74n, 224

Walcott, Derek 29, 30, 33, 218, 287, 296n, 313
Walmsley, Ann 24n
Walrond, Eric 141, **148–53**
waste 194, 225–26
water mumma spirit 244–45
Wegner, Philip E. 224
West Indian: as a term 24–25n; identity 149–51, 169; culture 11, 16, 17, 32, 35, 45–46, 56, 59, 66, 74, 124, 143, 156–58, 165, 255, 292; Federation 184, 283n (*see also* cricket)
West Indian Review, The 46
white people 34, 61–62, 64–65, 68, 70–71, 74n, 106, 117, 146, 150, 151, 170, 185–86, 202, 210, 215n, 225–26, 253, 259, 260 (*see also* race)
Whitfield, Esther 89, 92n
Wickham, John 23, 251
Williams, Eric 73–74, 132, 184, 194
Williams, Randolph 47
Williams, Raymond 42, 60
Winti 244, 250n (*see also* religion, spirituality)
women: 30–43, 44, 171, 177, 183, 185, 210, 220–29, 244–45, 258–59, 271, 273, 278–79, 282n; writers 31–43, 85, 87, 89, 111–113, 174, 219–220, 257, 270 (*see also* gender)
Woolf, Virginia 181–82n, 251
Woolford, Gordon 36
Wright, Richard 52
Wyndham, Francis 171
Wynter, Sylvia 31, 35, **40–42**, 43n

Yaatof, Olga 67
Yamamoto, Shin 260
Yáñez, Mirta 82, 87, 88, 92n
yard stories (*see* barrack-yard stories)
Yard Theatre Movement 33
Yelvington, Kevin 194, 266n

SHORT STORY COLLECTIONS
FROM PEEPAL TREE PRESS

Opal Palmer Adisa, *Until Judgement Comes: Stories About Jamaican Men*
9781845230425, £8.99
Angela Barry, *Endangered Species*   9781900715713, £8.99
Wayne Brown, *The Scent of the Past* [forthcoming]   9781845231538, £14.99
Jane Bryce, *Chameleon and other stories*   9781845230418, £7.99
Hazel Dorothy Campbell, *Singerman*   9780948833441, £8.99
Tanya Chan-Sam, *Mr Mohani and Other Stories*   9781845231194, £4.99
Merle Collins, *The Ladies Are Upstairs* [forthcoming]   9781845231798, £8.99
Cyril Dabydeen, *Berbice Crossing*   9780948833694, £8.99
Kwame Dawes, *A Place to Hide*   9781900715485, £9.99
Brenda Flanagan, *In Praise of Island Women*   9781845231279, £8.99
Curdella Forbes, *A Permanent Freedom*   9781845230616, £8.99
Beryl Agatha Gilroy, *Sunlight on Sweet Water*   9780948833649, £7.99
June Henfrey, *Coming Home and other stories*   9780948833670, £7.99
Manzu Islam, *The Mapmakers of Spitalfields*   9781900715089, £7.99
Meiling Jin, *Song of the Boatwoman*   9780948833861, £7.99
Cherie Jones, *The Burning Bush Women*   9781900715584, £7.99
Ismith Khan, *A Day in the Country*   9780948833090, £8.99
Rabindranath Maharaj, *The Writer and his Wife*   9780948833816, £8.99
E.A. Markham, *Taking the Drawing Room Through Customs: Selected Stories*
9781900715690, £9.99
Alecia McKenzie, *Stories from Yard*   9781900715621, £7.99
Mark McWatt, *Suspended Sentences: Fictions of Atonement* 9781845230012, £8.99
Rooplall Motilal Monar, *Backdam People*   9780948833007, £6.99
____*High House and Radio*   9780948833120, £8.99
Courttia Newland, *Music for the Off-Key: Twelve Macabre Short Stories*
9781845230401, £8.99
Anton Nimblett, *Sections of an Orange*   9781845230746, £8.99
Dayo Okunlola, *Without Extremeties*   9780948833427, £7.99
Geoffrey Philp, *Uncle Obadiah and the Alien*   9781900715010, £7.99
____*Who's Your Daddy? and other stories*   9781845230777, £8.99
Velma Pollard, *Considering Woman I & II*   9781845231699, £8.99
Jennifer Rahim, *Songster and other stories*   9781845230487, £8.99
Raymond Ramcharitar, *The Island Quintet: Five Stories* 9781845230753, £8.99
Jan Lowe Shinebourne, *The Godmother and other stories* 9781900715874, £7.99
Tell-Tales Collective, *Tell-Tales 4: The Global Village*   9781845230791, £8.99
N.D. Williams, *Julie Mango*   9781900715775, £9.99
____*The Crying of Rainbirds*   9780948833403, £8.99

Kamau Brathwaite
LX: the love axe/l Volume 1: Developing a Caribbean Aesthetic
9781845231750; 2011; 280pp; £18.99
LX: the love axe/l Volume 2: Notes and Commentary
9781845231767; 2011; £19.99

At once a manifesto for a revolutionary Caribbean aesthetics, a work of detailed literary analysis and a scholarly documentation of a vital period in Caribbean history, Kamau Brathwaite's long-awaited *Love Axe/l* is unique and indispensable work from one of the region's most distinguished writers and scholars. It deals not only with significant literary texts, but with the wider artistic, popular and intellectual movements which were part of the profound revolution in West Indian post-colonial consciousness.

Juanita Cox, ed.
In the Eye of the Storm: Edgar Mittelholzer 1909-2009, Critical Perspectives
9781845231286; 2012; £19.99

In the Eye of the Storm makes a substantial contribution to the celebration of the 100th anniversary of Edgar Mittelholzer's birth. The anthology brings together biographical essays, the best critical assessments of the past fifty years, a major new introduction, and an extensive bibliography of critical writing. With contributions from Jacqueline Ives (Ward), Frank Collymore, George Lamming, Frank Birbalsingh, J. Dillon Brown, A.J. Seymour and many others.

David Dabydeen & Letizia Gramaglia, eds
Coral Identities: Essays on Indo-Caribbean Literature
9781845231606; 2011; £16.99

Assembled to meet the growing interest in Indo-Caribbean literature, *Coral Identities* brings together fresh and incisive critical articles on diverse issues including gender and racial relations, religion, indenture, nature, cricket and madness. This lively and wide-ranging collection promises to stimulate dialogue and serve as a strong reference point for students and researchers in the field.

Olivier H.P. Stephenson, ed.
Visions and Voices: Conversations with Fourteen Caribbean Playwrights
9781845231736; 2011

In these fourteen interviews, conducted in the 1970s and 1980s, the Caribbean's most prominent playwrights discuss their own work and critique each other's, while providing fascinating insights into the politics, history and literary culture of the Caribbean. Interviewees include Derek and Roderick Walcott, Errol John, Dennis Scott and Carmen Tipling.

Silvio Torres-Saillant, *Caribbean Poetics*
9781845231071; 2011; 372pp; £19.99

Caribbean Poetics studies the literatures written in European languages in the Caribbean as a regionally unified corpus with its own identity. First published in 1997 and extensively revised for this edition, *Caribbean Poetics* is a seminal work in pan-Caribbean criticism.

Sylvia Wynter, *We must learn to sit down together and talk about a little culture: Decolonizing Essays, 1967-1984*
9781845231088; 2011; 260pp; £17.99

A practising novelist, playwright and scholar, and an incisive literary critic with a gift for the liveliest polemics, Sylvia Wynter's intellectual virtuosity shows in these wide-ranging essays, which include an exploration of C.L.R. James's writings on cricket, Bob Marley and the counter-cosmogony of the Rastafari, and the Spanish epoch of Jamaican history.

SELECTED BACKLIST ACADEMIC TITLES

Laurence A. Breiner, *Black Yeats: Eric Roach and the Politics of Caribbean Poetry*
9781845230470; 2008; £16.99

Stewart Brown, *Tourist, Traveller, Troublemaker: Essays on Poetry*
9781845230531; 2007; £16.99

Daryl Cumber Dance, *New World Adams: Interviews with West Indian Writers*
9781900715041; 2nd edn; 2008; £14.99

Kwame Dawes, *Natural Mysticism: Towards a New Reggae Aesthetic*
9781900715225; 1999; £14.99

Martin Zehnder, *Something Rich and Strange: Selected Essays on Samuel Selvon*
9781900715737; 2003; £14.99

All Peepal Tree titles are available from the website
www.peepaltreepress.com
with a money-back guarantee, secure credit card ordering